VISUAL QUICKPRO GUIDE

PREMIERE PRO 2

FOR WINDOWS

Antony Bolante

 Peachpit Press

Visual QuickPro Guide
Premiere Pro 2 for Windows
Antony Bolante

Peachpit Press
1249 Eighth Street
Berkeley, CA 94710
510/524-2178
800/283-9444
510/524-2221 (fax)

Find us on the Web at: www.peachpit.com
To report errors, please send a note to errata@peachpit.com

Peachpit Press is a division of Pearson Education

Editor: Matthew Purcell
Production Editors: Andrei Pasternak and Pat Christenson
Copyeditor: Tiffany Taylor
Compositor: WolfsonDesign
Indexer: Karin Arrigoni
Cover design: Peachpit Press

ISBN 0-321-38352-4

9 8 7 6 5 4 3 2 1

Printed and bound in the United States of America

This one's for my Mom.
Hi, Mom!

Acknowledgements

Everyone involved in creating the previous versions of this book; I hope this one does you proud.

Rebecca Gulick and Matt Purcell, the powerful editing tag-team.

Tiffany Taylor, our stalwart copy editor.

Aanarav Sareen, who provided the bulk of the screenshots, and Steven Goetz who supplied some lovely footage.

Andrei Pasternak, Lupe Edgar, Damon Hampson, Becky Morgan, and all the good people at Peachpit Press.

The clever folks at Adobe Systems, Inc.

Elena Day and Andy Sapora for the multi-camera footage of their excellent play, "Prisoners of Love."

Family and Friends who've let me share their beautiful photos and faces.

Shortstack.

My family, always.

TABLE OF CONTENTS

TABLE OF CONTENTS

EDITING, 2.0

"Version 2.0" is special. In some ways, it's more special than the software's debut, or even the versions to follow. Literally speaking, the designation, "version 2.0" denotes the second iteration of a program. But it's telling how "version 2.0" has acquired a more figurative meaning, as well. It has become a metaphor for any new and improved incarnation—especially one that represents a notable advancement. But we expect version 2.0 not only to update and add features to the initial version, but also to shed its predecessor's flaws. Cautious users patiently wait for others to road-test the initial release before adopting the more robust and retooled version 2.0. You might see version 2.0 not so much as a program's *second* release as it is the program's *first* major upgrade.

Given the high expectations associated with this milestone, users should be pleased with Premiere Pro 2.0. Although the latest version doesn't embody radical changes, it does include some significant innovations. The most evident enhancement is Premiere Pro 2.0's new and more efficient panel-based interface. Looking beneath the surface, you'll find multicamera editing, a DVD Layout feature, and a feature called Clip Notes that facilitates a collaborative workflow and review process. And though it's not a new feature, per se, Premiere Pro 2 ships with Adobe Bridge, a separate but tightly integrated program that not only allows you to browse for assets on your own hard disks, but also lets you shop in Adobe's extensive online catalog. And as you would expect from "version 2.0," Premiere Pro 2.0 corrects and augments features found in the previous version. It expands import options and supports professional deck control, permits you to create subclips and proxies, integrates titles into the project file and offers a wider array of title templates, includes new and enhanced effects and improves its keyframing controls, and allows you to integrate your workflow with other Adobe programs even better than before.

Whether you've chosen Premiere Pro 2.0 to create video programs for multimedia, broadcast, DVD, or the Web, you've chosen this QuickPro Guide because you're ready to get started. If version 2.0 is your first encounter with Premiere Pro, this book will get you up to speed; and if you're upgrading from the previous version, it will keep you up to date.

The Visual QuickPro Series

Chances are good you're already familiar with the QuickStart series of books from Peachpit Press. They're known for their concise style, step-by-step instructions, and ample illustrations.

The *Pro* in *QuickPro*, as in *Premiere Pro*, implies that the software under discussion appeals to more advanced users. For this reason, this QuickPro guide is designed for intermediate to advanced users and assumes that you have significant experience not only with computers, but also with the use of some form of digital media.

That said, the QuickPro series remains true to the essential QuickStart traditions. The approach still emphasizes step-by-step instructions and concise explanations. If the book looks a little thick for a "concise" guide, consider that it contains over 1,000 screen shots that clearly illustrate every task. Like other books in this series, *Premiere Pro 2: Visual QuickPro Guide* strives to be quick without failing to guide.

Using This Book

Although the text restricts itself to the task at hand, it doesn't hesitate to give you critical background information, usually in the form of *sidebars* that help you understand the concepts behind the task. If you're already familiar with the concept, feel free to skip ahead; if not, look to the sidebars for some grounding. Also keep an eye out for tips, which point out shortcuts, pitfalls, and tricks of the trade.

Chapters are organized to present topics as you encounter them in a typical editing project, but the task-oriented format and thumb tabs let you jump to the topic you need. By explaining how to use Premiere Pro, this book inevitably touches on a multitude of related topics: formats, editing aesthetics, special effects, audio sweetening, Web delivery, and so on. Discussing the fundamentals and background of each of these areas is far outside the scope of this book (and even books that don't have the word *quick* in their title). Nevertheless, this guide tries to provide enough information to keep you moving and point you in new directions.

How Premiere Pro Works

Premiere Pro is *digital nonlinear editing software*. A breakdown of this description can give you clues about how the program works:

Digital: Premiere Pro manipulates digital media: digital video and audio, scanned images, and digitally created artwork and animation stored in various formats. Regardless of the particular format, these materials are stored as files on your computer's hard disk. Strictly speaking, Premiere Pro doesn't convert analog video and audio to digital form, although it does contain controls that do so in conjunction with built-in hardware (such as the IEEE 1394 or USB 2 connection included in most computers) or add-on hardware (such as an analog video capture card).

Nonlinear: Editing in Premiere Pro is described as *nonlinear* because your sources aren't constrained to a linear medium, such as videotape. In other words, you can access any source clip instantly, without shuttling tape, and you can change the order of clips in a sequence without rerecording.

Software: As a software-only package, Premiere Pro can be installed on any personal computer system that meets or exceeds the program's minimum requirements and doesn't require specialized hardware. However, you can also purchase it bundled with a system or with other hardware options.

Terminology: Digital and Analog

When you record audio and video, sound and light are converted to electrical signals. *Analog* media record these signals as continuously changing values. *Digital* media, on the other hand, record audio and video as a series of specific, discrete values. A playback device converts these values back to audio and video. The accuracy of each conversion greatly influences the picture and sound quality.

Because digital recordings use discrete values, it's easy to reproduce them exactly, time after time. In addition, you can take advantage of the computer's ability to manipulate these values—which means you can more easily alter the sound, color, and brightness and add effects.

Editing Strategy: Offline and Online Editing

It can be argued that all projects begin at the same point: the end. Setting your output goal determines the choices you make to achieve it. Therefore, the editing strategy you develop always proceeds from the same question: What is my output goal (**Figure i.1**)?

Whether your movie is destined for film, broadcast video, CD-ROM, or the Web, familiarize yourself with the specifications of your output goal, such as frame size, frame rate, and file format. Often, you must reconcile your output goal with the capabilities and limitations of your system. These factors help determine your postproduction path—particularly whether you perform offline editing or online editing.

Online editing results in the final video sequence. You can edit online in Premiere Pro if your system is capable of acquiring, processing, and delivering a sequence at final-output quality. The higher the image quality, however, the greater the system requirements. To achieve your output goal, you may need a fast processor, a high-end capture card, and large, fast hard drives. If your system doesn't meet the output requirements, use another system for the online edit, and use Premiere Pro for your offline edit.

Offline editing prepares projects for an online edit. In an offline edit, you often edit with low-quality versions of the video. Rather than produce a final sequence at output quality, you produce an accurate draft version.

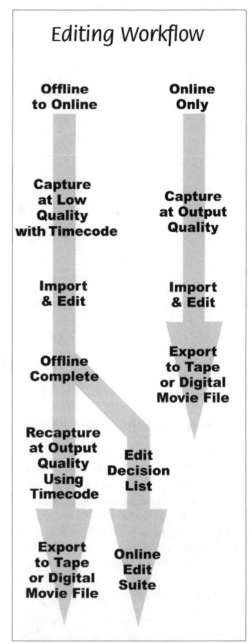

Figure i.1 This flow chart outlines the typical offline and online editing strategies.

The completed offline edit can produce a kind of transcript of all your edits, known as an *edit-decision list* (EDL). You can use the EDL and source tapes to re-create a sequence quickly and easily in a traditional tape-based online-editing suite. You can also use your offline edit and EDL to re-create a sequence on film. Premiere Pro can export a project in the widely accepted Advanced Authoring Format (AAF), which can contain EDL and other data as well as the CMX3600 EDL format.

Alternatively, you can edit offline and online on the same system. Because lower-quality clips are smaller, more of them fit on your hard drive, and your computer can process them faster. For the online edit, you can recapture at the final-output quality only the clips that you actually used in the sequence. Premiere Pro automatically uses the high-quality clips in your final sequence, and no re-editing is required.

For an offline edit to succeed, you must have some way to accurately match your low-quality offline clips with their high-quality counterparts. Without a frame-accurate reference, there's no way to easily reproduce the sequence you created in the offline edit. That frame-accurate reference is known as *timecode*.

Timecode numbers identify each frame of video on a source tape. Premiere Pro and other video technologies use timecode to track edits in the offline edit and accurately re-create them in the online edit. Without timecode, an EDL would be meaningless, and recapturing clips would be impossible.

✔ Tip

- Chapter 2, "Starting a Project," discusses timecode options, and Chapter 3, "Capturing and Importing Footage," explains how timecode is used to log and capture footage.

DV and Premiere Pro

For DV users, all this talk about offline and online editing may seem old-fashioned. DV is a high-quality, inexpensive video standard that not only has made video production more accessible, but simplifies postproduction, as well.

With DV, timecode is no longer a costly option found only in professional gear but is instead an integral part of the video signal. And *generational loss*—the progressive degradation of image and sound quality inherent in duplicating analog signals—isn't a concern with digital.

Because DV cameras record video in a digital format, there's no need to add a capture card to your computer to *digitize*, or convert an analog signal to a digital signal (for more about digitizing, see Chapter 3). With the help of an inexpensive IEEE 1394 (also called *FireWire* or *iLink*) or USB 2 (aka *fast USB*) interface, Premiere Pro can transfer your footage to the hard drive for editing.

Just as important, IEEE 1394 and USB 2 simplify postproduction. Whereas digitizing requires separate cables for video and audio, DV transfers both using a single cable. The cable also delivers DV's timecode information. Even device control (the ability to control a camera or deck from a computer) is accomplished over this same cable.

Compared to files digitized using older technology, DV footage consumes less storage space and requires only a modestly fast hard drive.

Whereas each type of analog capture card follows unique specifications, DV's characteristics are relatively consistent from one device to another. For this reason, Premiere Pro can include preset project and capture settings for DV, so you don't have to select video and audio settings manually.

✔ Tip

- For more detailed technical information about DV, IEEE 1394, and USB 2, see the corresponding sidebars in Chapter 3.

Your Desktop Editing Suite

All nonlinear editing systems use a graphical interface that to some degree refers to their predecessors: film- and tape-based editing tools. Yet as these traditional tools yield to newer technologies, the metaphors lose much of their meaning. These days, many editors have never seen a film splicer or a traditional video-editing suite. Nevertheless, it may help you to understand what Premiere Pro does if you realize what it's designed to replace.

Before programs like Premiere Pro, offline editing was synonymous with inexpensive, but very limited, editing equipment. In a typical offline suite, you'd create a simple *cuts-only* edit (no dissolves or other transitions) using low-quality copies of the camera originals called *window dubs*. In a window dub, timecode numbers were recorded over the picture (not actual timecode, but a "picture" of the timecode). When editing was complete, you could painstakingly transcribe the timecode numbers at the beginning and end of each shot to create the edit-decision list.

Only after you were armed with an EDL would you proceed to an online suite, with its expensive decks and special equipment. At this stage, you'd finally be able to add transitions, effects, and titles and mix audio.

Programs like Premiere Pro blur the line between online and offline editing by offering the online features at the offline stage (and price):

A/B roll editing: In a traditional tape-editing suite, any transition other than a cut required two sources: an *A roll* and a *B roll*. As the two tapes played, a video switcher could mix the signal from tape A with that from tape B for recording on the master tape. This way, you could create dissolves, wipes, and other effects. If two scenes were on the same source tape, one had to be copied onto the B roll before dissolves and other transitions could be applied (unless you had a deck with a preread feature, but that's another story). All this was possible only in an expensive online editing suite. Premiere Pro allows you to create an even wider range of transitions during the offline stage.

Audio mixing and sweetening: Just as a traditional offline suite permitted only simple cuts-only video editing, audio editing was usually limited to volume control. Better audio editing was left to the online edit or even to a separate audio post session. Premiere Pro allows you to apply complex audio editing and effects from the start, including audio processing to adjust the level, placement, and character of the sound. You can set audio In points based on audio samples, which are more precise than video frames. In addition, you can fade, boost, mix, and pan almost unlimited tracks of audio. Premiere Pro's audio mixer even resembles a traditional mixing board. Moreover, you can *sweeten* the audio, subtly correcting the sound and adding special effects.

Digital video effects (DVE): DVE is the generic term for a device used to process the video signal digitally, in real time, to accomplish all kinds of visual effects. DVEs can rotate, resize, and move an image; change the colors; and add other visual effects. Premiere Pro's effect settings can achieve the same results, as well as many effects you won't find in a DVE. They take more time to process on the desktop, but these kinds of visual effects used to be unavailable outside an online suite.

Character generator (CG): A CG is used to create text for video, usually to superimpose over other images. Premiere Pro's Titler brings the tools and ease of desktop publishing to character generation for video.

EDL import/export: This feature produces a transcript of the edits in the final sequence so that it can be reproduced on another system—typically, a traditional higher-end system. Alternatively, it can read an EDL from another system. Premiere Pro supports the AAF file format for exchanging data with other systems.

Batch capture: Batch capture uses timecode references to capture the proper clips automatically from a log or offline edit.

Workflow

Regardless of whether you choose an offline or online editing path, you should look at your editing workflow as proceeding from simple to complex. You don't need to adhere rigidly to the following outline, but gradually fleshing out the final sequence is usually more efficient than plunging into effects, going back again to rough-cutting, and then discovering that the effects need to be redone. The Premiere Pro workspace options provide for an incremental process, optimizing the interface for each stage of the project:

Logging: The most tedious (and, therefore, the most neglected) part of the editing process involves watching your source tapes and noting the *selects*—the shots you want to use in the project. Premiere Pro's Capture panel and device control can make the logging process nearly painless. If your tape has timecode, you can log shots directly to your project; this log can serve as a *batch list*, a list of timecode start and end numbers that can be used to automate the capture process.

Capture: If you're using an IEEE 1394 or USB 2 connection, capture involves transferring video from your camera or deck to the hard drive. Analog sources require a capture device that can digitize the video. If you have timecode and device control, Premiere Pro can capture shots from a batch list automatically.

Import: At this point, you add the footage you want to use to the project. You can import a variety of digital media: video, audio, stills, image sequences, and so on. Your project uses references to the source footage, not the footage itself.

Basic edit/rough-cutting: Arrange and adjust the sequence of clips into an edited sequence, using a variety of flexible and powerful editing tools. Because you're using file references, your decisions are non-destructive—that is, you can make as many changes as you want without permanently altering the source files.

Preview: Watch your sequences at any time, with or without transitions or special effects. Premiere Pro can render many effects in *real time*. That is, Premiere Pro can play transitions and other effects right away and at full playback speed using only your system's resources (and without special add-on hardware).

Fine-tuning/fine-cutting: Refine the edits in a sequence using any combination of editing controls, direct manipulation in the timeline, and the specialized Trim panel.

Effects and character generation: Add titles, superimpose clips, add motion or video and audio effects, and animate effects.

Audio sweetening: Cut audio with sample-rate precision, mix tracks using a full-featured audio mixer, and enhance audio clips and tracks using a variety of built-in effects or any VST effect. (VST stands for Virtual Studio Technology; see Chapter 11, "Mixing Audio," for details.)

Output: Export the finished sequence directly to tape or DVD, or save a file in any number of formats for playback on other computers, CD-ROM, or over the Web.

New Features

Some of the notable features introduced in Premiere Pro 2.0 include the following:

Improved user interface—Premiere Pro 2.0 incorporates a more efficient, panel-based user interface like that found in other Adobe programs. The new interface ensures the program always makes the most of your available screen space and optimizes your workflow.

Adobe Bridge—Premiere Pro 2.0 ships with Adobe Bridge, a separate but tightly integrated program that lets you browse for assets on your own hard disks and also acts as a gateway to Stock Photo, Adobe's extensive online library of images; you can use and evaluate these images before you buy them and incorporate them into your project.

Expanded import options—Premiere Pro 2.0 supports HD and HDV natively, and it can even accept 4K image files (a format with 4096 lines of vertical resolution). You can also control professional decks via RS-422 and RS-232 protocols.

Multicamera editing—Using one of Premiere Pro's most notable new features, you can synchronize and view footage from multiple cameras, and effortlessly cut that footage into a sequence.

Enhanced editing—Premiere Pro 2.0 lets you create and edit subclips and assign proxy footage for an improved workflow.

Integrated titles—Premiere Pro 2.0 now saves titles as part of the project file and includes a wider array of title templates.

Improved keyframing and effects—Premiere Pro 2.0 includes improved keyframing controls as well as new and enhanced effects.

Product integration—Changes you make in Premiere Pro 2.0 are instantly reflected in After Effects or Encore DVD—without rendering or re-importing footage—via a feature known as Dynamic Link.

Simplified DVD export—Premiere Pro now includes a DVD Layout feature for exporting a sequence to a DVD that includes scene navigation and motion menus and buttons.

Collaborative tools—Premiere Pro 2.0 facilitates a collaborative workflow with its new Clip Notes feature. Using Clip Notes, an editor can export a work in progress for review (automatically uploading it to a server, for example). Reviewers can attach comments to specific points in a sequence, so that the editor can make changes accordingly.

The Digital Video Collection

Although Premiere Pro is dedicated to editing video, you can use it to bring together a range of digital media. But even though Premiere Pro's features sometimes overlap with other types of software, the ideal workflow includes tools specialized for each job. Chances are good that Photoshop is already part of your still-image editing toolkit, and you use Illustrator for advanced typesetting and graphics. For moving media, Adobe hopes you will use Premiere Pro together with After Effects (for motion graphics and effects), Audition (for advanced audio editing and music creation), Encore DVD (for DVD authoring), and (with the recent acquisition of another company, Macromedia) Flash Professional (for Web content). You'll enjoy a discounted price if you purchase these programs together as what Adobe calls its Adobe Video Bundle.

In addition to selling these programs as a set, the folks at Adobe are trying their best to make the programs *work* as a set. As these software packages have matured, they have also become more integrated. Over time, it's become easier to move files from one program to another without performing intermediate steps or sacrificing elements of your work. Even the interfaces have grown more consistent with one another. (The landscape is similar; however, the customs aren't always the same. You may find that some shared features don't use exactly the same procedures or keyboard shortcuts.)

Your familiarity with other Adobe programs may give you a head start in learning Premiere Pro. Premiere Pro has a lot in common with its sibling, After Effects. If you're thinking about buying Premiere Pro or other Adobe programs, you may find their consistency or bundled pricing appealing. In any case, Adobe's eye toward product integration may be an important consideration for you.

THE DIGITAL VIDEO COLLECTION

System Requirements

To use Premiere Pro, your system must meet these requirements:

◆ Intel Pentium 4, 800 MHz or better (3 GHz recommended)

◆ Microsoft Windows XP Home (XP Professional recommended)

◆ 256 MB of RAM (1 GB of RAM or more recommended)

◆ 800 MB of available hard disk space for installation

◆ 1280 x 1024 32-bit color video display adapter (OpenGL card recommended)

◆ CD-ROM drive (for program installation)

◆ For CD creation: CD recorder (CD +/- R/RW)

◆ For Export to DVD: DVD recorder (DVD +/- R/RW)

◆ DirectX-compatible sound card (multichannel ASIO compliant for surround-sound support recommended)

◆ For DV capture: IEEE 1394 (also called FireWire or iLink) or USB 2 interface

◆ For DV media storage: Large-capacity 7200 RPM UDMA 66 IDE or SCSI hard disk or disk array

◆ For video capture using a third-party card: Adobe Premiere Pro 2.0 certified capture card (see Adobe's Web site)

✔ Tips

■ You'll need an Internet or phone connection to activate your copy of Premiere Pro.

■ Chapter 11, "Mixing Audio," contains more information about ASIO and surround sound.

Suggested System

These features aren't required, but they can make working with Premiere Pro a lot more satisfying:

Faster processor: The faster your system can make calculations, the faster it can process frames of video and create effects.

Additional RAM: Like all programs, Premiere Pro relies partly on RAM for performance and stability. In addition, the number of frames you can preview in real time without having to render depends entirely on the amount of RAM you can allocate to Premiere Pro.

Larger hard drives: Video files are notoriously large. Five minutes of DV footage, for example, consumes more than a gigabyte of storage space. Ample storage space allows you to work with more footage and with high-quality footage.

Faster hard drives: Your system's ability to play back footage smoothly relies partly on how quickly information can be read from the drives. Generally speaking, higher-quality footage requires faster drives. Drive arrays (RAIDs) use multiple drives to increase the overall transfer speed. To use DV footage, for example, your drives should sustain a data rate of around 5 MB per second.

24-bit displays: It almost goes without saying that it's best to work in True Colors.

Larger or multiple displays: Premiere Pro's interface can take up a lot of screen space. A large monitor can be more comfortable to work with. Many users like to spread out over two monitors, although others consider that arrangement to be overkill.

Professional System Additions

Other additions can elevate your editing system to a more professional level:

Video capture/playback device: Your computer needs an IEEE 1394 or USB 2 connection and a similarly equipped camera or deck to transfer and output video in the DV format. If you want to digitize material from an analog source (VHS, Hi8, or BetacamSP), you may opt for an add-on capture card. You'll also need a deck to play and record tapes in your format of choice.

Video monitor: Video monitors and computer monitors display images differently. If your work is destined for video or broadcast, a good monitor—preferably one with professional inputs and excellent color reproduction—allows you to judge it more accurately. A video capture device typically supports both your computer and video monitor.

Audio card: A standard built-in audio card is adequate for many applications, but you'll need a more advanced, ASIO-compliant audio card if you want to use Premiere Pro for multitrack recording or output to 5.1 surround. For more about ASIO and 5.1 surround, see Chapter 11.

Surround speakers: Although an advanced audio card helps process multitrack, high-data-rate audio in 5.1, you won't hear the full effect without a set of speakers to match. Like everything else, surround speakers vary greatly in price and quality.

DVD recorder: DVD recorders are quickly becoming as commonplace in a desktop editing suite as video tape decks. (Thankfully, they're becoming more affordable, as well.) You can use Premiere Pro to output your edited sequence to DVD. To produce more full-featured DVDs, you'll also need a dedicated authoring program like Adobe Encore DVD.

Third-party plug-ins: A multitude of third-party developers offer software plug-ins that expand Premiere Pro's capabilities. These products include improved or additional effects and transitions, audio effects, matchback tools to create EDLs for film, and tools that allow you to better evaluate and adjust the video signal.

Hardware acceleration: If rendering speed and turnaround time are of paramount importance, you may want to invest in a Premiere Pro system bundled with hardware to accelerate effects rendering.

PROFESSIONAL SYSTEM ADDITIONS

System Configurations

As the preceding sections suggest, your Premiere Pro setup can be simple or elaborate. As long as your computer meets the minimum requirements, you can install Premiere Pro and start editing. On the other hand, your system may include a television monitor and a camera or deck. Here's how a few common configurations might look:

DV camera configuration (Figure i.2): In this setup, a DV camera is used to transfer source video to your computer's hard drive over an IEEE 1394 or USB 2 connection. The completed, edited project can be played back and recorded to a tape in the camera.

Analog capture configuration (Figure i.3): In this setup, the computer is equipped with a qualifying video capture card to digitize video from an analog source (such as VHS, Hi8, or BetacamSP). The capture card converts the signal from analog to digital so that it can be stored on the hard drive.

Enhanced DV configuration (Figure i.4): In this setup, several recommended options have been added to the system. An external drive provides additional storage space for media, a dedicated playback and recording deck reduces wear on the camera's tape transport, a video monitor displays the sequences as they will appear on a television screen, and external speakers provide the audio.

✔ Tip

■ Looking for a complete system? Several vendors offer preconfigured editing systems. You may find their pricing and service agreements attractive. In addition, Premiere Pro is often bundled with capture cards and real-time acceleration cards and even offered as an option when you purchase a computer.

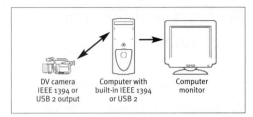

Figure i.2 This configuration includes a computer equipped for IEEE 1394 (also called FireWire or iLink) and a DV camera.

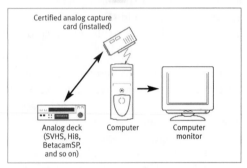

Figure i.3 This configuration includes a computer equipped with an Adobe-certified capture card and an analog video deck.

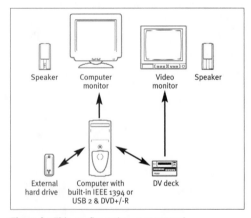

Figure i.4 This configuration uses several recommended options, such as a television monitor, speakers, DVD recorder, external hard drive, and deck.

PREMIERE PRO BASICS

Before embarking on a journey, it's useful to survey the landscape and learn a few local customs. In this chapter, you'll get oriented to the Premiere Pro interface and catch a glimpse of what's to come. In addition, you'll learn about the basic workings of the interface: how to use context menus, keyboard shortcuts, and commands, and how to undo mistakes. Once you're familiar with this little travel guide, you can get your passport stamped in Chapter 2, "Starting a Project."

Looking at the Interface

The Premiere Pro workspace consists of an integrated system of tabbed panels that can be arranged in preset or customized workspaces. Let's look at each panel, in the order you might encounter them in a typical workflow.

Capturing

Most projects begin with logging and capturing assets from a video/audio source (typically digital videotape) to your hard disk for use in a project.

The **Capture panel** may not be the first panel you see when you open a project, but it may be the first one you use (**Figure 1.1**). The Capture panel contains everything you need to review footage from a video/audio source and transfer, or *capture*, selected scenes to your hard disk. The Capture panel also allows you to create a log of the footage before capturing the segments you want automatically, in a *batch capture*. Chapter 3, "Capturing and Importing Footage," covers the process in detail.

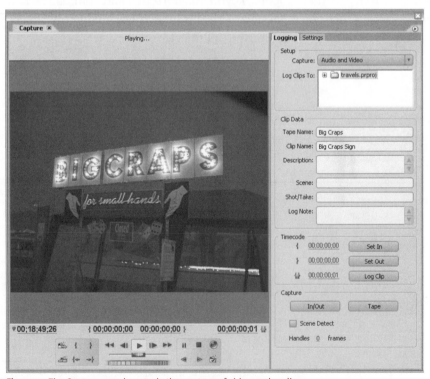

Figure 1.1 The Capture panel controls the capture of video and audio.

Editing

The bulk of a project is accomplished in a typical editing workspace, dominated by three panels: the Project, Monitor, and Timeline panels. However, there's still room for a few other ancillary panels (**Figure 1.2**).

Project panel   Source Monitor panel   Program Monitor panel

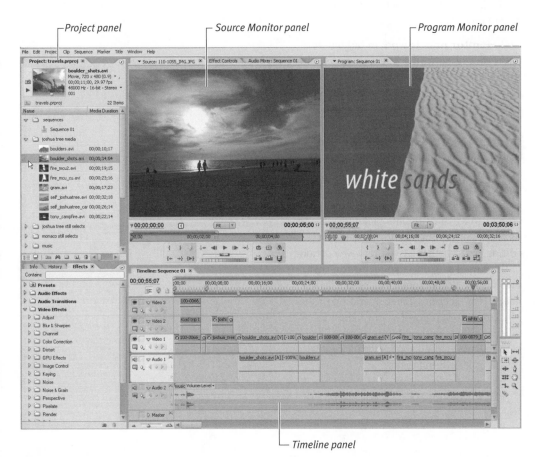

Timeline panel

Figure 1.2 The typical editing workspace is dominated by several panels: the Project panel, Source Monitor, Program Monitor, and Timeline panel.

The **Project panel** lists and organizes the assets you've captured or imported to use in your project as clips. It also lists *offline clips*— footage you've logged but haven't captured yet. An icon or thumbnail image helps you identify each clip, and you can even play it. The Project panel lets you view and organize clips according to various attributes, group them into folders, or use a search feature to locate a buried item. (These aspects of the Project panel are discussed in-depth in Chapter 4, "Managing Clips.")Although you usually open and edit a clip in the Monitor panel (explained next) before adding it to a sequence, you can add clips from the Project panel directly, using either a manual or auto-mated process.

The **Monitor panels** work in tandem for basic editing, so we'll address them together here. The **Source Monitor** displays the source clips and lets you specify the part you want to use before you add it to a sequence. To facilitate editing footage from a multicamera shoot, you can invoke a variation of the Source Monitor that lets you see up to four source clips at once. The **Program Monitor** displays the clips in an edited sequence and corresponds with the graphical representation embodied by the Timeline panel (explained next). The Program Monitor also includes editing controls that let you remove portions of the edited sequence, and a button that invokes the Trim panel (discussed a little later in this section). Basic operation of the Monitor panels is covered in Chapter 5, "Viewing Clips in the Monitor Panels," and subsequent chapters explain their central role in other editing tasks.

Figure 1.3 Selecting a tool from the Tools panel lets you use the mouse pointer for a specialized editing function.

Figure 1.4 The Audio Master Meters panel indicates the audio output levels.

Figure 1.5 The Info panel displays data related to the task at hand, such as the position of the mouse pointer in the timeline or a selected clip's attributes.

Figure 1.6 The History panel list recent actions and allows you to return the project to an earlier state.

The **Timeline panel** represents each sequence graphically, as a timeline. As in any timeline, time is measured along a horizontal graph, or *time ruler*. Edited video and audio clips appear as objects that you can arrange in vertically stacked tracks along the graph. The clips' order horizontally represents their place in time; their vertical placement corresponds to their stacking order: how image and sound overlap. It takes several chapters to reveal its many uses, but a detailed discussion of the Timeline panel begins in Chapter 6, "Creating a Sequence."

The **Tools panel** includes an assortment of editing tools that help you arrange and adjust clips in a sequence. It can be oriented vertically or horizontally (**Figure 1.3**).

The **Audio Master Meters panel** provides an objective, graphical measure of audio output levels. The height of the green bars depicts the levels of the left and right audio channels, measured in decibels (dB). Peak lights indicates when levels are too "hot" and may distort (**Figure 1.4**). The Audio Master Meters panel represents the output channels of the Audio Mixer, covered in Chapter 11, "Mixing Audio."

The **Info panel** displays information pertinent to the task at hand—such as the vital statistics of the selected clip or the current position of the mouse pointer (**Figure 1.5**). The Info panel is mentioned throughout the book, whenever it's particularly helpful for accomplishing a task.

The **History panel**, as in other Adobe programs, allows you to view and undo recent actions. It makes it much easier to get back on track if you make a mistake or change your mind (**Figure 1.6**). The History panel is explained later in this chapter.

More editing

As your project progresses, you'll call on other panels and features to fine-tune edits, mix audio, add effects, and finally export the completed sequence.

The **Multi-Camera Monitor** facilitates editing a sequence using footage from a *multicamera shoot*, in which multiple cameras record an event from several angles at once. Although it resembles the standard Source and Program Monitor setup, the Multi-Camera Monitor displays up to four source clips at once and lets you cut from one to another, allowing you to generate a seamless sequence (**Figure 1.7**).

The **Trim panel** provides special controls for fine-tuning the cut point between clips in a sequence (**Figure 1.8**). In contrast to the Monitor panel, the Trim panel's left view shows the frame before the cut, and the right view shows the frame after the cut. (See Chapter 8, "Refining the Sequence.")

Figure 1.7 The Multi-Camera Monitor makes it easy to edit a seamless sequence from several synchronized sources.

Figure 1.8 The Trim panel lets you fine-tune the cut point between clips in a sequence.

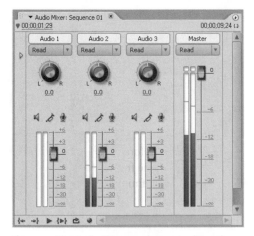

Figure 1.9 The Audio Mixer emulates a traditional mixing board.

The **Audio Mixer**, which emulates a traditional mixing board, allows you to fade and pan audio tracks in real time and sweeten the audio with effects such as noise reduction and equalization (**Figure 1.9**). (See Chapter 11.)

The **Titler** is a suite of related panels that lets you create text and graphics for use in your program (**Figure 1.10**). The Titler may also be referred to as the Title Designer. (See Chapter 12, "Creating Titles.")

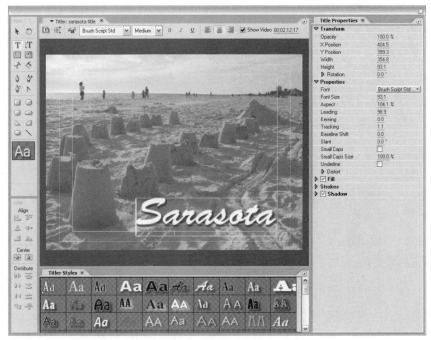

Figure 1.10 The Titler lets you create text and graphics.

The **Effects panel** lists and organizes video and audio transitions (see Chapter 9, "Adding Transitions") as well as video and audio filters (see Chapter 13, "Working with Effects") (**Figure 1.11**).

The **Effect Controls panel** consolidates everything you need to adjust transitions and effects in a single panel. It automatically displays the appropriate controls for adjusting a selected transition (**Figure 1.12**) or for setting and keyframing a clip's effects—whether they're inherent effects (motion, opacity, and volume) or filters (**Figure 1.13**). (See Chapter 9, "Adding Transitions," and Chapter 13.)

Figure 1.11 The Effects panel lists and organizes transitions and filters.

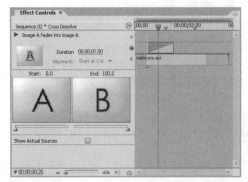

Figure 1.12 The Effect Controls panel provides controls for adjusting a selected transition...

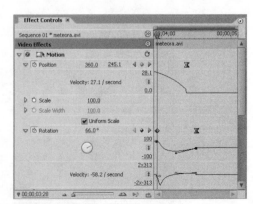

Figure 1.13 ...or helps you set and animate effects like motion, opacity, volume, and filters.

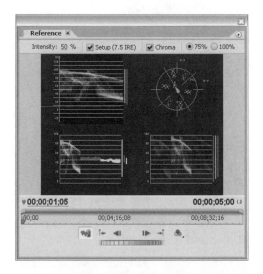

A **Reference Monitor** resembles the Program Monitor, but without the editing controls. A Reference Monitor provides an additional view of the sequence, which can be particularly helpful when color correcting or color matching shots (**Figure 1.14**). (See "Using the Color Corrector Filter" in Chapter 14, "Advanced Effects.")

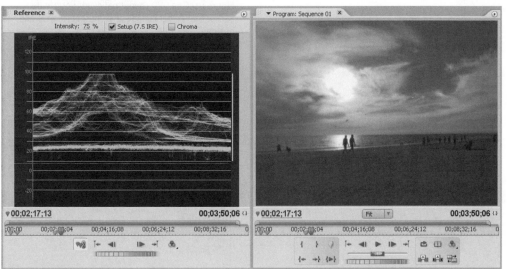

Figure 1.14 A Reference Monitor provides an additional view of a sequence and is helpful when you're correcting color. Here, the Reference Monitor (top) compares one part of the sequence with the frame shown in the Program Monitor (bottom).

Export and DVD authoring

Although some export formats require you to respond to relatively straightforward dialog boxes, a few export options benefit from dedicated panels. (See Chapter 15, "Creating Output.")The **DVD Layout panel** lets you select and customize DVD menu templates—complete with basic navigation menus and buttons—and burn an edited sequence to a DVD (**Figure 1.15**). When the DVD Layout panel is active, the Effect Controls panel displays controls pertinent to the task at hand (**Figure 1.16**).

Figure 1.15 The DVD Layout panel lets you create author a DVD that includes navigational menus and buttons.

Figure 1.16 You use the DVD Layout panel in conjunction with the Effect Controls panel, which toggles to show the appropriate controls.

Technically, the **Adobe Media Encoder** is just a specialized Export dialog box; however, its relatively elaborate interface earns it a status comparable to other panels. With its extensive controls and presets, the Media Encoder facilitates export to formats that require you to specify numerous settings (**Figure 1.17**).

✔ Tip

■ You can adjust the brightness of the interface by choosing Edit > Preferences > General and dragging the User Interface Brightness slider.

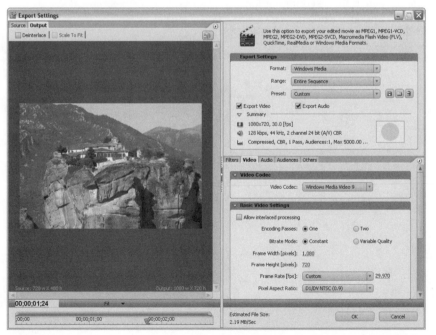

Figure 1.17 The Adobe Media Encoder facilitates encoding a sequence to formats that require you to specify numerous and often complex settings.

Arranging the Workspace

Premiere Pro lets you rearrange the panels on the screen to suit different editing tasks. Conveniently, Premiere Pro can memorize each configuration, or *workspace*. This allows you to switch to the most appropriate arrangement with a simple menu command.

Premiere Pro ships with four preset workspaces designed for specific tasks: Editing, Effects, Audio, and Color Correction. You can use them as they are or rearrange them to match your needs. When you save a custom workspace, it appears in the Workspace menu with the name you specify.

To choose a preset workspace:

◆ Choose Window > Workspace, and select one of the preset workspaces (**Figure 1.18**).

To save a custom workspace:

1. Arrange the panels in the configuration you want to save as a workspace.

2. Choose Window > Workspace > Save Workspace (**Figure 1.19**).

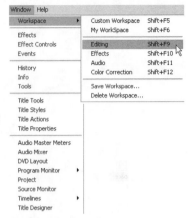

Figure 1.18 Choose Window > Workspace to select one of the preset workspaces.

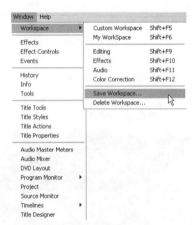

Figure 1.19 Choose Window > Workspace > Save Workspace.

Figure 1.20 Type a name for the new workspace, and click Save.

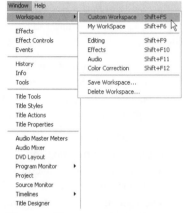

Figure 1.21 The new workspace is now available in the Window > Workspace menu.

3. In the Save Workspace dialog box, type a name for the workspace and click Save (**Figure 1.20**).

Your new workspace will now appear in the Window > Workspace menu above the supplied presets (**Figure 1.21**).

✔ Tips

■ The Workspace pull-down menu also contains commands for deleting a workspace and for assigning a keyboard shortcut to a workspace.

■ You can more quickly switch among your custom workspaces if you assign keyboard shortcuts as described in "Using Keyboard Shortcuts" later in this chapter.

ARRANGING THE WORKSPACE

Customizing the Workspace

Using the preset workspaces is convenient, not compulsory. By customizing the size and arrangement of the panels, you can optimize your workspace and your workflow. You just have to know a few things about frames, panels, and tabs.

The Premiere Pro interface consists of an interconnected system of *panels* contained within *frames*. Unlike a collection of free-floating windows that can be arranged like playing cards on a tabletop, frames are joined together in such a way that the interface may remind you of a mosaic or stained glass. Resizing one frame affects the adjacent frames so that, as a whole, the frames always fill the screen (or, more strictly speaking, Premiere Pro's main application window, which most users maximize to fill the screen). With frames and panels, it's easy to change the relative size of each part of the interface without wasting screen space. And you don't have to worry about one window disappearing behind another.

You can also customize a workspace by taking advantage of tabs. The tab that appears at the top of each panel looks a lot like its real-world counterpart in your office filing cabinet. By dragging a panel's tab into the same area as another panel, you *dock* the panels together. When panels are docked, it's as though they are filed one on top of the other. Like physical file-folder tabs, the tabs of the panels in the back are always visible along the top edge of the stack; but on the computer, you click a panel's tab to bring it to the front.

Just as docking reduces the number of spaces in the interface's mosaic of frames, dragging a panel between other panels creates an additional space, or frame.

Finally, you can separate a panel from the system of frames, creating a free-floating window. A floating window may be useful for tasks you don't perform often or when you can move it to a second computer screen.

To resize panels:

◆ Position the mouse pointer on the border between panels, so that the resize icon ↔ appears (**Figure 1.22**), and then drag.

The size of adjacent panels changes automatically, according to your adjustments (**Figure 1.23**).

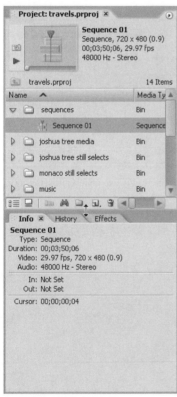

Figure 1.22 Position the mouse pointer over the border between panels so that the resize icon appears...

Figure 1.23 ...and drag to resize the panels that share that border. Note how resizing hides the optional areas of the Time Controls panel.

CUSTOMIZING THE WORKSPACE

To dock panels:

1. *Do either of the following:*

▲ To dock a panel, drag its tab or the textured area at the top of the panel.

▲ To dock a floating window, click and drag the top of the window.

2. Drag the mouse pointer within another panel, so that a highlighted area indicates the panel will appear docked as a tab (**Figure 1.24**), and then release the mouse.

The panels are docked together, so that they occupy the same area (or frame) in the interface's grid of panels (**Figure 1.25**). If the panel wasn't docked in its previous position, then docking it eliminates the frame.

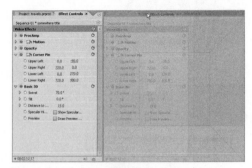

Figure 1.24 Dragging a panel into another panel...

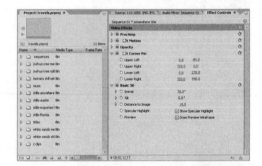

Figure 1.25 ...combines the two panels into a tabbed group.

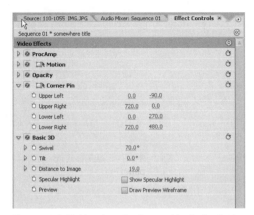

Figure 1.26 Clicking the tab of a panel in the back of the stack...

Figure 1.27 ...brings that panel to the front.

To view tabbed panels:

◆ To view a panel that's hidden behind another panel, click the tab of the panel you want to view (**Figures 1.26** and **1.27**).

◆ To view tabs that are don't fit within the width of the panel area, drag the thin scroll bar that appears above the tabs (**Figures 1.28** and **1.29**).

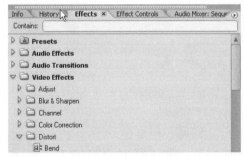

Figure 1.28 When the panel is too narrow to show all tabs, a thin scroll bar appears above the tabs.

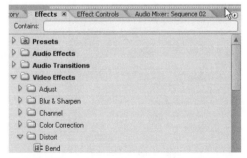

Figure 1.29 Drag the scroll bar to bring the hidden tabs into view.

CUSTOMIZING THE WORKSPACE

To create a new frame:

1. *Do either of the following:*

   ▲ To move a panel, drag its tab or the textured area at the top of the panel.

   ▲ To move a floating window, click and drag the top of the window.

2. Drag the mouse pointer near the side of any other panel, so that a highlighted area indicates where the panel will be inserted in the grid of frames (**Figure 1.30**), and then release the mouse.

   The panel occupies a new space in the grid of frames (**Figure 1.31**).

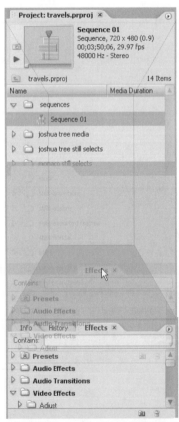

Figure 1.30 Dragging a panel between other panels...

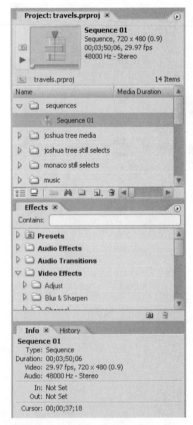

Figure 1.31 ...allows the panel to occupy a new space, or frame, in the grid of panels.

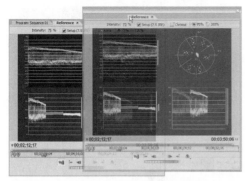

Figure 1.32 Dragging a panel to an empty area ...

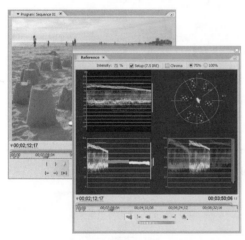

Figure 1.33 ...separates the panel from the others, converting it into a floating window.

To convert a panel into a floating window:

◆ Drag a panel's tab or the textured area at the top of the panel to the empty space above the interface, so that the highlighted area indicates where the floating window will appear (**Figure 1.32**), and then release the mouse.

The panel becomes a floating window (**Figure 1.33**). If the panel wasn't docked with other panels in its previous position, then undocking it eliminates the frame.

✔ Tip

■ When you move a panel, Premiere Pro highlights the destination, indicating the new placement. Initially, it can be tricky to distinguish the indicators, but you'll get it with a little practice.

Using Context Menus

In addition to accessing commands from the menu bar at the top of the screen, you can use context menus. Using the Windows operating system has already made you aware that right-clicking, or *context-clicking*, reveals a context menu near the mouse pointer.

As the name suggests, *context menus* contain commands relevant in a particular context or area of the screen. In other words, context-clicking a clip in the Timeline panel reveals a menu similar to the one you would see if you selected the clip and chose the Clip menu on the menu bar. The context menu for the Project panel contains commands that relate to it, such as the Import command. Like keyboard shortcuts, context menus can be real time savers.

To access a context menu:

1. Position the pointer on the appropriate window or item, and right-click.

   A menu relating to the panel or item appears (**Figure 1.34**).

2. Choose a command from the menu as you would from any other menu, and then release the mouse button.

   Premiere Pro executes the command.

Figure 1.34 Right-click to view a context menu, which is a menu that relates to the area where you clicked.

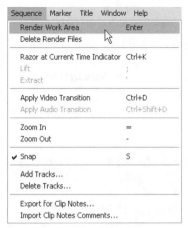

Figure 1.35 The keyboard shortcut for a menu command appears across from the command.

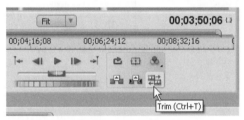

Figure 1.36 Hovering the mouse pointer over a button or icon reveals a tool tip, which identifies the item and its keyboard shortcut, if it has one.

Using Keyboard Shortcuts

One way to increase your speed and efficiency is to take advantage of keyboard shortcuts. A standard set of keyboard shortcuts, the Adobe Premiere Pro Factory Default shortcuts, is built in. Premiere Pro doesn't ship with a quick reference card for keyboard shortcuts, but the interface helps you learn them in other ways. The keyboard shortcut for a menu command appears across from the command in the right column (**Figure 1.35**). You may also have noticed that hovering the mouse pointer over a button or icon reveals a *tool tip*, a small box identifying both the item's name and its keyboard equivalent, if it has one (**Figure 1.36**). Other standard keyboard shortcuts are documented in the Help system. This book mentions the most common and useful shortcuts in the pertinent sections.

In addition to offering a standard set of shortcuts, Premiere Pro lets you create your own shortcut for practically every button, tool, and command. Moreover, you can save sets of shortcuts and easily switch among the sets. Sets are great when more than one editor uses the same Premiere Pro system. (Adjusting the chair height is still up to you.) And if you're accustomed to working on a version of Premiere prior to Premiere Pro, or even on a different editing system, you can create sets to match the shortcuts to the ones you're used to.

To view the keyboard shortcuts in Help:

1. Choose Help > Keyboard (**Figure 1.37**). Premiere Pro launches the Adobe Help Center (**Figure 1.38**).

2. In the Help system, click the appropriate related subtopics.

✔ Tip

■ Tool tips are turned on by default, but you can turn them off on the General panel of the Preferences dialog box.

To assign custom keyboard shortcuts:

1. Choose Edit > Keyboard Customization (**Figure 1.39**).

   The Keyboard Customization dialog box appears (**Figure 1.40**).

2. In the drop-down menu under the set name, choose the category of shortcut you want to view and edit:

   Application: Displays menu commands and other general shortcuts

   Windows: Displays shortcuts related to specific windows and their drop-down menus

   Tools: Displays shortcuts assigned to tools

Figure 1.37 Choose Help > Keyboard to learn about the keyboard shortcuts.

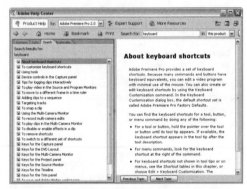

Figure 1.38 The Help feature launches in a browser window.

Figure 1.39 Choose Edit > Keyboard Customization.

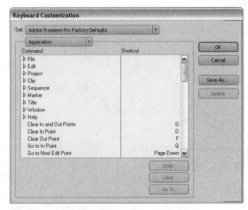

Figure 1.40 Create custom shortcuts using the Keyboard Customization dialog box.

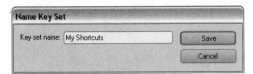

Figure 1.41 Click Save As to open the Name Key Set dialog box and save your custom set.

3. From the Command list, select the command or tool to which you want to assign a shortcut. If necessary, first click the triangle next to a subcategory to expand it and reveal the commands it contains.

4. *Do one of the following:*

▲ To assign a new shortcut to the selected item, type the shortcut.

▲ To remove the current shortcut from the selected item, click Clear.

5. If you want, *do one of the following when prompted:*

▲ To revert to the previous shortcut assignment, click Undo.

▲ To restore an undone shortcut, click Redo.

▲ To find the command that already uses the shortcut you assigned to the selected item (if any), click Go To.

6. Repeat steps 2–5 as needed.

To save a custom set of keyboard shortcuts:

1. In the Keyboard Customization dialog box, click Save As.

The Name Key Set dialog box appears (**Figure 1.41**).

2. Type a name for the key set, and click Save.

✔ Tip

■ In addition to the Adobe Premiere Pro Factory Default set, you can choose shortcuts for AVID Xpress DV and Apple Final Cut Pro.

USING KEYBOARD SHORTCUTS

Using the History Panel

Many people judge a program not only by how much it can do, but also by how much it can undo. The number of recent actions you can negate in Premiere Pro is limited only by the amount of available memory. If you change your mind yet again, you can redo the last undone action. The undo command's keyboard shortcut (Ctrl+Z) is practically universal and won't be covered in detail here. Instead, we'll correct mistakes using the History panel.

The History panel is like a super-undo— or a time machine. It lists your recent actions; each new action is added to the bottom of the list. By looking at the list, you can see exactly what you did and exactly where you went wrong. Clicking an action negates all the subsequent actions listed below it. When you resume editing, the undone actions are removed from the list, and history is rewritten.

To use the History panel:

1. If necessary, click the History tab to make the History panel visible.

   The panel lists the most recent actions, with the latest action at the bottom of the list (**Figure 1.42**).

2. Click the last action you want to retain (**Figure 1.43**).

   Actions below the selected action become dimmed in the list. The project reverts to the state it was in at the time the selected action was taken. To see the results of various selections, you can select the items even if they're currently dimmed.

3. If you're satisfied with your choice, resume other editing tasks.

   The dimmed actions disappear (**Figure 1.44**), and subsequent actions are added to the list.

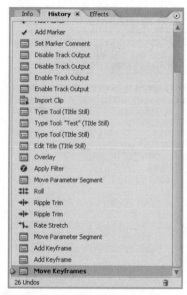

Figure 1.42 The History panel lists the actions you've taken; the most recent appears at the bottom.

Figure 1.43 Click an action in the list to return the project to the state it was in when that action was performed.

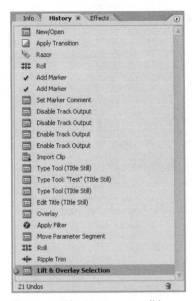

Figure 1.44 When you resume editing, the dimmed actions disappear, and your latest actions are added to the list.

To undo and remove actions from the History list:

1. On the History panel, select an action in the list.

   The project is returned to the state it was in at the time the selected action was taken.

2. *Do one of the following:*

   ▲ Click the Delete Redoable Actions icon (**Figure 1.45**).

   ▲ From the History panel menu, choose Delete.

3. When prompted, click Yes.

   The action and subsequent actions are removed from the list, and the project returns to the state it was in prior to the deleted actions (**Figure 1.46**).

Figure 1.45 On the History panel, select an action and click the Delete Redoable Actions icon.

Figure 1.46 The action and subsequent actions are removed from the list, and the project returns to the state it was in prior to the deleted actions.

To clear the History list without undoing actions:

◆ In the History panel menu, choose Clear History (**Figure 1.47**).

All items are removed from the list, but the project remains unchanged.

✔ Tips

■ The History panel doesn't list every move you make, just actions that affect the project.

■ Choosing File > Revert eliminates all the actions listed on the History panel since the project was last saved.

■ To cancel an action that Premiere Pro is processing (evidenced by a progress bar), press Esc.

■ When all else fails, you can open a project archived by the Auto-Save feature. For more information, see "Saving Projects Automatically," in Chapter 2.

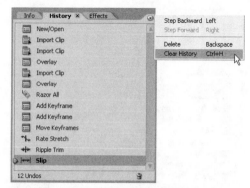

Figure 1.47 In the History panel menu, choose Clear History to clear the list without affecting the project.

STARTING A PROJECT

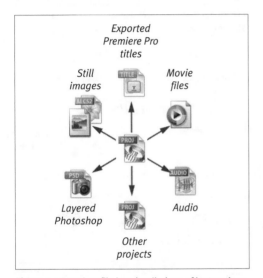

Exported
Premiere Pro
titles

Still
images

Movie
files

Layered
Photoshop

Audio

Other
projects

Figure 2.1 A project file is a detailed set of instructions that refers to—but doesn't contain—source files. Your hard drive must contain both the project (a small file) and the source files to which it refers (larger files).

When you edit with Adobe Premiere Pro, you're actually creating a detailed set of instructions called a *project* (**Figure 2.1**). A project contains a list of all the clips that you intend to use in your edited video program. It also contains a list of all your editing decisions, including the arrangement of the clips, transitions, audio levels, and effects.

You can think of a project as analogous to a musical score. Just as sheet music refers to instruments and indicates when they should play, the project refers to media files and indicates when they should play. A project doesn't contain the files themselves—only references to those files, called *clips*. As a result, you never alter the source files directly.

Hence, editing in Premiere Pro is sometimes referred to as *nondestructive editing*.

Because a project is simply a detailed set of instructions, a project file is small, sometimes less than 1 MB. The source files, on the other hand, tend to consume a lot of hard-drive space. For example, five minutes of DV footage with audio consumes more than 1 GB of storage. Returning to our analogy, you can slip sheet music into your pocket, but the actual orchestra is considerably more bulky.

In this chapter, you'll learn to start a new project, choose audio and video settings, and import a variety of source files as clips.

Starting a Project

After you launch Premiere Pro, a welcome screen prompts you to start a new project or open an existing one (**Figure 2.2**). Once you're working on a project, you can use a command on the menu bar to switch to another project or start a new one. You can have only one project open at a time, however.

The following steps outline how to start a project without detailing specific settings. For more about choosing project settings or specifying custom presets, continue reading this chapter.

To start a new project:

1. *Do one of the following:*

▲ Launch Premiere Pro. On the welcome screen, click New Project (**Figure 2.3**).

▲ With Premiere Pro running, choose File > New > Project (**Figure 2.4**).

The New Project dialog box opens (**Figure 2.5**).

2. In the New Project dialog box, *do one of the following:*

▲ To select the preset appropriate to your project, click the Load Preset tab.

▲ To specify settings (such as format, frame size, frame rate, and audio settings) suited to your project, click the Custom Settings tab.

A description of the preset's audio and video settings appears on the right side of the dialog box.

Figure 2.2 Premiere Pro's welcome screen makes starting a new or existing project easy.

Figure 2.3 To start a new project, click New Project on the welcome screen...

STARTING A PROJECT

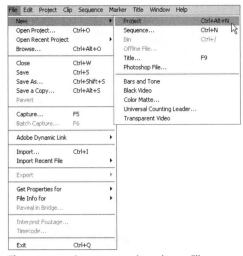

Figure 2.4 ...or, in an open project, choose File > New > Project.

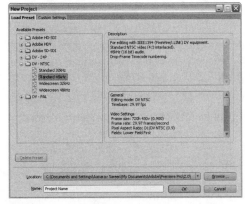

Figure 2.5 In the New Project dialog box, click the Load Preset tab to use presets, or click the Custom Settings tab to specify the settings manually.

3. Specify where you want to save the project file *by doing one of the following:*

  ▲ Enter the file path in the Location field.

  ▲ Click Browse to navigate to the location where you want to save the project file.

4. For Name, specify the name of the project. Premiere Pro automatically appends the .prproj extension to the file's name.

5. Click OK.

  Panels associated with the default workspace (Project, Monitor, Timeline, and so on) appear in the main application window. The Project pathname appears in the main application window bar.

✔ Tips

■ In contrast to older versions of Premiere, you may close the Project panel without closing the project itself.

■ When you launch Premiere Pro for the first time, it creates a Preferences file in the Application Data folder. If the Adobe Premiere Pro Preferences file becomes corrupted, causing the program to malfunction, delete the Preferences file to force the program to create a new, uncorrupted file.

STARTING A PROJECT

Specifying Project Settings

Project settings determine how Premiere Pro processes the audio and video as you edit. In most cases, you can choose one of the built-in presets that are optimized for several common scenarios, such as editing video in the DV format. However, you can also create custom settings to fit your particular needs.

Once you choose project settings, you can't change them for that project. Additionally, the project settings you choose apply to all the sequences in the project. Generally, your choice of settings is based on your source material, your capture device, your computer's ability to process video and audio, and your output goal.

The following sections explain how to select a built-in preset and then provide an overview to help you choose settings yourself.

✔ Tip

- If you discover that you've selected the wrong project settings after you've made significant progress on a sequence, don't panic. You can open a new project with the proper settings and import the sequence into it. Most of your editing decisions should remain intact. However, if the timebases of the two projects differ, clips in the sequence may be misaligned in the new project. In this case, double-check the In and Out points, and adjust them where necessary.

DV Is Easy

You could argue that the greatest advantage of the DV format isn't its high quality or affordability, but its ease of use. DV is digitized in the camera, it can be transferred to a hard drive over a single cable, it contains timecode, and it uses a consistent standard. For these reasons, DV users generally don't customize their project settings—they choose the appropriate DV preset and move on.

Unlike DV, which uses a widely accepted standard, capture cards generally use their own unique *codecs* (encoding/decoding schemes for storing and playing back video and audio). If you're using an analog video-capture card, chances are it comes with its own software, including a preset (which you can add to the list of available presets in the New Project dialog box). You can rely on the documentation that comes with your capture device, and you'll seldom need to stray from the settings designed for it.

If your current project isn't built around DV or a particular capture card, then your choices become more complex. Instead of choosing a ready-made preset, you have to select your own project settings.

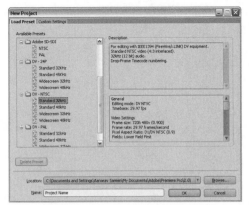

Figure 2.6 The Load Preset tab of the New Project dialog box presents a choice of built-in or custom-made project presets.

Choosing Built-in Presets

As you've learned, starting a new project opens the New Project dialog box, which includes a Load Preset tab and a Custom Settings tab.

When you select the Load Preset tab, the left side of the New Project dialog box lists project presets you can use. When you select a preset from the list, a description of the settings appears on the right side of the dialog box (**Figure 2.6**). The built-in presets include project settings optimized for common types of source footage, particularly DV:

◆ **Adobe HD-SDI:** Contains presets for editing High-Definition (HD) footage delivered via a Serial Digital Interface (SDI)—specifically, when using an AJA Xena HS system (developed jointly by Adobe and AJA Video).

◆ **Adobe HDV:** Contains presets for editing footage in the High Definition Video (HDV) format, which records high-definition, MPEG-2 video on standard DV media (DV or MiniDV tapes).

◆ **Adobe SD-SDI:** Contains presets for editing Standard-Definition (SD) footage delivered via an SDI—specifically, when using an AJA Xena HS system.

◆ **DV – NTSC:** Contains presets for DV footage (Digital Video format) shot in NTSC, the video standard used in North America, Japan, and other countries.

◆ **DV – PAL:** Contains presets for DV footage shot in PAL, the standard in most of Europe.

◆ **DV 24P:** Contains presets for footage shot using the 24P or 24P Advanced (24PA) format.

These folders each contain the following four options:

◆ **Standard 32kHz:** Used for DV footage shot in television's standard 4:3 aspect ratio, using 32-kHz audio, one of two audio sample rates supported by most DV cameras.

◆ **Standard 48kHz:** Used for DV footage shot in television's standard 4:3 aspect ratio, using 48-kHz audio.

◆ **Widescreen 32kHz:** Used for DV footage shot in a 16:9 aspect ratio, which is supported by some DV cameras and equipment, using 32-kHz audio.

◆ **Widescreen 48kHz:** Used for DV footage shot in a 16:9 aspect ratio, which is supported by some DV cameras and equipment, using 48-kHz audio.

✔ Tips

■ The DV presets' Default Sequence settings specify a stereo master track, which is suitable for most projects. Because you can't change a sequence's master track, you should use the custom settings to specify a different channel type (mono or 5.1) before you start a project (see the next section). Otherwise, you can create another sequence with the appropriate master audio track in the same project.

■ If you're not sure whether your DV footage was shot with 32-kHz or 48-kHz audio, check your camera's documentation or start a project and look at the clips' properties in the Project panel (see Chapter 4, "Managing Clips"). If you chose the wrong setting, start another project with the proper setting before you begin editing.

■ In video, the term *standard* can refer to image resolution—for example, *Standard Definition* as opposed to *High Definition*. It can also refer to image aspect ratio—for example, *standard* as opposed to widescreen.

Using Custom Project Settings

In the unlikely event one of the included presets doesn't match your footage, you can specify project settings manually on the Custom Settings tab of the New Project dialog box.

When the Custom Settings tab is selected, the left side of the dialog box lists four categories of settings: General, Capture, Video Rendering, and Default Sequence. For editing, you're primarily concerned with the General settings category. You'll learn more about the Capture, Video Rendering, and Default Sequence categories in later chapters.

This section explains only how to access the settings; for more complete explanations of each setting, consult Premiere Pro's Help system, or follow the instructions included with your capture card. Once you've specified settings appropriate to your situation, you can save the settings so they appear in the Available Presets list on the Load Preset tab of the New Project dialog box.

USING CUSTOM PROJECT SETTINGS

To select custom settings:

1. Start a new project.

   The New Project dialog box appears.

2. Select the Custom Settings tab.

3. To view settings to adjust them, click a category (**Figure 2.7**):

   ▲ **General:** Determines how Premiere Pro processes and displays video and audio. The General category also includes settings that specify safe zones and whether clips are scaled when added to a sequence.

   ▲ **Capture:** Sets the capture device.

   ▲ **Video Rendering:** Specifies the way video is compressed and whether stills are optimized for video display.

   ▲ **Default Sequence:** Sets the initial characteristics of new sequences in the project, such as the number of tracks and the type of audio tracks.

4. Select the settings that suit your project.

5. Specify Location and Name values, and click OK.

✔ Tip

■ Once you specify the channel type (mono, stereo, or 5.1) of a sequence's master track, you can't change it. However, you can create another sequence with a different type of master audio track in the same project.

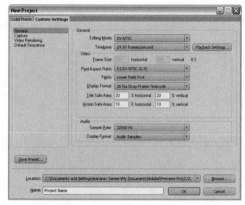

Figure 2.7 On the Custom Settings tab of the New Project dialog box, click a settings category from the list on the left.

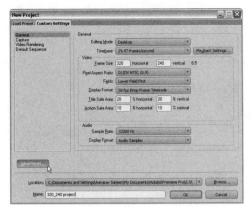

Figure 2.8 Once you've specified your settings, click Save Preset.

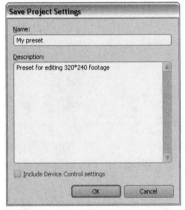

Figure 2.9 In the Save Project Settings dialog box, type a name and description for your preset.

To save custom project settings:

1. Specify the project settings as explained in the previous task, "To select custom settings."

2. On the Custom Settings tab of the New Project dialog box, click Save Preset (**Figure 2.8**).

   The Save Project Settings dialog box appears (**Figure 2.9**).

3. Type a name for your settings and a description that summarizes your choices.

4. To save settings pertaining to a capture device as part of the preset, select Include Device Control Settings.

5. Click OK to close the dialog box.

6. Click OK to close the New Project dialog box and start your project.

   From now on, your saved preset will appear in the Available Presets section of the Load Preset tab of the New Project dialog box. When you select this preset, the description you entered will appear in the Description area.

✔ Tip

■ You can delete a custom preset by selecting it and clicking the Delete Preset button.

USING CUSTOM PROJECT SETTINGS

Saving Projects

Because your project file embodies all your editing decisions, protecting it from possible mishaps is crucial. As with any important file, you should save your project often and keep backups. Premiere Pro can help you protect your project by automatically saving it in the Adobe Premiere Pro Auto-Save folder. In the event of a system crash or file corruption, you can retrieve one of the archived copies.

To save a project:

1. *Do one of the following:*

▲ Choose File > Save to save the project under the current name and location or to save the project for the first time.

▲ Choose File > Save As (**Figure 2.10**) to save the project under a new name or location and continue working on the new copy of the project.

▲ Choose File > Save a Copy to save a copy of the current project and continue working on the current project.

2. If you're prompted by a dialog box, specify a name and destination for the project (**Figure 2.11**).

3. Click Save to close the dialog box and save the file.

Figure 2.10 To save a file under a new name or in a different location, choose File > Save As.

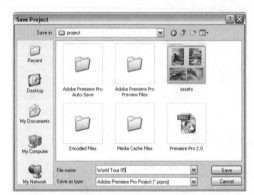

Figure 2.11 If prompted, specify a name and destination for the project.

Figure 2.12 Choose File > Revert to revert to the last-saved version.

Figure 2.13 When prompted, confirm your choice.

To revert to the last-saved version of a project:

1. Choose File > Revert (**Figure 2.12**).

   Premiere Pro prompts you to confirm your choice (**Figure 2.13**).

2. Click Yes to confirm that you want to revert to the last-saved version.

   The project returns to the state it was in when you last saved it.

Saving Projects Automatically

Premiere Pro can back up your project automatically as frequently as you choose. Backup files are saved in a folder called Adobe Premiere Pro Auto-Save, which is located in the same directory as the original project. Backup files use the original project name followed by a dash and a number (*filename*-1.prproj, *filename*-2.prproj, and so on).

To set automatic save:

1. Choose Edit > Preferences > Auto Save (**Figure 2.14**).

   The Auto Save panel of the Preferences dialog box opens.

2. Click the Automatically Save Projects check box, and type the time interval at which you want Premiere Pro to save the current project (**Figure 2.15**).

3. For Maximum Project Versions, enter the number of versions of each project that you want Premiere Pro to automatically save.

   When the maximum number of saved versions is reached, each additional saved version overwrites the oldest saved file.

4. Click OK to close the Preferences dialog box.

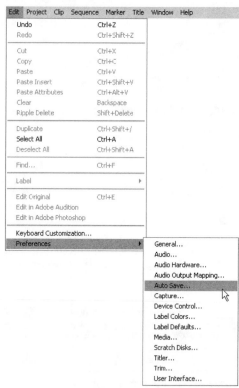

Figure 2.14 Choose Edit > Preferences > Auto Save to set the automatic save option.

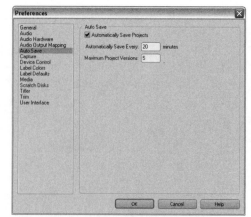

Figure 2.15 Select Automatically Save Projects and enter a time interval and the maximum number of project versions.

Figure 2.16 To open a project, click Open Project on the welcome screen...

Figure 2.17 ...or, in an open project, choose File > Open Project.

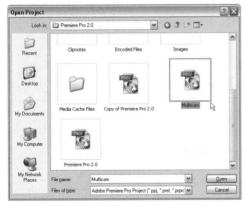

Figure 2.18 Navigate to the project you want to open, and select it.

Opening Projects

Premiere Pro's welcome screen makes it easy to open a project right after you launch the program. But, naturally, you can switch to another project at any time by using a menu command.

To open a project:

1. *Do one of the following:*

   ▲ On the welcome screen, click the Open Project icon (**Figure 2.16**).

   ▲ In an open project, choose File > Open Project (**Figure 2.17**).

   The Open Project dialog box appears.

2. Select the project file that you want to open (**Figure 2.18**).

   Auto-saved projects are located in the Adobe Premiere Pro Auto-Save folder, which resides in the Premiere Pro folder.

3. Click Open.

To open a recent project:

◆ *Do one of the following:*

▲ On the welcome screen, click the project's name in the Recent Projects list (**Figure 2.19**).

▲ In an open project, Choose File > Open Recent Project and choose the recently open project from the submenu (**Figure 2.20**).

The project opens.

✔ Tip

■ Closing a project returns you to the welcome screen, where you can quickly choose whether to start a new or existing project. Clicking Exit on the welcome screen quits Premiere Pro.

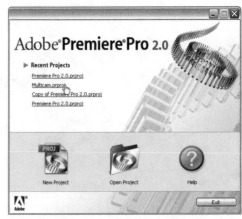

Figure 2.19 To open a recent project, click the name of the project on the welcome screen...

OPENING PROJECTS

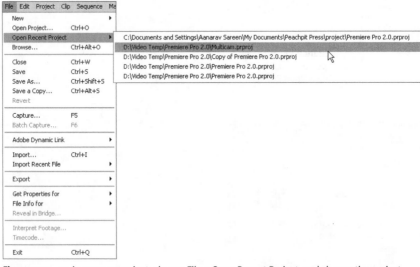

Figure 2.20 ...or, in an open project, choose File > Open Recent Project, and choose the project you want.

Locating Missing and Offline Files

As you learned at the beginning of this chapter, a project is simply a set of instructions that refers to files on a drive. When you open a project, Premiere Pro looks for the files to which the project refers. If the source files have been moved, deleted, or renamed since the project was last saved, Premiere Pro will have trouble finding them. Premiere Pro attempts to locate the missing clips and prompts you to confirm its choice. (Premiere Pro also attempts to find missing preview files; see Chapter 10, "Previewing a Sequence.")

Sometimes, a project refers to a file that is not currently available, or *offline*. Fortunately, you can tell Premiere Pro to insert a blank placeholder, or *offline clip*, to stand in until you can get the file back on your drive (or *online*) again. Naturally, when you use an offline clip, you can't view the file it's holding a place for, but using the offline clip permits the project to remember the name of the file and recall how you used it in your program.

Once you've accounted for missing files, resave the project. From then on, the updated project will open without incident, because you've told it where to find the files you want and not to look for the ones you don't want. If you say a clip is offline, it doesn't mean the clip is missing; the project just lists it as offline until you decide to capture it or to relink it with its source media file. For more about creating and capturing offline files, see Chapter 3, "Capturing and Importing Footage." For more about unlinking and relinking clips and media, see Chapter 4.

✔ Tips

- In this context, the term *offline* means unavailable, or not on a drive. Don't confuse offline clips with the term *offline editing*, which is the practice of creating a low-quality rough cut in preparation for *online editing*, which produces the final version.

- When the Project panel is set to list view, the Status column indicates a clip's status as Online, Offline, or Offline: File Missing. The clip's icon also indicates whether the clip is online or offline.

To open a project with missing files that are available:

1. Open a project using any of the methods described in the previous sections.

   If files are missing, the Where Is the File dialog box opens. The name of the missing file appears in quotation marks as part of the name of the dialog box (**Figure 2.21**).

2. To find a file, *do one of the following:*

   ▲ Allow Premiere Pro to automatically locate a file with the same name as the missing file.

   ▲ Manually locate the missing file or its replacement.

   ▲ Click Find to launch the Windows search feature to help locate the file.

3. When you locate the correct file, select it and click the Select button (**Figure 2.22**).

   The missing file is replaced with the selected file.

4. If necessary, repeat steps 2 and 3 when you're prompted to locate other missing clips. If missing clips aren't available on your hard drive, follow the instructions in the next task, "To open a project with missing files that are unavailable."

✔ Tips

■ As a rule, use a consistent organizational method for your files and avoid moving or renaming them until your project has been delivered and is ready to archive.

■ Unless you're in the bad habit of moving, renaming, or deleting files, there are only a few reasons Premiere Pro will prompt you for missing files—for example, if you have moved the project and media to another system or restored the files from a backup. In these cases, the media probably aren't on the same drive as when you saved the project.

Figure 2.21 If files are missing, the Where Is the File dialog box appears.

Figure 2.22 When you locate the correct file, select it and click Select.

Figure 2.23 If the file is unavailable, skip the file, designate it as offline, or cancel the search.

To open a project with missing files that are unavailable:

1. Open a project using any of the methods described in the previous sections.

   If files are missing, the Where Is the File dialog box opens. The name of the missing file appears in quotation marks as part of the name of the dialog box.

2. *Click one of the following buttons* (**Figure 2.23**):

   ▲ **Cancel** to close the dialog box without accounting for missing files. Premiere Pro will treat the files as missing the next time you open the project.

   ▲ **Skip** to remove the missing clip from the project. All instances of the clip disappear from the project, including the edited sequence.

   ▲ **Skip All** to have Premiere Pro remove all missing clips from the project without prompting you for confirmation.

   ▲ **Skip Previews** to remove all missing preview files from the project. Preview files are rendered audio and video effects, including transitions (see Chapter 10).

   ▲ **Offline** to list the missing file in the project as an offline clip.

   ▲ **Offline All** to have Premiere Pro list all missing files in the project as offline without prompting you for confirmation.

3. Repeat step 2 each time you're prompted to locate a missing file.

   Once you account for all missing files, the project opens.

4. Save the project to update the status of the missing clips.

CAPTURING & IMPORTING FOOTAGE

3

Once you've selected the proper settings for your project, it's time to begin adding footage to it. Usually, this means getting the video from a tape to your hard drive—a process known as video *capture*.

In Premiere Pro, all the controls you need for capture are integrated into a single Capture panel. You can control a camera or deck from within the Capture panel, which has built-in presets for controlling numerous devices, including most DV devices. The Capture panel also incorporates tabbed panels for viewing the current capture settings and for logging clips in a batch list.

But you aren't limited to using video footage in Premiere Pro. As explained in Chapter 2, "Starting a Project," you can import a wide range of digitally stored content: movie files in various formats; audio files; still images, including bitmapped and EPS files; numbered image sequences; and other Premiere Pro project files. Maybe you've already started using the files in Premiere Pro's sample folder. In addition, Premiere Pro generates commonly used footage items: black video, color fields, bars and tone, and a countdown. You can even create new Photoshop files from inside Premiere Pro. You can also generate titles, but we'll save that topic for Chapter 12, "Creating Titles."

Understanding Capture

It's not enough to have your video in a digital form; it must also be in a format that's practical to use for editing. In a digital file, every frame of standard (as opposed to high-definition) video consumes nearly 1 MB. Capturing and playing approximately 30 frames per second (the standard frame rate) is impossible for most processors and drives; the *data rate*, or flow of information, is simply too high, and the storage capacity needed to hold such enormous files is too great.

Some professionals use equipment that can process digital video in a relatively pristine, or *uncompressed*, form. However, most users either don't require or can't afford this level of quality; they use equipment that *compresses* the video for use on the computer. Compression is one way to reduce the file size (and thereby the data rate) of the video, making it easier to store, process, and play back. Other audio and video settings, such as frame size and frame rate, also affect the data rate. Along with your final output goal, the equipment you use helps determine the video and audio settings you choose for capturing video.

This chapter illustrates the capture process using a DV video source. Your particular capture device may require slightly different choices and dialog boxes, but the overall process won't vary. Consult the documentation that came with your hardware to learn about the options specific to your system.

USB 2, Fast USB

For many people, DV and IEEE 1394 are synonymous. The DV video standard emerged around the same time as the IEEE 1394 transfer protocol, and they worked in tandem to make video acquisition and editing easier than ever before.

However, IEEE 1394 isn't the only way to move data—including video data—quickly and easily. USB 2 (the second iteration of the Universal Serial Bus standard, aka Fast USB) is also up to the task. And in contrast to IEEE 1394, USB 2 connections are more often a standard feature of new computers. For this reason, manufacturers increasingly include a USB 2 port on DV camcorders.

IEEE 1394

IEEE 1394 provides simple, inexpensive, fast data exchange between electronic devices—most famously, between a video camera and a computer. If your computer doesn't already have an IEEE 1394 controller card, you can usually install one yourself. IEEE (pronounced "eye-triple-E") stands for the Institute of Electrical and Electronics Engineers, Inc., a non-profit association of professionals who develop standards to foster compatibility between devices. They dubbed their 1,394th effort—what else?—IEEE 1394. However, the folks at Apple dubbed it FireWire—a much snappier and more descriptive name. Sony uses name iLink for its IEEE 1394–capable devices. In the spirit of fairness, this book opts for the more generic (albeit more awkward) moniker IEEE 1394.

There are two forms of IEEE 1394. The original version is now known as IEEE 1394a, or FireWire 400, because its theoretical transfer rate is 400 Mbps. A newer iteration is called IEEE 1394b, or FireWire 800, because its theoretical transfer rate is 800 Mbps. There's a big difference between theoretical rates and actual transfer speeds, but even so, IEEE 1394b devices can move data much faster than their IEEE 1394a counterparts. In addition, IEEE 1394b cables—which use a different connector than IEEE 1394a cables—can be much longer.

These advantages don't come into play when you're capturing standard DV footage. IEEE 1394a easily handles DV's data rate, and a faster transfer rate won't make a videotape play any faster. However, the faster throughput could be handy if you're using formats with higher data rates, or when you need to move large files, like video files.

For the sake of simplicity, this book refers to both formats as IEEE 1394 unless there's a reason to distinguish them.

UNDERSTANDING CAPTURE

Capturing DV vs. Digitizing Analog

If you're using the widely accepted DV format, the capture process couldn't be much easier. DV cameras compress the video in the camera and record the resulting DV signal onto any of several DV tape formats, most commonly MiniDV. If your computer is equipped with the right port—known variously as FireWire, iLink, or IEEE 1394—you can transfer footage from a DV camera or deck to your hard disk in much the same way you copy files from one disk to another. But because an IEEE 1394 connection is often an optional addition to a computer, many cameras use a USB 2 (aka Fast USB) connection, which is a standard feature on most new computers. Both transfer methods can deliver DV video, audio, and timecode information to your hard disk over a single cable (**Figure 3.1**). Assuming that your system is fast enough to play DV (with its relatively lenient 3.6-MBps data rate), you're in business. The DV standard is just that: standard. It narrows what would otherwise be an intimidating selection of video and audio settings into a single set of options.

Figure 3.1 DV footage—including video, audio, and timecode—can be transferred over a single IEEE 1394 connection.

Despite the pervasiveness of DV, video and audio are still commonly recorded, stored, and delivered using an analog signal. Common lower-end formats include VHS and Hi8 videotape and conventional audio-cassette tapes.

To use analog media, most computers require a video capture card—add-on hardware that you can install in one of your computer's expansion slots. The capture card *digitizes* analog video and audio, converting it to digital form for storage on your computer. Generally, separate cables deliver the video, audio, and timecode (if timecode is present) (**Figure 3.2**). With some cards, the video is digitized using Motion-JPEG (MJPEG) compression. Other capture devices can convert analog sources

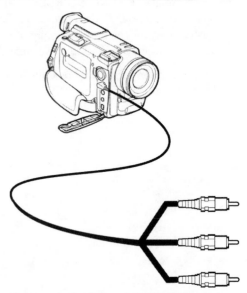

Figure 3.2 Analog footage is digitized with a capture card. Separate cables deliver the video and audio. A professional deck and a separate device-control cable are often required to deliver timecode.

DV or Not DV

Although *DV* stands for *digital video,* it actually refers to a specific type of signal that can be stored in certain formats.

You may encounter several flavors of DV. All these formats record the same type of DV signal, but each records it in a slightly different way:

MiniDV: This is the consumer version, often called simply *DV.* It's used by the DV cameras offered by consumer electronics vendors.

DVCam: Sony's professional variation of DV records a DV signal at a different *track pitch*, which uses more tape and provides a more reliable signal. Sony's cameras and decks can also read MiniDV.

DVCPro: Panasonic's professional variety of DV records the signal at an even greater track pitch and uses a more durable metal particle tape. Panasonic's equipment also supports DVCPro50, which doubles the standard data rate to achieve better color reproduction and more detail.

As far as capturing video in Premiere Pro is concerned, it doesn't matter which format you use, but you should understand the difference when you're choosing other equipment, such as cameras, decks, and tapes. Although the essential DV signals are the same, the quality and cost of the equipment differ greatly, and the equipment isn't interchangeable.

to the DV format. Through these processes, you can enjoy some of DV's editing advantages even if you didn't shoot or store the video in DV.

Of course, DV isn't the only digital format, and IEEE 1394 isn't the only digital interface used to transfer video. A film or broadcast professional may opt for a capture device that uses an uncompressed format, which in turn requires bigger, faster drives and high-speed interfaces. The capabilities, requirements, and prices of capture devices vary widely. When you choose a technology, do your homework and consider the implications from preproduction to distribution.

✔ Tips

■ Not all capture cards certified to work with earlier versions of Premiere have been certified to work with Premiere Pro. Be sure to check Adobe's Web site for an updated list of certified capture devices.

■ When you're putting together a DV editing system, be sure to get enough drive space for your needs: about 1 GB for every 5 minutes of video.

■ The maximum size for a single file isn't determined by Premiere Pro but by your operating system, your capture device, and the file system used by your hard disk. Hard disks formatted using FAT32 limit files to 4 GB each. Disks formatted using NTFS don't limit file size. Your capture device, however, may restrict file size; check its documentation.

CAPTURING DV VS. DIGITIZING ANALOG

Understanding Capture Options

At minimum, video capture requires a video source (a camera or deck) and a capture device (an IEEE 1394 or Fast USB connection or an analog capture card). Additional options like device control and timecode make features such as automated capture—or batch capture—available, and they also make it possible to employ an offline/online editing strategy. Most professionals don't consider these "options" at all, but crucial tools for a professional workflow.

Device control, timecode, and batch capture are summarized in this section. Later sections put these concepts into practice.

Device control

As the name indicates, *device control* gives Premiere Pro a means of controlling an external device—usually a videotape deck or camera, although it could also be a digital disk recorder or DAT player, for example. When you enable device control, Premiere Pro's Capture panel includes buttons that allow you to control the camera or deck from within Premiere Pro. Device control can also activate a camera or deck to record your finished program (see Chapter 15, "Creating Output"). Premiere Pro can control most DV devices via IEEE 1394, Fast USB, or most professional RS-422 and RS-232 interfaces; even so, some cameras and decks may require add-on hardware and software.

Timecode

Videotapes can be encoded with a signal called *timecode* that identifies each frame of video with a unique number, expressed in hours, minutes, seconds, and frames. Using timecode as a frame-accurate reference, you can create a *batch list*—a list of shots defined by start and end times. Premiere Pro can use timecode combined with device control to capture clips in the batch list automatically. Similarly, timecode makes it possible to recapture clips at different qualities, as when you replace offline-quality clips with clips captured at output quality. Timecode is always included in the DV signal, but for other video formats and devices, timecode is considered a professional option.

Batch capture

With device control and timecoded source tapes, Premiere Pro can capture clips automatically—a process known as *batch capture*. Device control enables Premiere Pro to cue and play the tape in the camera or deck; timecode makes it possible for Premiere Pro to locate the exact shot logged in the batch list.

✔ Tip

■ Unlike previous versions, Premiere Pro doesn't log clips in a separate batch list or file. Instead, clips are logged in the Project panel as *offline*. Nevertheless, *batch list* is still an industry term that refers to any list of shots awaiting batch capture.

Control without Timecode

To control a camera or deck, device control doesn't require that your tapes contain timecode or that your device read timecode. Some device controllers can even use your deck's counter numbers (which count frames using the tape's control track) to capture a specified shot, although the process won't be frame-accurate. Unlike timecode, counter numbers are arbitrary and can be reset at any time. Counter numbers aren't encoded into the captured clip and can't be used for batch lists or batch capturing.

Using the Capture Panel

The Capture panel includes two tabbed palettes: Logging and Settings. Selecting the Logging tab reveals controls you can use to set In and Out points, either to define the clips you want to capture right away or to log clips in the Project panel so they can be batch-captured later. Select the Settings tab to view and change capture settings or to set up *scratch disks* (disks you designate for particular tasks) and device control.

To open the Capture panel:

◆ Choose File > Capture (**Figure 3.3**).

The Capture panel appears (**Figure 3.4**).

Figure 3.3 Choose File > Capture to open the Capture panel.

Figure 3.4 The Capture panel.

USING THE CAPTURE PANEL

Figure 3.5
The Logging tab's
controls let you
log and capture
footage.

Figure 3.6
The controls on
the Settings tab
let you specify
settings and
scratch disks and
set up device
control.

To hide or show tabs in the Capture panel:

◆ In the Capture panel, *do one of the following:*

▲ To display controls for logging and capturing footage, select the Logging tab (**Figure 3.5**).

▲ To display controls for specifying the settings and scratch disks (the disks used to store captured audio and video) and for setting up device control, select the Settings tab (**Figure 3.6**).

▲ To hide the tabs, choose Collapse Window from the Capture panel's pull-down menu (**Figure 3.7**).

▲ To display the tabs, choose Expand Window from the Capture panel's pull-down menu (**Figure 3.8**).

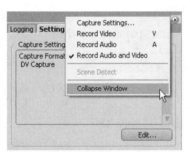

Figure 3.7 Choose Collapse Window to hide the tabs.

Figure 3.8 Choose Expand Window to display the tabs.

Choosing Capture Settings

As discussed in Chapter 2, "Starting a Project," the Project Settings dialog box includes a Capture category. You can access the Capture panel of the Project settings dialog box from the Capture panel. Usually, though, doing so isn't necessary, especially when you're capturing DV over an IEEE 1394 or USB 2 interface; once again, the DV presets take care of everything so you can get to work.

Even so, you should know where to find the settings, if only to tweak a few options. You might check the capture settings if you have more than one capture device installed, or if you want to specify whether to play video and audio in the Capture panel only or through your capture device to a television and external speakers as well.

To specify capture settings in the Capture panel:

1. In the Capture panel, select the Settings tab.

   The Settings panel appears.

2. In the Capture Settings area of the Capture panel's Settings panel, click the Edit button (**Figure 3.9**).

   The Capture panel of the Project Settings dialog box appears.

3. In the Capture Format pull-down menu, select an option.

   For systems using DV over an IEEE 1394 controller, the only option is DV Capture.

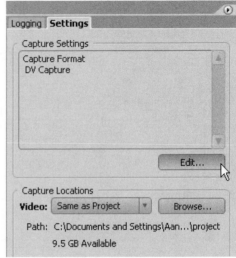

Figure 3.9 Click the Edit button in the Capture Settings area of the Capture panel's Settings panel.

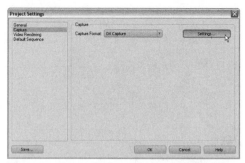

Figure 3.10 Choose the Capture Format option that matches your equipment, and then click the Settings button to specify capture settings.

Figure 3.11 Specify options in the DV Capture Options dialog box.

4. To specify playback settings when using the Capture panel, click Settings (**Figure 3.10**).

The Settings button appears only when you specify DV Capture as the Capture Format. The DV Capture Options dialog box appears (**Figure 3.11**).

5. In the DV Capture Options dialog box, specify whether you want to view the video and audio on the desktop while previewing or capturing footage.

Selecting an item plays the video or audio in the Capture panel; leaving it unchecked plays the video or audio on an external video monitor and speakers via the capture device only.

6. Click OK to close the DV Capture Options dialog box, and click OK again to close the Project Settings dialog box.

Choosing a Capture Location

Before you capture, choose the disks that Premiere Pro uses to save video and audio media files. If possible, specify a fast disk with ample storage space to help ensure that all frames are captured successfully.

To set the capture location:

1. In the Capture panel, select the Settings tab.

   The Capture panel's Settings panel appears, showing a summary of the capture settings and preferences.

2. In the Capture Locations area of the Settings panel, specify where you want to save captured clips *by doing one of the following:*

   ▲ Choose a folder from the Video pull-down menu (**Figure 3.12**).

   ▲ Click the Video Browse button to navigate to another folder or to create a new one (**Figure 3.13**).

   The path you chose as the location for saving media appears below the Video and Audio pull-down menus.

✔ Tips

■ To optimize your system for video editing, use your boot disk (C drive) for your system and software. Dedicate a different disk to media.

■ A capture location is essentially a type of scratch disk. Later in the book, you'll learn how to specify scratch disks for video and audio preview files and for conformed audio files.

Figure 3.12 To specify where to save captured media, choose a folder in the Video pull-down menu...

Figure 3.13 ...or click Browse to navigate to another folder or create a new one.

CHOOSING A CAPTURE LOCATION

Figure 3.14 In the Device Control section of the Settings tab, choose one of the options from the Device pull-down menu.

Using Device Control

DV devices can be controlled over the same IEEE 1394 or USB 2 cable that delivers video and audio, and the plug-ins for controlling most DV cameras and decks come built into Premiere Pro.

Other equipment may utilize *serial device control*, such as the standards known as RS-232 or RS-422. Serial device controllers usually include two components: a hardware cable to connect your computer to your deck and a software plug-in to put in the Premiere Pro Plug-Ins folder. However, Premiere Pro 2.0 usually eliminates the need for a separate plug-in by supporting RS-232 and RS-422 protocols natively. The controller's cable controls the deck and delivers timecode data only; video and audio are delivered over separate cables. Consult the documentation that came with your device-control equipment to make sure the equipment is set up properly.

To enable device control:

1. Make sure your device-control hardware is connected.

2. In the Capture panel, select the Settings tab.

   The Settings panel appears.

3. In the Device Control section of the Settings panel, choose an option from the Device pull-down menu (**Figure 3.14**):

   ▲ **None:** Capture without controlling a camera or deck.

   ▲ **DV/HDV Device Control:** Use Premiere Pro's built-in ability to control most DV and HDV cameras and decks.

   If software for other capture devices is installed in the Premiere Pro Plug-Ins folder, you can select that option from the list.

continues on next page

USING DEVICE CONTROL

4. To specify a particular camera or deck, click the Options button.

See the following task, "To set DV device-control options," for a detailed explanation.

✔ Tip

■ If your system doesn't support device control—either because your camera or deck lacks the capability or because you lack device-control hardware or software—you can still capture. The Capture panel's playback controls will appear dimmed, but the Stop and Record buttons will still work.

To set DV or HDV device-control options:

1. In the Device Control section of the Settings panel, choose DV/HDV Device Control from the Device pull-down menu.

2. Under the Device pull-down menu, click the Options button (**Figure 3.15**).

The Options dialog box appears (**Figure 3.16**).

3. Select the options appropriate to your system from the pull-down menus:

▲ **Video Standard:** The video standard used by your equipment. NTSC is the standard used in North America and Japan. PAL is the standard used in most of Europe.

▲ **Device Brand:** The brand of the camera or deck you're using (**Figure 3.17**). If your brand doesn't appear on the menu, choose Generic.

Figure 3.15 Click Options to open the Options dialog box.

Figure 3.16 The Options dialog box.

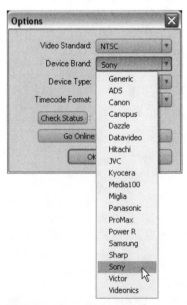

Figure 3.17 Choose the appropriate options from the pull-down menus, such as the brand of the device you're using.

▲ **Device Type:** The model of the camera or deck you're using. If your model doesn't appear on the menu, choose a closely related model, or choose Standard.

▲ **Timecode Format:** The counting method used by your tape and playback device. Most MiniDV equipment records drop-frame timecode. Other DV devices may offer a choice between drop-frame and non–drop-frame timecode. If you're unsure, choose Auto-Detect to have Premiere Pro determine the correct timecode format.

4. Click the Check Status button to see if device control is ready:

▲ **Online:** Indicates that the device is connected and ready to use.

▲ **Offline:** Indicates that the device isn't connected or isn't ready to use.

5. To open a browser and connect to Adobe's hardware guide for Premiere Pro, click Go Online for Device Info.

6. Click OK to close the DV Device Control Options dialog box.

The type of device you specified appears in the Device Control area of the Capture panel's Settings panel.

USING DEVICE CONTROL

To set other device-control options:

1. In the Capture panel, select the Settings tab.

   The Settings panel appears.

2. In the Device Control area of the Settings tab, specify the following options (**Figure 3.18**):

   ▲ **Preroll Time:** Enter the number of seconds the deck or camera rewinds before a specified point. Preroll allows the deck to reach normal playback speed before digitizing begins.

   ▲ **Timecode Offset:** If necessary, enter the number of frames to compensate for discrepancies between the timecode on the tape and that of the captured clips. Use this feature according to the documentation included with your capture device and device controller.

   ▲ **Abort Capture on Dropped Frames:** Select this option to stop capture whenever your system drops, or fails to capture, any frames of a clip.

✔ Tips

■ By default, Premiere Pro generates a report if any frames are dropped during capture. To change this setting, choose Edit > Preferences and select the Capture category in the Preferences dialog box.

■ Support for serial device control protocols —specifically, RS-232 and RS-422—is built into Premiere Pro 2.0. However, you may still have to calibrate your equipment to ensure the timecode on the captured clips matches the timecode on the source tapes. Do this by capturing footage from a timecode window dub and using the Timecode Offset feature to synchronize the actual timecode with the frame number displayed in the timecode window.

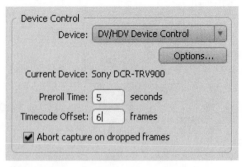

Figure 3.18 If necessary, specify the preroll time, timecode offset, and whether to abort capture on dropped frames.

Using Playback Controls in the Capture Panel

Once device control is set up, you can control a camera or deck from the Capture panel. Although most of the Capture panel's controls should be familiar to you, a few special features are worth reviewing (**Figure 3.19**).

Most notably, you can cue the tape to the frame at which the camera stopped and restarted recording. As you'll see, the Scene Detect feature not only makes it possible to quickly find different shots on the tape, but also allows you to capture an entire tape automatically—each shot becomes a separate clip.

You can also enter timecode numbers to set the current frame, In point, Out point, or duration.

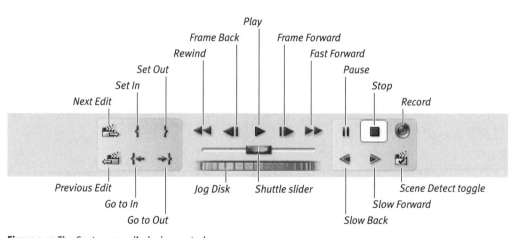

Figure 3.19 The Capture panel's device controls.

To cue a tape to a specified timecode:

1. Make sure your device-control hardware is connected.

2. In the Capture panel, click the current time display, enter a valid timecode, and press Enter (**Figure 3.20**).

   The tape cues to the frame you specified.

✔ Tips

■ The Scene Detect feature isn't available when you're using a serial device controller.

■ When the tape is stopped, the playhead is no longer engaged, so that it rewinds and fast-forwards faster but doesn't scan the tape. The Capture panel displays the last frame you viewed until you engage the playhead again by using another playback control.

■ Many cameras or decks enter a standby mode after several minutes of inactivity and disengage the playhead so as not to unnecessarily wear the tape.

Current time display

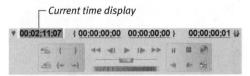

Figure 3.20 Click the current time display, enter a valid timecode, and press Enter.

Figure 3.21 Choose File > Capture to open the Capture panel.

Capturing Audio and Video

Even though it takes the next several tasks to cover the capture process, don't be alarmed: Premiere Pro's Capture panel makes capturing straightforward. The following sections explain the variations. You can capture clips on the fly by playing and recording the footage. Or, you can define a clip's start and end times (its In point and Out point, respectively) before you commit it to the hard drive. Finally, you can use Premiere Pro's Scene Detect feature to capture clips automatically, so that each camera shot becomes a separate clip. The methods are similar and, for the most part, intuitive.

Whatever process you choose, you should first specify the tape name. Then, each clip you capture or log will be associated with its source tape, which is essential for keeping track of your material and maintaining a grip on your sanity. You should also specify the tracks you want to capture from the tape: video, audio, or both.

To specify the tracks and tape name:

1. Choose File > Capture (**Figure 3.21**).

   If device control is set up properly, the Capture panel appears with buttons to control the camera or deck. Otherwise, you can use the camera's or deck's controls (sometimes called *local controls*).

2. In the Capture panel, select the Logging tab.

   The Logging panel appears.

   continues on next page

CAPTURING AUDIO AND VIDEO

3. In the Setup area of the Logging panel, choose the tracks you want from the Capture pull-down menu (**Figure 3.22**).

4. In the Clip Data area of the Logging panel, in the Tape Name field, specify a name for the tape (**Figure 3.23**).

5. Capture or log footage using any the methods explained in the following sections.

✔ Tips

■ You can also specify the tracks you want to capture in the Capture panel's pull-down menu.

■ You can record a voice-over track directly to a track in the timeline using the Audio Mixer. For details, see Chapter 11, "Mixing Audio."

■ It's impossible to record over a tape using the Capture panel, but it *is* possible from your deck or camera controls. Play it safe, and set the tape to "record inhibit" by sliding its tab into the save position (for formats like MiniDV) or by removing the tab (for formats like VHS).

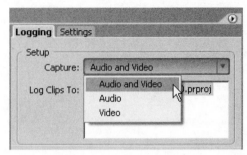

Figure 3.22 On the Logging tab, choose the tracks you want to capture from the Capture pull-down menu.

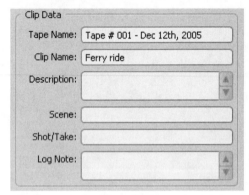

Figure 3.23 Specify the tape's name in the Tape Name field.

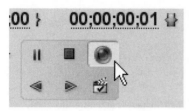

Figure 3.24 When the tape reaches the part you want to capture, click the Record button.

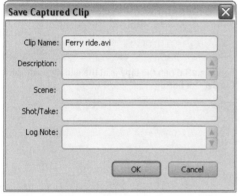

Figure 3.25 When you press Esc or click Pause or Stop, the Save Captured Clip dialog box opens.

Figure 3.26 After you save the captured file, it's listed as a clip in the Project panel.

To capture a clip without specifying an In point or Out point:

1. Open the Capture panel, and, on the Logging tab, specify the tape name and tracks, as explained in the previous task.

2. Using the playback controls in the Capture panel or on the deck, play the tape. When it reaches the part you want to capture, click the Capture panel's Record button ● (**Figure 3.24**).

3. When you've captured the footage you want to save as a clip, press Esc or click the Pause or Stop button.

   A Save Captured Clip dialog box appears (**Figure 3.25**).

4. In the Clip Name field, type a name for the captured media file.

   By default, Premiere Pro provides the proper file name extension, such as .avi.

5. If you want, enter additional information about the clip in the appropriate fields.

   These fields correspond to clip information categories in the Project panel.

6. Click OK to close the dialog box and return to the Capture panel.

   The Project panel lists the captured file as a clip (**Figure 3.26**).

✔ Tips

■ The status area at the top of the Capture panel displays information about the capture progress.

■ If no image appears in the Capture panel, the problem is usually something embarrassingly simple. Make sure the camera or deck is on, check your cable connections, and be sure the tape contains (or is cued to) video.

To capture a clip with a specified In point and Out point:

1. Choose File > Capture to open the Capture panel.

2. If necessary, set up device control, as explained in the section "Using Device Control" earlier in this chapter or in the documentation that shipped with the device controller.

   If device control is set up properly, the Capture panel appears with buttons to control the deck.

3. In the Capture panel, select the Logging tab and specify the tape name and tracks, as explained in the task "To specify the tracks and tape name," earlier in this chapter.

4. Use the playback controls in the Capture panel to cue the tape to the starting point, and *do one of the following:*

   ▲ In the Logging panel, click the Set In button (**Figure 3.27**).

   ▲ In the Capture panel's playback controls, click the Set In button {.

   The current time appears as the In point for the captured clip.

5. Use the controls in the Capture panel to cue the tape to the end point, and *do one of the following:*

   ▲ In the Logging panel, click the Set Out button (**Figure 3.28**).

   ▲ In the Capture panel's playback controls, click the Set Out button }.

   The current time appears as the Out point for the capture.

Figure 3.27 When the tape is at the starting point, click the Set In button.

Figure 3.28 When the tape is at the ending point, click the Set Out button.

CAPTURING AUDIO AND VIDEO

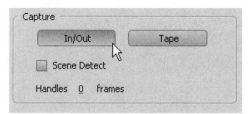

Figure 3.29 Click the In/Out button to capture the footage you specified.

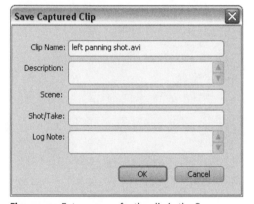

Figure 3.30 Enter a name for the clip in the Save Captured Clip dialog box, and then click OK.

6. In the Capture area of the Logging panel, click the In/Out button (**Figure 3.29**).

Premiere Pro automatically captures the video you defined. When it cues the tape, Premiere Pro uses the preroll you specified on the Settings tab (see "To set other device-control options" earlier in this chapter). When digitizing is complete, the Save Captured Clip dialog box appears.

7. Enter a name for the clip, and click OK (**Figure 3.30**).

The captured clip appears in the selected bin of the Project panel.

✔ Tips

- If your deck isn't reaching normal speed before the In point, the device-control software may issue an error message. Try increasing the preroll time on the Settings tab of the Capture panel. See "To set other device-control options," earlier in this chapter.

- Some decks have a switch that toggles the controls between local and remote modes. In local mode, you can control the tape only using buttons on the deck. To use any type of device control, set the switch to remote.

- In addition to using buttons to set the current frame as an In point or Out point, you can use the In Point, Out Point, and Duration timecode displays. Drag the number, or click it and enter a timecode. Changing the duration alters the Out point.

- If Premiere Pro fails to capture, or *drops*, one or more frames, you can take certain steps: confirm that your system meets or exceeds the minimum requirements for your project settings; disable non-essential system features and file sharing; and specify a fast scratch disk. Try quitting other applications; they may be consuming system resources. Finally, you may need to perform some maintenance, such defragmenting your hard disks or checking for computer viruses.

CAPTURING AUDIO AND VIDEO

Capturing using the Scene Detect feature

As you've seen, Premiere Pro can detect *scene breaks*, which are points on the tape where the camera stopped recording and then restarted—you know, where the director called "Roll camera" and "Cut!" You can use the Scene Detect feature to capture an entire tape automatically, so that each shot on the tape is captured as a separate media file. The clips use the name you specify plus a sequential number: *filename*01, *filename*02, and so on.

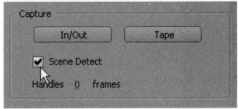

Figure 3.31 Select Scene Detect in the Capture area of the Logging tab.

To capture using Scene Detect:

1. Set up device control, as explained in "Using Device Control" earlier in this chapter or in the documentation that shipped with the device controller.

2. Choose File > Capture.

3. Using the Capture panel's playback controls, cue the tape to the point at which you want to start capturing.

   To capture the entire tape, rewind it to the beginning.

4. In the Capture panel, select the Logging tab.

   The Logging panel appears.

5. In the Setup area of the Logging panel, choose the tracks you want from the Capture pull-down menu.

6. In the Clip Data area of the Logging panel, specify the name of the tape by entering a name in the Tape Name field.

7. In the Capture area of the Logging tab, select Scene Detect (**Figure 3.31**).

CAPTURING AUDIO AND VIDEO

Figure 3.32 For Handles, enter the number of frames you want before the In point and after the Out point.

Figure 3.33 Click Tape to capture each shot as a clip using the Scene Detect feature.

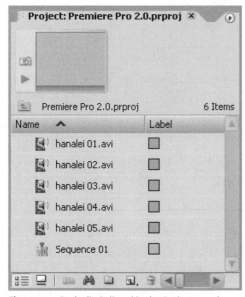

Figure 3.34 Each clip is listed in the Project panel.

8. To specify the number of frames, or *handles*, you want to capture beyond the beginning and end of each clip, enter a value for Handles (**Figure 3.32**).

9. Click Tape (**Figure 3.33**).

Premiere Pro captures each shot on the tape as a separate file, and each file is listed in the Project panel as a clip (**Figure 3.34**).

✔ Tips

- It's a good practice to shoot about 30 seconds of black (or color bars, if your camera can generate them) at the very beginning of the tape. This way, you can capture the first shot with a handle at the beginning and not miss any footage. Also, the beginning of a tape is more prone to physical damage.

- If you don't like the naming scheme, you can change the name of the source clip (or an individual instance of the clip in the Timeline panel). See Chapter 4, "Managing Clips," for details.

CAPTURING AUDIO AND VIDEO

Logging clips for batch capture

You can log clips to a batch list in two ways. When you use device control, you can create a batch list as you view the timecoded tape in Premiere Pro's Capture panel. If the tape is unavailable (or if a timecode-capable deck is unavailable), you can log a batch list manually. To log manually, you need a written list of accurate timecode starting and ending numbers. Logging manually can help you remain productive (saving you time and money) if you don't always have access to a system that has a deck and device control.

To log clips for batch capture:

1. Set up device control, as explained in the section "Using Device Control" earlier in this chapter.

2. Choose File > Capture.

3. In the Capture panel, click the Logging tab.

   The Logging panel appears.

4. For Tape Name, enter the name of the tape you're using.

   Each tape you use should have a unique name.

5. Use the playback controls in the Capture panel to cue the tape to the frame where you want to start the capture, and then click the Set In button (**Figure 3.35**).

   The current timecode appears in the In field.

6. Use the deck controls in the Capture panel to cue the tape to the frame where you want to stop the capture, and then click the Set Out button (**Figure 3.36**).

   The current timecode appears in the Out field.

Figure 3.35 When the tape is at the starting point, click the Set In button.

Figure 3.36 When the tape is at the ending point, click the Set Out button.

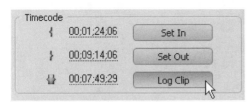

Figure 3.37 Click the Log Clip button.

Figure 3.38 In the Log Clip dialog box, enter the name of the clip and any other information you want to appear in the Project panel.

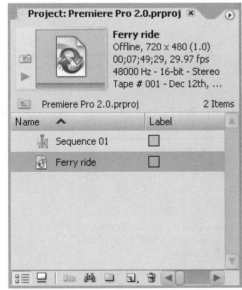

Figure 3.39 The specified clip is listed as offline in the Project panel.

7. Click Log Clip (**Figure 3.37**).

   A Log Clip dialog box appears.

8. Enter a name for the clip (**Figure 3.38**).

9. If you want, enter additional information to be logged with the clip.

10. Click OK.

   The specified clip appears in the Project panel. A media-offline icon ⬛ indicates that the clip isn't yet linked to a file (**Figure 3.39**).

11. Repeat steps 5–10 for every clip you want to capture from this tape.

   If you change tapes, be sure to enter a new tape name.

✔ Tip

■ You don't need to have your source tape to log a clip using the Capture panel. Just use the In Point, Out Point, and Duration timecode displays to define the clip. Naturally, you need a reliable list of timecode numbers to work from.

To create an offline file without a tape:

1. In the Project panel, click the New Item button 🔳, and choose Offline File (**Figure 3.40**).

    The Offline File dialog box appears (**Figure 3.41**).

2. Choose an option from the Contains pull-down menu (**Figure 3.42**): Audio and Video, Audio, or Video.

3. For Tape Name, enter the name of the tape that contains the footage you want to capture.

4. For File Name, type the name of the clip.

5. If you want, specify any of the information in the remaining fields in the General section.

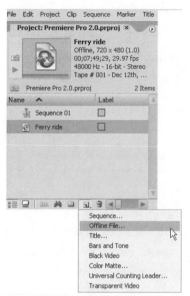

Figure 3.40 Click New Item, and choose Offline File.

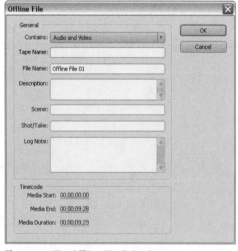

Figure 3.41 The Offline File dialog box.

Figure 3.42 In the Offline File dialog box, choose an option from the Contains pull-down menu.

Figure 3.43 Specify the Media Start, Media End, and Media Duration timecode numbers.

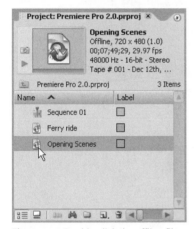

Figure 3.44 Double-click the offline file in the Project panel.

Figure 3.45 Edit the information as needed, and click OK.

6. In the Timecode area of the dialog box, specify the Media Start, Media End, and Media Duration timecode numbers *by doing one of the following* (**Figure 3.43**):

▲ Click the timecode number to highlight it, and enter a valid timecode number.

▲ Drag the timecode number.

Changing the In point or Out point automatically affects the duration. Changing the duration makes a corresponding change in the Out point.

7. Click OK to close the dialog box.

The clip is listed in the Project panel as offline.

To edit an offline file's information:

1. In the Project panel, double-click the offline file (**Figure 3.44**).

The Edit Offline File dialog box appears.

2. Edit the information as needed, and click OK (**Figure 3.45**).

✔ Tip

■ The same information (tape name, file name, description, and so on) can be edited in the Project panel when it's set to list view.

CAPTURING AUDIO AND VIDEO

Batch capturing

Before you batch capture, check the scratch disk, available disk space, capture settings, device-control settings, and deck, if necessary. (These topics are covered earlier in this chapter.) If everything is set properly, you need to attend to the batch capture only when you're required to change source tapes. With a reasonably powerful PC, you can even work in other applications without interrupting the batch capture or causing it to drop frames.

The clips you log appear in the Project panel with the offline icon ⬛. The Media Type and Clip Status columns of the Project panel also identify these clips as offline. Clips that have been (intentionally or unintentionally) unlinked from their source media files also appear as offline.

To batch capture:

1. In the Project panel, select the offline clips you want to capture (**Figure 3.46**).

2. Choose File > Batch Capture (**Figure 3.47**). The Batch Capture panel appears.

3. *Select any of the following* (**Figure 3.48**):

    ▲ **Capture with Handles:** To specify the handles, the number of frames you want to capture beyond the beginning and end of each clip's defined start and end points.

    ▲ **Override Capture Settings:** To enable the Edit button, which allows you to open a dialog box (similar to the one for the capture settings) and specify custom capture settings.

    In most cases, you won't need to edit the capture settings of a clip to make them different from the project capture settings.

Figure 3.46 Select the offline clips you want to capture.

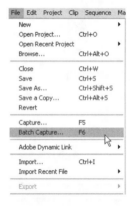

Figure 3.47 Choose File > Batch Capture to open the Batch Capture panel.

Figure 3.48 In the Batch Capture panel, you can usually leave Override Capture Settings unchecked, and click OK.

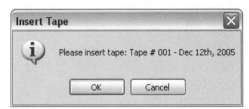

Figure 3.49 When prompted, make sure the proper tape is in the deck, and click OK.

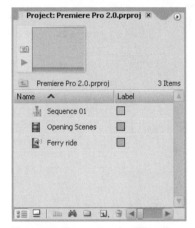

Figure 3.50 The previously offline clips now appear with the movie icon in the Project panel.

4. When you're prompted for a tape, make sure the proper tape is in the deck, and click OK (**Figure 3.49**).

The Capture panel appears, and Premiere Pro captures the selected clips automatically.

5. When Premiere Pro notifies you that the batch capture is finished, click OK. If necessary, close the Capture panel.

Previously offline clips appear with the proper movie icon in the Project panel (**Figure 3.50**). In addition, Premiere Pro saves a batch-capture log alongside the captured files and lists the log file in the Project panel.

✔ Tips

■ A *gap* (unrecorded area) in the tape, or a *break* (a discontinuity) in the tape's timecode, of longer than three seconds can cause Premiere Pro to abort the batch-capture process. By making sure you understand how your camera works, you can avoid timecode breaks while you shoot. Otherwise, you may have to copy, or *dub*, a camera original containing troublesome gaps to another tape. Alternatively, you can capture the items where the timecode is continuous and cue the tape manually to prevent Premiere Pro from encountering a timecode break.

■ Capturing handles (frames beyond the clips' specified In and Out points) can give you an extra measure of flexibility during editing—for example, by providing frames you may need to accomplish a transition.

■ Premiere Pro can import a batch list from Premiere 6.x or a tab-delimited text file and translate the list into a bin of clips in the Project panel. Conversely, you can export a batch-list file for use in an older version of Premiere or in another program. See the Premiere Pro User Guide or Help system for more details.

Importing Footage

When you want to use a file in your project, you import the file as a clip. You can import one clip at a time, several clips at a time, or an entire folder of clips. You can even import another project into the current project.

Premiere Pro can support a variety of video and audio formats and file dimensions up to 4096 pixels by 4096 pixels. Adobe and other manufacturers may also offer plug-in software modules to provide additional file-format support.

To import files as a clips in the project:

1. In the Project panel, specify where you want to import the clip *by doing one of the following:*

   ▲ Navigate to the bin into which you want to import or to the topmost level of the Project panel.

   ▲ In list view, select the bin into which you want to import.

2. Choose File > Import (**Figure 3.51**). The Import dialog box appears.

Figure 3.51 Choose File > Import.

Figure 3.52 Select one or more files and choose Open; or, to import a folder of files, select it and click Import Folder (shown here).

Figure 3.53 The clips appear in the Project panel. A folder of clips appears as a bin in the Project panel (shown here).

3. *Do one of the following:*

▲ To import a single file, double-click the file.

▲ To import multiple files, select the files and click Open.

▲ To import a folder of files, select the folder and click Import Folder (**Figure 3.52**).

The dialog box closes, and the clips appear in the Project panel. If you imported an entire folder, then the folder appears as a bin of clips in the Project panel (**Figure 3.53**).

✔ Tips

■ There are many ways to import files, and chances are, you'll be doing a lot of importing. Now's a good time to learn (or create) shortcuts for the Import command. Use a contextual menu or keyboard shortcut. Instead of choosing File > Import, you can double-click an empty part of the clip area of the Project panel.

■ Bins in the Project panel work like folders on the operating system. For more about using the Project panel, see Chapter 4.

Importing Stills

You import still images as you would any type of media. However, specifying a few preferences beforehand will determine the images' initial duration and scale, which can save you editing time.

A still image consists of a single frame that, if used alone in a sequence, would play for only an instant. However, any still you import uses the current *default duration*, which defines its initial duration when you add it to a sequence. If you know how long you want still images to play in a sequence, then setting their default duration before you import them spares you from setting each image's duration manually. (If you change your mind, you can edit a clip's duration at any time, using techniques covered later in this book.)

You can also determine whether the stills are imported at their native size or scaled so that the largest dimension fits within the image size of the project's sequences. Letting Premiere Pro scale the images automatically can spare you from scaling clips manually using motion effects (see Chapter 13, "Working With Effects").

To set the default duration and scale for still images:

1. Choose Edit > Preferences > General (**Figure 3.54**).

   The General panel of the Preferences dialog box opens.

Figure 3.54 Choose Edit > Preferences> General.

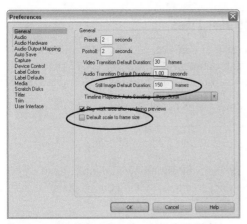

Figure 3.55 For Default Duration, type the initial duration of still images, in frames. To scale imported stills to match the project's frame size, select Default Scale to Frame Size.

2. To set the initial duration of imported still images, type the duration, in frames, for Still Image Default Duration (**Figure 3.55**).

   Hereafter, all still images imported into the project will use the default duration. Still images that are already in the project or program remain unaffected. You can change the duration of a still-image clip at any time.

3. To automatically scale imported images to match the project's frame size, select Default Scale to Frame Size.

   When this option is unchecked, stills are imported at their native scale and appear at that size when added to a sequence.

4. Click OK to close the Preferences dialog box.

✔ Tip

■ When you're creating still images for use in video projects, be aware of the differences in pixel aspect ratios. Image-editing programs often display artwork using square pixels, or a pixel aspect ratio (PAR) of 1. In contrast, video formats often use nonsquare pixels, such as DV's .9 PAR. Usually, Premiere Pro correctly interprets an image's PAR and displays the image without distortion. However, when an image that uses square pixels is saved using image dimensions common to a nonsquare pixel format, Premiere Pro interprets the footage incorrectly, and the image appears distorted.

IMPORTING STILLS

Importing Illustrator Files

Premiere Pro can *rasterize* Illustrator files—a process that converts path-based (vector) art to Premiere Pro's pixel-based (bitmapped) format. The program *anti-aliases* the art, so that edges appear smooth; it also interprets blank areas as transparent (**Figures 3.56** and **3.57**).

Set crop marks in the Illustrator file to define the dimensions of the art that will be rasterized by Premiere Pro.

✔ Tips

■ The term *aliasing* refers to the hard, jagged edges many objects show in digital, pixel-based images. *Anti-aliasing* subtly adds transparency to edges, making them appear smoother.

■ Technically speaking, Premiere Pro interprets blank areas in Illustrator artwork as an alpha channel *premultiplied* with white. You can learn more about alpha channels in Chapter 14, "Advanced Effects."

Figure 3.56 An image viewed in Illustrator as artwork only...

Figure 3.57 ...appears rasterized and anti-aliased in Premiere Pro.

Figure 3.58 Choose File > Import.

Importing Layered Photoshop Files

As you probably know, a Photoshop file can consist of multiple image layers. You can import the combined, or *merged*, layers as a single clip, or import any layer as a separate clip. You can even import the file as a *layered sequence*, a sequence in which Premiere Pro automatically arranges each layer in separate track. Importing a layered sequence can facilitate certain effects, such as building a graphic gradually, layer by layer. For example, your video program might include a graph to illustrate data; using a layered sequence, you could the bars of the graph one by one. Premiere Pro recognizes a Photoshop file's *alpha channels*, which define transparent areas that reveal images in lower tracks (see Chapter 14).

To import a layered Photoshop file:

1. In the Project panel, specify where you want to import the clip *by doing one of the following*:

   ▲ Navigate to the bin into which you want to import or to the topmost level of the Project panel.

   ▲ In list view, select the bin into which you want to import.

2. Choose File > Import (**Figure 3.58**), or double-click an empty area of the main clip area of the Project panel.

   The Import dialog box appears.

3. Locate a layered Photoshop file to import, and click Open (**Figure 3.59**).

   The Import Layered File dialog box opens.

4. In the Import As pull-down menu, choose Footage (**Figure 3.60**).

Figure 3.59 Locate a layered Photoshop file to import, and click Open.

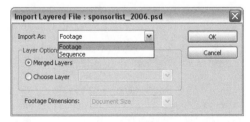

Figure 3.60 In the Import As pull-down menu, choose Footage.

continues on next page

5. For Layer Options, *choose one of the following:*

▲ To import the image after merging all layers into a single layer, select Merged Layers.

▲ To import the single layer as a clip, select Choose Layer and choose a layer (**Figure 3.61**).

6. If you chose a layer in step 5, choose an option for Footage Dimensions (**Figure 3.62**):

▲ **Document Size:** Imports the layer at the document's pixel dimensions. The layer appears in its proper position; any empty areas are imported as an alpha channel (**Figure 3.63**).

▲ **Layer Size:** Imports the layer at its individual pixel dimensions (**Figure 3.64**).

7. Click OK.

Depending on your choice, the single layer or merged layer appears in the selected bin.

Figure 3.61 To import a particular layer, select Choose Layer and choose a layer from the pull-down menu.

Figure 3.62 Single layers can be imported at the document size or the layer size.

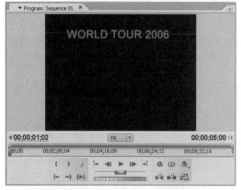

Figure 3.63 Choosing the Document Size option imports the layer using the pixel dimensions of the entire Photoshop document. This makes it easy to reassemble the layers as they appeared in the Photoshop document.

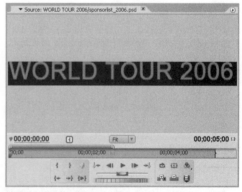

Figure 3.64 Choosing the Layer Size option uses the layer's individual pixel dimensions.

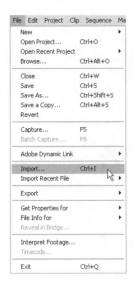

Figure 3.65 Choose File > Import.

To import a file as a layered sequence:

1. Choose File > Import (**Figure 3.65**), or double-click an empty area of the main clip area of the Project panel.

   The Import dialog box appears.

2. Locate a layered Photoshop file to import, and then click Open (**Figure 3.66**).

   The Import Layered File dialog box opens.

3. In the Import As pull-down menu, choose Sequence (**Figure 3.67**).

   continues on next page

Figure 3.66 Locate a layered Photoshop file to import, and click Open.

Figure 3.67 In the Import As pull-down menu, choose Sequence.

4. Click OK.

A bin appears in the Project panel containing each layer as a clip and a sequence that uses the same name as the layered file (**Figure 3.68**).

5. Double-click the sequence to open it in the Timeline panel.

In the sequence, each layer appears in a different track (**Figure 3.69**).

✔ Tip

■ You can also launch Photoshop from within Premiere Pro, as explained in the section "Creating a Photoshop File," later in this chapter.

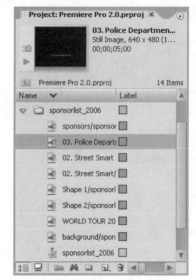

Figure 3.68 The imported file appears as a bin containing each layer and a sequence.

Figure 3.69 In the sequence, each layer appears in a different track.

Figure 3.70 Choose File > Import.

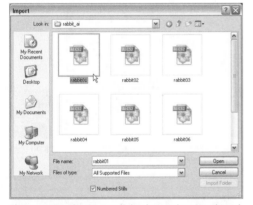

Figure 3.71 In the Import dialog box, select Numbered Stills.

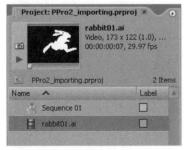

Figure 3.72 The image sequence appears in the selected bin as a single clip.

Importing Still-Image Sequences

In addition to (or instead of) exporting a single movie file, many programs export movies as a sequence of still images. Don't worry—Premiere Pro has no trouble importing a numbered sequence as a single clip.

To import numbered still images as a single clip:

1. Confirm that each image in the numbered sequence has the correct extension and that the file names contain an equal number of digits at the end (seq000.bmp, seq001.bmp, and seq002.bmp, for example).

2. In the Project panel, specify where you want to import the clip *by doing one of the following:*

   ▲ Navigate to the bin into which you want to import or to the topmost level of the Project panel.

   ▲ In list view, select the bin into which you want to import.

3. Choose File > Import (**Figure 3.70**). The Import dialog box appears.

4. Select the first file in the numbered sequence.

5. Select the Numbered Stills check box (**Figure 3.71**).

6. Click Open.

   The image sequence appears in the selected bin as a single clip (**Figure 3.72**).

✔ Tip

■ By default, Premiere Pro assumes that the imported image sequence uses the same frame rate as your project. To tell Premiere Pro that the footage uses a different frame rate, use the Interpret Footage command, explained in Chapter 4.

Importing Projects

In addition to importing media files, you can import an entire project, including all of its clips and sequences. An imported project appears as a bin in the current project, which in turn contains all of its bins, clips, and sequences.

Why would you import a project rather than just reopen it? Maybe you want to join sequences that were created in different projects or use a boilerplate project in several other projects. In Chapter 2, you learned that many of a project's attributes—such as its timebase and audio-sample rate—can't be changed later. However, you can easily work around this restriction by importing the entire project into another project that uses different settings. Finally, you can open projects created in Premiere 6.*x.* However, not all of your edit decisions will translate seamlessly into Premiere Pro; see the user guide or Help system for details.

To import another project into the current project:

1. In the Project panel, specify where you want to import the clip *by doing one of the following:*

   ▲ Navigate to the bin into which you want to import or to the topmost level of the Project panel.

   ▲ In list view, select the bin into which you want to import.

2. Choose File > Import (**Figure 3.73**). The Import dialog box appears.

3. To make finding the project to import easier, in the Files of Type pull-down menu, choose the type of project you want to open (**Figure 3.74**): either Adobe Premiere 6 Projects (*.ppj) or Adobe Premiere Pro Projects (*.prproj).

4. Select a project, and click Open (**Figure 3.75**).

Figure 3.73 Choose File> Import.

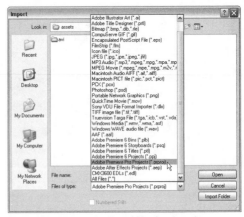

Figure 3.74 Narrow the list of files by choosing an option in the Files of Type pull-down menu.

Figure 3.75 In the Import dialog box, select a project and click Open.

IMPORTING PROJECTS

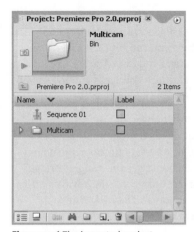

Figure 3.76 The imported project appears as a bin containing sequences and source clips.

The imported project appears in the Project panel as a bin with the same name as the project file. The bin contains any clips and sequences used in the project (**Figure 3.76**).

5. Open the imported bin, and double-click the sequences you want to view.

For more about sequences, see Chapter 6, "Creating a Sequence."

Dynamic Link

If you're using the Premiere Pro as part of the Adobe Production Studio or Video Collection, you can integrate your workflow using a feature called *Dynamic Link*.

It's not hard to imagine a project that requires work in different programs: editing in Premiere Pro; compositing, effects, and animation in After Effects; and DVD authoring in Encore DVD. In the past, your workflow would have required that you render an element in one program (a composition in After Effects, for instance) and then import it into the other (edit into a Premiere Pro sequence). And making changes meant repeating the process. Dynamic Link allows you to connect compositions in After Effects with Premiere Pro or Encore DVD. Changes you make in one program are reflected in the other—without rendering or even saving the changes. The two programs interact more seamlessly.

Using Dynamic Link is straightforward: In Premiere Pro, you choose File > Adobe Dynamic Link to create or import an After Effects composition. But because Dynamic Link involves both programs, it's a little outside the scope of this book. Consult your Production Studio User Guide and Help for more details.

Importing with Adobe Bridge

Chances are, you've accumulated a seemingly countless number of assets on your hard disks. It can be a chore to find the one you need. Fortunately, Premiere Pro and other Adobe programs ship with a companion program—a research assistant, if you will—called Adobe Bridge.

Bridge facilitates asset management by providing a convenient way to search for, sift, and preview files. Bridge also lets you see information embedded in the file, or *metadata*. You can even apply your own metadata, label, rating, and keywords to a file, adding ways to distinguish the needle from the rest of the haystack (**Figure 3.77**).

Bridge also provides an access point to Adobe Stock Photos, an online resource for stock footage you can preview and use in your projects. If you own Adobe's Creative Suite 2, Bridge also connects you to Version Cue, Adobe's file-version manager.

This book can't cover all the features of another full-fledged program; this section focuses on browsing and importing using Bridge. You should get the hang of Bridge's familiar and intuitive interface with a little experimentation and a quick visit to its Help system.

Figure 3.77 Bridge is a companion program that facilitates file management.

Figure 3.78 To find any file using Bridge, choose File > Browse.

To import a file or project template using Bridge:

1. *Do either of the following:*

   ▲ To open any file, Choose File > Browse.

   ▲ To navigate to project templates directly, Choose File > Browse (**Figure 3.78**).

   Premiere launches its companion program, Adobe Bridge.

2. To navigate to the file you want to view, *do either of the following:*

   ▲ Use the navigation tools at upper-right in the Bridge window to select a disk volume or folder (**Figure 3.79**).

   ▲ Select an item in the Favorites tab or the Folders tab (**Figure 3.80**).

   The selected item's content appears in Bridge's large main panel. You can also open a folder by double-clicking it in the main panel. (The appearance of items in the main panel depends on the position of the icon size and viewing mode, which you can set using controls at lower-right in the panel.)

   continues on next page

Show previous folder or volume

Go up one level in hierarchy

Show next folder or volume

Select item in pull-down menu

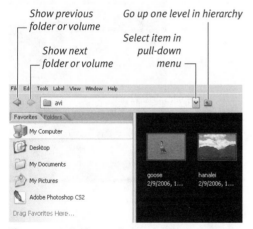

Figure 3.79 In Bridge, navigate using the browser-style navigation tools at the top of the window...

Figure 3.80 ...or select an item in the Favorites or Folders tab.

IMPORTING WITH ADOBE BRIDGE

3. To see a preview image and other information about the item, select the item.

The item's image appears in Bridge's Preview tab. Motion footage and templates include standard playback controls. The item's metadata and keywords appear in the corresponding tabbed areas (**Figure 3.81**).

4. In Bridge's main panel, double-click the item you want to import (**Figure 3.82**).

Premiere Pro may prompt you to specify options according to the type of item you import. (Refer to the section in this chapter pertaining to the file type.) The item appears in the Project panel (**Figure 3.83**).

Figure 3.81
The selected item appears in the Preview tab; additional information appears in the Metadata and Keywords tabs.

Figure 3.82 Double-clicking the item in Bridge's main panel...

Figure 3.83 ...imports it into Premiere Pro.

Figure 3.84 Choose File > New > Photoshop File.

Figure 3.85 Specify a name and destination for the new Photoshop file, and click Save.

✔ **Tip**

■ As usual, Premiere Pro never alters source files. Importing a layered Photoshop file as merged, for example, doesn't actually merge the layers in the Photoshop document.

Creating a Photoshop File

If both programs are installed on your computer, you can launch Photoshop from within Premiere Pro. (Your computer must have enough memory to run both Premiere Pro and Photoshop simultaneously.) Photoshop opens a file automatically and sets its image dimensions and PAR according to the current Premiere Pro project. In Premiere Pro, the imported file reflects any changes you make to it in Photoshop.

To create a Photoshop file:

1. Choose File > New > Photoshop File (**Figure 3.84**).

   The Save Photoshop File As dialog box appears.

2. Specify a name and destination for the new Photoshop file (**Figure 3.85**).

3. To import the file to Premiere Pro automatically, select Add to Project (Merged Layers).

   Selecting this option combines, or merges, multiple layers in the imported clip. Alternatively, you can leave this option unchecked and import the merged layers, an individual layer, or all the layers as a sequence using the methods described earlier in this chapter.

4. Click Save to close the Save Photoshop File As dialog box.

   Photoshop opens a new file and sets the image dimensions and PAR according to the Premiere Pro project. If you selected Add to Project in step 3, the file appears in Premiere Pro as a clip.

5. Use Photoshop's image-creation and -editing tools, and save the changes as needed.

   Any changes you make to the file in Photoshop are reflected in Premiere Pro. If you didn't select Add to Project in step 3, then you must import the file manually.

Generating Synthetic Media

In addition to accepting a wide variety of source files, Premiere Pro can generate useful clips of its own. The Project panel's New Item button ⬛, includes options for creating a title, bars and tone, black video, a color matte, a standard countdown, or a transparent video clip. You can think of these items as "synthetic" media, because they exist only as part of the project file, not as independent media files.

This section doesn't cover items that aren't synthetic media, per se (sequences and offline files), or titles, which have an entire chapter devoted to them (Chapter 12, "Creating Titles"). Transparent video clips have a special use that's best explained in Chapter 13.

To create bars and tone or black video:

1. In the Project panel, specify where you want to import the clip *by doing one of the following:*

   ▲ Navigate to the bin into which you want to import or to the topmost level of the Project panel.

   ▲ In list view, select the bin into which you want to import.

2. Click the New Item button, and choose one of the following (**Figure 3.86**):

   ▲ **Bars and Tone:** Creates an NTSC color bars pattern and a 1-kHz audio tone.

   ▲ **Black Video:** Creates black video that registers 7.5 IRE on a waveform monitor. (See the sidebar "Using a Waveform Monitor," in Chapter 5, "Viewing Clips in the Monitor Panel.")

   The footage item you chose appears in the Project panel and uses the duration you specified for still images (**Figure 3.87**).

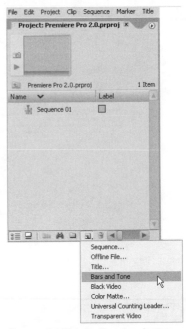

Figure 3.86 Click the New Item button, and choose Bars and Tone or Black Video.

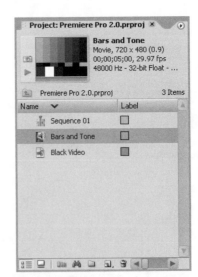

Figure 3.87 The item you select appears in the Project panel and uses the default duration for still images.

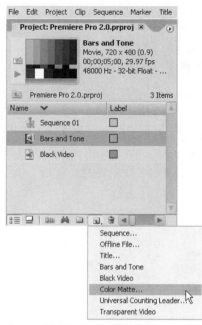

Figure 3.88 Click the New Item button, and choose Color Matte.

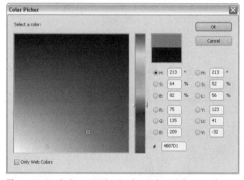

Figure 3.89 Select a color in the Color Picker, and click OK.

Figure 3.90 Type a name for the color matte, and click OK.

To create a color matte:

1. In the Project panel, specify where you want to import the clip *by doing one of the following:*

   ▲ Navigate to the bin into which you want to import or to the topmost level of the Project panel.

   ▲ In list view, select the bin into which you want to import.

2. Click the New Item button, and choose Color Matte from the pull-down menu (**Figure 3.88**).

   A Color Picker dialog box appears.

3. Choose a color, and click OK (**Figure 3.89**).

   A Choose Name dialog box appears.

4. Type a name for the color matte, and click OK (**Figure 3.90**).

   The color matte appears in the Project panel and uses the duration you specified for still images (**Figure 3.91**).

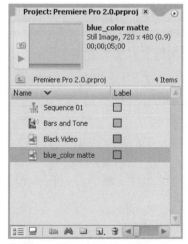

Figure 3.91 The color matte appears in the Project panel and uses the default duration for still images.

GENERATING SYNTHETIC MEDIA

To create a countdown:

1. In the Project panel, specify where you want to import the clip *by doing one of the following:*

   ▲ Navigate to the bin into which you want to import or to the topmost level of the Project panel

   ▲ In list view, select the bin into which you want to import

2. Click the New Item button, and choose Universal Counting Leader from the pull-down menu (**Figure 3.92**).

   The Universal Counting Leader Setup dialog box appears.

3. Specify the following options (**Figure 3.93**):

   ▲ To open the color picker for each element of the countdown, click the color swatch next to each element.

   ▲ To display a small circle in the last frame of the leader, select the Cue Blip on Out check box.

   ▲ To play a beep at the two-second mark of the countdown, select the Cue Blip on 2 check box.

   ▲ To play a beep at each second of the countdown, select the Cue Blip at All Second Starts check box.

Figure 3.92 Click the New Item button, and choose Universal Counting Leader.

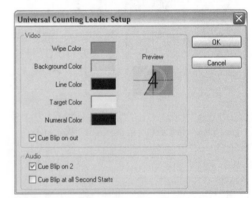

Figure 3.93 Specify options in the Universal Counting Leader Setup dialog box.

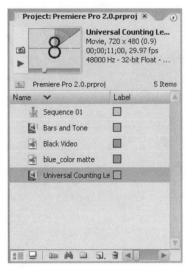

Figure 3.94 The countdown appears in the Project panel.

4. Click OK to close the dialog box.

A Universal Counting Leader clip appears in the selected bin of the Project panel (**Figure 3.94**).

✔ Tips

- To make a slate (containing information such as client, producer, and total running time), you can create a title card, as explained in Chapter 12.

- Although an empty space in a sequence appears as black, it doesn't allow you to perform certain edits, and it doesn't appear in edit-decision lists. To gain these advantages, add a black video clip.

- Double-clicking black video, color bars, or a counting leader opens the footage in the source view. However, double-clicking a color matte reopens the color picker.

Creating a Leader

You can use the New Item button's synthetic media options to create a *leader,* a series of shots that typically appear at the beginning of a master tape. The *master tape* is used to make duplicates (or *dubs*) and usually contains the following:

- **30 seconds of black:** A black screen without sound keeps the program away from the *head,* or beginning, of the master tape, which is more prone to damage.

- **60 seconds of bars and tone:** The color bars and reference tone are used by video technicians to faithfully reproduce your program's video and audio levels.

- **10 seconds of black:** Here, black acts as a buffer between the bars and the slate.

- **10 seconds of a slate:** A title screen contains pertinent information about the program and the tape itself, such as the name of the program, the producer, whether the audio is mixed, and so on.

- **8 seconds of countdown:** The visible countdown originally helped a film projectionist know when the program was about to start. It can serve a similar purpose for videotape operators. The standard countdown starts at 8 and ends at 2 (where there is usually a beep, or *2 pop,* to test the sound).

- **2 seconds of black:** Black video immediately precedes the program.

GENERATING SYNTHETIC MEDIA

MANAGING CLIPS

All the *assets* you intend to use in your project—video clips, audio clips, still pictures, and synthetic media such as leaders and mattes—are listed in the Project panel. The more complex the project, the lengthier and more unwieldy the list becomes. Fortunately, the Project panel includes features that help you keep your clips organized and easy to find, as you'll see in this chapter.

You'll also learn how to perform other media-management tasks, such as specifying how Premiere Elements interprets a clip's inherent attributes, and reuniting an offline clip with its previously missing source file. Finally, you'll learn how to use the Project Manager to do a little project housekeeping, which includes assembling assets in one location and trimming them down to only the footage critical to the project.

Working with the Project Panel

The Project panel is the receptacle for all the clips you intend to use. So you can work efficiently, it's vital that the clips be organized, easy to find, and easy to evaluate. Premiere Pro's Project panel helps you achieve these goals (**Figure 4.1**).

To help you change the view options or access common commands quickly, several buttons are conveniently located at the bottom of the

Project panel. As in all the primary panels, you can also access commands associated with the panel from an integrated menu named after the panel—in this case, the Project panel menu. (Some like to call these types of menus *fly-out* or *wingtip* menus.)

The preview area displays vital information about selected bins, sequences, and clips, as well as a sample image. You can play movie files in the preview area. In addition, you can choose any frame of a movie clip to represent the clip in the Project panel views.

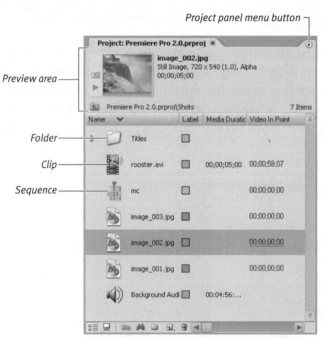

Figure 4.1 The Project panel helps you organize, find, and evaluate your clips. You can specify how you want the Project panel to depict clips; this is just one set of options.

Figure 4.2 In icon view, Project panel items are arranged in a grid.

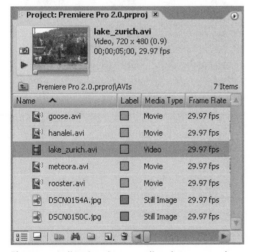

Figure 4.3 In list view, items are listed as rows and columns of information.

List view   Icon view

Figure 4.4 Click the appropriate button at the bottom of the Project panel to switch views.

Working with Project Panel Views

You can view the clips in the Project panel in two ways: as icons or as a list. In icon view, items in the Project panel are arranged in a grid (**Figure 4.2**). This view tends to take up more space, but it lets you lay out the items like photos on a table. You can use icon view to create a kind of storyboard, which you can assemble into a sequence automatically (using the Automate to Sequence feature, explained in Chapter 6, "Creating a Sequence"). In list view, on the other hand, items are listed with rows and columns of information, which can help you sort and organize your clips (**Figure 4.3**). List view can show more items at once, and its columns are key to managing a large number of clips.

Both view types allow you to choose whether to represent each clip as an icon representing the type of footage or as a thumbnail image of the footage. You can even set the size of the items.

The sections that follow explain how to work with each view, so you can customize the Project panel for the task at hand.

To change the Project panel view:

◆ At the bottom of the Project panel, click the button that corresponds to the view you want to use (**Figure 4.4**).

To toggle thumbnails in the Project panel:

◆ In the Project panel menu, choose Thumbnails > Off (**Figure 4.5**).

When Off is selected, items appear as icons (**Figure 4.6**); when Off isn't selected, items appear as thumbnail images (**Figure 4.7**).

Figure 4.5 In the Project panel menu, choose Thumbnails > Off.

Figure 4.6 When Off is selected, items appear as icons.

Figure 4.7 When Off isn't selected, items appear as thumbnail images.

Figure 4.8 In the Project panel menu, choose Thumbnails and select a size.

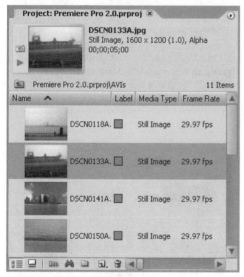

Figure 4.9 Items in the Project panel appear at the relative size you specify.

To change the size of items in the Project panel:

◆ In the Project panel menu, choose Thumbnails and select a size (**Figure 4.8**).

Items in the Project panel appear at the relative size you specify (**Figure 4.9**).

WORKING WITH PROJECT PANEL VIEWS

Working with Icon View

In icon view ⬛, items in the Project panel appear as larger icons arranged in a grid (something like the tiles view in Windows XP). Some editors prefer this view or like to switch to it when working with a client.

Icon view also lends itself to a workflow you might call *storyboard editing*. You can arrange the clips in order, much like the sketches in a storyboard, and then assemble them into a sequence automatically using Premiere Pro's Automate to Sequence command. (See Chapter 6 for more about the Automate to Sequence feature.)

To arrange items in icon view:

1. With the Project panel set to icon view, select one or more items.

2. Drag the selected items to another cell in the grid.

   A bold line between grid cells indicates where the moved items will be inserted (**Figure 4.10**). When you release the mouse, subsequent items are shifted to the right to make room for the moved items (**Figure 4.11**).

Figure 4.10 When you select items to move to a new position in the grid, a bold line between grid cells indicates where the moved items will be inserted.

Figure 4.11 Subsequent items are shifted to the right to make room for the moved items.

Figure 4.12 Choose Clean Up in the Project panel menu.

To clean up icon view:

◆ With the Project panel set to icon view, choose Clean Up in the Project panel menu (**Figure 4.12**).

   Items in the Project panel are arranged in the visible cells of the grid from left to right and from top to bottom, so that there are no empty cells between items (**Figure 4.13**).

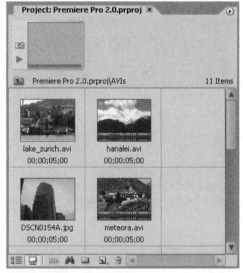

Figure 4.13 Items are rearranged so that there are no empty cells between items.

Working with List View

List view ⊞ lets you organize items according to a number of categories that appear as columns in the Project panel. You can select which columns you want to include and add your own custom columns. You can also resize and rearrange the columns to suit your organizational method. However, you can rename or permanently remove only custom columns, and the Name column is always the first column.

To hide or show columns in list view:

1. In the Project panel menu, choose Edit Columns (**Figure 4.14**).

   The Edit Columns dialog box appears.

2. Select the headings for the type of information you want to view when the Project panel is set to list view (**Figure 4.15**).

3. Click OK to close the Edit Columns dialog box.

   Only the columns you specified appear in the Project panel.

To add custom columns:

1. In the Project panel menu, choose Edit Columns.

   The Edit Columns dialog box appears.

2. Click Add (**Figure 4.16**).

   An Add Column dialog box appears.

Figure 4.14 In the Project panel menu, choose Edit Columns.

Figure 4.15 In the Edit Columns dialog box, select the headings for the type of information you want to view.

Figure 4.16 In the Edit Columns dialog box, click Add.

Figure 4.17 In the Add Column dialog box, type the name of the custom column.

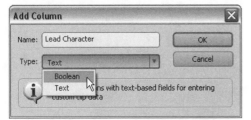

Figure 4.18 Choose an option in the Type pull-down menu.

Figure 4.19 Select a column name and choose to rename, remove, or move the column.

3. Type the name of the custom column (**Figure 4.17**).

4. Choose an option from the Type drop-down menu (**Figure 4.18**):

Text: Creates a column of text fields in which you can enter information.

Boolean: Creates a column of check boxes, which you can use to indicate a yes or no state.

5. Click OK to close the Add Column dialog box.

The new column appears in the Edit Columns dialog box.

6. When you've finished editing columns, click OK to close the Edit Columns dialog box.

To edit columns:

1. In the Project panel menu, choose Edit Columns.

The Edit Columns dialog box appears.

2. Select a column name, and *click any of the following buttons* (**Figure 4.19**):

▲ **Rename:** Renames a custom column.

▲ **Remove:** Removes a custom column.

▲ **Move Up:** Moves a column one item higher in the list, which moves it to the left in the Project panel.

▲ **Move Down:** Moves a column one item lower in the list, which moves it to the right in the Project panel.

3. Click OK to close the dialog box.

The Project panel reflects your choices.

✔ Tip

■ You can't rename or remove any of the default columns, but you can hide them.

To rearrange headings in list view:

◆ With the Project panel set to list view, drag a heading in the Project panel to the left or right to place it where you want (**Figures 4.20** and **4.21**).

To adjust a column's width in list view:

◆ With the Project panel set to list view, drag the right edge of a heading in the Project panel to resize it (**Figures 4.22** and **4.23**).

Figure 4.20 Dragging a heading to the right or to the left (shown here)...

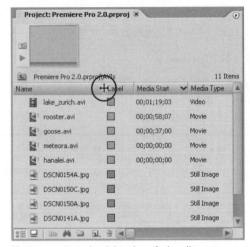

Figure 4.22 Drag the right edge of a heading to resize it.

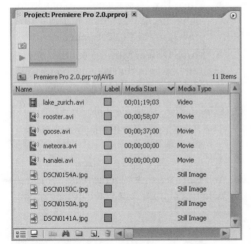

Figure 4.21 ...changes its relative position in the Project panel.

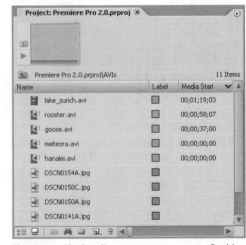

Figure 4.23 The heading appears narrower or (in this case) wider.

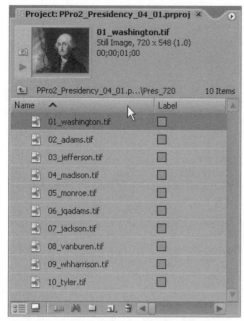

Figure 4.24 Click a column heading to sort clips by that heading. (Note the small arrow next to the Name column points up.)

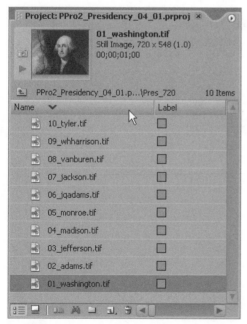

Figure 4.25 Click the heading a second time to reverse the sort order. (Here, the small arrow points down.)

To sort items in list view:

◆ With the Project panel set to list view, *do one of the following:*

▲ To sort clips by a particular column heading, click the heading (**Figure 4.24**).

▲ To reverse the sort order, click a column heading twice (**Figure 4.25**).

A small triangle next to the column name indicates whether items are sorted in ascending or descending order.

✔ Tips

■ In list view, the Label column identifies each item using a small color swatch. Different colors represent the six types of items: Bin, Sequence, Video, Audio, Movie, and Still. You can assign any of eight colors to represent these six types by choosing Edit > Preferences > Label Colors. An item's label color is also reflected in the Timeline panel.

■ Offline files, counting leaders, and bars and tone use the same label color as sequences. Color mattes, black video, and titles use the same label color as stills.

Selecting and Deleting Items in the Project Panel

You can select items in the Project panel in much the same way as you select files in the operating system. However, when you delete an item from the Project panel, bear in mind that you're deleting only a *reference* to a file on the hard disk, not the file itself. If you delete a clip, the project will no longer require that clip, but its source media remains on the hard disk. When you attempt to delete a clip that's in a sequence, or a sequence that has clips in it, Premiere Pro prompts you to confirm the action.

To select items in the Project panel:

1. If necessary, open the bin that contains the clips you want to view.

2. To select a clip or clips, *do one of the following:*

   ▲ Click an item.

   ▲ Shift-click a range of items.

   ▲ Ctrl-click several noncontiguous items.

   ▲ Drag a marquee around two or more items (**Figure 4.26**).

   ▲ Choose Edit > Select All to select all items.

   ▲ Choose Edit > Deselect All to deselect all items.

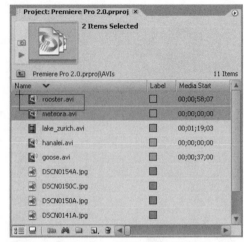

Figure 4.26 Select items by clicking, or select a range of items by dragging a marquee (shown here).

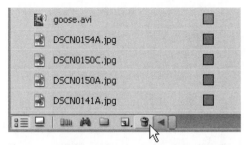

Figure 4.27 Clicking Delete removes selected items from the project but doesn't remove related media files from the disk.

To delete items from the Project panel:

1. In the Project panel, select one or more items.

2. In the Project panel, click the Delete button ⬚, or press Delete on your keyboard.

   Deleting a clip removes it from the project, but the source file remains on the hard disk (**Figure 4.27**). If the clip is used in a sequence, Premiere Pro prompts you to confirm your choice.

✔ Tip

■ You can use the Project Manager to help with basic housekeeping: It will remove unused clips and collect all the clips you're using in a new location. See "Using the Project Manager" later in this chapter.

Using the Preview Area of the Project Panel

The preview area of the Project panel displays a sample image of the selected bin or clip. The preview area also displays the number of clips in a bin or the vital statistics of a clip—its name, file type, image dimensions, and so on.

If the selected clip is a movie file, you can play the clip—with sound—directly in the Project panel. In addition, you can set any frame of the clip as the *poster frame,* the image used to represent the clip when you're viewing thumbnails of the clips in the Project panel. This allows you to choose the most appropriate image to represent the clip.

To display a preview of an item in the Project panel:

◆ In the Project panel, click a clip to select it.

A sample frame and information appear in the preview area of the Project panel. Clip information can include the clip's name, file type, image size, duration, frame rate, data rate, and audio settings; the number of times the clip has been used in sequences; and so on (**Figure 4.28**).

To show detailed usage information for a clip:

1. In the Project panel, click a clip to select it.

2. Click the small arrow to the right of the clip's video or audio usage information (**Figure 4.29**).

A menu lists information about each instance of a clip in a sequence, including the name of the sequence, the name of the clip, and the clip's In point.

Figure 4.28 The preview area of the Project panel displays a thumbnail-sized version of the clip and other clip data.

Figure 4.29 Click the small arrow to the right of the clip's video or audio usage information.

Figure 4.30 Play the preview image by clicking its Play button...

Figure 4.31 ...or cue to a frame by by dragging its slider or clicking on the slider's track.

To play a movie clip in the preview area:

1. In the Project panel, click a movie clip to select it.

   A sample image and information appear in the preview area of the Project panel.

2. To play the preview image, *do one of the following:*

   ▲ To the left of the preview image, click the Play button (**Figure 4.30**).

   ▲ Press the spacebar.

3. To stop playback, click the Play button or press the spacebar again.

4. To shuttle through the preview image, drag the slider below the image (**Figure 4.31**).

5. To cue the preview image to a frame, click on the slider's track.

USING THE PREVIEW AREA OF THE PROJECT PANEL

To set the poster frame for a movie clip:

1. In the Project panel, click a movie clip to select it.

   A sample image and information appear in the preview area of the Project panel.

2. Below the preview image, drag the slider to cue the preview to the frame you want to set as the poster frame (**Figure 4.32**).

3. To the left of the preview image, click the Set Poster Frame button ▣.

   The current frame of the preview becomes the poster frame—the image used to represent the clip when you view thumbnail images of clips in the Project panel (**Figure 4.33**).

✔ Tips

- In Premiere Pro's predecessor, called Premiere, setting the poster frame set the zero marker for a clip. In Premiere Pro, the poster frame and the zero marker are independent of each other.

- If you haven't set a poster frame for a clip by clicking the Set Poster Frame button ▣, the poster frame is the In point of the clip. If you've set the poster frame and it's before the In point, then it changes to the In point. If you set it after the In point, then it remains where you set it.

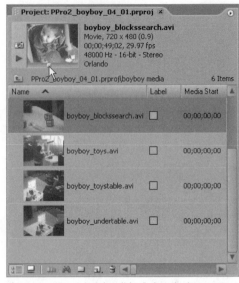

Figure 4.32 Dragging the slider below the image a frame...

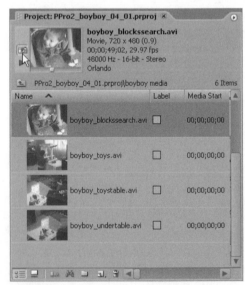

Figure 4.33 ...and clicking the Set Poster Frame button makes thumbnails of the clip use the frame you specified to represent the clip.

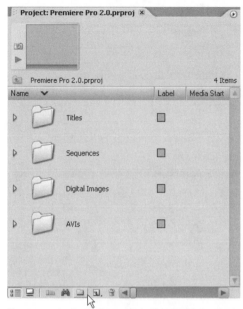

Figure 4.34 In the Project panel, click the Bin button.

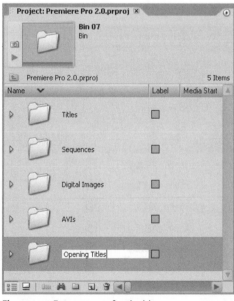

Figure 4.35 Enter a name for the bin.

Organizing Clips in Bins

Premiere Pro allows you to manage clips in the project in much the same way that you manage files on your computer operating system. The Project panel's clip area can list individual items, or you can create folder-like containers known as *bins*. You can specify whether to list imported clips in the topmost level of the Project panel's organizational hierarchy or nested inside a bin. You can move clips in and out of bins at any time.

To create a bin:

1. In the Project panel, click the Bin button 🗀 (**Figure 4.34**).

   A bin appears in the Project panel. By default, new bins are named Bin01, Bin02, and so on. However, the name is highlighted, ready for you to change it.

2. Enter a name for the bin (**Figure 4.35**).

To view the contents of a bin:

◆ *Do one of the following:*

▲ In list view, click the triangle next to the bin icon to expand the bin and view its contents in outline form (**Figure 4.36**).

▲ In list view or icon view, double-click the bin to open it and view its contents in the main clip area of the Project panel (**Figure 4.37**).

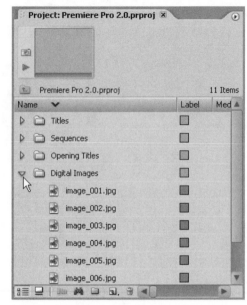

Figure 4.36 In list view, clicking the triangle next to the bin icon expands the bin and lets you view its contents in outline form.

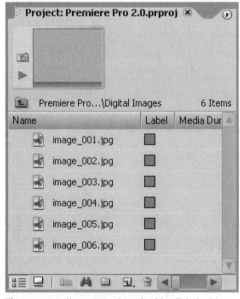

Figure 4.37 In list or icon view, double-click the bin to open it and view its contents in the main clip area of the Project panel.

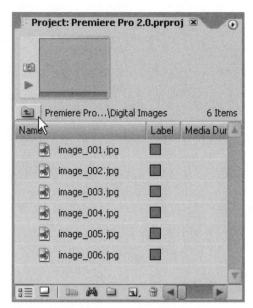

Figure 4.38 In list view or icon view, click the Exit Bin button.

To hide the contents of a bin:

◆ *Do one of the following:*

▲ In list view, click the triangle next to the bin icon so that the bin's contents are hidden.

▲ In list view or icon view, click the Exit Bin button above the main clip area (**Figure 4.38**). The button looks and works like the Up One Level button in Windows XP.

Clips and Bins (Not Files and Folders)

Premiere Pro often employs film-editing metaphors. Film editors use bins to store and organize their clips ("clipped" from reels of film). The film dangles from hangers into a bin until the editor pulls down a strip of film and adds it to the sequence. Premiere Pro's bins may be less tactile than film bins, but they're also a lot less messy.

If you've never seen a film bin, you may find it more useful to compare clips stored in bins with files stored in folders on a drive. In fact, bins were called folders in older versions of Premiere. If you import a folder of files, the folder appears in the project as a bin containing clips.

Unlike some other editing programs, Premiere Pro saves bins as part of the project file, not as separate files.

To move clips into a bin:

1. In list view or icon view, make sure the clips you want to move and the destination bin are both visible in the main clip area of the Project panel.

2. Select one or more items.

3. Drag the selected items to another bin (**Figure 4.39**).

   The items are moved into the destination bin (**Figure 4.40**).

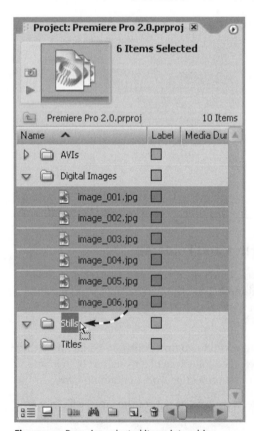

Figure 4.39 Dragging selected items into a bin...

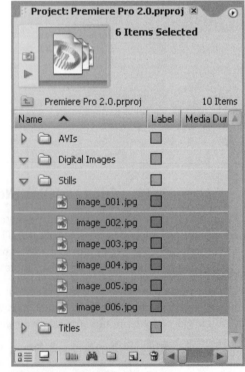

Figure 4.40 ...moves them into that bin.

To move items out of a bin in list view:

1. Set the Project panel to list view.

2. Click the triangle next to a bin to expand the bin and view its contents.

3. Select the items you want to remove from the bin.

4. Drag the selected items down to an empty part of the main clip area (**Figure 4.41**).

   When you release the mouse, the selected items are moved out of the folder and placed one level up in the bin hierarchy (**Figure 4.42**).

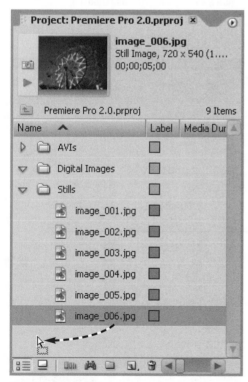

Figure 4.41 When you drag items to an empty part of the main clip area...

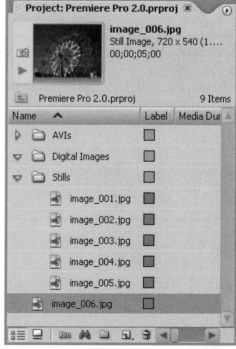

Figure 4.42 ...the selected items are moved out of the folder and placed one level up in the bin hierarchy. Now that the selected clip is no longer within a folder, it doesn't appear indented in the list of items.

Duplicating and Copying Source Clips

You can duplicate any item in the Project panel. A duplicate item appears alongside the original, with *Copy* appended to its name.

Alternatively, you can use the Cut, Copy, and Paste commands. This method is useful when you want to replicate a clip in a different bin. A pasted clip uses the same name as the original.

As you can guess by now, duplicating a clip doesn't create a new source media file; it only creates another reference to the same file.

To duplicate clips:

1. Select one or more clips.

2. Choose Edit > Duplicate (**Figure 4.43**).

   A duplicate clip appears in the Project panel. It uses the name of the source clip with the word *Copy* appended to it (**Figure 4.44**).

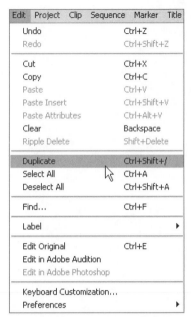

Figure 4.43 Selecting a clip and choosing Edit > Duplicate...

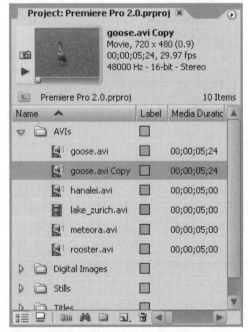

Figure 4.44 ...creates a duplicate clip with the word *Copy* appended to its name.

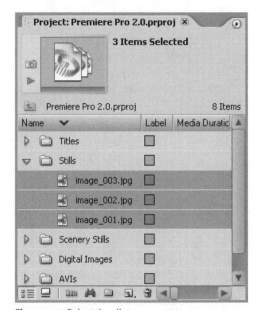

Figure 4.45 Select the clips you want to copy.

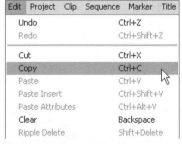

Figure 4.46 Choose Edit > Copy.

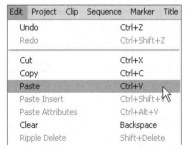

Figure 4.47 Navigate to a destination in the Project panel, and choose Edit > Paste.

To copy and paste clips:

1. Select one or more clips (**Figure 4.45**).

2. *Do one of the following:*
   ▲ Choose Edit > Cut.
   ▲ Choose Edit > Copy (**Figure 4.46**).

3. View the destination in the main clip area of the Project panel.
   If necessary, open the destination bin.

4. Choose Edit > Paste (**Figure 4.47**).

continues on next page

5. A duplicate of the clip appears in the selected destination. The clip uses exactly the same name as the original (**Figure 4.48**).

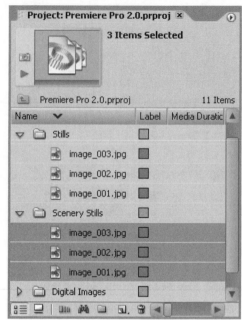

Figure 4.48 The pasted item uses the same name as the original.

Duplicate Clips and Subclips

In most cases, there's no need to copy a clip in the Project panel; you can add the same clip to any sequence again and again (changing its In point and Out point each time, if you want). However, on some occasions you may want the same clip listed more than once. For example, you may want to interpret each copy of a clip differently, perhaps ignoring the alpha channel for one and not the other (see "Interpreting Footage" later in this chapter). More commonly, you may want to make a copy for organizational purposes. For example, copies let you use parts of the same clip more than once in a storyboard (see "Storyboard Editing" in Chapter 6).

Initially, you may be tempted to think of clip copies as *subclips*. On the contrary, copies are full-fledged, independent clips that refer to the same media file. Copies aren't dependent on the original clip, so deleting one copy of a clip has no effect on other copies. (But, of course, deleting a source clip does delete any instance of that clip in a sequence.) In addition, clip copies access the same full range of source media; you can't limit a copy to a shorter segment.

Subclips, in contrast, are created from a defined segment of a source clip. For more about subclips, see Chapter 6.

Figure 4.49 Right-click a clip, and choose Rename in the context menu.

Figure 4.50 Enter a new name for the clip.

Renaming Clips

After you import a file as a clip, you shouldn't rename the file on your hard disk. Doing so will ruin your project's reference to the file, and Premiere Pro won't be able to locate the file the next time you open the project. Nevertheless, you may still need to identify a clip by another name. Fortunately, you can rename a clip in a project for the purposes of editing. Renaming the clip doesn't affect the source file's name or interfere with your project's references.

To rename a clip:

1. In the Project panel, *do one of the following:*

   ▲ Click the clip's name, and then click it again (don't double-click).

   ▲ Select a clip, and then choose Clip > Rename.

   ▲ Right-click a clip, and choose Rename in the context menu (**Figure 4.49**).

   The clip's name becomes highlighted.

2. Enter a new name (**Figure 4.50**).

3. Press Enter, or click away from the clip.

   The clip takes another name in the project. The source file on the drive isn't renamed, however.

✔ Tip

■ If you want to know the original name of a renamed clip, you can right-click the clip and choose Properties from the menu. In the Properties panel, look at the file path to discover the source media file's name, which is the default name of the clip.

Finding Clips

Even the most organized editor can lose track of a clip, particularly when a project contains a lot of clips. Here's how to find one from the Project panel.

To find a clip:

1. In the Project panel, click the Find button  (**Figure 4.51**).

    The Find dialog box appears. It contains two lines of search criteria (**Figure 4.52**).

2. From the Column pull-down menu, choose a category by which to search.

    Find options match the columns of the Project panel's list view.

3. From the Operator pull-down menu, choose a limiting option.

4. In the Find What field, enter search content.

5. To narrow the search, specify another column, another operator, and more search content in the next line.

6. For Match, choose either All or Any.

7. To find only items that match the capitalization of the item you're searching for, select Case Sensitive.

8. Click Find.

    If a clip meets your criteria, it's selected in the Project panel (**Figure 4.53**).

9. To search for other clips that meet the search criteria, click Find again.

    If an additional clip meets your criteria, it's selected in the Project panel.

10. Repeat step 9 until you find the clip you're searching for or finish searching.

11. Click Done to close the Find dialog box.

Figure 4.51 In the Project panel, click the Find button.

Figure 4.52 In the Find dialog box, enter search criteria.

Figure 4.53 If a clip meets your criteria, it's selected in the Project panel.

Figure 4.54 Select a clip, and choose File > Interpret Footage.

Figure 4.55 To use a frame rate different from that of the file, select Assume This Frame Rate and enter the rate, expressed in frames per second.

Interpreting Footage

In most cases, Premiere Pro correctly *interprets* imported clips, accurately processing characteristics such as frame rate, pixel aspect ratio, and alpha channel. Nevertheless, sometimes you must override Premiere Pro's assessment and specify how these characteristics should be interpreted. For example, a still image sequence may be designed to play at a particular frame rate that you need to set. Or an imported still image may appear distorted—a sure sign that its pixel aspect ratio (PAR) hasn't been interpreted correctly. Finally, you may need to manually specify how to handle a clip's alpha channel. In these situations, use the Interpret Footage command to set things right. As usual, Premiere Pro doesn't alter the source media file; it just processes it differently.

To set the frame rate of a clip:

1. Select a clip, and choose File > Interpret Footage (**Figure 4.54**).

   The Interpret Footage dialog box appears.

2. Select an option:

   ▲ **Use Frame Rate from File:**
   Uses the file's inherent frame rate.

   ▲ **Assume This Frame Rate:**
   Uses the frame rate that you enter here (**Figure 4.55**).

To set the pixel aspect ratio of a clip:

1. Select a clip, and choose File >
   Interpret Footage.

   The Interpret Footage dialog box appears.

2. In the Pixel Aspect Ratio area of the
   Interpret Footage dialog box, select an
   option:

   ▲ **Use Pixel Aspect Ratio from File:**
   Uses the PAR Premiere Pro assumed.

   ▲ **Conform To:** Uses the alternative
   PAR you select from the drop-down
   menu (**Figure 4.56**).

To ignore or invert a clip's alpha channel:

1. Select a clip, and choose File > Interpret
   Footage.

   The Interpret Footage dialog box appears.

2. In the Alpha Channel area of the
   Interpret Footage dialog box, select the
   options you want (**Figure 4.57**):

   ▲ **Ignore Alpha Channel:** Disregards
   the clip's alpha channel so that it doesn't
   define transparent areas when the clip
   is added to video track 2 and higher.

   ▲ **Invert Alpha Channel:** Reverses the
   transparent and opaque areas defined
   by the clip's alpha channel.

✔ Tip

■ If you need detailed information about
any media file (whether it's in the current
project or not), choose File > Get Properties
For > File and select a file in the Get
Properties dialog box. When you select
a movie file, the Properties panel also
analyzes the movie's data rate, which can
help you troubleshoot a file that isn't
playing back properly.

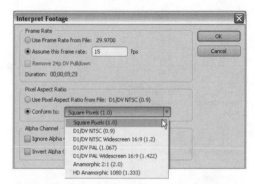

Figure 4.56 To change the PAR, select Conform To and select an option from the drop-down menu.

Figure 4.57 In the Interpret Footage dialog box, specify whether to ignore or invert the clip's alpha channel.

INTERPRETING FOOTAGE

Figure 4.58 Select one or more clips.

Figure 4.59 Choose Project > Make Offline.

Unlinking and Relinking Media

By now, you should appreciate the relationship between clips and media. You should know, for example, that a clip you log remains offline until you batch-capture the actual media to which it refers. Moreover, you should understand that deleting a clip doesn't remove the media from the hard disk—and, conversely, that deleting media results in clips with missing references. To truly manage your assets, however, you need control over the connection, or *link*, between clip and media.

Premiere Pro allows you to unlink a clip from its corresponding media file and relink the two again. Suppose you've been editing with low-quality proxy versions of your media (what some call *offline quality*). You can unlink the clips from the proxies and then link them to the high-quality versions (*online quality*). Alternatively, you can unlink media and remove it from the hard disk. Doing so lets you free up storage space and still retain the clip information in the form of an offline clip—ensuring that you can recapture the media if you decide you need it later.

To unlink clips from media:

1. In the Project panel, select one or more clips (**Figure 4.58**).

2. Choose Project > Make Offline (**Figure 4.59**).

   The Make Offline dialog box appears.

   continues on next page

UNLINKING AND RELINKING MEDIA

3. *Select one of the following* (**Figure 4.60**):

▲ **Media Files Remain on Disk:**
Breaks the clip's reference to the
media file without deleting the file.

▲ **Media Files Are Deleted:** Breaks
the clip's reference to the media file,
and deletes the file.

The selected clips' icons change to indicate that they're offline, unrelated to
media on the hard drive (**Figure 4.61**).

Figure 4.60 In the Make Offline dialog box, select the
appropriate option.

Figure 4.61 The selected clips become offline, and the
corresponding media files are either retained or
deleted, depending on your choice.

Figure 4.62 Select offline clips, and choose Project > Link Media.

Figure 4.63 Locate the correct media file, and click Select to link the clip to the file.

To link clips with media:

1. In the Project panel, select one or more offline clips.

2. Choose Project > Link Media (**Figure 4.62**).

   The Attach Which Media to *clipname* dialog box appears.

3. Find and select the media file you want to attach to the clip, and click Select (**Figure 4.63**).

   If you selected more than one clip in Step 1, Premiere Pro relinks the remaining clips automatically, as long as the corresponding media files are in the same location. If the corresponding media is in a different location, Premiere Pro prompts you with another Attach Which Media to *clipname* dialog box.

4. Repeat step 3 for clips with media in other locations on the hard disk.

   When all the clips you selected in Step 1 are relinked, Premiere Pro no longer prompts you to locate the media. In the Project panel, the selected clip's icon indicates that it's linked to media.

UNLINKING AND RELINKING MEDIA

Using the Project Manager

Because video files can consume large amounts of precious storage space, it's particularly important to manage them efficiently. You can organize your media and reduce storage requirements with the Project Manager. With the Project Manager, you can collect and trim your project.

Collecting a project moves all of the project's media to a single location. This is useful when it's time to archive your project or move it to another editing system—especially if your assets aren't well organized and are scattered over one or more hard disks.

Trimming a project identifies the clips you used in sequences and creates a duplicate project that includes only those clips. Moreover, their corresponding media files are trimmed, or shortened, to the range of footage present in sequences. This way, the footage you used consumes less storage space, and you can more easily delete the footage you didn't use.

Whether you collect or trim a project, note that Premiere Pro saves a new project separately, leaving the original version untouched. This is consistent with the idea of nondestructive editing, explained in Chapter 2, "Starting a Project."

To use the Project Manager:

1. Choose Project > Project Manager (**Figure 4.64**).

   The Project Manager dialog box appears (**Figure 4.65**).

   continues on next page

Figure 4.64 Choose Project > Project Manager to open the Project Manager.

Figure 4.65 With the Project Manager, you can collect and trim your project.

Figure 4.66 The Calculate Progress panel appears briefly while Premiere Pro calculates the required disk space.

Figure 4.67 Use the Browse for Folder dialog box to select a destination.

Figure 4.68 The Project Manager Progress panel shows the project being trimmed...

Figure 4.69 ...or copied.

2. *Do one of the following:*

▲ To create a new trimmed project, select Create New Trimmed Project

▲ To collect all of the project's assets into a common location, select Collect Files and Copy to New Location.

3. Specify other options.

These options are explained in detail in the next section, "Choosing Project Manager Options."

4. In the Disk Space area of the Project Manager, click Calculate to calculate the disk space required to store the new files.

The Calculate Progress panel appears briefly while the required disk space is being calculated (**Figure 4.66**).

5. In the Project Destination area of the Project Manager, click the Browse button and specify a destination.

The Browse for Folder dialog box appears (**Figure 4.67**).

6. Specify the location for the collected or trimmed files.

7. Click OK to create the new files.

The Project Manager Progress panel appears, indicating that the project is being trimmed (**Figure 4.68**) or copied (**Figure 4.69**). When processing is complete, the original project is still open. To use the new project, close the original project and open the new project.

USING THE PROJECT MANAGER

129

Choosing Project Manager Options

The Project Manager includes a number of options, depending on whether you trim or collect your project:

◆ **Exclude Unused Clips:** Excludes media from the new project that you didn't use in the original project.

◆ **Make Offline:** Marks as offline any footage that you can recapture later. Select this option when you want the Project Manager to retain reel names and time-code to facilitate quick batch capture. This option is available only if Create New Trimmed Project is selected.

◆ **Include Handles:** Specifies the number of frames retained before the In point and after the Out point of each trimmed clip.

◆ **Include Preview Files:** Specifies that effects you rendered in the original project stay rendered in the new project. When this option is selected, the new project requires more disk space; so, unless the footage requires extensive rendering, leave this option unchecked when backing up projects. This option is available only if you select Collect Files and Copy to New Location.

◆ **Include Audio Conform Files:** Specifies that the audio you conformed in the original project remains conformed in the new project. When this option is selected, the new project requires more disk space, but the audio doesn't need to be conformed again when you open the project. This option is available only if you select Collect Files and Copy to New Location.

◆ **Rename Media Files to Match Clip Names:** Renames the copied clips with the same names as the captured clips. Select this option if you rename your captured clips in the Project panel and want the copied footage files to have the same names.

✔ Tips

■ *Handles* are extra frames that allow you to make additional small adjustments to the edits in a new project.

■ In cases where multiple clips use segments from the same captured footage file, and you rename each project, the Project Manager renames the footage file using the name of the first clip in the project.

■ If you select the Make Offline option and then rename captured clips, the copied project retains and displays the original file name, not the new name.

VIEWING CLIPS IN THE MONITOR PANELS

5

As their names imply, the Source and Program Monitors let you see your footage much as you would on the video monitors in a traditional video-editing suite or the screens on a flatbed film-editing table. The Monitors are modeled after an *entire* editing station, complete with editing controls to play back your clips and assemble them into a sequence. Not that the Monitor panels merely emulate their predecessors—they have features and advantages you can find only in a digital, nonlinear editing program.

This chapter focuses on using the Monitor panels to view clips. You'll learn to open and play clips and specify a number of viewing options. With these features under your belt, you'll be prepared to use the Monitors' editing features, covered in the next chapter.

VIEWING CLIPS IN THE MONITOR PANELS

131

Using the Monitor Panels

In the default editing workspace, the two Monitor panels tend to command the most attention. Arranged side by side, they're nearly identical in appearance and, in most ways, function the same; however, they're complimentary in purpose.

On the left is the *Source Monitor*, where you view source clips and set their edit marks before adding them to a sequence. On the right is the *Program Monitor*, where you view an edited sequence (the same sequence depicted graphically in the Timeline panel). The Program Monitor also contains editing controls—but in this case, for specifying where footage will be added to or removed from a sequence (**Figure 5.1**).

Some editors will recognize the Monitors as the nonlinear equivalent of a traditional video-editing suite (and, to a lesser extent, a flatbed film-editing table). This time-tested paradigm lets you see the source and sequence side by side, which can help you make editing decisions. You can even *gang* the Source and Program Monitors, so that footage in the source and sequence play synchronously. This feature is invaluable when you need to preview the timing of certain edits or see other editing relationships.

Source Monitor   Program Monitor

Figure 5.1 In the default editing workspace, the Source Monitor and Program Monitor appear side by side. The Source Monitor displays and controls source clips; the Program Monitor displays and controls an edited sequence.

Once you've assembled a rough cut, however, your need for a Source Monitor diminishes. Fortunately, Premiere Pro's flexible panel-based interface makes it easy to replace the Source Monitor with the panel most appropriate to the task at hand, such as the Effect Controls panel or the Audio Mixer. (See Chapter 1, "Premiere Pro Basics," for more about customizing the workspace.)

Premiere Pro also includes a few related panels that include "Monitor" in their names. The *Reference Monitor* provides a secondary view of a sequence that's useful in comparing and color-correcting shots (**Figure 5.2**).

Figure 5.2 Other editing tasks may require related panels. For color correction, you may employ a Reference Monitor. Here, the video in the Program Monitor (on the right) can be analyzed using a Reference Monitor (on the left), which displays a color-measurement tool.

The *Multi-Camera Monitor* facilitates editing footage from a *multicamera shoot*, in which several cameras record an event from different angles at once. By synchronizing the shots in a sequence and nesting it as a multicamera source, you can see all the shots at once and select the one you want to use (**Figure 5.3**). Although editing with the Multi-Camera Monitor is fully explained in Chapter 6, "Creating a Sequence," the playback controls it shares with other Monitors are covered here.

✔ Tips

■ Prior to Premiere Pro 2.0, a single Monitor window contained a Source view and a Program view. The current interface allows you to view the source footage and edited sequences in separate panels, a far more flexible and user-friendly design.

■ You can set up a Premiere Pro editing system that includes a television that shows the same image as in the currently selected Monitor panel. This not only provides a larger view for you and your client, but also more accurately represents how the footage will appear to viewers (if you plan to present your project on television). See Chapter 10, "Previewing a Sequence," to learn more about your options.

Figure 5.3 For editing synchronized footage from several camera angles, you can use a Multi-Camera Monitor.

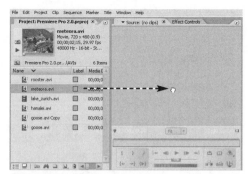

Figure 5.4 Double-click a clip or drag it to the Source Monitor, as shown here.

Figure 5.5 The clip opens in the Source Monitor, and its name appears on the Source tab.

Viewing Clips

When you open any kind of clip—a movie, a still image, or audio—it appears in the Source Monitor, where you can play it and mark frames for editing. The name of the open clip appears in a tab at the top of the Source Monitor, the *source tab*. Clicking the small triangle on the source tab reveals a *source menu*; this menu lists all the clips you've opened in order, starting with the most recent. You can quickly reopen a clip by selecting it from the Source menu. When the menu becomes unwieldy, you can clear items from the list.

To open a clip in the Source Monitor:

◆ *Do one of the following:*

▲ Double-click a clip in the Project panel, the preview image, or the Timeline panel.

▲ Drag a clip from the Project panel or the preview image into the Source Monitor (**Figure 5.4**).

The clip's image or audio waveform appears in the Source Monitor, and its name appears on the Source tab (**Figure 5.5**).

VIEWING CLIPS

To load several clips into the Source menu at once:

1. In the Project panel, select one or more clips (**Figure 5.6**).

2. Drag the selected clips to the Source Monitor (**Figure 5.7**).

   The clips appear in the Source menu in order, so that the last clip selected is first and its video or audio waveform appears in the Source Monitor.

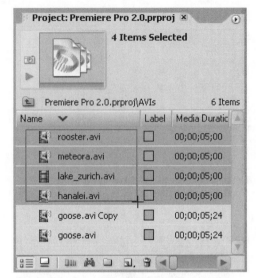

Figure 5.6 In the Project panel, select one or more clips...

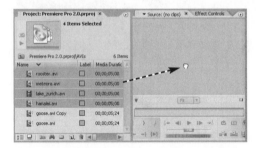

Figure 5.7 ...and drag them to the Source Monitor to load them into the Source menu.

Opening Source Clips and Clip Instances

When you open a clip from the Project panel, you're opening a *source* clip. As you'll learn in the next chapter, you open a source clip to view and edit it before adding it to a sequence.

Each time you add a source clip to a sequence, you create a new *instance* of the source clip, also called a *sequence clip*. Opening a clip instance allows you to view that particular use of the clip in the Source Monitor, and any edits you make are instantly reflected in the Timeline panel (although once the clip is in a sequence, there are numerous other ways to edit it).

For now, note that the Source menu lists source clips by name. It lists clip instances by a kind of path name that includes the sequence name, the clip name, and the clip's current In point in the sequence.

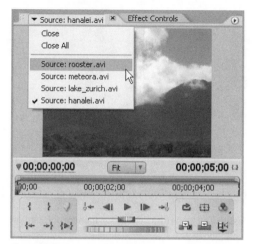

Figure 5.8 From the Source menu, choose the name of the clip you want to view.

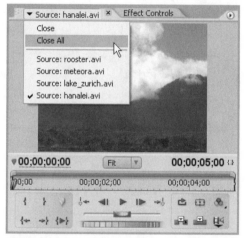

Figure 5.9 To remove all clips from the Source menu, choose Close All.

To view clips using the Source menu:

◆ In the Source menu, choose the name of a clip (**Figure 5.8**).

The selected clip appears in the image area of the Source Monitor.

To remove clips from the Source menu:

◆ *Do one of the following:*

▲ To close the open clip and clear it from the Source menu, click the Close button ⊠ on the Source tab or choose Close from the Source menu.

▲ To clear all the clips from the Source menu, choose Close All from the Source menu (**Figure 5.9**).

Depending on your choice, one or more clips are removed from the Source menu. However, closed clips remain listed in the Project panel.

✔ Tips

■ You can also open nested sequences in the Source Monitor for editing. See Chapter 6 for details.

■ Double-clicking a selection of multiple clips won't load all the selected clips into the Source menu, just the one you double-click.

VIEWING CLIPS

137

Opening Audio Clips

The Source Monitor works the same for audio clips as for movie clips, except that instead of showing the current frame of the video, it depicts the audio as a *waveform*— a kind of graph of the audio's power over time. A monophonic track appears as a single waveform; a stereophonic track appears as two waveforms (**Figures 5.10** and **5.11**). Often, you can identify particular sounds by examining the audio waveform. Powerful beats in a song are depicted as spikes in the waveform; silence or pauses between lines of dialogue result in flat horizontal lines in the waveform.

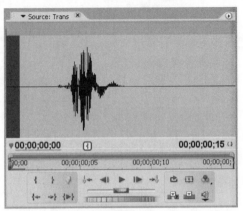

Figure 5.10 In the Source Monitor, monophonic audio clips appear as a single waveform...

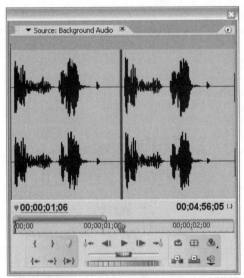

Figure 5.11 ...whereas stereophonic clips appear as a dual waveform.

Clip marker icon   Current time indicator
In point icon   Out point icon

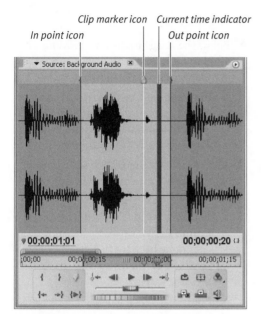

Figure 5.12 In addition to a waveform, the Source Monitor shows other information for audio clips differently than it does for video.

Figure 5.13 In the Source Monitor's pull-down menu, choose Audio Waveform.

Because the waveform depicts audio over a span of time (as opposed to a single video frame), the Source Monitor can display other information as well. A vertical line indicates the current time—the position of the playback head, if you will. In addition, icons for clip markers and In and Out points appear at the top of the Source Monitor, with vertical lines extending from them to help you see their positions in terms of the waveform. Furthermore, the area between the current In and Out points is shaded lighter so you can see your selection as well as hear it (**Figure 5.12**). For more about markers and In and Out points, see Chapter 6.

To view the audio portion of a video:

◆ In the Source Monitor's pull-down menu, choose Audio Waveform (**Figure 5.13**).

The audio waveform linked to the video file appears in the image area of the Source Monitor.

✔ Tips

■ You can switch the Source Monitor's time ruler to show audio samples rather than video frames. See Chapter 6 for details.

■ As you'll see in Chapter 6, audio clips can be added to a sequence only in a track of the same channel type. In other words, mono audio clips can be added only to a mono track in the sequence, and stereo clips can be added only to a stereo track.

■ You can separate, or *break out*, the mono channels from a stereo track. See Chapter 11, "Mixing Audio," for more information.

Using Playback Controls

Whether you're playing a clip in the Source Monitor or an edited sequence in the Program Monitor, the basic playback controls work the same.

Most playback controls also have preset keyboard shortcuts, which are well worth learning. Before you use keyboard playback controls, however, make sure you select the appropriate Monitor. As usual, the selected panel appears highlighted, outlined with a colored border.

Also bear in mind that the Program Monitor corresponds to the sequence in the Timeline panel. As you change the current time in the Program Monitor, watch how it affects the current time indicator in the Timeline panel (and vice versa). The same keyboard playback commands that work in the Program Monitor also work when the Timeline panel is selected.

To use the playback controls:

◆ Below the image in the Source Monitor and Program Monitor, click the appropriate playback control (**Figure 5.14**):

▲ **Play/Stop:** Plays the clip or sequence until it reaches the last frame. Click the control again to stop playback. The icon toggles accordingly.

▲ **Frame Advance:** Moves the current time one frame forward in time (or forward by the timebase division you selected for the time display).

▲ **Frame Back:** Moves the current time one frame back (or backward by the timebase division you selected for the time display).

▲ **Loop:** Repeats a playback operation (play or play In to Out) until you click Stop.

▲ **Play In to Out:** Plays the portion of the clip or program between the selected In and Out points.

▲ **Jog Disk:** Advances or reverses the clip by small amounts as you drag and release the control.

▲ **Shuttle:** Scans the clip more quickly the further you drag the control from its center position. Releasing the control returns it to its center position and stops playback.

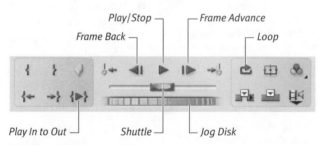

Figure 5.14 Most playback controls work the same in the Source and Program Monitors.

Table 5.1

Default Keyboard Shortcuts for Playback	
ACTION	RESULT
Press L	Play.
Press K	Pause.
Press J	Play in reverse.
Press J or L repeatedly	Increase speed. (Most media plays at 2x, 3x, and then 4x normal speed.)
Press Shift+J or Shift+L repeatedly	Play slowly. (Most media plays at 0.1x and then 0.2x normal speed.)
Spacebar	Toggle between play and stop.

To use keyboard shortcuts to control playback:

1. Make sure the appropriate Monitor is active.

2. *Do one of the following* (see **Table 5.1**):

▲ To play in reverse, press J.

▲ To stop playback, press K.

▲ To play forward, press L.

▲ To increase playback speed, press J or L again. For most media types, speed increases by increments of 1x, 2x, 3x, and 4x normal speed.

▲ To play forward slowly, press Shift+L.

▲ To play in reverse slowly, press Shift+J. For most media types, clips play at 0.1x and 0.2x normal speed.

▲ To toggle between play and stop, press the spacebar.

✔ Tips

■ The J-K-L keyboard combination is worth getting used to. In the next chapter, you'll see how you can use J-K-L along with other keyboard shortcuts for speedy keyboard-based editing. This keyboard combination has become standard in several popular editing programs. You can think of J-K-L as the *home keys* of nonlinear editing (just as certain home keys are the basis of touch typing).

■ Pressing Alt toggles the Play In to Out button to the Play Around button. Play Around plays frames just before and after the current time indicator. The number of frames is defined by the preroll and postroll values you specify in the Preferences.

■ If you use a mouse with a scroll wheel, you can use the wheel as a jog-disk control for the active Monitor.

USING PLAYBACK CONTROLS

Cuing Clips Numerically

You can use the time displays to cue the Source and Program Monitors to a particular frame number, or *absolute time*. Or you can cue to a *relative time*—in other words, add frames to or subtract frames from the current time. Like most user-defined values in Premiere Pro and other Adobe products, the time display is *scrubbable hot text*—you can adjust the value by dragging the number.

To cue a Monitor to an absolute time:

1. Click the Monitor panel's current time display to highlight the number (**Figure 5.15**).

2. Enter the number of the frame that you want to view, and press Enter (**Figure 5.16**).

   As long as the frame number that you entered exists, the view displays that frame (**Figure 5.17**).

Figure 5.15 Click a view's current time display to highlight the number.

Figure 5.16 Type a valid frame number (typically, expressed in timecode), and press Enter...

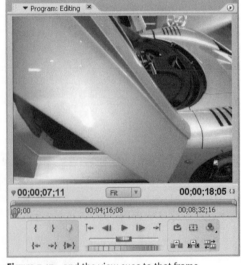

Figure 5.17 ...and the view cues to that frame.

Cuing Clips Numerically

Figure 5.18 Here, the time display is set to cue the current time 20 frames forward.

Figure 5.19 You can also drag the current time display to change its value. This is true for underlined values in all Adobe programs.

To cue a Monitor to a relative time:

1. Click the Monitor's current time display to highlight the number.

2. Type a plus (+) or a minus (–) sign and a number (**Figure 5.18**).

   To cue the clip 30 frames after the current frame, for example, type +30. To cue the view 60 frames before the current frame, type –60.

To cue a Monitor by scrubbing the current time:

◆ *Do one of the following:*

   ▲ Drag the current time display to the right to increase the number and advance the current time (**Figure 5.19**).

   ▲ Drag the current time display to the left to decrease the number and reverse the current time.

CUING CLIPS NUMERICALLY

✔ **Tips**

■ You can highlight individual numbers in the current-time readout and change them to cue the current frame.

■ If the time that you enter in the current time display doesn't exist, the Monitor is cued to the nearest available frame: either the first or the last frame of the clip or sequence.

■ The frame-counting method displayed in the time display is determined by the Project settings (see Chapter 2, "Starting a Project"). For most users (and for most screenshots in this book), the display uses drop-frame timecode.

CUING CLIPS NUMERICALLY

Entering Frame Values

Any duration value that you enter in Premiere Pro has a *threshold* of 100. That is, numbers 99 and below are interpreted as frames; numbers 100 and above are expressed in the units of the selected time display. In a project that uses a timecode display, for example, the number 99 is interpreted as 99 frames, or 3 seconds and 9 frames; the number 100 is interpreted as seconds and frames, or 1 second and 00 frames.

Using a Monitor's Time Ruler Controls

A *time ruler* in each Monitor panel provides another way to navigate through a clip or sequence (**Figure 5.20**). The full width of the ruler represents the entire length of the clip in the Source Monitor or the entire length of a sequence in the Program Monitor. Tick marks and numbers measure time using the unit of measure you specified in the project settings, although you can toggle the ruler to measure audio samples as well. The frame displayed in the Monitor's image area corresponds to a blue triangular marker in the ruler, called the *current time indicator (CTI)*.

Each time ruler also displays icons for its corresponding Monitor's markers and In and Out points. You can move the current time, markers, and In and Out points by dragging the appropriate icon in a time ruler.

Just above each time ruler is a thin bar with curved ends, called the *viewing area bar*. By changing the width of the viewing area bar, you can control the scale area of the time ruler. Expanding the bar to its maximum width reveals the entire span of its time ruler, and contracting the bar zooms into the ruler for a more detailed view. Dragging the center of the bar scrolls through the time ruler without changing its scale.

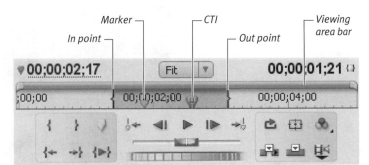

Figure 5.20 A time ruler in each view provides another way to navigate through a clip or sequence.

To view the time ruler in more or less detail:

◆ *Do one of the following:*

▲ To show a Monitor's time ruler in more detail, drag the ends of the viewing area bar closer together (**Figures 5.21** and **5.22**).

▲ To show more of a Monitor's time ruler, drag the ends of the viewing area bar farther apart.

Dragging one end of the viewing area bar scales the bar from its center.

Figure 5.21 Here, the viewing area bar is set to show the full span of time. Note how the tick marks and icons appear at the current scale.

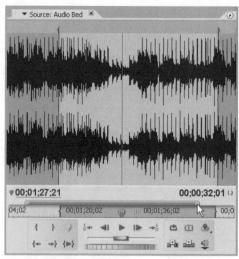

Figure 5.22 To view the ruler in more detail, drag the ends of the viewing area bar closer together. Again, note how the tick marks and icons look at the new scale.

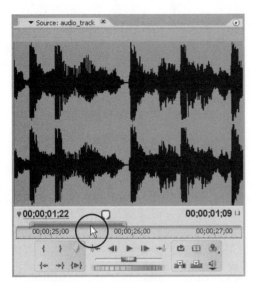

Figure 5.23 Drag the viewing area bar from the center to view a different part of the time ruler.

Figure 5.24 To set the current time, click the time ruler or drag the CTI.

To change the visible area of a Monitor's time ruler:

◆ Drag the center of the viewing area bar to the left to see an earlier part of the time ruler or to the right to see a later part (**Figure 5.23**).

To set the current time in a time ruler:

◆ *Do one of the following:*

▲ Click the time ruler to cue the current time.

▲ Drag the blue CTI (**Figure 5.24**).

✔ Tip

■ Because the Program Monitor and Timeline panel correspond to the same sequence, they show the same current time, markers, and In and Out points. However, their viewing area bars operate independently; the part of the time ruler you view in the Program Monitor can be different than the part you see in the Timeline panel.

Viewing Video Safe Zones

A Monitor panel displays the entire video frame, but television monitors are likely to crop off the outer edges of the image. If your program is destined for full-screen display on a television, you may need to check whether certain parts of the image fall within the video *safe zones*.

In video, the inner 90 percent of the complete image is considered to be *action safe*—that is, everything within that area is likely to appear on most television screens. The inner 80 percent is considered to be *title safe*. Because you can't afford to let any of the title's content be lost, the title-safe area defines a necessary safety margin. The safe-zone guides are for your reference only; they aren't added to the source image and don't appear in the program output.

To view safe zones:

◆ In the Source or Program Monitor, click the Safe Margins button ▦ (**Figure 5.25**).

Safe-zone guides appear in the corresponding Monitor panel (**Figure 5.26**). Deselect the button to hide the safe-zone guides.

✔ Tips

■ As you may guess, safe zones are particularly useful when you're creating titles or moving images through the screen. See Chapter 12, "Creating Titles," or Chapter 13, "Working with Effects," for more information.

■ You can change the position of the safe-margin guides in the General panel of the Project settings, but 10 percent and 20 percent margins (to demarcate the 90-percent and 80-percent zones) are standard.

Figure 5.25 In the Source or Program Monitor, click the Safe Margins button.

Action safe (90 percent)

Title safe (80 percent)

Figure 5.26 Safe-zone guides appear in the view.

Figure 5.27 In the Source or Program Monitor, click the output button and choose a quality setting from the pull-down menu.

Choosing a Quality Setting

You can set the relative quality of the video image in each Monitor panel. Even though you may prefer the highest quality—which displays all the pixels in each frame of video—using a lower quality setting can be useful. By reducing a Monitor panel's resolution, you reduce the processing demands on your computer and make it easier for your system to play video at the proper frame rate. This is particularly useful in the Program Monitor; lowering its quality setting enables your system to play effects or other processing-intensive parts of a sequence right away, without pausing to render (see Chapter 10, "Previewing a Sequence").

But even at the highest quality setting, the methods used to process images in the Monitor panels are inferior to those used to export the final video. All of the quality settings use a bi-linear pixel resampling method to resize the video image, and none of them process interlaced fields. When it's exporting a sequence, on the other hand, Premiere Pro processes interlaced fields and uses a cubic resampling method, which is superior to bi-linear.

To set a Monitor's image quality:

◆ In the Source or Program Monitor, click the output button and choose a quality option from the menu (**Figure 5.27**):

  ▲ **Highest Quality:** Displays video in the Monitor panel at full resolution.

  ▲ **Draft Quality:** Displays video in the Monitor panel at one-half resolution.

  ▲ **Automatic Quality:** Measures playback performance, and dynamically adjusts the video quality.

Changing the Magnification

Whatever size you make a Monitor panel, the video in each Monitor automatically scales to fit in the available space. However, you can see the video in more detail by increasing a Monitor's *magnification setting*. Alternatively, you can decrease the magnification setting to reduce the image relative to the empty, or *pasteboard*, area around it, so you can adjust motion effects more easily, for example. The magnification setting is for viewing purposes only; it doesn't alter the video's appearance for output or change the source file in any way.

To set a Monitor's magnification:

◆ Under the Source or Program Monitor's video image, click the Magnification button and choose an option from the pull-down menu:

  ▲ To fit in the available area of a Monitor panel, choose Fit.

  ▲ To magnify a Monitor's image, choose a percentage value (**Figure 5.28**).

Figure 5.28 To magnify a view, choose a magnification setting from the pull-down menu.

Figure 5.29 Here, the image is reduced so that motion effects can be adjusted more easily.

Increasing the magnification setting zooms into the video image; using a lower magnification setting reduces the image relative to the Monitor panel's pasteboard area (**Figure 5.29**).

Scroll bars appear when you magnify the Monitor's image over 100 percent. You can change the visible part of the image by using the scroll bars (**Figure 5.30**) or by selecting the Hand tool and dragging the image.

Figure 5.30 Scroll bars appear when you magnify the view over 100 percent.

Choosing a Display Mode

Ordinarily, the video in each Monitor panel appears as it would on any television screen (albeit before television's safe zones effectively crop the outer edges). However, you can set a Monitor's *display mode* to show the video's *alpha channel*—its transparency information as represented by a grayscale image. In addition, you can set the display mode to show several iterations of a *waveform monitor* and *vectorscope*, tools that precisely measure the video's luminance and chrominance values. The waveform monitor and vectorscope (often collectively referred to as *scopes*) are invaluable for color correction and for ensuring that your video meets broadcast specifications. If you're unfamiliar with these tools, turn to the sidebars "Using a Waveform Monitor" and "Using a Vectorscope," later in this chapter.

To set the display mode:

◆ In the Source or Program Monitor, click the Display Mode button 🌢, and choose an option from the menu (**Figure 5.31**):

▲ **Composite Video:** Displays the normal video image, sometimes referred to as the *composite* of the *luminance* (grayscale) and *chrominance* (color) components of the video.

▲ **Alpha:** Displays the image's transparency information (called the *alpha channel* in digital formats) as a grayscale image, so that the range of black to white corresponds to the range of transparency to opacity (**Figure 5.32**).

▲ **All Scopes:** Displays all four measurement devices—YC Waveform monitor, vectorscope, YCbCr Parade, and RGB Parade—one in each corner of the view.

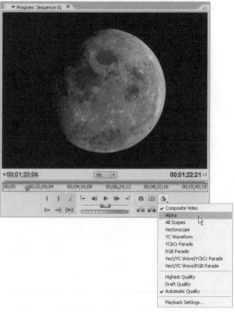

Figure 5.31 In the Source or Program Monitor, click the Display Mode button and choose an option.

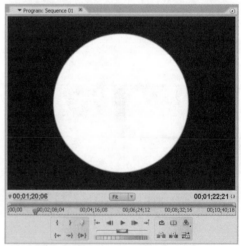

Figure 5.32 The Alpha option shows transparency information as a grayscale image in which white represents opaque areas and black represents transparent areas.

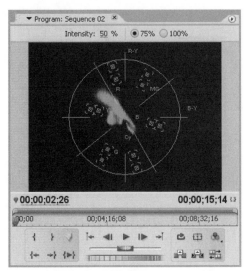

Figure 5.33 A vectorscope measures the video's chrominance.

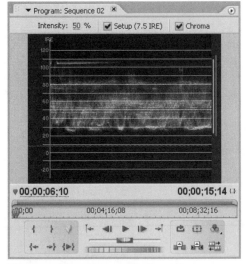

Figure 5.34 A waveform monitor is used to measure the video's luminance levels.

▲ **Vectorscope:** Displays a standard vectorscope, a device used to measure the video's chrominance levels, which include hue and saturation (**Figure 5.33**).

▲ **YC Waveform:** Displays a standard waveform monitor, a device used to measure the video's luminance levels in units called IRE (pronounced letter by letter and named for the Institute of Radio Engineers) (**Figure 5.34**).

▲ **YCbCr Parade:** Displays a variation of the waveform monitor that charts the components of the video image separately, in terms of a YCbCr color model.

▲ **RGB Parade:** Displays a variation of the waveform monitor that charts the components of the video image separately, in terms of an RGB color model.

▲ **Vect/YC Wave/YCbCr Parade:** Displays three scopes: a standard waveform monitor and vectorscope in the top half of the view and YCbCr Parade in the bottom half.

▲ **Vect/YC Wave/RGB Parade:** Displays three scopes: a standard waveform monitor and vectorscope in the top half of the view and RGB Parade in the bottom half.

CHOOSING A DISPLAY MODE

Setting Waveform and Vectorscope Display Options

You can use the display mode options in the Monitor panels to modify your view of the YC Waveform and Vectorscope displays (**Figure 5.35**). These options appear at the top of the Monitor panel when the Vectorscope, YC Waveform, and All Scopes display modes are selected.

Intensity lets you change the brightness of the selected display, which can help you discern aspects of the scope's pattern. This setting affects both the YC Waveform and Vectorscope displays and is set to 50 percent by default.

Setup limits, or *pins*, a YC Waveform display's black level to 7.5 IRE when selected, or 0 IRE when unselected. Setup specifies the voltage level that corresponds to black in an image. In the United States, NTSC standards place the setup (also known as *pedestal*) at 7.5 IRE; Japan's implementation of NTSC standards places the setup at 0 IRE. A Monitor panel's Setup setting affects the Waveform's display pattern only; it doesn't affect the actual footage. If you're using an analog output device, it may add a pedestal of 7.5 IRE, so this option gives you a similar view.

Chroma superimposes a chrominance, or *chroma*, waveform pattern (in blue) over the luminance waveform (in green). Deselecting Chroma excludes the video's color components in the waveform pattern, which can make it easier to identify the image's luminance values. This setting applies to the YC Waveform display only.

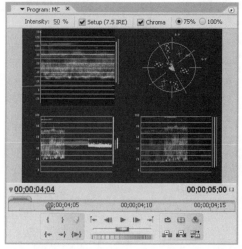

Figure 5.35 The All Scopes mode has all three display mode options.

Using a Waveform Monitor

You can use a waveform monitor to measure the video's brightness—or, more precisely, its luminance component. You can read the waveform monitor just as you would read a graph. Horizontally, the graph corresponds to the video image; vertically, it measures luminance in IRE units. The video produces a waveform pattern (bright green areas) on the graph, so that bright objects produce a waveform near the top of the graph, and darker areas produce a waveform near the bottom (**Figure 5.36**).

For NTSC video in the United States, luminance levels should range from 7.5 to 100 IRE. Japan's implementation of NTSC standards permits a luminance range from 0 to 100 IRE. Allowing video levels to stray outside these limits, or NTSC-safe levels, may ruin more than the video's appearance; it could interfere with parts of the signal that keep the picture stable and make it ineligible for broadcast.

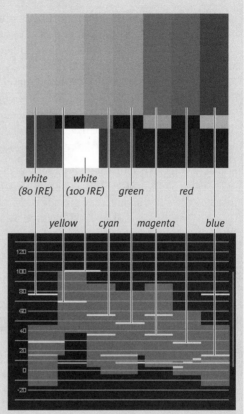

Figure 5.36 The top image shows a standard color bars pattern in a view set to the composite display mode. The bottom image shows the same color bars as seen in a waveform monitor. Note how the bars and the pattern in the waveform monitor correspond.

WAVEFORM/VECTORSCOPE DISPLAY OPTIONS

The Waveform Monitor and Vectorscope Are Not Surf Reports

In Chapter 3, "Capturing and Importing Footage," you learned that a *leader* (the boilerplate information on the first few minutes of a master tape) always includes a color-bars test pattern. Video technicians use the color bars as a reference to faithfully reproduce your video's color and brightness levels (in much the same way that a service bureau uses a color-chip chart or PANTONE colors to reproduce printed material). To accurately calibrate their equipment to the color bars, technicians use hardware devices known as a *waveform monitor* and a *vectorscope*. The *scopes*, as they're sometimes called, accurately measure the video's brightness and color (in technical terms, its luminance and chrominance). Using a waveform monitor and vectorscope ensures that the bars—and the rest of the video program—are copied exactly.

Similarly, you can use Premiere Pro's software waveform monitor and vectorscope to accurately judge video levels and make precise adjustments, such as color correction. Because the scopes measure the video signal, they provide more accurate information than does judging the video by eye. Even the keenest eye is subjective; even the best monitor can be poorly calibrated and inaccurate.

If you've never used scopes to evaluate video, see the sidebars "Using a Waveform Monitor" and "Using a Vectorscope."

I Love a Parade: RGB and YCbCr

Even those familiar with the waveform monitor may be confused by two of the viewing mode options: RGB Parade and YCbCr Parade. These describe the components of video using two different color models: one native to most computer applications, the other native to digital video. For many users, the basic waveform and vectorscope will suffice, and the parade options will be of little interest. For the rest of you—well, you asked for it. Here's a brief explanation.

Most computer programs process and display video using the RGB color space. However, video is often processed using a YUV model (which itself is derived from another model). When converted into the digital realm, YUV becomes YCbCr. For this reason, YUV and YCbCr are sometimes used interchangeably, although the results aren't entirely accurate.

In most cases, video must be translated from its native tongue, YCbCr, to the local dialect, RGB. And as with spoken languages, there's always something lost in the translation. In literal terms, one system must be mathematically scaled and converted into the other, losing a degree of precision in the process.

Premiere Pro can process video using YCbCr—provided that everything in your project uses it, including all your footage and effects. Otherwise, Premiere Pro processes everything in RGB. But you probably shouldn't worry about this too much. Only the most demanding applications (or finicky users) will suffer from the conversion to RGB. Your energy will be better spent maintaining image quality at other points in the production and post-production processes.

Using a Vectorscope

You can use a vectorscope to measure a video signal's color—or, more precisely, its *chrominance*. A vectorscope maps chrominance to a circular chart according to chrominance's two components: saturation and hue (**Figures 5.37** and **5.38**).

Saturation is measured from the center of the chart outward, so that more saturated, vivid colors produce a pattern near the edges of the chart, whereas a grayscale image produces only a dot at the center of the chart. The color, or hue, in the image determines the angle of the pattern in the vectorscope.

Fully saturated magenta, blue, cyan, green, yellow, and red—all present in a color-bars test pattern—should each register in a corresponding box on the vectorscope. In NTSC video, chrominance levels should never overshoot these target areas, the NTSC-safe color range. In video, oversaturated colors tend to bleed. That is, colors shift horizontally, so that the video resembles pictures in a coloring book belonging to a kid who doesn't color within the lines.

Figure 5.37 This video of a campfire contains bright yellows and reds.

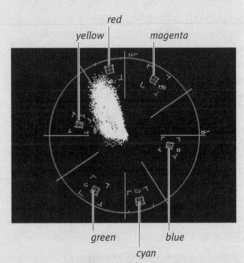

Figure 5.38 Here is the same video in a vectorscope. Hue is indicated by the angle of the pattern, whereas saturation is measured from the center outward. Target boxes show where fully saturated colors (as in color bars) should produce a pattern.

Using a Reference Monitor

A *Reference Monitor* acts much like a secondary Program Monitor that opens in a separate window (which, like all windows, can be docked as a panel). You can use the Program Monitor and Reference Monitor to compare different frames of a sequence side by side or to view the same frame of a sequence using different display modes.

For example, by cueing the Program Monitor and Reference Monitor to different clips in the sequence, you can correct the scenes using the color-matching filter. On the other hand, you can *gang* the Program Monitor and Reference Monitor, so that their playback controls are locked together and always show the same frame. This allows you to set the Program Monitor to a composite display mode and the Reference Monitor to a waveform monitor or vectorscope—the ideal setup for using the color-correction filter.

The Reference Monitor has many of the same controls as the Source and Program Monitors, but because it's used as a reference, it lacks editing controls. You can open only one Reference Monitor, and it always displays the same sequence as the Program Monitor.

To open a Reference Monitor:

1. In the Program Monitor, select the sequence from which you want to create a Reference Monitor.

2. In the Program Monitor's pull-down menu, choose New Reference Monitor (**Figure 5.39**).

   A Reference Monitor appears for the current sequence (**Figure 5.40**).

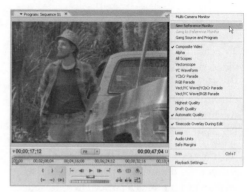

Figure 5.39 In the Program Monitor's pull-down menu, choose New Reference Monitor.

Figure 5.40 Here, the Reference Monitor is set to a different frame of the sequence for purposes of comparison.

Figure 5.41 Click the Reference Monitor's Gang to Program Monitor button to synchronize the Monitor with the Program Monitor.

Figure 5.42 Here, the Reference Monitor is ganged to the Program Monitor, and its display mode is set to a Waveform Monitor to check the luminance levels.

To gang a Reference Monitor to a sequence:

◆ *Do one of the following:*

▲ In the Reference Monitor, click the Gang to Program Monitor button to select it (**Figure 5.41**).

▲ In the Reference Monitor's pull-down menu, choose Gang to Program Monitor.

▲ In the Program Monitor's pull-down menu, choose Gang to Reference Monitor.

The Reference Monitor and Program Monitor are linked so that the playback controls used in one affect the other (**Figure 5.42**).

Ganging the Source and Program Monitors

In some circumstances, you need to preview the relationship between a source clip and a sequence visually. You may want to preview to see which frames will be replaced by an overlay edit, for example, before you perform the edit (this and other editing techniques are covered in Chapter 6, "Creating a Sequence").

For these situations, you can calculate durations, or you can gang the Source and Program Monitors. Ganging the Source and Program Monitors synchronizes them, so that playing one plays the other. This way, you can see how the frames of the Source Monitor correspond to those of the Program Monitor to help you decide where to set editing marks.

To gang the Source and Program Monitors:

1. In the Monitor panel, cue each view to the frame from which you want to synchronize. For example, cue the views to the In points you're considering for the next edit.

2. In the Source or Program Monitor's pull-down menu, select Gang Source and Program (**Figure 5.43**).

3. Use the playback controls in either the Source or Program Monitor.

   The views move in sync (**Figure 5.44**). To make each view work independently, deselect Gang Source and Program in either view's pull-down menu.

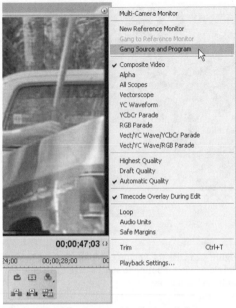

Figure 5.43 In the Program Monitor's pull-down menu, choose Gang Source and Program.

Figure 5.44 When you jog or shuttle either view, they move together in a synchronized relationship. Here, ganging a wide and medium shot helps identify the best cut point.

CREATING A SEQUENCE

You may have heard film editing referred to as *cutting*. This, of course, refers to the fact that you literally cut the work print of a film. In some circles, however, editing is called *joining*, which refers to the process of splicing film segments together. The term you prefer may say something about your attitude toward editing—emphasizing either the elimination or the union of footage. Literally speaking, editing involves both cutting and joining clips. You select portions of the source footage and arrange them into one or more sequences.

The basic editing methods covered in this chapter fall into three categories: drag-and-drop editing; editing with the controls in the Source and Program Monitors; an automated process sometimes called *storyboard editing*; and multicamera editing. The number of choices can make the process seem more complex than it really is. Editing can always be reduced to two simple tasks: defining the part of the clip you want to use, and adding that part to a particular point in the sequence.

This chapter takes you through the rough cut; the following two chapters cover fine-tuning the sequence. Although each chapter tends to emphasize a particular part of the interface, the divisions are based on the general editing tasks: cutting and joining, rearranging, and trimming clips. The tools and techniques you use to accomplish these tasks are varied, flexible, and interrelated. When you've mastered the material in these chapters, you'll be able to integrate all the techniques smoothly.

Comparing Editing Methods

You can add clips to a sequence in several ways. You can drag them to the Timeline panel and assemble a sequence in a manner akin to splicing film (albeit much faster). Or you can use the editing controls in the Source and Program Monitor panels, which is comparable to using an editing controller in a traditional video-editing suite (only much easier). Alternatively, you can use the Project panel to plan the sequence in storyboard fashion and have Premiere Pro execute your plan automatically. Finally, you can use the Multi-Camera Monitor to create a sequence using footage from several camera angles. Each method has its advantages, so it's to your benefit to learn them all. Don't worry, though: You'll find that the same fundamental editing principles underlie all the editing methods.

Drag-and-drop

The drag-and-drop method takes advantage of the computer's ability to display clips as objects that you can move and place using the mouse (**Figure 6.1**). Most users find this technique the most intuitive and reassuringly similar to the way that the operating system works. You can argue that Premiere Pro's design encourages this method—especially because you can apply the same techniques to refine and rearrange clips in the Timeline panel (fully explained in Chapter 8, "Refining the Sequence").

Figure 6.1 Using the drag-and-drop method, you drag a clip from the Project panel or the Source Monitor (shown here) to a sequence in the Timeline panel.

Figure 6.2 Use the Monitors' editing controls to perform traditional three-point and four-point edits. Here, the Insert button (circled) was used to add the clip to the sequence.

Figure 6.3 In the Project panel, you can arrange clips in storyboard fashion and use the Automate to Sequence feature (circled) to quickly assemble them into a sequence.

Monitor controls

Although this method isn't as intuitive as dragging and dropping clips into the timeline, using the Monitor panels enables you to employ a traditional editing technique called *three-point editing* (**Figure 6.2**). You can also perform four-point edits. (For more information on both techniques, see "Performing an Edit Using Monitor Controls," later in this chapter.) Because the Monitor panels' editing controls have single-stroke keyboard shortcuts, some editors find they can edit more quickly than when they drag with the mouse. Other editors prefer editing this way because doing so is similar to using traditional edit controllers or other nonlinear editing interfaces.

Automate to sequence

Instead of building a sequence shot by shot, you can assemble an entire sequence automatically, according to how you've arranged the clips in the Project panel—a technique often called *storyboard editing*. With the Project panel set to icon view, you can arrange the clips in storyboard fashion and use the Automate to Sequence command to assemble them into a sequence (**Figure 6.3**). You can even have Premiere Pro apply a default transition between video and audio clips. If your footage lends itself to storyboarding, this method provides a fast way to generate a rough cut. It's also well suited to editors who prefer a storyboard's visual layout or who are working with a client who does.

COMPARING EDITING METHODS

Multicamera editing

Many productions employ a film-style shooting technique, in which a single camera records the action. But some events (such as a sporting event or concert) can only be captured fully from several camera angles at once, in a *multicamera shoot*.

Prior to Premiere Pro 2, there was no simple way to edit footage from multiple sources. But with the Multi-Camera Monitor, you can view up to four synchronized camera views at once and easily edit them into a seamless sequence (**Figure 6.4**).

✔ Tip

■ You can use yet another method to add a clip to a sequence: Drag clips from the Source Monitor or Project panel to the Program Monitor. The clips are overlaid or inserted at the sequence's current time. This method combines the drag-and-drop method with the Monitor editing controls—but it's less elegant than either of those approaches.

Figure 6.4 The Multi-Camera Monitor helps you view footage from several synchronized camera sources at once and edit them into a single, continuous sequence.

Figure 6.5 Cue to the starting frame, and click the Set In Point button.

Setting In and Out Points

Setting In points and Out points is central to all editing. An *In point* is where you want the clip to start playing, and an *Out point* is where you want the clip to stop playing. The length of time between the In and Out points is called the *duration*.

When you edit, you can set In and Out points for both individual clips and a sequence. In Premiere Pro, you can accomplish this essential editing task in many ways. This section focuses on setting In and Out points for clips using controls in the Source Monitor (a technique used in all editing approaches). However, you apply the same techniques to setting In and Out points for the sequence using the Program Monitor (required for three-point and four-point edits, as well as for lift and extract edits).

You can open a clip that's already in the sequence in the Source Monitor, to adjust its In and Out points. Any changes you make to the clip are instantly reflected in the Timeline panel. However, adjacent clips may prevent you from extending a clip this way. In the chapters to follow, you'll learn many other ways to change the In and Out points of clips already in a sequence.

To mark In and Out points in a Monitor panel:

1. *Do one of the following:*

   ▲ To set edit points in a clip, open a clip in the Source Monitor.

   ▲ To set edit points in the sequence, activate the Program Monitor or the Timeline panel.

2. Cue the current time to the frame where you want the clip to start, and click the Set In Point button ⟦ or press I (**Figure 6.5**). An In point icon ⟦ appears at the current time indicator (CTI) in the Monitor's time ruler.

continues on next page

3. Cue the current time to the frame where you want the clip to end, and click the Set Out Point button [ ] or press O (**Figure 6.6**).

An Out point icon [ ] appears at the CTI in the Monitor's time ruler. In the Monitor's time ruler, the area between the In point and Out point is shaded.

To clear an In or Out point in a Monitor panel:

◆ Do one of the following:

▲ To clear an In point, Alt-click the Set In Point button [ ].

▲ To clear an Out point, Alt-click the Set Out Point button [ ] (**Figure 6.7**).

▲ To clear both the In and the Out points, select the appropriate Monitor and press G.

Figure 6.6 Cue to the ending frame, and click the Set Out Point button.

Figure 6.7 To clear an In or Out point, Alt-click the Set In Point or Set Out Point button (shown here).

Figure 6.8 You can change an In or Out point by dragging the appropriate icon directly in the Monitor's time ruler. Here, the In point is being dragged to a different time. Note how the mouse pointer changes.

To change In and Out points in a Monitor's time ruler:

◆ In a Monitor's time ruler, *do one of the following:*

▲ To change the In point, drag the In point icon (the mouse pointer becomes a trim head icon ✛) (**Figure 6.8**).

▲ To change the Out point, drag the Out point icon (the mouse pointer becomes a trim tail icon ✛).

▲ To change both the In and the Out points without changing the duration, drag the textured area between the In and Out points (**Figure 6.9**). (When the mouse is over the textured area, the hand tool ✋ appears; otherwise, clicking cues the CTI.)

Figure 6.9 To change both the In and Out points without changing the duration, drag the textured area between the In and Out points.

✔ Tips

■ When you use the Source Monitor to change the In or Out point of a clip that's already in the sequence, adjacent clips may prevent you from extending the duration. In this case, adjust the clip directly in the Timeline panel or by using the Trim panel (see Chapter 8).

■ The In and Out points you set in the Program Monitor are also reflected in the Timeline panel's time ruler. For more about using the Timeline panel, see Chapter 7, "Editing in the Timeline."

■ To set In and Out points around selected clips in the Timeline panel, select one or more contiguous clips, and choose Marker > Set Sequence Marker > In and Out Around Selection.

■ When you set In and Out points for a *linked clip*—a clip that contains both video and audio tracks—both tracks share the same In point and Out point. However, you can set separate edit marks for the video and audio tracks to create what's known as a *split edit* (also known as *L-cuts* and *J-cuts*). Split edits cause the video of one clip to overlap with the audio of an adjacent clip (and vice versa), which can make edits seem smoother to the viewer. Although the Marker menu includes commands for setting split edit marks before you add a clip to a sequence, most editors create split edits after the clips are already in sequence, in the fine-tuning stage. Consequently, this book addresses split edits in later chapters.

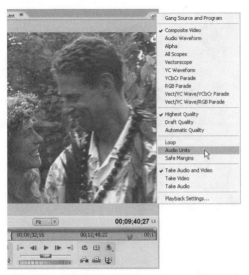

Figure 6.10 In the Source Monitor or Program Monitor pull-down menu, choose Audio Units.

Figure 6.11 The time ruler's scale changes to audio samples, as indicated by the time display and musical note icon.

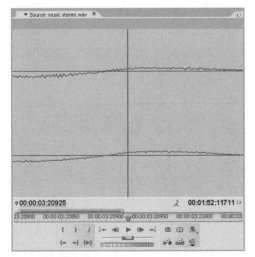

Figure 6.12 You can zoom the time ruler to the sample level.

Setting Precise Audio In and Out Points

Setting an In or Out point can be compared with cutting film between image frames. In Premiere Pro, frame divisions are set by the timebase of the project, which is based on one of several standard frame rates: 24 fps film, 25 fps PAL video, 29.97 fps NTSC video, or 30 fps video. Naturally, you would never cut through the middle of a picture frame.

Digital audio, however, isn't based on video frame rates, but on audio *sample rates*. A CD-quality sample rate is 44.1 kHz, or approximately 44,100 samples per second. Therefore, it's possible to cut audio much more finely than video.

In Premiere Pro, you can take advantage of audio's more-precise time divisions by setting audio In points based on samples rather than frames.

To toggle the time ruler between frames and audio units:

◆ In the Source Monitor or Program Monitor pull-down menu, choose Audio Units (**Figure 6.10**).

The time ruler's scale changes to audio samples, permitting you to navigate and set edit marks based on audio timebase divisions (**Figures 6.11** and **6.12**).

✔ Tip

■ As you'll see in the next chapter, you can set the Timeline panel's time ruler to audio units as well. And although the Program Monitor and Timeline panel are related, you can set one time ruler to video frames while the other is set to audio units.

Creating Subclips

When a clip is particularly lengthy, it can be difficult to find the part you want to use (despite features like instant-access playback controls and clip markers). Fortunately, you can break a clip into several shorter, more manageable portions, called *subclips*. Each subclip includes only the range of frames you specify, sparing you from searching through a long source clip for the shot you want. And because each subclip appears in the Project panel as a separate item using a name you specify, you can organize subclips using the methods you learned in Chapter 4, "Managing Clips."

Note that subclips refer to their corresponding source, or *master clip* (which, in turn, refers to a media file). Consequently, you can't delete a master clip without also removing the subclips created from it. However, this also means that you can always redefine the range of frames a subclip includes (up to the full duration of its master clip). In the Project panel, a master clip's icon is distinct from a subclip's icon.

Figure 6.13 Open a clip, and define its In and Out points.

To create a subclip:

1. In the Project panel, double-click a clip to open it.

   The clip appears in the Source Monitor.

2. In the Source Monitor, cue to the frame you want the subclip to begin, and click the Set In button

3. Cue to the frame you want the frame you want the subclip to end, and click the Set Out button (**Figure 6.13**).

Figure 6.14 Choose Clip > Make Subclip.

Figure 6.15 Specify a name in the Make Subclip dialog box, and then click OK.

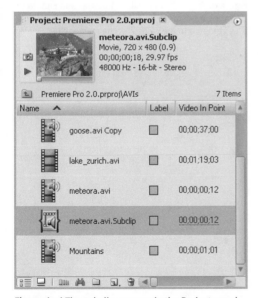

Figure 6.16 The subclip appears in the Project panel using the name you specified. Compare the source clip's and subclip's durations and icons.

4. *Do either of the following:*

▲ Choose Clip > Make Subclip (**Figure 6.14**).

▲ Right click the image in the Source Monitor, and choose Make Subclip from the context menu.

A Make Subclip dialog box appears. By default, the Name field appends ".Subclip" and an incremental number to the source clip's name.

5. In the Make Subclip dialog box, enter a name for the subclip, and click OK (**Figure 6.15**).

The subclip appears in the selected bin of the Project panel using the name you specified (**Figure 6.16**).

To edit a subclip:

1. In the Project panel, double-click a subclip.

The subclip opens in the Source Monitor.

2. *Do either of the following:*

▲ Choose Clip > Edit Subclip (**Figure 6.17**).

▲ Right-click the image in the Source Monitor, and choose Edit Subclip in the context menu.

The Edit Subclip dialog box appears.

3. In the Subclip area of the Edit Subclip dialog box, specify values for Start and End (**Figure 6.18**).

The Start Shift, End Shift, and Duration values adjust accordingly. You can compare the subclip's values with those of the master clip.

4. Click OK to close the dialog box.

The subclip reflects the values you specified.

Figure 6.17 Open a subclip, and choose Clip > Edit Subclip.

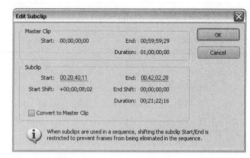

Figure 6.18 Specify new values for Start and End. Note how the new values affect the other displays, and how they compare to the values for the master clip.

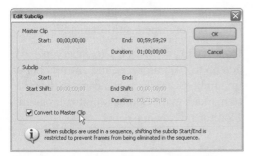

Figure 6.19 Selecting Convert to Master Clip makes the subclip a master clip. Henceforth, the clip includes only the current range of footage, and can you can no longer restore the original master clip's footage.

To convert a subclip into a master clip:

1. In the Project panel, double-click a subclip.

The subclip opens in the Source Monitor.

2. Choose Clip > Edit Subclip.

The Edit Subclip dialog box appears.

3. In the Subclip area of the Edit Subclip dialog box, select Convert to Master Clip (**Figure 6.19**).

The Start and End values are dimmed.

4. Click OK to close the dialog box.

The subclip's icon becomes a master clip icon. Henceforth, the clip includes only the current range of footage. The complete range of footage present in the originating master clip can't be restored.

✔ Tip

■ Prior to Premiere Pro 2, subclips were more like clip duplicates than true subclips. Although each subclip appeared as a separate item using a name you specified, it still included the same range of frames as the originating master clip.

Setting Clip Markers

During the editing process, you often need a way to mark important points in time. *Markers* allow you to visibly stamp these points both in individual clips and in a sequence's time ruler in the Timeline panel (**Figures 6.20** and **6.21**). For example, markers can help you visually identify beats in a song, synchronize video with a sound effect, or note where a title should fade up.

In each clip and in each sequence, you can add up to 100 numbered and any number of unnumbered markers. You can cue the CTI to markers in the Source Monitor, Program Monitor, or Timeline panel.

Markers

Figure 6.20 Clip markers appear in the Source Monitor's time ruler; sequence markers appear in the Program Monitor's time ruler.

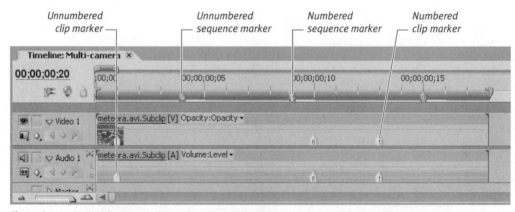

Figure 6.21 In the Timeline panel, clip markers appear in each clip; sequence markers appear in the sequence's time ruler.

Figure 6.22 In a Monitor, click the Marker button.

When you add a clip to a sequence, the clip's markers are visible in the timeline. However, adding or changing a clip's markers in the Source Monitor doesn't affect clips already in a sequence. In other words, each instance of a clip in a sequence has its own unique set of markers.

This section concentrates on using the Source Monitor to add clip markers. You use similar controls in the Program Monitor and Timeline panel to add sequence markers. But because sequence markers appear in a sequence's time ruler and have a few special features, they're discussed in the next chapter.

To add an unnumbered clip marker in the Source Monitor:

1. Open a clip in the Source Monitor.

2. Cue the current frame to the point where you want to add a marker.

3. In the Source Monitor, click the Marker button ▮ (**Figure 6.22**).

   An unnumbered marker appears in the Source Monitor's time ruler. When the clip is added to a sequence, the marker also appears in the clip in the Timeline panel (provided that the marker is between the clip's In and Out points).

To add numbered clip markers:

1. *Do one of the following:*
   - ▲ Open a clip in the Source Monitor.
   - ▲ Select a clip in the Timeline panel.

2. *Do one of the following:*
   - ▲ For a clip in the Source Monitor, cue the CTI to the frame you want to mark.
   - ▲ For a selected clip in the Timeline panel, cue the CTI in the Program Monitor or Timeline panel.

3. Choose Marker > Set Clip Marker, and *do one of the following* (**Figure 6.23**):
   - ▲ To mark the frame with the next consecutive number not already present in the clip, choose Next Available Numbered.
   - ▲ To mark the frame with the number of your choice, choose Other Numbered.

4. Enter the number for the marker in the Set Numbered Marker dialog box, and click OK (**Figure 6.24**).

   The marker you specified appears at the current time in the Monitor's time ruler (**Figure 6.25**). In the Timeline panel, the clip marker's number is visible (**Figure 6.26**).

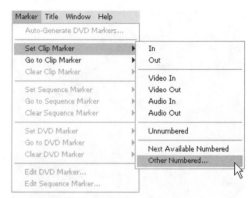

Figure 6.23 Choose Marker > Set Clip Marker, and choose an option. Here, Other Numbered is selected.

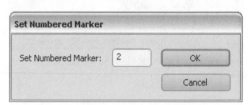

Figure 6.24 If you chose Other Numbered, a Set Numbered Marker dialog box appears. Enter a number, and click OK.

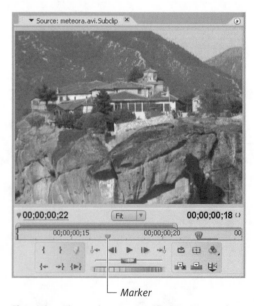

— *Marker*

Figure 6.25 The marker you specified appears at the current time in the Monitor's time ruler (here, the CTI has been moved aside so you can see the marker).

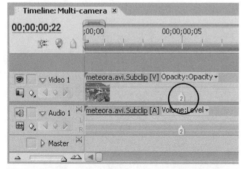

Figure 6.26 The clip marker appears with a number when added to the sequence in the Timeline panel.

Figure 6.27 Each time you press the asterisk key (on the numeric keypad), an unnumbered marker appears. Here, the technique is being used to mark the beats of a music clip.

To add unnumbered clip markers on the fly:

1. Open a clip in the Source Monitor.

2. Play the clip.

3. Press the asterisk key (*) on the numeric keypad (not Shift+8 on the main keyboard).

   Each time you press the asterisk key, a marker appears in the Source Monitor's time ruler (**Figure 6.27**). If you opened a clip instance from a sequence, markers also appear in the clip as it appears in the Timeline panel.

✔ Tips

■ Each numbered marker (0–99) can appear only once in the same clip. Setting any number to a different frame eliminates its previous position.

■ You can't set a marker on the same frame as another marker (the option appears dimmed in the menu). You must clear the existing marker first and then set the new marker.

■ Markers are helpful for marking where lines of dialogue or voice-over begin and end. Try using a numbered marker at the beginning of a spoken line and an unnumbered marker at the end of the line. This technique makes it easy to identify pauses between lines (which often need to be cut).

■ The 0 marker also has a special use with the Frame-Hold command (see "Creating a Freeze Frame" in Chapter 7). You may want to reserve the 0 marker for this purpose.

SETTING CLIP MARKERS

Cuing to and Clearing Clip Markers

You can cue the CTI to consecutive markers by using buttons in the Source Monitor. (Note that the buttons occupying corresponding positions in the Program Monitor have a different purpose: They cue the sequence's CTI to cuts in a sequence.) Clearing markers is best accomplished via a command on the menu bar (unless you use the keyboard customization feature to map the command to a keyboard shortcut).

To cue the Source Monitor to clip markers:

1. Open a clip in the Source Monitor.

2. In the Source Monitor, *click one of the following buttons:*

   ▲ ↓← Go to Previous Marker

   ▲ →↓ Go to Next Marker (**Figure 6.28**)

   The Source Monitor's CTI moves to the previous or next marker, depending on your choice.

To clear clip markers:

1. Open a clip in the Source Monitor.

2. *Do one of the following:*

   ▲ To clear a particular marker, cue the clip to a marker, and choose Marker > Clear Clip Marker > Current Marker.

   ▲ To clear all markers in the clip, choose Marker > Clear Clip Marker > All Markers (**Figure 6.29**).

   The clip markers you cleared disappear from the Source Monitor's time ruler (and from the Timeline panel, if the clip is in a sequence).

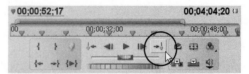

Figure 6.28 Cue to clip markers by clicking the Go to Previous Marker button or Go to Next Marker button (shown here).

Figure 6.29 To clear all markers in the clip, choose Marker > Clear Clip Marker > All Markers.

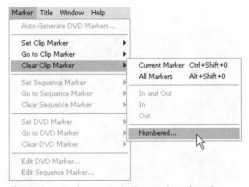

Figure 6.30 To clear a particular numbered marker, choose Marker > Clear Clip Marker > Numbered.

Figure 6.31 In the Clear Numbered Marker dialog box, select the marker you want to clear, and click OK.

To clear specific numbered markers:

1. Open a clip in the Source Monitor.

2. Choose Marker > Clear Clip Marker > Numbered (**Figure 6.30**).

   The Clear Numbered Marker dialog box appears.

3. Select the marker you want to clear, and click OK (**Figure 6.31**).

   You can select only one marker at a time. The selected numbered marker disappears from the Source Monitor's time ruler (and from the Timeline panel, if the clip is in a sequence).

Specifying Source and Target Tracks

Video and audio materials are often described as discrete tracks of information, due to the way they're physically stored on traditional media, such as magnetic tape. Digital files don't encode video and audio the same way tape does, of course. Nevertheless, it's helpful to think of video and audio as occupying tracks that you can manipulate separately.

By selecting source and target tracks, you can add video, audio, or both to any appropriate track in the sequence.

Whatever editing method you use, you choose the source tracks by clicking the Source Monitor's Take Audio and Video button (**Figure 6.32**) (as explained in the following task, "To specify source tracks"). How you choose the destination, or *target*, tracks depends on the editing method you use.

In drag-and-drop editing, you determine the target track *as* you perform the edit, by dragging the clip to an appropriate track in the Timeline panel. When you edit with the Monitor panels' editing controls, however, you must specify target tracks *before* you perform an edit, by selecting the track in the Timeline panel (**Figure 6.33**). After all, you can choose any of several tracks in the sequence, and Premiere Pro can't make this decision for you.

Note that you can neither target nor drag a clip to a locked track (see "Locking and Unlocking Tracks" in Chapter 7). Also, remember that source and target audio tracks must be of the same channel type.

Figure 6.32 You choose the source tracks by clicking the Source Monitor's Take Audio and Video toggle button.

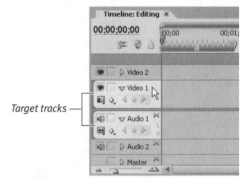

Figure 6.33 To perform edits with the Monitors' editing controls, you must specify target tracks by clicking them in the Timeline panel.

Figure 6.34 In the Source Monitor, click the Take Audio and Video toggle button to specify whether you want to use both video and audio...

Figure 6.35 ...video only...

Figure 6.36 ...or audio only.

To specify source tracks:

◆ In the Source Monitor, click the Take Audio and Video toggle button until it displays the icon corresponding to the tracks you want (**Figures 6.34**, **6.35**, and **6.36**):

▲ 🖳 Video and audio

▲ 🖳 Video only

▲ 🔊 Audio only

If the source clip doesn't contain a track, the corresponding icon won't appear when you toggle the button.

To specify target tracks:

◆ In the Timeline panel, *do one of the following*:

▲ Click the track you want to target in the track's header area, near the track name.

▲ Click a targeted track's header area to deselect it.

The selected track's header area is shaded lighter than other tracks and has rounded corners.

Comparing Overlay and Insert Edits

Whenever you add a clip to a sequence, you must determine how the new clip affects the clips already in the sequence. Specifically, you must specify whether to replace material with an overlay edit or shift material with an insert edit.

An *overlay edit* works like adding a clip using videotape, recording the new clip over any existing material on the master tape. When you *overlay* a clip, the source clip is added at the designated point in the time-line, replacing any material that was already there (**Figures 6.37** and **6.38**).

An *insert edit* works much like adding a clip using film, inserting the new clip without removing material that is already on the pro-gram reel. When you *insert* a clip, the source clip is added at the designated point in the timeline, and subsequent clips are shifted later in time to make room for the new clip. If the insertion point in the sequence occurs at a point where clips already occupy the timeline, the clips in the timeline are split, and the portions after the edit are shifted later in time. Depending on your choice, an insert edit can shift clips in all tracks or just in the target tracks (the tracks to which you add the new clip) (**Figures 6.39** and **6.40**).

✔ Tip

■ In versions of Premiere prior to Premiere Pro, overlay edits were not the default. In fact, you weren't permitted to perform an overlay edit by dragging a clip to the timeline; you had to use the Monitor panels' editing controls. If you're accus-tomed to older versions of Premiere, the current method will take some getting used to, but in the end you'll find it to be far superior to the old one.

Figure 6.37 This figure shows a clip in a sequence. A new clip will be added, starting at the CTI (the vertical line).

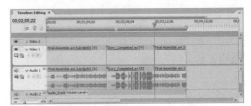

Figure 6.38 In an overlay edit, the new material replaces the old material.

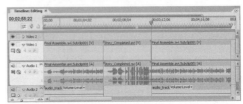

Figure 6.39 In an insert edit, everything after the edit point shifts forward in time to make room for the new material. If necessary, clips are split at the edit point.

Figure 6.40 Alternatively, you can perform an insert edit that shifts material in the target tracks only.

In point — Out point — Take Audio and Video

Figure 6.41 In the Source Monitor, set a clip's edit marks and specify the source tracks.

Adding Clips by Dragging

You can add a source clip to a sequence by dragging it to the appropriate track in the Timeline panel. Drag the clip from the Source Monitor if you want to set its edit marks before adding it to a sequence. If you want to use the clip's most recent edit marks, you can drag it directly from the Project panel.

You can drag a linked clip (a clip containing both audio and video) to either a video or audio track. When you do, the video or audio components appear in a corresponding track. For example, dragging a clip to video 1 makes the linked audio appear in audio 1.

However, you can add an audio clip only to a compatible audio track. In other words, the clip and the target track must be of the same channel type: mono, stereo, or 5.1. If the audio doesn't match the channel type of the target track, the audio appears in the next compatible track, or a compatible track is created automatically. (The default tracks are determined by the project settings, covered in Chapter 2, "Starting a Project." See Chapter 7 for more about adding tracks to a sequence.)

To add a clip to a sequence by dragging:

1. Open a clip in the Source Monitor.

2. Set the In point and Out point in the source clip.

   You may also want to set numbered or unnumbered markers. See "Setting Clip Markers," earlier in this chapter.

3. Click the Take Audio and Video toggle button so that it shows the icon for the source tracks you want (**Figure 6.41**).

continues on next page

4. Drag the clip from the Source Monitor to the appropriate track of the sequence in the Timeline panel, using *one of the following methods*:

▲ To perform an overlay edit, drag the clip so that the pointer appears with the overlay icon 🖱 (**Figure 6.42**).

▲ To perform an insert edit that shifts all tracks, Ctrl+drag the clip so that the mouse pointer appears with the insert icon 🖱 and arrows appear at the edit point in all tracks (**Figure 6.43**).

▲ To perform an insert edit that shifts target tracks only, Ctrl+Alt+drag the clip so that the mouse pointer appears with the insert target icon 🖱 and arrows appear at the edit point in the target tracks (**Figure 6.44**).

A shaded area indicates where the clip will appear when you release the mouse.

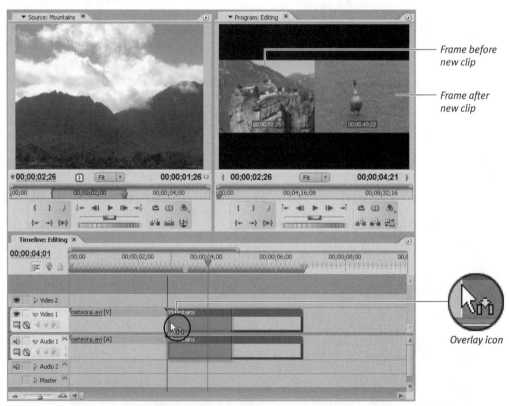

Frame before new clip

Frame after new clip

Overlay icon

Figure 6.42 To perform an overlay edit, drag the clip to the track you want. Note that visual feedback in the Program Monitor shows the frames before and after the new clip.

Insert all tracks icon

Figure 6.43 To perform an insert edit that shifts material in all tracks, Ctrl+drag the clip to the track you want.

Insert target tracks icon

Figure 6.44 To perform an insert edit that shifts target tracks only, Ctrl+Alt+drag the clip to the track you want.

✔ Tips

■ When you drag and drop a linked clip, be sure you're not inadvertently overwriting material in one of the corresponding tracks. For example, if you pay attention only to where you're dragging the video, you may end up overwriting something in the audio track.

■ To precisely align clips as you drag them, make sure the Timeline panel's Snap button 🖼 is selected. As you drag a clip with snap on, a vertical line appears whenever In points, Out points, or markers align. For more about the snap feature, see Chapter 7.

■ To zoom in or out on a clip when you drag it to the timeline, continue to hold down the mouse button, and press the + key to zoom in or the – key to zoom out until you've zoomed in or out as far as you want.

To add clips to a sequence from the Project panel:

1. Select one or more clips in the Project panel.

2. Drag the selection from the Project panel to the appropriate track of the sequence in the Timeline panel, using *one of the following methods:*

   ▲ To perform an overlay edit, drag the clip so that the pointer appears with the overlay icon ⬚ (**Figure 6.45**).

   ▲ To perform an insert edit that shifts all tracks, Ctrl+drag the clip so that the mouse pointer appears with the Insert icon ⬚ and arrows appear at the edit point in all tracks.

   ▲ To perform an insert edit that shifts target tracks only, Ctrl+Alt+drag the clip so that the mouse pointer appears with the insert target icon ⬚ and arrows appear at the edit point in the target tracks.

   A shaded and transparent "ghost" version of the clips indicates where they'll appear when you release the mouse. Multiple clips are added to the sequence in the order in which you selected them in the Project panel.

✔ Tip

■ You can drag clips to the Source Monitor, the Program Monitor, or the timeline directly from the thumbnail viewer at the top of the Project panel just like you can from the list view or icon view. This procedure is useful if you're in the habit of using the thumbnail viewer to look at clips before using them in your project.

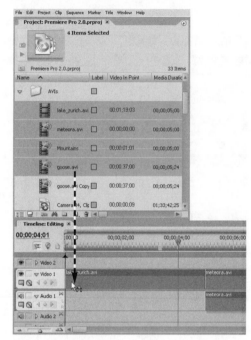

Figure 6.45 You can drag one or more clips from the Project panel to the Timeline panel to perform overlay and insert edits.

Editing with Monitor Panel Controls

As suggested earlier in this chapter, editing with the Monitor panels' controls isn't as intuitive as editing using the drag-and-drop method. However, the Monitor panels' editing controls use a paradigm familiar to those who have used traditional video edit controllers or other nonlinear systems. In addition, this method lets you rely less on the mouse and more on single-stroke keyboard shortcuts, which could mean faster editing.

Before you proceed, you need to understand a few basic concepts:

◆ **Insert and overlay:** Methods for determining how a three-point or four-point edit affects the clips in the sequence. You're already familiar with these concepts from the previous sections.

◆ **Three-point and four-point editing:** Methods for determining where clips begin and end in both the source and the sequence.

◆ **Lift and extract:** Methods for removing frames from the program; roughly the reverse of the insert and overlay methods.

The following sections explain these concepts and then put them into practice. Don't worry—these ideas are as easy to grasp as they are essential. Taking a moment to learn them will be well worth the effort. If you prefer, you can skip ahead to the editing tasks and then turn back to see the full explanations.

Three-Point Editing

The *point* in the term *three-point editing* refers to In points and Out points. In points and Out points in a clip define where the clip starts and ends. Similarly, In and Out points in a sequence define where a clip starts and ends in the sequence.

In drag-and-drop editing, you set the source In and Out points in the Source Monitor, but the sequence's In and Out points were implied by where you dragged the clip into the Timeline panel (see "Drag-and-drop," earlier in this chapter). In the following sections, you mark both the source and sequence editing points in the Monitor panels.

Technically, every edit has four points: source In, source Out, sequence In, and sequence Out. To add a clip to the sequence, you must define at least three of these four points in the Source and Program Monitors. If you provide three points, Premiere Pro figures out the fourth. Hence the term *three-point editing*.

Most often, this means that you mark two In points and one Out point. **Figure 6.46** shows a typical edit, in which the source In point and source Out point define a portion of the clip, and the sequence In point defines where the clip starts in the sequence. The sequence Out point is implied by the duration of the clip.

Figure 6.46 Typically, the three edit points include two In points and an Out point—in this example, the source In, source Out, and sequence In points. Note the shading after the program In point.

Sometimes, however, it's more important to set where the clip ends than to set where it begins. In such a case, you mark two Out points and only one In point. In **Figure 6.47**, the next shot will follow the last clip in the program: a typical program In point. However, a particular frame of the new shot (the source Out point) must coincide with a particular cue in the sound track, at marker 1 (the sequence Out point). That defines three edit points: sequence In point, source Out point, and sequence Out point. The editor doesn't need to mark the source In point, because it's determined by the other three points.

Figure 6.47 Sometimes where the clip ends is more important than where it begins. In this case, you can set two Out points and one In point. Note the shading before the program Out point.

Four-Point Editing

As you've seen, every edit uses four points, but you need to set only three of them. Premiere Pro always figures out the missing variable to balance out the editing equation. Actively marking all four points forces Premiere Pro to balance the equation in another way. If the source duration differs from the program duration, Premiere Pro asks whether you want to shorten the source clip, change the speed of the source clip to fit, or ignore one of the sequence edit points and perform a three-point edit.

Typically, you use a four-point edit to change the speed of the source to match the duration defined by the sequence's In and Out points. This technique is frequently called *fit to fill*, because you *fit*, or change, the speed (and duration) of the source to *fill* the duration you specified in the sequence.

Suppose that you require a two-second cutaway or reaction shot, but your source clip includes only one second of footage. A four-point edit can stretch the one second of source footage to fill two seconds in the program. In the sequence, the clip plays in slow motion—in this case, at half normal speed (**Figure 6.48**).

✔ Tip

- You can change the speed of a clip after it's in the timeline by using the Speed/Duration command or the Rate Stretch tool. For more information about using editing techniques in the timeline, see Chapter 7.

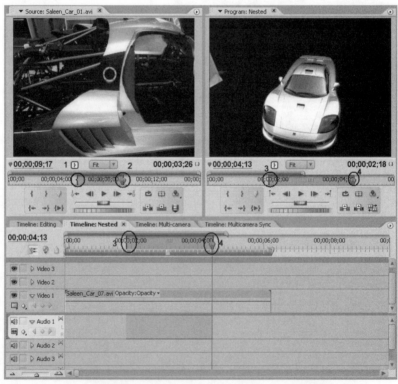

Figure 6.48 Here, the editor defined all four edit points. Because the durations differ, you have to resolve the difference. Usually, this means changing the speed of the clip.

Figure 6.49 In the Source Monitor, set the edit marks and specify source tracks.

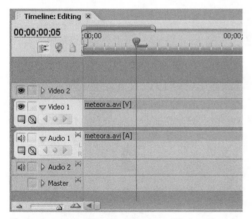

Figure 6.50 In the Timeline panel, specify target tracks.

Performing an Edit Using Monitor Controls

Now that you understand the essential concepts behind an edit, it's time to put them into practice.

To perform a three-point edit:

1. Open a clip in the Source Monitor.

2. Click the Take Audio and Video toggle button so that it shows the icon for the source tracks you want (**Figure 6.49**).

3. Specify the target tracks in the sequence by clicking in the track header area, near the track's name in the Timeline panel (**Figure 6.50**).

   The track header area of the targeted tracks appears darker than that of the other tracks.

   continues on next page

4. Set any combination of three In and Out points in the Source and Program Monitors (**Figure 6.51**).

Sequence In and Out points appear both in the Program Monitor's time ruler and in the sequence's time ruler in the Timeline panel.

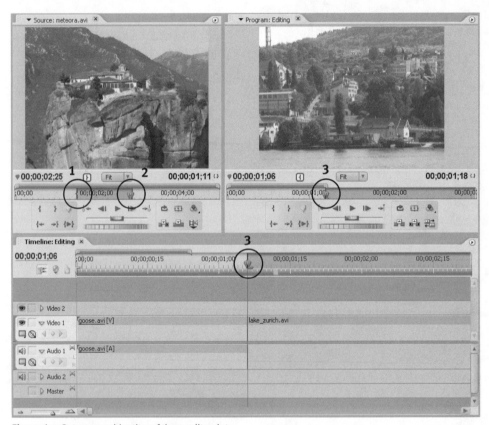

Figure 6.51 Set any combination of three edit points.

Figure 6.52 In the Source Monitor, click the Overlay or Insert button (circled).

Figure 6.53 The clip appears in the sequence in the position and tracks you specified.

5. In the Source Monitor, *do one of the following:*

▲ To replace material in the specified area of the sequence, click the Overlay button.

▲ To shift subsequent clips in all tracks, click the Insert button (**Figure 6.52**).

▲ To shift subsequent clips in target tracks only, Alt+click the Insert button.

The clip appears in the timeline in the position and tracks you specified (**Figure 6.53**). Premiere Pro cues the sequence's current time to the end of the new clip and clears the sequence's In and Out points.

✔ Tips

■ If you don't specify an In or Out point in the Program Monitor, the current time in the Program Monitor (and in the Timeline panel) serves as the In point. After an edit, Premiere Pro cues the current program time to the end of the new clip in the sequence and clears any sequence In and Out points. You can save time by using the sequence's current time as the In point, especially when you want to assemble clips into a sequence quickly.

■ You can quickly set the In and Out points around the area you've selected in the timeline by pressing the forward slash (/) key.

■ When you perform an insert edit that shifts material in target tracks only, use caution: It's easy to inadvertently shift linked video and audio out of sync this way.

■ You've lost sync between linked video and audio when a number appears before the clip's name in the Timeline panel. For now, use the Undo command to restore sync. To learn more about linked clips and sync, see Chapter 7.

To perform a four-point edit:

1. Mark all four edit points in the Source and Program Monitors (**Figure 6.54**).

2. Select the source tracks by clicking the Source Monitor's Toggle Take Audio and Video button.

3. Specify the target tracks in the sequence by clicking the tracks in the track header area in the Timeline panel.

   The track header area of the targeted tracks appears darker than that of the other tracks.

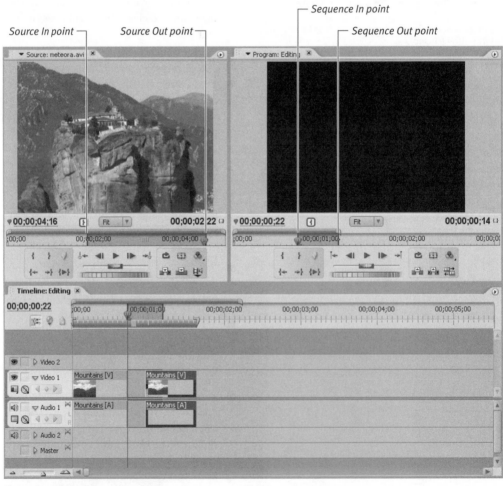

Figure 6.54 Mark all four edit points.

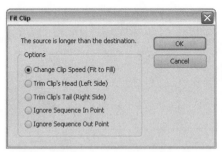

Figure 6.55 If the source duration and sequence duration differ, Premiere Pro prompts you to resolve the discrepancy.

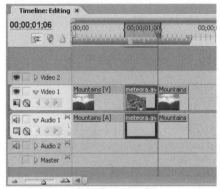

Figure 6.56 Change Clip Speed alters the speed of the clip so that it matches the sequence's duration.

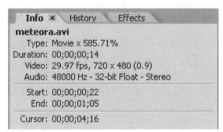

Figure 6.57 You can learn the clip's exact speed by selecting the clip and viewing its information on the Info panel.

✔ Tip

■ You can set a sequence edit point beyond the last frame of the last clip by using the arrow keys to move the CTI later in time. Press Shift+arrow to move in increments of five frames.

4. Click the Insert ⊞ or Overlay ⊞ button.

5. If the source duration and sequence duration differ, Premiere Pro prompts you to choose one of the following options (**Figure 6.55**):

▲ **Change Clip Speed (Fit to Fill):** Changes the speed of the source clip to fit the specified duration in the sequence. Only the speed changes; the In and Out points stay the same. In **Figure 6.56**, the source clip has been slowed, making its duration long enough to fit in the range defined by the program In and program Out points. If the source clip were too long, its speed would increase so that its duration would match the program duration. You can learn the clip's exact speed by selecting the clip and viewing its information on the Info panel (**Figure 6.57**) or by hovering the cursor over the clip until a tool tip appears.

▲ **Trim Clip's Head (Left Side):** Changes the source In point to fit the specified duration in the program. The Out point and the speed of the clip are unaffected. (In other words, this option ignores the source Out point and works like a three-point edit.)

▲ **Trim Clip's Tail (Right Side):** Changes the source Out point to fit the specified duration in the program. The In point and the speed of the clip are unaffected.

▲ **Ignore Sequence In Point:** Disregards the sequence In point, and performs a three-point edit.

▲ **Ignore Sequence Out Point:** Disregards the sequence Out point, and performs a three-point edit.

The clip is added to the sequence according to your selection.

Lift and Extract

Just as the Source Monitor has two buttons for adding frames to a sequence, the Program Monitor has two buttons for removing frames from a sequence: Lift and Extract. You can think of lift and extract edits as being the opposite of insert and overlay edits, respectively:

◆ **Lift:** Removes the defined range from the timeline, leaving a gap in the timeline.

◆ **Extract:** Removes the defined range from the timeline and shifts all the later clips earlier in the timeline, closing the gap.

Unfortunately, an extract edit isn't the perfect opposite of an insert edit: It won't shift linked audio and video out of sync. Suppose you try to extract frames of video from the beginning or middle of a clip and leave the audio track untargeted. Extracting the video should shift it and subsequent material in that track back to close the gap—and out of sync with any linked audio. Instead, extract works just like lift in this case. Some would argue that Premiere Pro helps prevent you from inadvertently losing sync; others complain that the extract functions inconsistently. If you want to shift material out of sync, you have to drag in the Timeline panel using techniques covered in Chapter 8.

To lift a segment from a sequence:

1. Set an In point and an Out point in the Program Monitor to define the range to be removed from the sequence.

    You can see the editing marks in both the Program Monitor's time ruler and the Timeline panel (**Figure 6.58**).

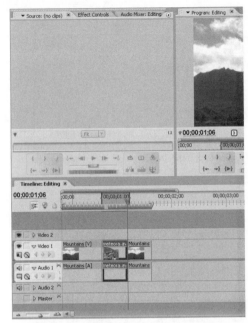

Figure 6.58 Set sequence In and Out points. Here, sequence In and Out marks surround the second clip, but you can remove any range of frames, including portions of clips.

Figure 6.59 Deselect all tracks to remove frames from all tracks, or select particular tracks. Here, only the video 1 track is targeted.

2. *Do one of the following:*

▲ To remove material from particular tracks in the defined range, target the tracks by clicking in the track header area in the Timeline panel (**Figure 6.59**).

▲ To remove material from all tracks in the defined range, deselect all tracks so none are targeted.

3. In the Program Monitor, click the Lift button ⬛ (**Figure 6.60**).

The frames between the In and Out points in the selected tracks of the program are removed, leaving an empty space (**Figure 6.61**).

Figure 6.60 In the Program Monitor, click the Lift button.

Figure 6.61 The frames between the In and Out points in the selected tracks of the program are removed, leaving an empty space.

To extract a segment from a sequence:

1. Set an In point and an Out point in the Program Monitor to define the range to be removed from the sequence (**Figure 6.62**).

2. *Do one of the following:*
   ▲ To remove material from particular tracks in the defined range, target the tracks by clicking in the track header area in the Timeline panel.
   ▲ To remove material from all tracks in the defined range, deselect all tracks so none are targeted (**Figure 6.63**).

3. Click the Extract button 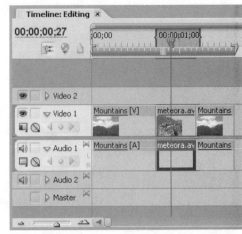 in the Program Monitor (**Figure 6.64**).

Figure 6.62 Set sequence In and Out points.

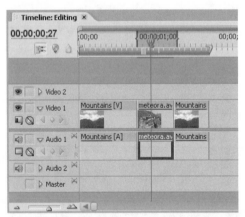

Figure 6.63 To remove material from all tracks in the defined range, deselect all tracks so none are targeted.

Figure 6.64 In the Program Monitor, click the Extract button.

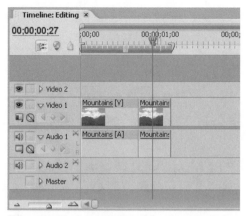

Figure 6.65 The frames between the In and Out points are removed, shifting subsequent material in target tracks to close the gap.

The frames between the In and Out points are removed, shifting subsequent material in the target tracks to close the gap (**Figure 6.65**). If no tracks are targeted, material in all tracks shifts. If shifting material would move linked clips out of sync, then a lift edit is performed instead.

✔ Tip

■ Unless Adobe modifies the extract and track targeting functions in Premiere Pro, it's probably best to use extract to remove material from all tracks. See the sidebar "Extraction Exception" in Chapter 8.

Editing with the Home Keys, or Three-Finger Editing

As any typist will tell you, the basis for touch-typing is learning to keep your fingers over the home keys. Well, desktop editing programs have developed their own version of home keys: J, K, and L (**Figure 6.66**). Keeping one hand on your editing home keys and the other on the mouse is the secret to blazing-fast Monitor panel editing. This technique works in other popular editing programs as well. Learning it can produce joy and speed akin to typing 60 words per minute. But if you insist, you can use onscreen buttons for the equivalent of hunt-and-peck editing.

Figure 6.66 You can think of the J-K-L combo as the home keys of nonlinear editing. They give you quick three-finger control over the main playback and editing features.

Storyboard Editing

Before shooting any footage, filmmakers usually create a *storyboard*—a series of sketches that depicts each shot in the finished sequence. Planning each shot in a storyboard can save you enormous amounts of time, money, and energy in production. In postproduction, you can use a similar storyboarding technique to plan a rough cut and instantly assemble it into a sequence, again saving time and energy.

As you learned in Chapter 3, "Capturing and Importing Footage," setting the Project panel to icon view allows you to arrange clips in a storyboard fashion. If you want, you can open the clips in the Source Monitor to set In and Out points, as well. Once your storyboard is complete, use the Automate to Sequence command to assemble the selected clips into a sequence. Premiere Pro can even add the default video and audio transitions between clips.

Although the Automate to Sequence feature is best suited to storyboard editing, you can also use it to add clips to a sequence according to the order in which you select clips in the Project panel. Also, note that it ignores target tracks and always adds clips to video track 1 and audio track 1.

To add clips using the Automate to Sequence command:

1. In the Project panel, *do one of the following:*

    ▲ Sort the clips in the order you want them to appear in the sequence (from left to right and top to bottom in icon view, or from top to bottom in list view), and select them (**Figure 6.67**).

    ▲ Select the clips in the order you want them to appear in the sequence.

Figure 6.67 With the Project panel set to icon view, arrange the clips as on a storyboard and select the ones you want to add to the sequence.

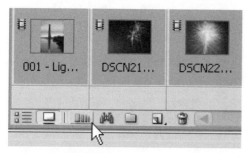

Figure 6.68 Click the Automate to Sequence button.

2. In the Project panel, click the Automate to Sequence button ▦ (**Figure 6.68**). An Automate to Sequence dialog box appears.

3. Choose an option from the Ordering pull-down menu (**Figure 6.69**):
   - ▲ **Sort Order:** Arranges clips in the order in which they're sorted in the Project panel.
   - ▲ **Selection Order:** Arranges clips in the order in which they're selected in the Project panel.

4. Specify how the clips are added to the program by making a choice from the Placement pull-down menu (**Figure 6.70**):
   - ▲ **Sequentially:** Adds the clips in the timeline one after the other.
   - ▲ **At Unnumbered Markers:** Adds the clips in the timeline at unnumbered sequence markers.

continues on next page

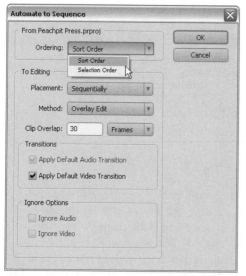

Figure 6.69 If you've arranged the clips in storyboard fashion, select Sort Order from the Sort Order pull-down menu.

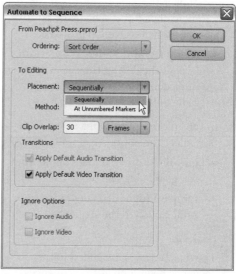

Figure 6.70 In most cases, you'll choose Sequentially from the Placement pull-down menu.

STORYBOARD EDITING

5. Specify the editing method used to add each clip to the sequence by choosing an option in the Method pull-down menu (**Figure 6.71**):

▲ **Insert Edit:** Adds the selected clips to the sequence beginning at the current time, using insert edits.

▲ **Overlay Edit:** Adds the selected clips to the sequence beginning at the current time, using overlay edits.

6. Make a choice from the Clip Overlap pull-down menu to specify the length of transitions between clips and the time unit:

▲ **Frames:** Interprets the value you enter as frames, at the frame rate you set in the project settings.

▲ **Seconds:** Interprets the value you enter as seconds.

If you want only cuts between clips, with no overlap, enter 0.

7. In the Transitions area of the dialog box, select the options you want:

▲ **Apply Default Audio Transition:** Applies the default transition between audio clips if you specified a positive value for Clip Overlap in step 6.

▲ **Apply Default Video Transition:** Applies the default transition between video clips if you specified a positive value for Clip Overlap in step 6.

8. In the Ignore Options area of the dialog box, select the options you want:

▲ **Ignore Audio:** Excludes audio from being added to the sequence.

▲ **Ignore Video:** Excludes video from being added to the sequence.

9. Click OK.

The selected clips are added to the sequence beginning at the sequence's current time according to the options you specified (**Figure 6.72**).

Figure 6.71 In the Method pull-down menu, choose whether to add the clips using insert or overlay edits. Then, specify the other options you want.

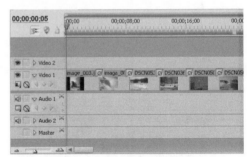

Figure 6.72 The selected clips are added to the sequence beginning at the sequence's current time according to the options you specified.

✔ Tip

■ Automate to Sequence ignores target tracks and always adds clips to video track 1 and audio track 1 (unless they're locked). But, as usual, if the audio clips don't match the audio 1 track's channel type (mono, stereo, or 5.1), they're added to the next compatible track, or a compatible track is created automatically.

About Multiple and Nested Sequences

So far, you've assembled clips into a single configuration, called a *sequence*. But Premiere Pro allows you to create any number of sequences in a single project. The obvious implication is that you can edit multiple versions of your masterpiece—to try out ideas, cater to different audiences, or meet various presentation requirements.

But even more important, you can embed an entire sequence into another sequence, a process called *nesting*. This doesn't mean copying and pasting the *contents* of one sequence into another (which you can do); it means adding the sequence as a *single item*, just like any other clip. The concept of nesting is simple, but its practical implications are powerful and far reaching.

Using Multiple Sequences

As discussed previously, each sequence appears as an item in the Project panel. When you open a sequence, it appears as a tab in the Program Monitor and in the Timeline panel. Clicking a sequence's tab in either the Timeline or the Program Monitor makes it the active sequence in both panels; clicking a tab's Close button removes it from both panels.

You can create any number of sequences, each with any number and type of tracks. But as you learned in Chapter 2, all the sequences in a project must use the same timebase, which can't be changed.

To create a new sequence:

1. *Do one of the following:*

   ▲ Choose File > New > Sequence.

   ▲ In the Project panel, click the New Item button 🔲, and choose Sequence (**Figure 6.73**).

   The New Sequence dialog box appears, using the default settings for the number and type of the master audio tracks.

2. Name the sequence (**Figure 6.74**).

3. In the Tracks area of the dialog box, *do any of the following:*

   ▲ Enter the number of video tracks.

   ▲ Enter the number of each type of audio track, including audio submix tracks.

   ▲ In the Master pull-down menu, specify the type of master audio track.

Figure 6.73 Click the New Item button, and choose Sequence.

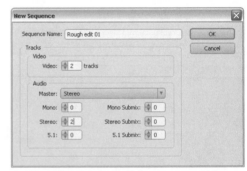

Figure 6.74 In the New Sequence dialog box, enter a name for the sequence and specify the number and type of tracks.

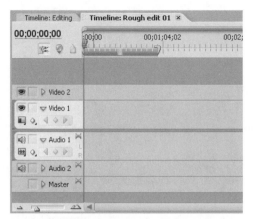

Figure 6.75 The new sequence appears as the active tab in the Timeline panel.

4. Click OK.

The new sequence appears as a tab in the Program Monitor and in the Timeline panel (**Figure 6.75**).

To duplicate a sequence:

1. In the Project panel, right-click a sequence, and choose Duplicate from the context menu (**Figure 6.76**).

A duplicate of the sequence appears in the Project panel. It uses the original sequence's name with the word *Copy* appended to it (**Figure 6.77**).

continues on next page

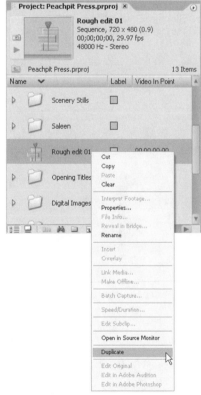

Figure 6.76 In the Project panel, Right-click a sequence and choose Duplicate from the context menu.

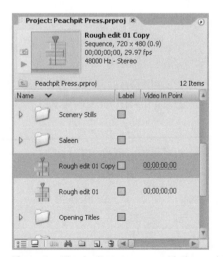

Figure 6.77 The duplicate appears with the word *Copy* appended to its name.

USING MULTIPLE SEQUENCES

2. To give the copied sequence a unique name, *do one of the following:*

▲ Click the sequence, and then click it again to highlight its name.

▲ Right-click the sequence, and choose Rename from the context menu.

3. Type a new name, and press Enter (**Figure 6.78**).

✔ Tip

■ You can specify the default settings for a sequence by choosing Project > Project Settings > Default Sequence. This command determines the initial settings in the New Sequence dialog box.

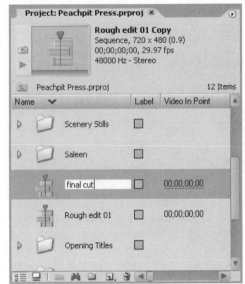

Figure 6.78 Click the sequence's name twice (don't double-click) to highlight it and enter a new name.

USING MULTIPLE SEQUENCES

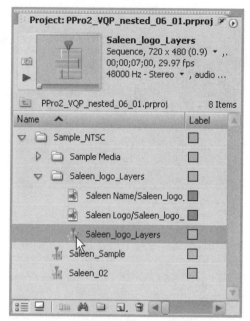

Figure 6.79 In the Project panel, Ctrl+double-click a sequence. You can also Ctrl+double-click a nested sequence in a Timeline panel.

Figure 6.80 The sequence opens in the Source Monitor.

Nesting Sequences

You use the same techniques to nest a sequence that you use to add a clip to a sequence. You can drag and drop the sequence from the Project panel or open the sequence in the Source Monitor and add it from there. No matter how many clips and tracks a sequence contains, it appears as a single linked clip when you nest it in another sequence. Once it's nested, you can edit the sequence like any other clip; you can move and trim it, apply speed changes and filters, adjust its audio and transparency levels, apply motion settings, and so on. Any alterations you make to the content of the source sequence are instantly reflected in its related nested sequences. Not only can you nest a sequence as many times and in as many sequences as you want, but you can also nest sequences to any *depth*, like Russian dolls. Nesting lets you group elements and create hierarchies to get effects you can't achieve any other way.

If you nest a sequence with sequence markers in a new sequence, the markers appear as clip markers with a slightly different color than the other clip markers in the new sequence. To adjust the location of the markers, display the original sequence and drag the markers to adjust them.

See the sidebar "Crowing about Nesting" for some examples; see the sidebar "Nesting Rules" for a list of restrictions.

To open a sequence in the Source Monitor:

◆ *Do one of the following:*

▲ Ctrl+double-click the sequence in the Project panel (**Figure 6.79**).

▲ Ctrl+double-click a nested sequence in a Timeline panel.

The sequence opens in the Source Monitor and functions like a single clip (**Figure 6.80**).

NESTING SEQUENCES

To nest a sequence:

◆ Add a sequence from the Program panel
or Source Monitor to the active sequence
using any of the editing methods you've
learned in this chapter (**Figure 6.81**).

You can use the same editing controls
and drag-and-drop methods with a
sequence that you use with a single clip.
Although a nested sequence acts like
any other sequence clip, it refers to its
source sequence.

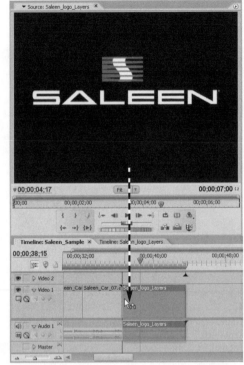

Figure 6.81 You nest a sequence the same way you
add a clip to a sequence. Here, a title sequence is
being dragged from the Source Monitor into the main
sequence.

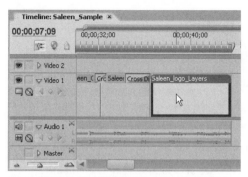

Figure 6.82 Double-clicking a nested sequence...

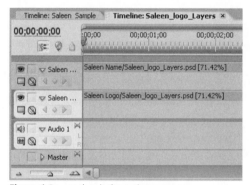

Figure 6.83 ...makes it the active sequence.

To open the source of a nested sequence:

◆ In the Timeline panel, double-click a nested sequence (**Figure 6.82**). The source of the nested sequence becomes the active sequence. Any changes you make to the source sequence are reflected in all of its instances nested in other sequences (**Figure 6.83**).

✔ Tips

■ If you're familiar with Premiere Pro's sibling, After Effects, you'll instantly recognize the nesting concept and appreciate what it means for your project. Conversely, knowing how nesting works in Premiere Pro will give you a head start when you learn After Effects.

■ Nesting makes the virtual clip feature found in versions of Premiere prior to Premiere Pro obsolete.

NESTING SEQUENCES

Nesting rules

Here are a few things to keep in mind when you use nesting:

◆ You can't nest a sequence within itself (think about it; it doesn't work).

◆ Nesting can increase processing demands on your system, and thereby the time it takes to see certain effects at the full frame rate.

◆ A nested sequence includes empty space at the beginning of its source sequence but not at the end.

◆ Whereas a nested sequence reflects changes you make to its source sequence, it does not reflect changes to duration. Therefore, you must use standard trimming methods to lengthen a nested sequence and reveal material added to its source sequence. Conversely, trim back the Out point of the nested sequence to remove black video and silent audio resulting from shortening its source sequence.

Crowing about nesting

Essentially, nesting lets you group sequences and arrange them into hierarchies. With nesting, you can streamline a workflow that otherwise would be elaborate and create effects that otherwise would be impossible. Nesting lets you do the following:

◆ Break a complex or lengthy project into manageable sequences, and then bring them together into a single sequence

◆ Easily repeat material in a sequence, such as a complex transition

◆ Reuse material in several sequences, such as an opener or other boilerplate elements

◆ Easily update multiple instances of the nested material by changing the content of its source sequence

◆ Apply an effect to a sequence, thus altering all the clips within it, such as letterboxing the entire program or applying a speed adjustment to the sequence as a whole

◆ Apply different effects to each instance of the nested sequence

◆ Reduce a complex sequence to a single clip, streamlining the timeline and preventing you from making inadvertent changes or shifting elements out of sync

◆ Create complex hierarchies and layering of effects. You can create transitions-within-transitions. Or use motion and transparency settings to show multiple nested sequences onscreen at once, as in a split screen or picture-in-picture effect.

Editing Multiple-Camera Footage

Typically, a production employs a *single camera* or *film-style* shoot. That is, a single camera records the action, stopping whenever it's time to change angles, change scenery, or accommodate a union-mandated break. But some events—sporting events, concerts, theatrical performances, and even wedding ceremonies—can't be captured fully from a single angle. Stopping the camera to change the angle risks missing a fleeting, unrepeatable action. These situations require a *multicamera shoot.*

In a multicamera shoot, cameras record the action from several angles at once. In some productions (live broadcasts, for example), a director chooses which angle the audience sees on the fly, using a device called a *switcher.* But when live broadcast isn't required, the footage from each camera can be edited together at a later time, using a system such as Premiere Pro.

In Premiere Pro, viewing and switching angles is accomplished using a tool designed for the task, the *Multi-Camera Monitor* (**Figure 6.84**). The Multi-Camera Monitor resembles the Source and Program Monitors, but instead of displaying a single source's image, you can view up to four sources at once. Preparing for and editing a multicamera sequence is explained over the next several tasks, so the process may seem more complex than it really is. The procedure breaks down into three parts:

◆ Synchronize footage from each camera.

◆ Nest the synched sequence, and designate it a multicamera clip.

◆ Use the Multi-Camera Monitor as a switcher, cutting the multicamera clip from one shot to another.

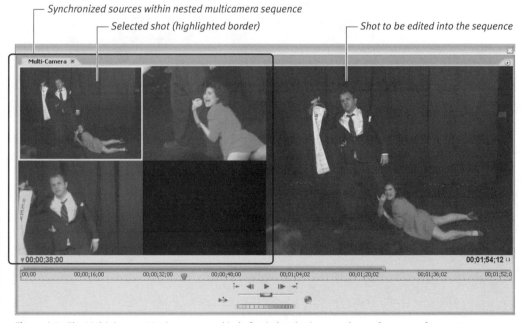

Synchronized sources within nested multicamera sequence

Selected shot (highlighted border)

Shot to be edited into the sequence

Figure 6.84 The Multi-Camera Monitor acts as a kind of switcher, letting you choose from up to four sources.

To synchronize clips:

1. Open each camera's clip, and specify an edit mark you can use to synchronize the shots (**Figure 6.85**).

    For example, set the shots' In points to the same point in the recorded action, or set clip markers you can use to synchronize the shots.

2. Edit each camera's footage into a separate track of a sequence in the Timeline panel.

3. Select the clips, and do either of the following:

    ▲ Choose Clip > Synchronize

    ▲ Right-click a selected clip and choose Synchronize from the context menu (**Figure 6.86**).

    A Synchronize Clips dialog box appears.

Figure 6.85 Mark each camera's footage, and mark a frame to synchronize them. Here, a marker is set at the frame to be synchronized.

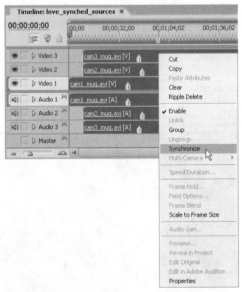

Figure 6.86 Stack the clips in the timeline, right-click the clips, and select Synchronize in the context menu.

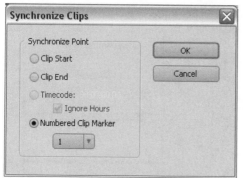

Figure 6.87 In the Synchronize Clips dialog box, specify a method to synchronize the clips.

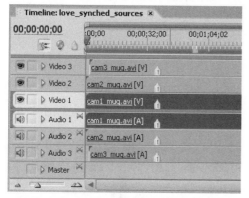

Figure 6.88 The clips are synchronized according to your choice (in this case, a numbered marker).

4. Specify how you want Premiere Pro to synchronize the clips, and then click OK (**Figure 6.87**).

The clips are synchronized according to your choice (**Figure 6.88**). You can also synch the clips manually. If the Timeline's snap button ▣ is selected, then clip edges and markers tend to align as you drag the clips. For more information, see Chapter 7.

To specify a multicamera clip:

1. Nest the sequence containing the clips you synchronized into the new sequence (**Figure 6.89**).

   Use methods described in the task, "To Nest a sequence," earlier in this chapter. The nested sequence appears as a single linked clip in the current sequence.

2. Right-click the nested sequence, and choose Multi-Camera > Enable (**Figure 6.90**).

   The nested sequence clip becomes a multicamera clip, and its name is preceded by *[MC1]* (**Figure 6.91**). You can edit the clip using the Multi-Camera Monitor, as described in the next task.

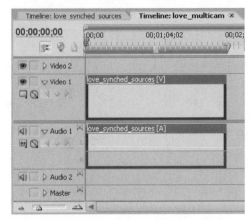

Figure 6.89 Nest the sequence containing the synchronized shots into another sequence...

Figure 6.90 ...and then right-click the nested sequence clip and choose Multi-Camera > Enable...

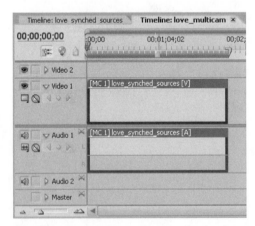

Figure 6.91 ...to make it a multicamera clip. The clip's name in the timeline is preceded by *[MC1]* to indicate that it's a multicamera clip.

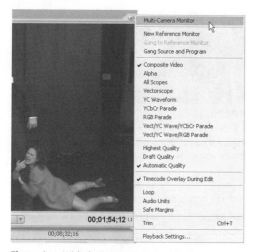

Figure 6.92 With the sequence containing a multicamera clip active, choose Multi-Camera Monitor from the Program Monitor's pull-down menu.

To open the Multi-Camera Monitor:

1. Make the sequence containing a multi-camera clip the active sequence.

   See the preceding task, "To specify a multicamera clip."

2. In the Source Monitor's pull-down menu, choose Multi-Camera Monitor (**Figure 6.92**).

   A Multi-Camera Monitor appears (**Figure 6.93**). Each clip contained in the multicamera sequence appears in the left view of the Multi-Camera Monitor; the right view shows the selected clip.

Figure 6.93 The Multi-Camera Monitor appears. It displays all the shots contained by the multicamera clip (the shots synchronized in its source sequence).

To edit a multicamera clip into a series of shots:

1. In the Multi-Camera Monitor, select the camera view you want to use, and cue it to the point you want it to begin in the sequence.

   The active camera appears with a yellow border in the Multi-Camera Monitor's left view and becomes the current image in the right view (**Figure 6.94**). In the Timeline panel, the multicamera clip's name reflects the active camera (the clip's name in the nested sequence).

2. Click the Multi-Camera Monitor's Record button ● (**Figure 6.95**).

3. Using the Multi-Camera Monitor's playback controls, play the multicamera clip to the point at which you want to cut to a different camera angle, and then stop playback.

   As the multicamera clip plays, watch the other images to see when you want to switch to a different angle.

4. In the Multi-Camera Monitor's left view, select the camera view you want to use next (**Figure 6.96**).

   In the Timeline panel, the multicamera clip is cut at the current time. The previously selected shot appears before the cut; the new shot appears after the cut (**Figure 6.97**).

Figure 6.94 In the Multi-Camera Monitor, select the image you want to use in the sequence.

Figure 6.95 To commit the active view to the sequence, click the Multi-Camera Monitor's Record button.

Figure 6.96 Use the Multi-Camera Monitor's playback controls to play the clip to the point you want the current shot to end. Selecting a new shot...

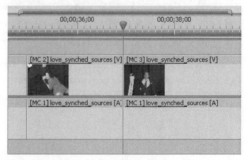

Figure 6.97 ...cuts the multicamera clip at the current time, so that the current shot becomes the clip after the cut.

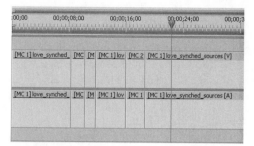

Figure 6.98 Every time you select a new shot, the multicamera clip cuts to the shot. The result is a seamless, continuous sequence created from the multicamera footage.

5. Repeat steps 3 and 4 to turn the multicamera clip into a series of edited shots.

As long as the Record button ● is active, selecting a different shot cuts the multicamera clip at the current time and makes the clip following the cut match the selected shot (**Figure 6.98**).

6. To use the Multi-Camera Monitor without affecting the multicamera clip, deselect the Record button ● .

7. When you're finished, you can close the Multi-Camera Monitor and fine-tune the sequence as you would any other sequence of clips.

✔ Tips

- In a typical film production, a *slate* (or *clapper board*) is used not only to identify a shot visually but also to synchronize picture (the sight of the clapper closing) with audio (the sound of the clapper closing). You can also use a slate to synchronize the shots from multiple cameras. If a slate wasn't used, another onscreen source of a (preferably) percussive sound can provide a synch point.

- Generally, the point of multicamera editing is to switch angles while maintaining the continuous flow of action. When you fine-tune a multicamera sequence, you should use *rolling edits*, which adjust the end of one clip and the beginning of the next by the same amount. For more about rolling edits, see Chapter 8.

- After making a rough cut using the multicamera feature, you may want to superimpose images taken from different angles. Move the clip you want to superimpose into a higher video track, and then trim the higher and lower shots so they overlap (without losing synch). Finally, adjust the higher clip's opacityto blend the shots.

Overlay and Insert Keyboard Modifiers and Icons

As you gain experience editing in Premiere Pro, you'll notice a pattern in how you perform overlay and insert edits using the mouse: Overlay edits are the default and never require a keyboard modifier; insert edits are accomplished by pressing the Ctrl key. This is true not only when you add a new clip to a sequence, but also when you rearrange clips already in a sequence (see Chapter 8).

Ordinarily, insert edits shift material in all tracks. This is usually the desired behavior, because it tends to keep everything in sync. However, there are times when you want an insert edit to shift only the target tracks. In this case, add another keyboard modifier: the Alt key. When you edit clips already in a sequence by manipulating them in the Timeline panel, the Alt key modifier serves another purpose: It allows you to select and trim one track of a linked clip.

The editing conventions for overlay and insert edits are reinforced by visual feedback in the Timeline panel. When you perform overlay edits and insert edits with the mouse, a corresponding icon appears next to the mouse pointer. See **Table 6.1** for an overview.

And while we're on the subject, similar icons are invoked when you move and rearrange clips by dragging them in the Timeline panel. You'll learn about that in Chapter 8.

Table 6.1

Overlay and Insert Icons		
EDIT	MODIFIER	ICON
Overlay	None	
Insert (all tracks)	Ctrl	
Insert (target tracks)	Ctrl+Alt	

EDITING IN THE TIMELINE

7

As you saw in Chapter 6, "Creating a Sequence," you can view an edited sequence in two ways: in the Program Monitor or in the Timeline panel. The Program Monitor shows the frame at the current time, much as it would appear on a television display; the Timeline panel graphically represents all of the sequence's clips arranged in time.

In the timeline, the sequence looks a lot like edited film. Like film, the timeline lays out the instances of clips before you. Unlike film, however, the timeline allows you to view any segment of the sequence instantly or to view the entire sequence. Yet the timeline doesn't provide simply another way to look at or navigate through the sequence; it also gives you a way to edit. Editing in the timeline can feel almost as tactile as editing film but can be far more flexible and efficient than using razors and tape.

This chapter discusses how to use the Timeline panel and how to manipulate clips in this panel to perform a number of basic editing tasks. For now, you'll concentrate on manipulating clips as discrete objects in the timeline. You'll learn how to select and group clips; disable and delete them; split, copy, and paste them; and alter their playback speed. You'll discover ways to make more subtle changes in Chapter 8, "Refining the Sequence."

Customizing the Time Ruler

As in any other timeline, the Timeline panel measures time horizontally, along a *time ruler*. By default, the time ruler starts at zero, but you can set the ruler to start at any number you choose. The time ruler uses the counting system you specified in the project settings—which for most DV projects is drop-frame timecode. However, you can toggle the ruler between video frames and audio units. In Chapter 6, you learned that changing the Source Monitor's timeline to audio units enables you to set more precise audio In and Out points. In the same way, you can set the Timeline panel's time ruler to audio units to view audio clips in greater detail and make precise, sample-based adjustments.

To set a sequence's starting time:

1. In the Timeline panel menu, choose Sequence Zero Point (**Figure 7.1**).

   The Sequence Zero Point dialog box appears.

2. Set the time at which the sequence's time ruler starts (**Figure 7.2**).

   You can change the number by dragging it or clicking the number and entering a new value.

3. Click OK.

   The number you set becomes the sequence's starting time, as reflected in the Program Monitor and Timeline panel time rulers and time displays (**Figure 7.3**).

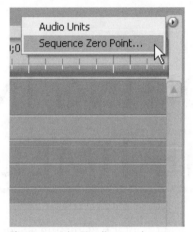

Figure 7.1 In the Timeline panel menu, choose Sequence Zero Point.

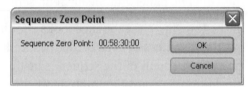

Figure 7.2 In the Sequence Zero Point dialog box, enter a starting time for the sequence's time ruler.

Figure 7.3 The number you enter becomes the sequence's starting time.

Figure 7.4 In the Timeline panel menu, select Audio Units.

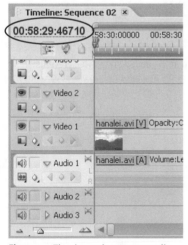

Figure 7.5 The time ruler counts audio samples.

To toggle the timeline time ruler between video frames and audio samples:

◆ In the Timeline panel menu, select Audio Units (**Figure 7.4**).

The Timeline panel time ruler changes to audio units (**Figure 7.5**). Deselect Audio Units to change the time ruler's scale to video frames.

✔ Tip

■ A typical two-minute leader starts at 00;58;00;02, so that the actual program content starts at 01;00;00;00. (See the sidebar "Creating a Leader" in Chapter 3.)

Customizing Track Views

You can view the contents of each track in a sequence in more or less detail, according to your preferences or the task at hand. *Collapsed* tracks show the least information, displaying each clip as a relatively narrow band of color containing only the clip's name. Collapsed tracks also consume the least vertical space, allowing you to view the greatest number of tracks at once and providing a clean interface that updates and scrolls quickly.

Expanding a track makes the track and the clips it contains wider, revealing options for viewing additional clip information. An *expanded* video track can display *thumbnails* (small images taken from each clip's video content). The clips in an expanded audio track can display a *waveform*, a visual representation of the audio. Expanded tracks also reveal controls for viewing and navigating keyframes, which you can use to control video and audio effects such as filters, transparency, and audio fades. For more about keyframes, see Chapter 13, "Working with Effects."

To expand or collapse a track:

◆ Click the triangle to the left of a track's name to toggle it between expanded and collapsed states (**Figures 7.6** and **7.7**).

Additional display options appear in the track header area of expanded tracks.

Figure 7.6 Clicking the triangle to the left of a track's name toggles it from a more compact collapsed state...

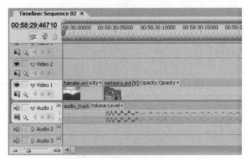

Figure 7.7 ...to an expanded state, which reveals additional controls and information about the clips in the track.

Figure 7.8 In an expanded video track, click the Set Display Style button, and choose an option from the menu.

Figure 7.9 Each video track shown uses a different display style: (from top to bottom) Head and Tail, Head Only, Show Frames, and Show Name Only.

To set a video track's display style:

1. If necessary, expand the track.

   Additional buttons, including the Set Display Style button, appear in the track's header area.

2. Click the Set Display Style button (under the track's eye icon), and choose an option from the pull-down menu (**Figure 7.8**):

   ▲ **Show Head and Tail** 🖫: Displays a thumbnail image at the beginning and end of each clip in the expanded track.

   ▲ **Show Head Only** 🖫: Displays a thumbnail image at the beginning of each clip in the expanded track.

   ▲ **Show Frames** 🖩: Displays thumbnail images for each time unit in the clips in the expanded track.

   ▲ **Show Name Only** 🖵: Displays the name of the clips in the expanded track without thumbnail images.

   The Set Display Style button's icon reflects your choice. The clips in the expanded track use the display style you specify (**Figure 7.9**).

CUSTOMIZING TRACK VIEWS

To show and hide audio waveforms in an audio track:

1. If necessary, expand the track.

   Additional buttons, including the Set Display Style button, appear in the track's header area.

2. Click the audio track's Set Display Style button, and choose an option from the pull-down menu (**Figure 7.10**):

   ▲ **Show Waveform:** Displays an audio waveform in each clip in the expanded track.

   ▲ **Show Name Only:** Displays the audio clip's name only in the expanded track, without a waveform.

   The Set Display Style button's icon reflects your choice. The clips in the expanded audio track use the display style you specify (**Figure 7.11**).

✔ Tips

- To maximize both screen space and performance, display only the information you need. Large icons, detailed track formats, and waveforms not only use up valuable screen space, but also take longer to appear on the screen. Excessive detail can result in an overcrowded screen and slow scrolling in the timeline.

- You can resize the height of each track to aid in the use of keyframes or other controls, or just to aid your eyesight. You can also resize the track header area to minimize its width or, more likely, to accommodate longer custom track names. Just position the mouse on the border you want to resize, and drag.

- When there are more tracks than the Timeline panel can show at once, you can adjust the border between the video and audio tracks to favor the tracks you need the most. Again, drag the border between video and audio tracks.

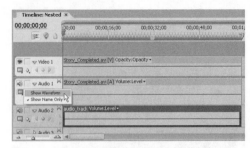

Figure 7.10 In an expanded audio track, click the Set Display Style button, and choose an option from the menu.

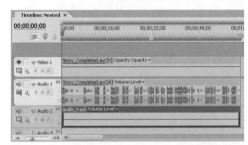

Figure 7.11 The clip in audio track 1 is set to Show Waveform; the clip in audio track 2 is set to Show Name Only.

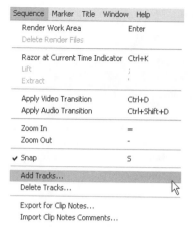

Figure 7.12 Choose Sequence > Add Tracks.

Figure 7.13 In the Add Tracks dialog box, enter the number of video, audio, and audio submix tracks you want to add.

Figure 7.14 For each type of track you add, choose an option in the Placement pull-down menu.

Adding, Deleting, and Renaming Tracks

As you learned in Chapter 2, "Starting a Project," the Default Sequence settings determine the initial number of tracks in a sequence. For many projects, you need only a modest number of tracks: video tracks for the main content and for superimposed images; audio tracks for dialogue, sound-track, and sound effects. However, Premiere Pro permits you to have as many as 99 video and 99 audio tracks in the timeline. What's more, you can name all those tracks, so you can easily distinguish the sound-effects track from the music and dialogue tracks, for example.

Similarly, you can remove either a particular track (and all the clips it contains) or empty tracks only. You can't remove the master audio track, however.

To add tracks:

1. Choose Sequence > Add Tracks (**Figure 7.12**).

   The Add Tracks dialog box appears (**Figure 7.13**).

2. Specify the number of video, audio, and audio submix tracks you want to add.

3. For each type of track you add, specify an option in the Placement pull-down menu: Before First Track, After Target Track, or After Last Track (**Figure 7.14**).

continues on next page

4. For audio tracks, choose an option in the Track Type pull-down menu: Mono, Stereo, or 5.1 (**Figure 7.15**).

5. When you've finished specifying the track options, click OK.

The number and type of tracks you specified appear in the sequence (**Figure 7.16**).

To delete tracks:

1. To delete a particular video or audio track, target the track by clicking its header area (near the track's name).

You can target one video and one audio track, including audio submix tracks. You can't target the master audio track.

2. Choose Sequence > Delete Tracks (**Figure 7.17**).

The Delete Tracks dialog box appears (**Figure 7.18**).

Figure 7.15 In the Track Type pull-down menu, choose the type of audio track you want to add.

Figure 7.16 The additional tracks appear in the positions you specified.

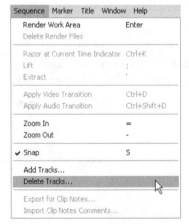

Figure 7.17 Choose Sequence > Delete Tracks.

Figure 7.18 In the Delete Tracks dialog box, choose the types of tracks you want to delete.

Figure 7.19 For each type of track you want to delete, specify whether you want to delete all empty tracks or only the targeted track.

Figure 7.20 Right-click the track's header area, and choose Rename from the menu.

Figure 7.21 Type a new name for the track, and press Enter.

3. Choose the types of tracks you want to delete by checking the appropriate boxes.

4. For selected video or audio tracks, choose an option from the corresponding pull-down menu (**Figure 7.19**):

▲ **Target Track:** Removes the currently targeted track (and any clips it contains).

▲ **All Empty Tracks:** Removes all video or audio tracks that don't contain clips.

If you selected audio submix tracks, then all unassigned submix tracks will be removed.

5. Click OK.

The tracks you specified are removed from the sequence.

To rename a track:

1. Right-click the track's name, and choose Rename from the menu (**Figure 7.20**).

The track's name is highlighted with a text-insertion cursor.

2. Type a new name for the track, and press Enter (**Figure 7.21**).

The track uses the name you entered.

✔ Tips

■ You can also access the Add Tracks and Remove Tracks dialog boxes by right-clicking the track header area.

■ If none of the available audio tracks matches a new clip's audio channel type, Premiere Pro adds a compatible audio track automatically. See Chapter 6 for details.

Monitoring Tracks

When used as a noun, the term *monitor* can refer to a video screen or an audio speaker. It's also used as a verb, meaning to see or hear, as in "to monitor the video and audio." In Premiere Pro, you can monitor any combination of the tracks in the timeline. Only monitored tracks are included during playback and when you preview or export the program. Although you usually monitor all the tracks, at times you may want to monitor only certain tracks. You may want to hear the dialogue track without the music and effects tracks, for example.

To monitor tracks:

◆ In the Timeline panel, *do one of the following:*

▲ Click a video track's Track Output toggle button to hide or reveal the eye icon 👁.

▲ Click an audio track's Track Output toggle button to hide or reveal the speaker icon 🔊.

The Track Output toggle button is the first box in the track's header area. When a track output icon (eye or speaker) is visible, you can see or hear the clips in the corresponding track; when the icon is hidden, clips in the track are excluded from playback (**Figure 7.22**).

✔ Tips

■ Shift+click next to the track name in the timeline to reveal or hide all the speaker icons or all the eye icons.

■ Isolating a single audio monitor can be especially helpful when you're synching sound effects to video. (On an audio mixer, this procedure is called *soloing* the track.) The other sound tracks often prevent you from hearing whether a sound effect is synched properly.

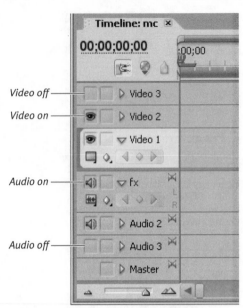

Figure 7.22 Tracks with the eye icon are visible during playback, and tracks with the speaker icon can be heard.

■ The Audio Mixer panel includes switches for monitoring audio tracks during mixing. For more information, see Chapter 11, "Mixing Audio."

MONITORING TRACKS

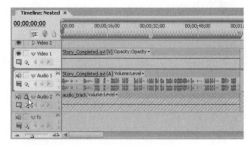

Figure 7.23 Click to make the lock icon appear and lock the track. The contents of the track appear with a pattern of slashes. Click the lock icon to make it disappear and unlock the track.

Locking and Unlocking Tracks

Locking a track protects the clips in the track from accidental changes. You can't add clips to a locked track, and you can't move or modify the clips that are already in the locked track. Moreover, clips in locked tracks don't shift in time after an insert edit is performed. Locking a track makes a lock icon appear in the track's header area and marks the track under the time ruler with a pattern of slashes.

Although you can't alter the clips in a locked track, you can still monitor those clips, and the track is included when you preview or export the program.

To lock and unlock tracks:

◆ Click the track's Track Lock toggle button (the second square in the track's header area) to show or hide the lock icon 🔒 (**Figure 7.23**).

This icon indicates that the corresponding track is locked and can't be modified. Locked tracks also appear with a pattern of slashes. If no icon appears, the track is unlocked.

LOCKING AND UNLOCKING TRACKS

Getting Around the Timeline

You can navigate the sequence in the time-line in several ways. You can zoom in, zoom out, and scroll through the timeline. In addition to using the standard zoom tools and scroll bars, you can take advantage of the Timeline panel's *viewing area bar*.

You're already familiar with the Source and Program Monitors' viewing area bar from Chapter 5, "Viewing Clips in the Monitor Panels." The Timeline panel's viewing area bar works just like its counterparts: The width of the viewing area bar corresponds with the area of the sequence visible in the Timeline panel. Drag the ends of the viewing area bar to view the sequence in more detail; drag them farther apart to see more of the sequence. Dragging the center of the bar left or right scrolls the visible area.

Whereas the Zoom tool magnifies the part of the timeline you click or drag, the time unit slider, zoom buttons, and viewing area bar use the current time indicator (CTI) as the center of changes in scale. In other words, using these controls zooms into the CTI or out from the CTI. Note how the time ruler zooms smoothly, rather than by large, discrete increments.

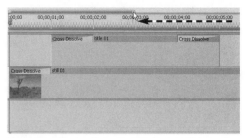

Figure 7.24 To view the sequence in more detail, you can drag the ends of the viewing area bar closer together...

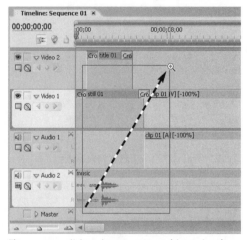

Figure 7.25 ...click or drag a marquee (shown here) with the Zoom tool...

Figure 7.26 ...or drag the zoom slider to the right (shown here), or click the Zoom In button.

To view part of the sequence in more detail:

◆ *Do one of the following:*

▲ Above the Timeline panel's time ruler, drag the ends of the viewing area bar closer together (**Figure 7.24**).

▲ In the Tools panel, select the Zoom tool 🔍, and then click the part of the timeline that you want to see in more detail.

▲ In the Tools panel, select the Zoom tool 🔍 and then drag a marquee around the area of the timeline that you want to see in detail (**Figure 7.25**).

▲ At the bottom left of the Timeline panel, drag the zoom slider to the right (**Figure 7.26**).

▲ To the right of the zoom slider, click the Zoom In button.

To view more of the sequence in the timeline:

◆ *Do one of the following:*

▲ Above the Timeline panel's time ruler, drag the ends of the viewing area bar farther apart (**Figure 7.27**).

▲ In the Tools panel, select the Zoom tool 🔍, and then Alt+click the part of the timeline that you want to center in the wider view (**Figure 7.28**).

When you press Alt, the Zoom tool icon appears with a minus sign to indicate that it will zoom out.

▲ At the bottom left of the Timeline panel, drag the zoom slider to the left (**Figure 7.29**).

▲ To the left of the zoom slider, click the Zoom Out button.

✔ Tips

■ To zoom out quickly to view the entire program in the timeline, press the back-slash key (\).

■ To select the Zoom tool quickly, press Z.

■ When you zoom into the time ruler closely enough for the ruler to measure video frames, a short blue line extends from the right side of the CTI. This represents the duration of the frame.

■ As you would expect, you can scroll the visible part of the timeline by dragging the standard scroll bar or pressing the scroll buttons. Depending on your preference, the timeline can scroll automatically to keep the CTI in view (see the task "To specify the timeline scrolling option," later in this chapter).

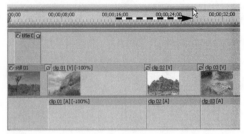

Figure 7.27 To view more of the sequence, you can drag the ends of the viewing area bar farther apart...

Figure 7.28 ...Alt+click with the Zoom tool...

Figure 7.29 ...or drag the zoom slider to the left (shown here), or click the Zoom Out button.

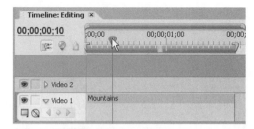

Figure 7.30 Click the Timeline panel's time ruler to cue the CTI to that point.

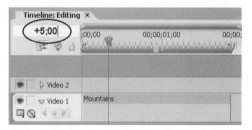

Figure 7.31 Select the Timeline panel's time display, and enter an absolute time or a number relative to the current time. You can also drag the time display to change the number.

Playing the Sequence in the Timeline

In Chapter 4, "Managing Clips," you learned to use playback controls in the Monitor panels to cue the current video frame. In the Timeline panel, a small blue triangle in the time ruler, the CTI, looks and works like its counterpart in the Program Monitor. However, a vertical line extends from the Timeline panel's CTI through the tracks of the sequence. This makes it easy to see the current frame in relationship to the clips in the sequence. Furthermore, the vertical line makes it even easier to align clips with the CTI, and vice versa. You can cue the Timeline panel's CTI by clicking or dragging the time ruler or by using the Timeline panel's time display.

You can also snap the Timeline panel's CTI to an edit point by pressing Shift while dragging the CTI.

Remember that the Timeline panel's CTI and the Program Monitor's CTI show the same frame of the sequence and move in tandem; however, their time rulers can show different parts of the same sequence at different scales and using different time units.

To cue the Timeline panel CTI:

◆ *Do one of the following:*

▲ In the Timeline panel, click the time ruler to move the CTI to that point in the sequence (**Figure 7.30**).

▲ In the Timeline panel, click the current time display to select it, and then type a relative or absolute time and press Enter (**Figure 7.31**).

▲ In the Timeline panel, drag the current time display to change the number.

▲ In the Program Monitor, use the playback controls (or a keyboard shortcut) to cue the current program frame. (See "Using Playback Controls" in Chapter 5.)

To snap the Timeline panel CTI to an edit point:

◆ In the Timeline panel, press Shift, and drag the CTI to an edit point in the sequence (**Figure 7.32**). Edit points can be clip edges or markers.

When you drag to the edge of a clip, the CTI snaps to the edge, and an indicator ▾ appears at the corner of the clip.

When you drag to a marker or the edge of the work area bar, an indicator ▲ appears under the timeline ruler.

When the edge of a clip and the edge of the timeline ruler (or marker) coincide, both indicators appear.

To specify the timeline scrolling option:

1. Choose Edit > Preferences > General (**Figure 7.33**).

   The General pane of the Preferences dialog box appears.

2. In the Timeline Playback Auto-Scrolling pull-down menu, choose an option (**Figure 7.34**):

   ▲ **No Scroll**: The Timeline doesn't scroll until playback is stopped.

   ▲ **Page Scroll**: Scrolls the Timeline in increments equal to the width of the visible area of the Timeline.

   ▲ **Smooth Scroll**: Scrolls the Timeline during playback so that the CTI never moves beyond the visible area of the Timeline.

3. Click OK to close the Preferences dialog box.

✔ Tip

■ You can also drag the vertical line extending from the Timeline panel's CTI, as long as there are no clips at the point where you grab the CTI.

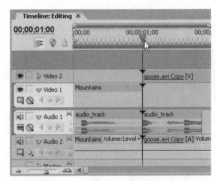

Figure 7.32 Hold down the Shift key, and drag the CTI to an edit point in the sequence.

Figure 7.33 Choose Edit > Preferences > General.

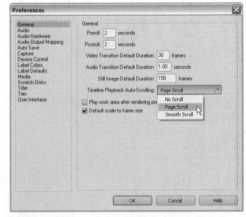

Figure 7.34 Specify an option in the Timeline Playback Auto-Scrolling pull-down menu.

PLAYING THE SEQUENCE IN THE TIMELINE

Figure 7.35 Select the tracks containing the edits to which you want to cue the CTI.

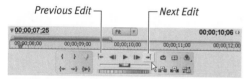

Previous Edit — ⌐ Next Edit

Figure 7.36 In the Program Monitor, click the Previous Edit or Next Edit button.

Cuing to Edits

An *edit* is the point between two clips or the point directly before or after a clip in a selected track. (You may also refer to the visual transition at the edit as a *cut*.) You can instantaneously cue the CTI to an edit point by clicking the Previous Edit and Next Edit buttons, making it that much easier to navigate through and edit the sequence.

To cue to the next or previous edit:

1. Target the tracks containing the edits to which you want to cue the CTI (**Figure 7.35**).

2. In the Program Monitor, *click either of these buttons* (**Figure 7.36**):

   ▲ **Previous Edit** |←: Cues the CTI to the previous edit in a selected track.

   ▲ **Next Edit** →|: Cues the CTI to the next edit in a selected track.

✔ Tip

■ You can also use the playback controls in the Program Monitor to cue the CTI to an absolute or relative time position or to an In point, an Out point, or a sequence marker. See "Using Playback Controls" in Chapter 5 for details.

Using Sequence Markers

Just as clip markers can help you identify important frames in the source clips, you can use *sequence markers* to specify important points in the timeline.

In most respects, sequence markers work exactly the same way as clip markers. The commands you use to set, delete, and cue to sequence markers are equivalent to the commands you use for source clip markers. However, sequence markers appear in a sequence's time ruler, rather than in clips. Apart from these minor differences, the methods you learned in Chapter 6 can be applied to sequence markers.

However, sequence markers have a few unique features that merit separate explanations. First, a sequence marker can include a text message. Comments are for your reference only and can be accessed only through the Marker dialog box; they don't appear during playback, nor are they exported.

In addition, a sequence marker can contain a Web link or chapter link that's embedded in the exported movie file. When the movie reaches a Web link marker, it automatically opens a Web page in your browser. A chapter link specifies points to which you can cue the movie when exporting to certain formats.

Note that you can export a DVD directly from Premiere Pro. Premiere Pro's DVD Layout feature uses special DVD markers—not sequence markers—to specify points for the main menu, scenes, and the end of the DVD. See Chapter 15, "Creating Output," for details.

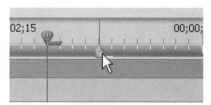

Figure 7.37 Double-click a sequence marker.

Figure 7.38
Double-click the
Set Unnumbered
Marker button.

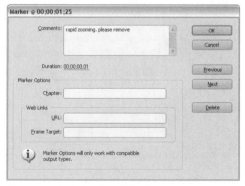

Figure 7.39 In the Marker dialog box, enter a comment and duration.

To add a comment to a sequence marker:

1. To access the Marker dialog box, *do one of the following:*

   ▲ In the Timeline panel's time ruler, double-click a sequence marker (**Figure 7.37**).

   ▲ With the CTI cued to an existing marker, double-click the Set Unnumbered Marker button 🗓 on the left side of the timeline ruler (**Figure 7.38**).

   A dialog box for the marker appears.

2. In the Marker dialog box, enter information in the following fields (**Figure 7.39**):

   ▲ **Comments:** A text message that will appear in the Program Monitor.

   ▲ **Duration:** The amount of time the marker lasts, beginning at the marked time in the program.

3. Click OK to close the Marker dialog box.

   In the time ruler, a line extending from the marker indicates the comment duration you specified.

To add a Web or chapter link to a sequence marker:

1. To access the Marker dialog box, *do one of the following:*

   ▲ In the Timeline panel's time ruler, double-click a sequence marker.

   ▲ With the CTI cued to an existing marker, double-click the Set Unnumbered Marker button.

2. In the Marker Options section of the dialog box, *do one of the following* (**Figure 7.40**):

   ▲ To set a chapter link, enter the name of the chapter in the Chapter field.

   ▲ To set a Web link, enter the Web address in the URL field.

   ▲ To activate a particular frame of the site in a Web link, enter the file name of the frame in the Frame Target field.

3. Click OK to close the Marker dialog box.

✔ Tips

■ DVD authoring guidelines restrict the proximity of chapter links. When you set markers for use as chapter links, make sure they're spaced at least 15 frames apart or by the number of frames your authoring software requires.

■ Double-clicking the Set Unnumbered Marker button on the left side of the timeline ruler allows you to set a marker and add a comment and/or Web link in one step.

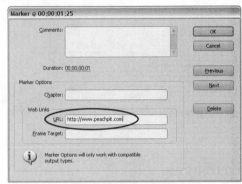

Figure 7.40 To set a chapter link, enter the name of the chapter in the Chapter field. To set a Web link, enter a URL (circled) and, if you want, a file name for the frame target.

USING SEQUENCE MARKERS

Using Linked Clips

When a clip contains both video and audio material, it's known as a *linked clip*. When you move a linked clip in the timeline, the video and audio portions of the clip move together. Similarly, when you change a linked clip's edit marks, the video and audio tracks both change— unless you deliberately treat them separately.

The link helps you keep the video and audio synchronized. Even if your video and audio were recorded separately (as in a film shoot), you can create an artificial link between them. If you've ever edited film and magnetic tape, you know how convenient linked clips are.

Nevertheless, it's possible to lose sync between the tracks of a linked clip. Fortunately, Premiere Pro alerts you to the loss of sync by tagging the affected clips in the timeline. Premiere Pro even tells you by exactly how much the clips are out of sync and provides easy ways to restore sync.

Although the link is usually an advantage, Premiere Pro permits you to override it if necessary. You can even break the link if you want.

To perform the tasks described in this chapter, you need to understand how linked clips behave in the timeline. In the next chapter, you'll learn to tackle more advanced tasks related to sync and links.

Selecting Clips in the Timeline

Not surprisingly, whenever you want to manipulate or affect a sequence clip in any way, you have to select it first.

Clicking a linked clip selects both the video and audio portions of the clip. To select or otherwise manipulate only the video or audio portion of a linked clip, use the Alt keyboard modifier.

To select clips in the Timeline panel:

◆ *Do any of the following:*

  ▲ To select a clip, click the clip in the timeline (**Figure 7.41**).

  ▲ To add or subtract from the selection, Ctrl+click clips.

  ▲ To select a range of clips, drag a marquee around a range of clips (**Figure 7.42**).

  ▲ To select only the video or audio portion of a linked clip, Alt+click the clip (**Figure 7.43**).

When a clip is selected, its border is highlighted.

Figure 7.41 To select clips in the Timeline panel, click a clip...

Figure 7.42 ...or drag a marquee around multiple clips. Make sure you start dragging in an empty track; otherwise, you could move a clip.

Figure 7.43 Alt+click to select only the video or audio portion of a linked clip.

Figure 7.44 In the Tools panel, select the Track tool.

Figure 7.45 Click a clip with the Track tool to select that clip and all subsequent clips in that track (including their linked counterparts in unlocked tracks).

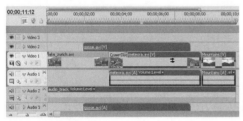

Figure 7.46 Pressing Shift toggles the Track tool to the Multitrack tool, which selects a clip and all subsequent clips in all tracks.

■ Because selecting a track of clips also selects any linked audio or video, keep an eye on the clips in linked tracks when you move a selection. Otherwise, you may overwrite other clips without noticing.

To select all the clips in one or more tracks:

1. In the Tools panel, choose the Track tool ▓ (**Figure 7.44**).

2. *Do one of the following:*

   ▲ To select all clips in the track from a particular clip forward, including the linked audio or video in other tracks, click the clip (**Figure 7.45**).

   ▲ To select all clips in the track from a particular clip forward, not including the linked audio or video in other tracks, Alt+click the clip.

   ▲ To select all clips in all tracks from a particular clip forward, Shift+click the clip (**Figure 7.46**).

   Pressing Shift changes the Track tool into the Multitrack tool ▓.

✔ Tips

■ You can't select clips in locked tracks. This isn't a restriction, but an advantage. Lock tracks to protect the clips in a track from inadvertent changes.

■ Although it looks the same, the Track tool doesn't function as it did in previous versions of Premiere. In Premiere Pro, Shift+clicking with the Track tool toggles to the Multitrack tool. Therefore, you can select either one track or all tracks. And unlike in past versions, selecting a track of clips also selects any linked audio or video unless you press the Alt modifier key.

■ When you select multiple contiguous clips in the timeline, the Info panel indicates the number of clips selected and the total duration of the clips. If you select noncontiguous clips, the duration is calculated from the In point of the first clip to the Out point of the last clip.

Grouping Clips

Even though you can select and move any number of clips (even a noncontiguous range of clips), at times it may be more convenient to group clips. *Grouping* clips allows you to select and move the clips as a single clip.

You can adjust the outer edges—the In point of the first clip or the Out point of the last clip—of the group, but not the interior In and Out points. Unlike with individual clips, you can't apply clip-based commands (such as speed changes) or effects to a group. However, you can select individual members of the group and apply effects to them without ungrouping the clips. And, of course, you can ungroup the clips at any time.

To group clips:

1. Select more than one clip in the Timeline panel (**Figure 7.47**).

2. Choose Clip > Group (**Figure 7.48**).

    The clips are grouped together. Clicking any member of the group selects the entire group.

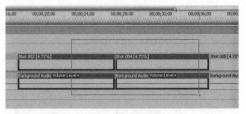

Figure 7.47 Select more than one clip in a sequence for your group.

Figure 7.48
Choose Clip > Group.

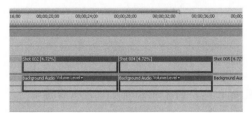

Figure 7.49 Select a grouped clip.

Figure 7.50
Choose Clip > Ungroup.

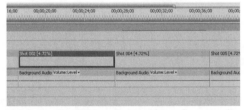

Figure 7.51 Alt+click to select members of a group clip without ungrouping them.

To ungroup clips:

1. Select a grouped clip in the Timeline panel (**Figure 7.49**).

2. Choose Clip > Ungroup (**Figure 7.50**). The clips are ungrouped so that you can select and manipulate each clip independently.

To select individual clips in a group:

◆ *Do one of the following:*

▲ Alt+click individual clips in a group (**Figure 7.51**).

▲ Shift+Alt+click to add to or subtract from the selection.

✔ Tip

■ You can't apply an effect to a group clip, but you can apply an effect to a nested sequence. For more about nested sequences, see Chapter 6.

Deleting Clips and Gaps from the Timeline

Whatever you can select, you can delete. That includes both clips and gaps between clips. Delete commands work much like the lift and extract edits you learned about in Chapter 6. When you delete a clip, the result is like a lift edit, leaving an empty space behind and leaving surrounding clips unaffected. The result of a Ripple Delete command is comparable to an extract edit. Ripple-deleting a clip removes the clip and closes the gap, shifting all subsequent clips back in time by the duration of the clip. You can also select and ripple-delete a gap between clips. However, you can't select a gap and a clip simultaneously. Also, the Ripple Delete command always shifts clips in all tracks. To limit the ripple effect to the tracks containing the deleted clip, you'll need to lock the other tracks or use a variation of an extract edit, explained in Chapter 6.

To delete clips from the timeline:

1. Select one or more clips in the timeline (**Figure 7.52**).

2. Press Backspace (or Delete, on an extended keyboard).

   The selected clips are removed from the timeline (**Figure 7.53**).

Figure 7.52 Select one or more clips in the Timeline panel.

Figure 7.53 Pressing Backspace (or Delete) is like performing a lift edit, removing the selection and leaving empty space.

Figure 7.54 Right-click selected clips (or a gap between clips), and choose Ripple Delete. Because a ripple delete doesn't split clips in other tracks to perform the ripple edit, other tracks must be locked.

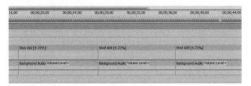

Figure 7.55 The selection or gap is extracted, and subsequent material in the sequence shifts back in time by the number of frames that were removed.

To ripple-delete a clip or a gap between clips:

◆ Right-click a clip or gap in the timeline, and choose Ripple Delete from the menu (**Figure 7.54**).

The subsequent clips shift back in the timeline to close the gap (**Figure 7.55**). The command doesn't split clips in other tracks to perform the ripple edit, and if other clips are unlocked, the command appears dimmed. Lock tracks containing other clips to enable the command.

✔ Tips

■ Delete and Ripple Delete are great for removing entire clips or gaps. To remove portions of clips or to remove frames from several clips and tracks, perform a lift or extract edit. See "Lift and Extract" in Chapter 6.

■ You can Alt+click to select only the video or audio portion of a linked clip and then delete or ripple-delete just that part.

Enabling and Disabling Clips

Disabling a clip in the sequence prevents it from appearing during playback and when you preview or export the program. Disabling a clip is useful if you want to keep the clip in the program but exclude it temporarily. You may want to disable a single audio clip to hear what the program sounds like without it, for example. You can still move and make other changes to a disabled clip.

To disable or enable clips:

1. Select one or more clips in the timeline (**Figure 7.56**).

2. Choose Clip > Enable (**Figure 7.57**).

   A check mark indicates that the clip is enabled. If no check mark appears, the clip is disabled. Disabled clips appear dimmed in the Timeline panel (**Figure 7.58**).

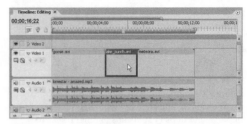

Figure 7.56 Select one or more clips in the Timeline panel.

Figure 7.57 Choose Clip > Enable to uncheck the option.

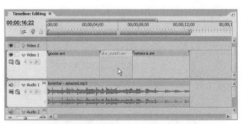

Figure 7.58 Disabled clips appear dimmed in the Timeline panel and don't appear in the Program Monitor or in exported movies.

Figure 7.59 Select the Razor tool.

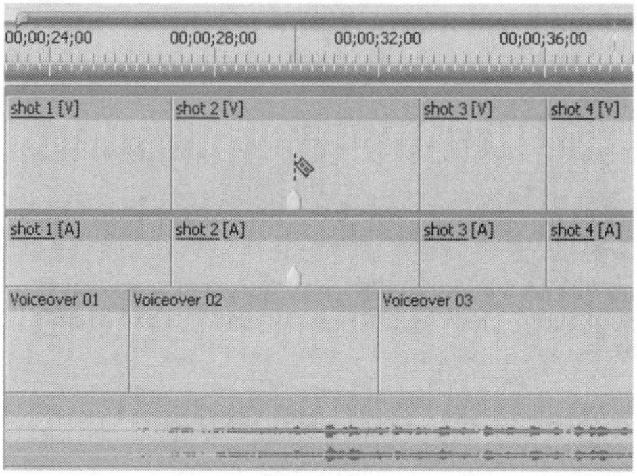

Figure 7.60 Clicking a clip with the Razor tool...

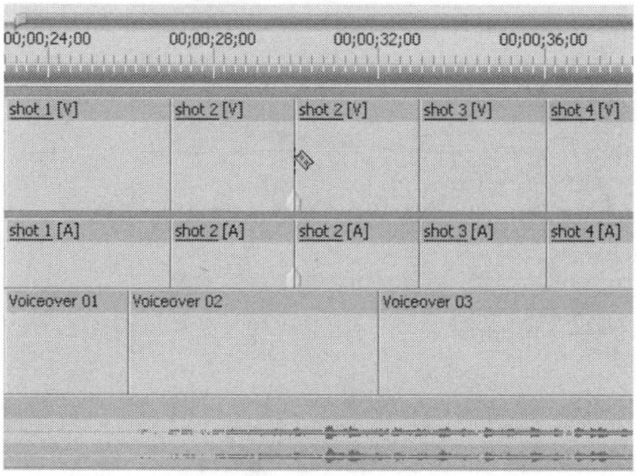

Figure 7.61 ...splits it into two clips at the point you click.

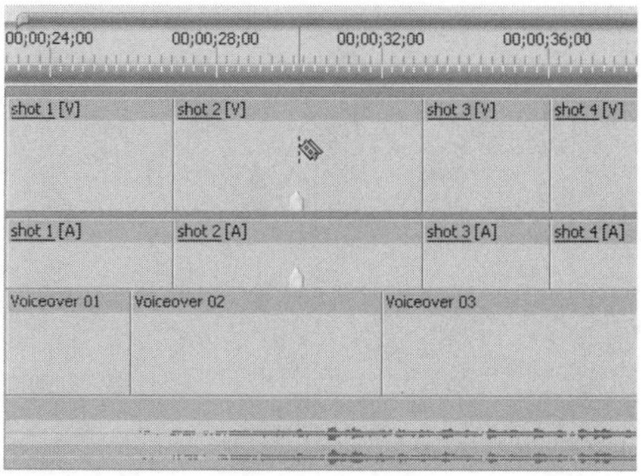

Figure 7.62 Pressing Shift toggles the Razor tool to the Multirazor tool. Clicking with the Multirazor tool...

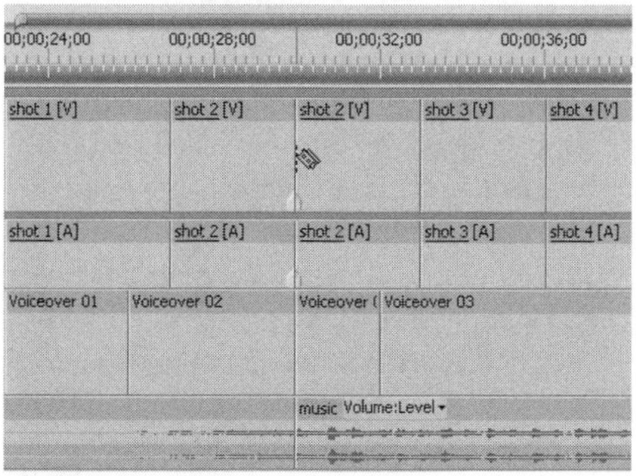

Figure 7.63 ...splits clips in all tracks.

Splitting Clips

Sometimes you need to cut a clip in the timeline into two or more pieces. You may want to apply an effect to one part of a shot but not to another, for example. When you split a clip, each piece becomes an independent sequence clip or clip instance. When you split a linked clip, both the video and audio tracks are split.

To split a clip with the razor:

1. In the Tools panel, select the Razor tool 🔪 (**Figure 7.59**).

2. Click a clip in the timeline at the point where you want to split it (**Figure 7.60**). The clip is split into two individual clips at that point (**Figure 7.61**).

To split clips in multiple tracks:

1. In the Tools panel, select the Razor tool 🔪.

2. Shift+click the point in the timeline where you want to split the clips in all tracks (**Figure 7.62**).

Pressing Shift changes the Razor tool to the Multirazor tool 🔪. Shift+clicking splits all clips in all unlocked tracks at the same point in time (**Figure 7.63**).

SPLITTING CLIPS

To split clips at the CTI:

1. Position the CTI at the point where you want to split the clips (**Figure 7.64**).

2. Choose Sequence > Razor at Current Time Indicator (**Figure 7.65**).

   All unlocked clips in all unlocked tracks are split at the same point in the timeline (**Figure 7.66**).

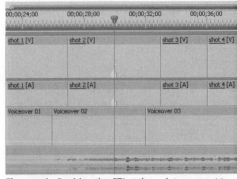

Figure 7.64 Position the CTI at the point you want to split clips. The Program Monitor displays the frame after the cut point.

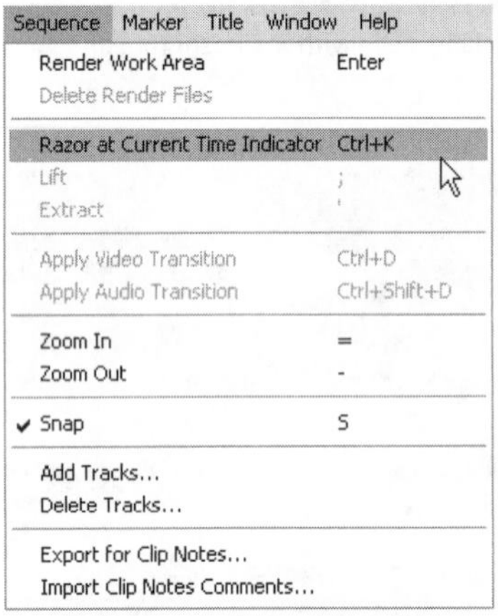

Figure 7.65 Choose Sequence > Razor at Current Time Indicator.

Match-Frame Edits

Splitting a clip creates a cut that is visible in the Timeline panel but invisible during playback. This kind of cut is called a *match-frame edit*. In traditional tape-based editing, match-frame edits are essential to A/B roll editing. In Premiere Pro, match-frame edits can be useful if you want to add an effect or a speed change in one part of a shot but not another. Because the viewer can't detect a match-frame edit, the effect appears to be seamless.

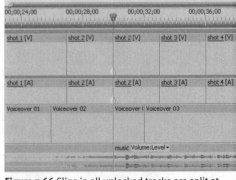

Figure 7.66 Clips in all unlocked tracks are split at the CTI.

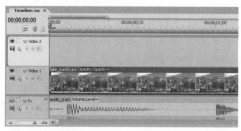

Figure 7.67 Select one or more clips in the Timeline panel.

Figure 7.68
Choose Edit > Cut or Edit > Copy (shown here).

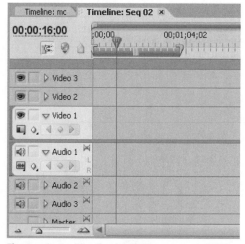

Figure 7.69 Position the destination sequence's CTI where you want the pasted selection to start.

Cutting, Copying, and Pasting Clips

As you would expect of any computer program, Premiere Pro offers copy and paste functions. You may be pleasantly surprised by Premiere Pro's powerful paste commands. You can paste any number of clips in any number of tracks within the same sequence or from one sequence to another. The standard Paste command works like an overlay edit, whereas the Paste Insert command works like an insert edit. (For more about overlay and insert edits, see Chapter 6.)

In this section, you'll learn how to copy and paste the contents of a clip.

To paste clips:

1. Select one or more clips in a sequence (**Figure 7.67**).

2. *Do one of the following:*
   - ▲ Choose Edit > Cut.
   - ▲ Choose Edit > Copy (**Figure 7.68**).

3. Open the sequence in which you want to paste the selection, and position the CTI where you want the pasted clips to begin (**Figure 7.69**).

continues on next page

CUTTING, COPYING, AND PASTING CLIPS

4. *Do one of the following* (**Figure 7.70**):

▲ Choose Edit > Paste.

▲ Choose Edit > Paste Insert.

The selection appears in corresponding tracks beginning at the CTI (**Figure 7.71**). If there aren't enough tracks or the appropriate type of audio tracks to accommodate the pasted selection, Premiere Pro creates the necessary tracks automatically.

Figure 7.70
Choose Edit > Paste (shown here) or Edit > Paste Insert.

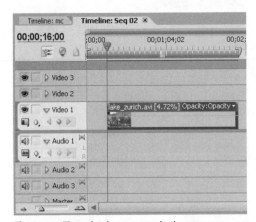

Figure 7.71 The selection appears in the sequence, starting at the CTI. In this example, the selection was pasted into a different sequence.

Playing Clips at a Different Speed or in Reverse

In Premiere Pro, you can change the speed of a clip by choosing a menu command or by dragging directly in the timeline. A clip's speed correlates inversely with duration: Increasing speed reduces duration; decreasing speed increases duration. The clip's In and Out points, however, remain intact. In other words, if the clip shows a 10-second countdown, increasing the speed won't cut out any of the shot. You'll still see all 10 numbers—they'll just go by in less than 10 seconds. You can also use the Speed/Duration command to reverse playback at the specified speed, which will make the 10-second countdown in the example count *up*.

Note that a speed change applies to the entire clip. If you want to affect only part of a clip, split the clip and apply the speed change to one part only. If you want the speed to change over the course of the clip—making its playback accelerate or decelerate—you need to use a program like Adobe After Effects.

Unlike some editing programs, Premiere Pro doesn't create a new media file at the new speed; it merely plays back the clip at the specified speed in the project. The source media is unaffected. (If you want a new media file, you can change the clip's speed and then export it as a new movie file.)

Copying and Pasting between Premiere Pro and Adobe After Effects

It's not unusual to use the same footage in both Premiere Pro and After Effects, in order to take advantage of each program's unique strengths. Since Premiere Pro 1.5 and After Effects 6.5, you can copy and paste clips and sequences—analogous to layers and compositions in After Effects—between the two applications' Timeline panels. With some minor limitations, almost everything in Premiere Pro can be copied to After Effects. However, features unique to After Effects—3D layers, masks, text layers, and transfer modes—can't be pasted into Premiere Pro. Similarly, not all of the effects available in one application are available in the other. The Adobe Help Center details how items copied from one program are pasted into the other. And by the way—make sure Premiere Pro is running before you copy items in After Effects.

You're not limited to copying and pasting individual elements. You can transfer your After Effects work into Premiere Pro by importing an entire After Effects project (as explained in Chapter 3, "Capturing and Importing Footage"). If your project requires an even more integrated workflow, you can have one program reflect changes you make in the other, by utilizing the Dynamic Link feature (mentioned in the sidebar "Dynamic Link," in Chapter 3).

To change the speed of a clip using the Speed/Duration command:

1. Select a source clip in the Project panel or a sequence clip in the Timeline panel (**Figure 7.72**).

2. Choose Clip > Speed/Duration (**Figure 7.73**).

   The Clip Speed/Duration dialog box appears (**Figure 7.74**).

3. Click the chain icon so that speed and duration values are linked.

   A link icon 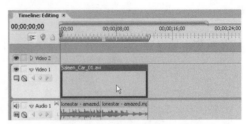 indicates that speed and duration are linked; an unlink icon indicates that speed and duration values operate independently.

4. Enter a value for either of the following:

   ▲ **Speed:** Enter a speed for the clip, expressed as a percentage of the normal speed. A value less than 100 percent decreases the clip's speed; a value greater than 100 percent increases the clip's speed.

   ▲ **Duration:** Enter a total duration for the clip. Durations shorter than the original increase the clip's speed; durations longer than the original decrease the clip's speed.

5. Select the options you want:

   ▲ **Reverse Speed:** Plays the clip in reverse at the speed you specify.

   ▲ **Maintain Audio Pitch:** Shifts an audio clip's pitch to compensate for pitch changes caused by speed adjustments.

6. Click OK to close the Clip Speed/Duration dialog box.

   In the timeline, the clip's speed—and therefore its duration—change according to the values you specified (**Figure 7.75**). The source In and Out points aren't changed, only the speed of the clip.

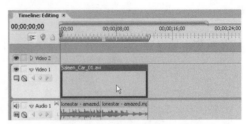

Figure 7.72 Select a source clip in the Project panel or a sequence clip in the Timeline panel (shown here).

Figure 7.73 Choose Clip > Speed/Duration.

Figure 7.74 In the Speed/Duration dialog box, make sure the chain icon shows that speed and duration values are linked. Enter a value for the speed, and check the other options you want.

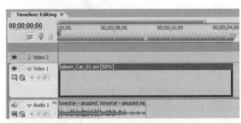

Figure 7.75 The clip's speed (and consequently, its duration) changes according to your choices. In this example, the clip's speed is 50 percent, and therefore the clip is twice as long as it was in Figure 7.72.

PLAYING CLIPS AT A DIFFERENT SPEED/IN REVERSE

Figure 7.76 Select the Rate Stretch tool.

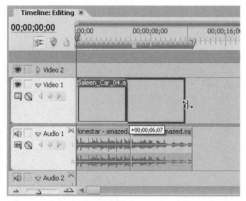

Figure 7.77 With the Rate Stretch tool, drag the edge of a clip in the Timeline panel.

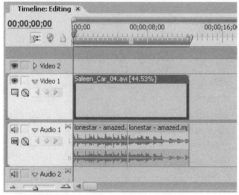

Figure 7.78 In this example, the clip's duration is stretched to match the Out point of the music clip. The clip displays the new frame rate as a percentage, if the clip is wide enough at the current scale of the time ruler to include this information. (Or, you can hover the mouse over the clip to view the speed in a tool tip.)

To change the speed of a clip using the Rate Stretch tool:

1. In the Tools panel, select the Rate Stretch tool ⭲ (**Figure 7.76**).

2. Position the Rate Stretch tool at the edge of a clip in the timeline, and drag the edge (**Figure 7.77**).

   Dragging the edge to shorten the clip increases its speed; dragging the clip to lengthen it decreases its speed. The clip's In and Out points aren't changed, only its speed. A clip set to a speed other than 100 percent display its speed value next to its name (provided the view of the timeline is zoomed-in enough to include it) (**Figure 7.78**).

✔ Tips

- You can also use the Speed/Duration command to change a clip's duration without affecting its speed. Doing so changes the clip's Out point so that the clip becomes the length you specify. Because there are numerous (and better) ways to change a clip's duration, this section doesn't cover this option.

- You can change the speed of an entire sequence by nesting the sequence in another sequence. Because a nested sequence appears as a single linked clip, you can apply the Speed command to it, just as you would to any other clip. You can use this technique to make a program meet a specified running time, provided the speed change isn't too drastic. For more on nesting sequences, see Chapter 6.

Slow-Mo Mojo

The quality of a slow-motion effect is limited by your source material. When shooting film, you can create a slow-motion effect in the camera by *overcranking*. Overcranking sets the frame rate higher than the film's standard frame rate, thereby capturing more images per second. When the film is played back at the normal frame rate, the image appears to move in slow motion. On most video cameras, however, you can't increase the frame rate; instead, you must use a program such as Premiere Pro to create a slow-motion effect by repeating the existing frames. Because overcranked film captures a greater number of unique frames, the slow-motion image appears to be much smoother than a similar image created using a video effect, which merely duplicates frames.

Figure 7.79 Select a clip.

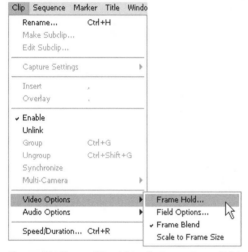

Figure 7.80 Choose Clip > Video Options > Frame Hold.

Creating a Freeze Frame

Using the Frame Hold command, you can make any frame of a clip appear for the entire duration of the clip. Because the held frame is based on the clip's current In point, Out point, or zero marker, you can easily change the held frame. However, you have to be careful not to change the held frame inadvertently.

When you use Frame Hold, you may need to take extra steps to achieve certain effects. For example, if you want the frame to remain longer than the clip's full duration, you'll have to use more than one copy of the clip with the same Frame Hold effect applied. Creating what is commonly known as a *freeze frame*—playing the video at normal speed and then halting the motion and holding on that frame—also requires two copies of the clip. The Out point of the first clip must match the held frame of the second clip. Because a match-frame edit is undetectable, it appears as though a single clip plays and freezes on a frame.

If you find the way the Frame Hold command works too cumbersome, you can use a still image instead. Just export a frame as a still-image file, and then import the still. See Chapter 15 for more about exporting a frame of a sequence as a still image file.

To use the Frame Hold command:

1. Select a clip in the Timeline panel (**Figure 7.79**).

2. Choose Clip > Video Options > Frame Hold (**Figure 7.80**).

   The Frame Hold Options dialog box appears.

   continues on next page

3. Select Hold On, and choose an option from the pull-down menu (**Figure 7.81**):

▲ **In Point:** Displays the clip's current In point frame.

▲ **Out Point:** Displays the clip's current Out point frame.

▲ **Marker 0:** Displays the frame with marker 0, if present.

4. Select other options you want:

▲ **Hold Filters:** Uses any effect settings at the held frame; otherwise, keyframed effects animate.

▲ **Deinterlace:** Removes one field from an interlaced video frame and doubles the remaining field, to remove interlace artifacts (such as combing).

5. Click OK to close the dialog box.

The specified frame appears for the duration of the clip. Changing the specified frame (In point, Out point, or zero marker) changes the held frame.

Figure 7.81 In the Frame Hold Options dialog box, select Hold On, and choose the frame you want to hold. Specify other options you want, and click OK.

✔ Tips

■ Speed changes, freeze frames, and other effects can sometimes result in *field artifacts*—defects in the image caused by the way that video fields (the alternating lines of every frame) are processed. Deinterlacing removes a field and, consequently, field artifacts.

■ If the freeze frame you want consists of more than one clip—the result of transparency and compositing techniques—you must either export the frame of the sequence as a still image or nest the sequence and apply the Frame Hold command to it.

REFINING THE SEQUENCE

After you assemble a rough cut, you can refine it by making adjustments to the In and Out points of the clips in the sequence—a process known as *trimming*. Although you already know several ways to trim clips in the sequence, the techniques in this chapter will expand your repertoire.

Just as you assembled the sequence using a combination of overlay, insert, lift, and extract edits, you can rearrange and refine the clips in a sequence using comparable techniques, this time by dragging the sequence's clips in the Timeline panel. You'll also learn various other ways to fine-tune edit points in the sequence, both by manipulating clips directly in the Timeline and by using a panel optimized for trimming edits, called (appropriately enough) the Trim panel. In addition, this chapter covers techniques that deal with the connection between the audio and video components of linked clips. You'll learn how to trim linked audio and video separately to accomplish a common editing technique known as a *split edit*, or *L-cut*. You'll also find out how to break the link between video and audio so you can handle each component separately and, conversely, how to create a link between previously unrelated video and audio clips. And should linked video and audio inadvertently shift out of their synchronized relationship, you'll be able to detect and correct the problem.

Using the Snapping Feature

When you move clips in the timeline, you usually want to align them precisely. In a sequence of clips in a single track, alignment generally isn't a problem: You can easily drag clips to butt up against one another without overlaying another clip or leaving a gap. At times, however, aligning clips isn't as straightforward. You may want a title in video track 2 to start right after the clip in track 1 ends, for example. When you're placing a sound effect, you may want to align a marker in a video clip with a marker in an audio clip. Or you may want to move a clip to exactly where you placed the current time indicator (CTI).

The timeline provides an easy way to align clips through a feature called *snapping*. When you activate snapping, clips behave as though they're magnetized; they tend to snap to the edge of another clip, to a marker, and to the CTI. A vertical line with black arrows, or *snap line*, confirms that elements are flush (**Figure 8.1**). Snapping also works when you're trimming clips in the timeline.

A red snap line indicates that the frame division used by the clip's edge (In or Out point) doesn't match the frame division used in the timeline. In other words, one is based on audio samples, and the other is based on video frames For example, when the timeline is set to *audio units*, it's possible to cut or trim an audio clip to a point that doesn't coincide with a frame boundary. If you then attempt to snap one audio clip to another while the ruler is set to show frame divisions, the clip aligns with the frame boundary instead of the sample boundary— and leaves a gap in the audio track. The red snap line may also appear when you drag clips to the work area In and Out points, sequence markers, and sequence In and Out points (**Figure 8.2**).

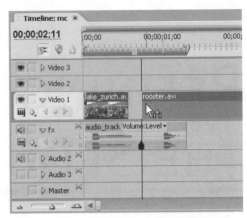

Figure 8.1 When snapping is on, a vertical line appears when clips are aligned with edges, markers, or the CTI.

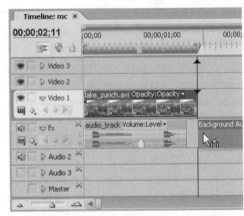

Figure 8.2 Here, the audio clip's Out point is sample-based, but the time ruler is set to count video frames. The snap line appears red, and the clips won't align.

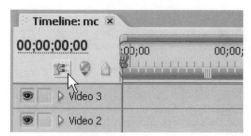

Figure 8.3 In the Timeline panel, click the Snap button (with the magnet icon) to toggle it on and off.

(For more about setting audio edit marks based on audio units, see Chapter 6, "Creating a Sequence"; for more about specifying the time ruler's counting method, see Chapter 7, "Editing in the Timeline.")

When snapping is off, clips move smoothly past one another as you drag them in the timeline. Because snapping is so convenient, you'll probably leave it on most of the time.

To toggle snapping on and off:

◆ At the top left of the Timeline panel, click the Snap button ⊞ to toggle snapping on and off (**Figure 8.3**).

✔ Tips

■ When snapping is on, it's easy to use clip markers to cut video to the beat of music or to sync sound effects to video.

■ Occasionally, several edges may be so close together that snapping makes it difficult to place the clip properly. In these infrequent cases, you should zoom in to the timeline so that competing edges appear farther apart. Alternatively, you can turn off snapping and disable its magnetic effect.

■ By default, you can toggle snapping by pressing the S key. This feature works even while you're dragging a clip.

USING THE SNAPPING FEATURE

Editing by Dragging

You can move clips in the timeline much as you rearrange clips of film: You can drag and move each clip almost as though it were a physical object. But, obviously, clips aren't bits of celluloid, so they aren't constrained by the laws of the physical world. In Premiere Pro, you aren't limited to rearranging clips like so many building blocks. Moving a clip from its current position performs a lift or extract edit; placing it somewhere new performs an overlay or insert edit. (For an explanation of overlay, insert, lift, and extract edits, see Chapter 6.)

To perform edits by dragging, you need to learn a simple set of *keyboard modifiers*, keys you press to toggle editing functions. You'll find that these modifiers work consistently throughout Premiere Pro—in fact, you've already applied them in earlier chapters.

Lift and overlay edits are accomplished by dragging and dropping. Add the Ctrl key to perform an extract or insert edit (**Figures 8.4–8.8**). Add Ctrl+Alt to perform an insert edit that shifts only clips in the destination tracks. The Ctrl+Alt combination is also called a *rearrange edit* or *recycle edit*; it offers a quick and easy way to swap the position of clips in a sequence.

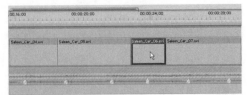

Figure 8.4 This figure shows the sequence before the edit. The selected clip (Saleen_car_o6) will be moved back in time.

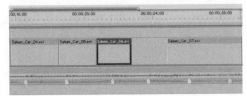

Figure 8.5 The selection you made in Figure 8.4 has been lifted and dropped into its new position using an overlay edit.

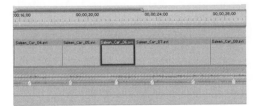

Figure 8.6 Here the selection has been extracted and overlaid...

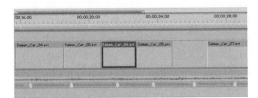

Figure 8.7 ...lifted and inserted...

Figure 8.8 ...and, finally, extracted and inserted. In these examples, the audio track containing the soundtrack is locked to make extract edits possible (see the sidebar "Extraction Exception").

Table 8.1

FUNCTION	ACTION	ICON
Editing by Dragging		
Lift	Drag	No icon
Extract	Ctrl+click+drag	
Overlay	Drop	
Insert	Ctrl+drop	
Rearrange/Recycle	Ctrl+Alt+drop	

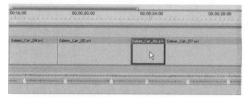

Figure 8.9 Select the clips you want to move. You must make a selection first if you want to move multiple clips at once.

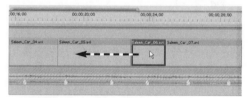

Figure 8.10 Click and then drag a selection to lift it from its original position.

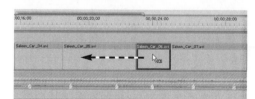

Figure 8.11 Ctrl+click, and then drag a selection to extract it. Note the extract icon and the pattern of slashes in audio 1, indicating that it's locked.

As you discovered in Chapter 6, an icon associated with each type of edit accompanies the mouse pointer, confirming that you're pressing the correct keys for the edit you want (**Table 8.1**). In addition, the Program Monitor provides helpful visual feedback, displaying the frames involved in the edit as you make it. And when you drag a clip in the timeline, a tool tip tells you how many frames the clip has traveled from its starting point.

As usual, if you want to limit the edit to either the video or audio portion of a linked clip, first Alt+click either the video or audio portion to select it; then, perform the edit. Also, make sure you lock any tracks you don't want to shift as a result of an insert edit (or, to limit shifting to the destination tracks, use the Ctrl+Alt combo described earlier). Finally, there's one caveat when it comes to extracting; see the sidebar "Extraction Exception," later in this chapter.

To perform an edit by dragging:

1. In the Timeline panel, select one or more clips that you want to move (**Figure 8.9**).

   Alt+click the video or audio portion of a linked clip to affect only that part of the clip.

2. *Do one of the following:*
   - ▲ To lift the selection, click it and drag (**Figure 8.10**).
   - ▲ To extract the selection, Ctrl+click the selection before dragging it (**Figure 8.11**).

continues on next page

EDITING BY DRAGGING

3. Drag the clip to its new position, using the visual feedback in the Program Monitor as a reference (**Figure 8.12**).

You don't have to hold down any modifier keys as you drag.

4. *Do one of the following:*

▲ To overlay the selection, drop the clip at any point in an appropriate track (**Figure 8.13**).

▲ To insert the selection, Ctrl+drop the clip at any point in an appropriate track (**Figure 8.14**).

The selection is repositioned according to the methods you used. Insert edits shift all material in unlocked tracks by the duration of the selection, splitting clips if necessary (refer to Figures 8.4 through 8.8).

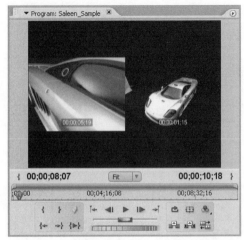

Figure 8.12 The Program Monitor helps you position the clip by showing the frame preceding the selection on the left and the frame after the selection on the right.

Figure 8.13 Dropping the selection overlays it, as the icon indicates.

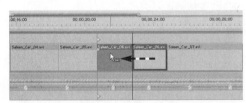

Figure 8.14 Pressing Ctrl as you drop the selection inserts it in the new location. Again, note the icon and the pattern of slashes in the audio track, indicating that it's locked to prevent it from being split at the edit point.

EDITING BY DRAGGING

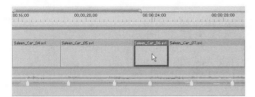

Figure 8.15 Select the clips you want to move.

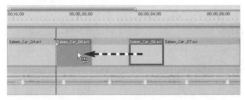

Figure 8.16 Press Ctrl+Alt as you drop the selection in its new location. Note the icon.

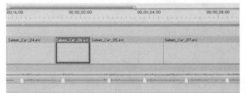

Figure 8.17 The selection is extracted from its original position and inserted into its new position. Clips in other tracks aren't affected, even in unlocked tracks. This figure illustrates how you can use a recycle edit to quickly exchange the order of clips—in this case, shots 5 and 6.

To perform a recycle edit:

1. In the Timeline panel, select one or more clips that you want to move (**Figure 8.15**).

   Alt+click the video or audio portion of a linked clip to affect only that part of the clip.

2. Click and drag the selection to its new position, using the visual feedback in the Program Monitor as a reference.

   You don't have to use a keyboard modifier until you're ready to drop the selection.

3. Press Ctrl+Alt so that the recycle icon appears, and then drop the selection (**Figure 8.16**).

   The selection is extracted from its original position and inserted into its new position (**Figure 8.17**). The edit affects only material in the destination tracks. Because the extracted material and the inserted material are of equal duration, the total duration of the sequence remains the same.

✔ Tips

- You can change keyboard modifiers as you drag; just make sure you have the correct combination before you drop the clip.

- Versions of Premiere prior to Premiere Pro permitted much more limited building-block editing in the timeline. Users upgrading to Premiere Pro will quickly discover that its full-featured drag-and-drop editing model is superior to the older editing model.

EDITING BY DRAGGING

Extraction Exception

Whereas inserting a clip splits clips in all unlocked tracks and shifts subsequent material forward, extracting a clip *does not* extract material in other tracks and shift subsequent material back.

A rearrange edit lets you extract-insert in the destination tracks only. Similarly, you can extract-overlay, but only if other tracks are empty, or if you first lock other tracks—otherwise, the edit works like a lift-overlay (**Figures 8.18–8.20**). To extract material from all tracks, you must perform additional edits, use different editing methods, or both.

The corollary to this behavior is that locking other tracks enables an extract edit but disables an insert edit from shifting clips in all tracks. Conversely, leaving other tracks unlocked disables an extract edit but enables insert edits to shift clips in all tracks.

Because there are plenty of ways to edit the clips in a sequence, this idiosyncrasy doesn't pose an unsolvable problem. Even so, many editors expect extract edits to work like the inverse of insert edits and would welcome more consistent behavior in a future release of Premiere Pro.

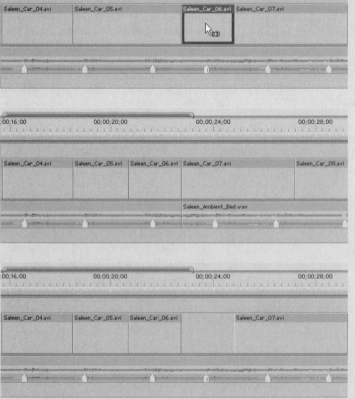

Figure 8.18 This example is similar to the extract-overlay edit shown in Figures 8.4 and 8.6 except that in this figure, the audio track is left unlocked, which prevents an extract edit from working.

Figure 8.19 If you could drag-extract across all tracks, the edit would look like this. (Note that the portion of the audio clip containing marker number 1 has been extracted.)

Figure 8.20 Instead, the audio clip prevents the extract edit from working, resulting in a lift edit.

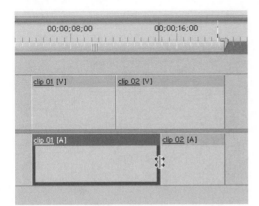

Figure 8.21 You can trim clips in the timeline by dragging with the mouse...

Figure 8.22 ...or you can trim clips using the Trim panel.

✔ Tips

- Extending the duration of a clip is often referred to as *trimming out* the In or Out point; reducing the clip's duration is called *trimming in*.

- Because the Timeline panel represents clips graphically, a clip's In and Out points are also called *edges*. The beginning of a clip is also known as the *head*, and the end is also known as the *tail*.

Choosing a Trimming Method

Making an adjustment to a clip's In or Out point—particularly a small adjustment—is called *trimming*. You can trim a clip by manipulating it directly in the timeline or by using the Trim panel. Although you can use either method to perform some editing tasks, each has unique features.

Trimming in the timeline relies on the mouse to move the edges of a sequence's clips, thereby changing their In or Out point (**Figure 8.21**). By selecting various tools, you can perform specialized trimming tasks known as *ripple edits*, *rolling edits*, and *simple trimming*. You can also *slip* or *slide* clips—something you can't accomplish in the Trim panel.

Like all timeline editing, trimming in the timeline is graphically clear and intuitive. The precision of the edit, however, depends partly on the detail of your view of the timeline. Also, this kind of trimming doesn't permit you to preview the changes before you make them final.

Alternatively, you can open the Trim panel, designed for trimming clips in the sequence (**Figure 8.22**). Like trimming in the timeline, trimming in the Trim panel lets you perform ripple edits and rolling edits. Although using the Trim panel isn't as intuitive as editing directly in the timeline, the Trim panel always gives you precise control. Trim view also provides a large view of the edit as you make adjustments and allows you to preview the changes.

Whether you trim in the timeline or in the Trim panel, you can't extend a clip beyond the limits of its source media. When a clip's edge reaches the end of the source media, the top corner of that edge appears curved.

The following sections explain trimming techniques, first in the timeline and then in the Trim panel.

Trimming Clips in the Timeline

To perform simple trimming in the timeline, you don't need to select a special tool. The default tool, the Selection tool, automatically switches to a trim tool when you position it at a clip edge in the timeline.

Simple trimming affects only one edge of a single clip and doesn't affect adjacent clips. Trimming a clip in this way doesn't shift subsequent clips in time, nor does it allow you to extend the clip to overlay an adjacent clip. (You'll learn other techniques to accomplish these tasks later in this chapter.) In other words, shortening a clip leaves empty space behind; you can extend a clip only up to the edge of an adjacent clip (or to the beginning of the time ruler, or to the limit of the clip's source media).

The Program Monitor displays the edge frame as you trim. To gain more precise control, you can zoom in to the sequence before you start trimming.

To trim a clip in the timeline:

1. Using the Selection tool, *do one of the following:*
   ▲ To trim the In point, position the pointer on the left edge of a clip in the timeline.
   The pointer becomes the Trim Head tool (**Figure 8.23**).
   ▲ To trim the Out point, position the pointer on the right edge of a clip in the timeline.
   The pointer becomes the Trim Tail tool (**Figure 8.24**).

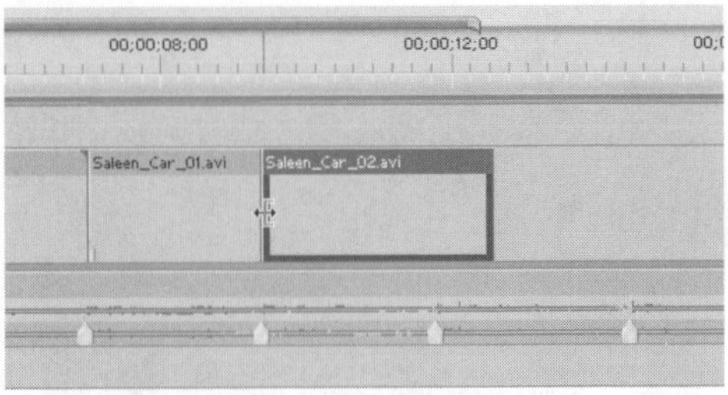

Figure 8.23 Position the mouse at the left edge of the clip to trim its In point, or head...

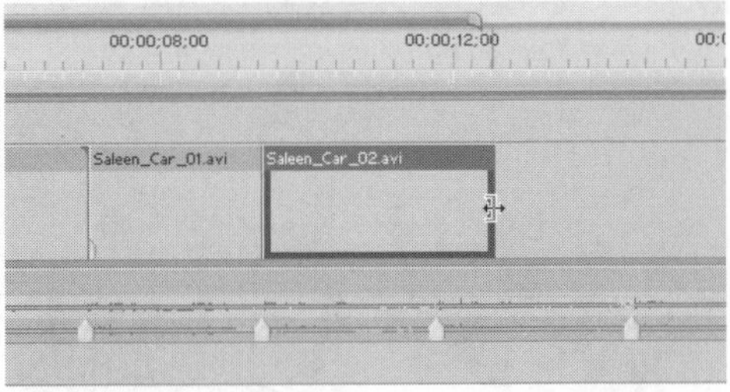

Figure 8.24 ...or position the mouse at the right edge to trim the Out point, or tail.

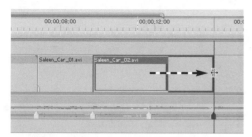

Figure 8.25 Drag to shorten (trim in) or lengthen (trim out) the clip. In this figure, the clip's Out point is being dragged to the right to extend the clip's duration.

2. Drag to the left or right to change the clip's In or Out point (**Figure 8.25**).

The Program Monitor displays the edge frame (In point or Out point) as you adjust it.

When you release the mouse button, the clip's In or Out point changes.

✔ Tips

■ If snapping is on, edges snap to other edges, markers, or the CTI as you trim. This setting is often advantageous, but if it prevents you from trimming to the frame you want, turn off snapping. (See "Using the Snapping Feature," earlier in this chapter.)

■ When you place the mouse pointer near the edge of short clips that don't have adjacent clips in the timeline, the pointer changes to the trim icon. This makes it easier to work with short clips without zooming in.

■ If you've internalized the pattern of keyboard modifiers, you've already guessed that pressing Ctrl changes the trimming tool to a ripple edit tool, which makes trimming work like an extract or insert edit (depending on which way you're trimming). Ripple editing is covered in the next section.

Making Ripple and Rolling Edits

Whereas the basic trimming method affects only a single clip, ripple edits and rolling edits affect the cut point between clips. You might think of ripple and rolling edits as the trimming equivalents of insert and overlay edits, respectively. You can make rolling edits or ripple edits by using tools in the Timeline panel or by using the Trim panel.

In a *ripple edit,* you change the duration of one clip but don't affect the duration of the adjacent clips. After you ripple-edit the edge of a clip, all subsequent clips shift in the timeline to compensate for the change, in a ripple effect. Therefore, the total length of the sequence changes.

In a *rolling edit,* you change the Out point of one clip while you change the In point of the adjacent clip. Put another way, you make one clip shorter while you make the adjacent clip longer; one clip rolls out while the other rolls in. Because both edges are trimmed by the same amount, the total length of the sequence remains the same.

The Program Monitor displays the frames of the changed cut as you perform a ripple or rolling edit.

✔ Tip

■ Because overlay edits are the default (and don't require a keyboard modifier), earlier sections covered overlay edits first and then insert edits. Technically, rolling edits and slide edits are derived from overlay edits; ripple edits and slip edits are descended from insert edits. Even so, the following sections cover the insert family first and then the overlay family—*ripple and roll* and *slip and slide* are catchier and easier to remember than saying them the other way around.

Figure 8.26 Select the Ripple Edit tool.

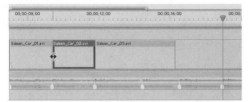

Figure 8.27 Position the mouse over a clip's left edge to ripple-edit its In point...

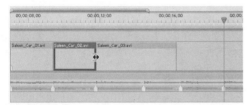

Figure 8.28 ...or position the mouse over a clip's right edge to ripple-edit its Out point.

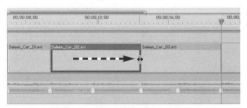

Figure 8.29 In this example, a ripple edit has been used to extend the duration of the clip and shift subsequent clips later in time.

To perform a ripple edit in the timeline:

1. In the Tools panel, select the Ripple Edit tool ⬌ (**Figure 8.26**).

2. *Do one of the following:*

   ▲ To ripple-edit an In point, position the mouse over the left edge (In point) of a clip in the timeline.

   The pointer becomes the Ripple Edit In tool ⬌ (**Figure 8.27**).

   ▲ To ripple-edit an Out point, position the mouse over the right edge (Out point) of a clip in the timeline.

   The pointer becomes the Ripple Edit Out tool ⬌ (**Figure 8.28**).

3. Drag to the left or right to trim the clip's edge.

   The subsequent clips shift in the timeline by the number of frames you trimmed (**Figure 8.29**).

To perform a rolling edit in the timeline:

1. In the Tools panel, select the Rolling Edit tool 〓 (**Figure 8.30**).

2. Position the pointer between the two adjacent clips you want to change.

   The pointer becomes the Rolling Edit tool ‡‡ (**Figure 8.31**). Blank space in the track can also act as one of the clips, but this method is then functionally equivalent to using the basic trimming method.

3. Drag to the left or right to trim the Out point of the first clip and the In point of the second clip by the same number of frames (**Figure 8.32**).

   The Program Monitor displays the edge frames as you perform the rolling edit.

✔ Tips

- You can use a rolling edit to adjust the point at which you split a clip with the razor. If you weren't precise when you split the clip, use the Rolling Edit tool to move the cut point to the left or right.

- You can make a rolling or ripple edit between a clip and an empty space (or gap) in the track. The gap will function like another clip.

Figure 8.30 Select the Rolling Edit tool.

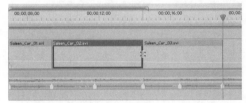

Figure 8.31 Position the mouse between two clips so that the rolling-edit icon appears.

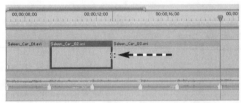

Figure 8.32 A rolling edit trims the Out point of the first clip and the In point of the second clip by the same amount, effectively moving the edit point. In this example, the cut from Figure 8.31 has been moved back in time.

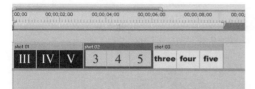

Figure 8.33 Notice how the frames of the center clip look before a slip edit. This figure uses numbers to represent image frames and better illustrate the effect.

Figure 8.34 Dragging the center clip with the Slip Edit tool changes its In and Out points simultaneously, maintaining its duration.

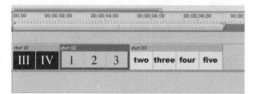

Figure 8.35 A slide edit retains the In and Out points of the center clip while changing the In point of the preceding clip and the In point of the following clip.

Making Slip and Slide Edits

When you have three clips side by side in the timeline, you can perform specialized editing techniques called slip edits and slide edits. Slip and slide edits can be described as ways to adjust two edit points simultaneously; but they're much easier to understand visually, by watching them in action in the Timeline panel. This may explain why these edits can be accomplished only in the Timeline panel and not in the Trim panel.

In a *slip edit,* you change both the In point and the Out point of a clip at the same time without altering the adjacent clips. It's as if you're viewing part of the clip through a space between the two other clips; when you slip the center clip back and forth, you get to see a different part (**Figures 8.33** and **8.34**).

In a *slide edit,* the clip's In and Out points remain the same as you shift the clip in the timeline. When you drag, or slide, the clip to the left, the preceding clip gets shorter, and the following clip gets longer. When you slide the clip to the right, the preceding clip gets longer, and the following clip gets shorter (**Figure 8.35**).

MAKING SLIP AND SLIDE EDITS

To slip a clip:

1. In the Tools panel, select the Slip Edit tool ⊢⊣ (**Figure 8.36**).

2. Position the pointer on a clip that's between two other clips in a track of the timeline.

   The mouse pointer changes to the slip edit icon ⊢⊣.

3. Drag left or right to change the clip's In and Out points without changing the clip's duration or position in the timeline (**Figure 8.37**).

   The Program Monitor displays the frames at the edit points of the slip edit and reports the number of frames by which you're shifting the clip (**Figure 8.38**).

Figure 8.36 Select the Slip Edit tool.

Figure 8.37 Drag a clip positioned between two clips to perform a slide edit.

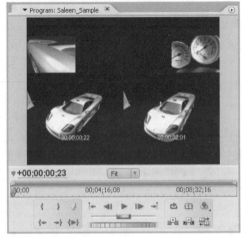

Figure 8.38 The Program Monitor displays the frames affected by the slip edit.

Figure 8.39 Select the Slide Edit tool.

Figure 8.40 Drag a clip positioned between two clips to perform a slide edit.

Figure 8.41 The Program Monitor displays the frames affected by the slide edit.

To slide a clip:

1. In the Tools panel, select the Slide Edit tool ⬌ (**Figure 8.39**).

2. Position the pointer on a clip that's between two other clips in the timeline.

   The pointer changes to the slide edit icon ⬌.

3. Drag right or left to shift the clip in the timeline (**Figure 8.40**).

   The Program Monitor displays the frames at the edit points of the slide edit and reports the number of frames by which you're shifting the clip (**Figure 8.41**).

Using the Trim Panel

To some extent, the current scale of the time ruler determines the precision of the edits you make in the Timeline panel: The closer you're zoomed in, the easier it is to make precise adjustments. When your work is focused on fine-tuning edits, however, you should take advantage of a panel optimized for trimming tasks: the aptly named Trim panel. The Trim panel's two views may remind you of the Monitor panels. But instead of a showing a source and a sequence, the Trim panel shows two adjacent clips in the sequence.

The Out point of the first clip appears on the left; the In point of the second clip appears on the right. An array of controls allows you to perform precise ripple and rolling edits (**Figure 8.42**).

Although you can perform the same edits in the timeline, the Trim panel has several unique advantages. In the Trim panel, you can see both sides of the edit in a large viewer and trim them with numerical precision. Also, the Trim panel lets you play back the adjusted edit before you finalize it.

Outgoing clip's (clip before the cut) last frame   *Incoming clip's (clip after the cut) first frame*

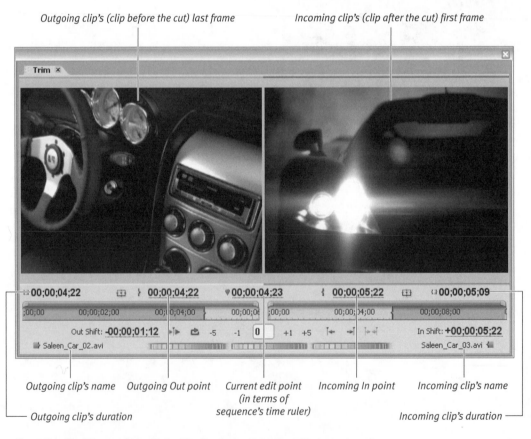

Outgoing clip's name   Outgoing Out point   Current edit point   Incoming In point   Incoming clip's name
(in terms of
sequence's time ruler)
Outgoing clip's duration   *Incoming clip's duration*

Figure 8.42 The Trim panel is optimized for fine-tuning the cut point between two clips.

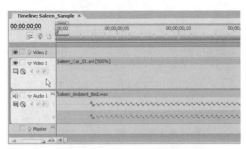

Figure 8.43 Target the tracks containing the clips you want to trim.

Figure 8.44 In the Program Monitor, click the Trim button.

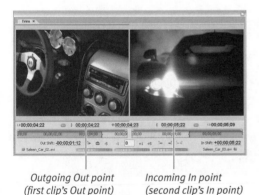

Outgoing Out point
(first clip's Out point)

Incoming In point
(second clip's In point)

Figure 8.45 The Trim panel opens. The frame to the left of the edit point appears on the left; the frame to the right of the edit point appears on the right.

To prepare to edit in the Trim panel:

1. In the Timeline panel, specify the target tracks by clicking the tracks' header areas.

   By default, the header areas of targeted tracks appear lighter than those of other tracks (**Figure 8.43**).

2. Cue the CTI to an edit point by *doing one of the following:*

   ▲ In the Timeline panel, position the edit line (the program's current time) on or before the cut you want to trim, and open the Trim panel.

   If the edit line isn't positioned on a cut point, the Trim panel cues to the next cut in the timeline.

   ▲ In the Trim panel, click the Previous Edit button ⌊← or the Next Edit button →⌋.

   If you alter an edit in the Trim panel, the changes are finalized by cueing to another cut point.

3. To open the Trim panel, *do one of the following:*

   ▲ In the Program Monitor, click the Trim button ▦ (**Figure 8.44**).

   ▲ Press Ctrl+T.

   The Trim panel opens (**Figure 8.45**). In a typical editing workspace, the Trim panel opens directly over the Monitor panels.

To perform a ripple edit numerically in the Trim panel:

1. In the Trim panel, *do one of the following:*

   ▲ To trim the first clip's Out point, click the image on the left (**Figure 8.46**).

   ▲ To trim the In point of the second clip, click the image on the right.

   Blue bars appear above and below the active image.

2. To trim frames in the active view, *do one of the following:*

   ▲ Click the Trim Back One Frame button ⏴ to trim one frame to the left (earlier in time).

   ▲ Click the Trim Back by Large Trim Offset button ⁻⁵ to trim several frames to the left (earlier in time).

   ▲ Click the Trim Forward One Frame button ⁺¹ to trim one frame to the right (later in time).

   ▲ Click the Trim Forward by Large Trim Offset button ⁺⁵ to trim several frames to the right (later in time).

   ▲ Click the Out Shift or In Shift time display, type a relative or absolute time to trim that view, and press Enter.

   As you trim frames, the number of trimmed frames appears in the Out Shift field or the In Shift field. Trimming to the left subtracts from an Out point or adds to an In point. Trimming to the right adds to an Out point or subtracts from an In point. You can see the effects in the timeline.

Blue bar indicates active view ⎯

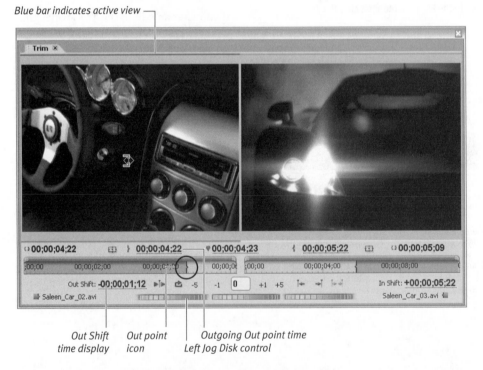

Out Shift   Out point   Outgoing Out point time
time display   icon   Left Jog Disk control

Figure 8.46 Click a view's image to make it active for ripple editing with numerical trim buttons, or drag its image or other controls to apply a ripple edit. This figure shows a ripple edit being applied to the left view (Out point of the first clip); use corresponding controls to ripple-edit the right view (In point of the second clip).

To perform a ripple edit in the Trim panel by dragging:

◆ In the Trim panel, *do one of the following:*

▲ Position the mouse pointer in the view you want to trim so that a ripple-edit icon (◀ or ▶) appears; then, drag left or right.

▲ Drag the Jog Disk control below the view you want to trim.

▲ Drag the Out point icon in the left view's time ruler or the In point icon in the right view's time ruler.

▲ Drag the Out Shift or In Shift time display left or right.

As you trim frames, the number of trimmed frames appears in the Out Shift field or the In Shift field. Trimming to the left subtracts from an Out point or adds to an In point. Trimming to the right adds to an Out point or subtracts from an In point. You can see the effects in the timeline.

To perform a rolling edit numerically in the Trim panel:

1. In the Trim panel, click between the two views.

   Blue bars appear above and below both views.

2. To trim frames in both views, *do one of the following:*

   ▲ Click the Trim Back One Frame button -1 to trim one frame to the left.

   ▲ Click the Trim Back by Large Trim Offset button -5 to trim several frames to the left.

   ▲ Click the Trim Forward One Frame button +1 to trim one frame to the right.

continues on next page

USING THE TRIM PANEL

▲ Click the Trim Forward by Large Trim Offset button +5 to trim several frames to the right.

▲ Highlight the roll edit display, type a positive number to move the edit forward in time or a negative number to move the edit back in time, and then press Enter.

▲ Click the Edit Point Position time display (the center time display), type a relative or absolute time to move the edit in time, and then press Enter.

As you trim frames, the number of trimmed frames appears in the Out Shift and In Shift fields. A rolling edit moves both the In Shift and Out Shift values by the same amount (**Figure 8.47**). Trimming to the left moves the cut earlier in time; trimming to the right moves the cut later in time. You can see your changes in the timeline.

To perform a rolling edit in the Trim panel by dragging:

◆ In the Trim panel, *do one of the following:*

▲ Place the pointer between the two views so that the pointer becomes the rolling-edit icon ⇹, and then drag left or right.

▲ Drag the Edit Point Position time display to the left or right.

▲ Drag the center Jog Disk control left or right.

As you trim frames, the number of trimmed frames appears in the Out Shift and In Shift fields. A rolling edit moves both the In Shift and Out Shift values by the same amount. Trimming to the left moves the cut earlier in time; trimming to the right moves the cut later in time. You can see your changes in the timeline.

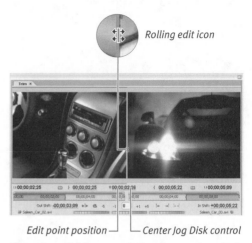

Rolling edit icon

Edit point position ⎯ ⎿ *Center Jog Disk control*

Figure 8.47 Click between the images to activate both views and apply a rolling edit using numerical trim buttons. You can also drag between the views or use the center trimming controls to apply a rolling edit.

✔ Tips

■ By default, the multiframe trim buttons (-5 and +5) trim 5 frames or 100 audio samples. However, you can change this amount by choosing Edit > Preferences > Trim and entering a new value for the large trim offset.

■ In the Trim panel, you can switch between ripple and rolling edits before you apply the edit.

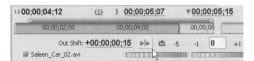

Figure 8.48 Clicking the Play button plays the edit.

Previewing and Applying Edits in the Trim panel

After you've made your adjustments in the Trim panel, you can play them back—complete with audio and transitions—before you finalize your changes. After you look at your handiwork, you can use the Previous Edit or Next Edit button to trim other edits, or you can close the Trim panel and resume other editing tasks. If you don't like what you've done, you can undo your actions as usual. Using the Undo command closes the Trim panel and cancels the most recent trim. Choose Undo again or use the History panel to cancel previous edits.

To preview the edit in the Trim panel:

♦ *Do one of the following:*
  ▲ Click the Play Edit button ▶|▶ (**Figure 8.48**).
  ▲ Press the spacebar.
  To loop the edit, click the Loop button 🔁, and click the Play Edit button ▶|▶ or press the spacebar.

  The Trim panel shows a single image and plays a short segment of the sequence that includes the edit. The preroll and postroll times (specified on the General panel of the Preferences dialog box) determine the duration of the segment.

To apply the trimmed edit and trim other edits:

♦ In the Trim panel, *do one of the following:*
  ▲ To trim the next edit in a selected track of the timeline, click the Next Edit button →|.
  ▲ To trim the previous cut in a selected track of the timeline, click the Previous Edit button |←.

  The current frame of the program (CTI) is cued to the next or previous cut, which is displayed in the Trim panel. Trim the cut as usual.

Working with Links

As you learned in earlier chapters, a linked clip contains both video and audio. Although the video and audio portions of the clip appear in different tracks of the timeline, a link between the two portions of the clip helps maintain their synchronized relationship. (See the sidebar "Using Linked Clips," in Chapter 7.)

At times, however, you want to manipulate the two parts of a linked clip separately. For example, you may want to employ a traditional editing technique called the *split edit* (also known as L-cuts and J-cuts). Or you may want to break the link altogether, so you can manipulate the video and audio independently. Sometimes you may want to create a link between audio and video clips that weren't captured together—in film production, for example, the image and sound are recorded separately; after they're digitized, you can create a link to synchronize the two elements in the timeline.

The following sections describe how to manipulate linked clips in the timeline.

Creating Split Edits

In a split edit, or L-cut, the video and audio have different In points or Out points. A dialogue scene serves as a good example. First you see and hear a person talking, with the video and audio in sync. Then you hear the person's voice but see the person being addressed; in this case, the video Out point occurs earlier than the audio Out point, and in the timeline, the video and audio form an L shape—hence the name *L-cut.* (When the situation is reversed, it's sometimes called a *J-cut.*) Split edits are a great way to make your edits feel much smoother. Watch a movie closely, and you'll find that split edits far outnumber *straight cuts,* in which the video and audio share the same In and Out points.

By now, you know numerous ways to create a split edit. The following tasks outline a few ways to create a split edit from a straight cut in the timeline.

To split edit clips in the timeline:

1. In the Tools panel, select the Rolling Edit tool ⚌ (**Figure 8.49**).

2. Position the Rolling Edit tool between two clips in the timeline in either the video or audio track, and Alt+click (**Figure 8.50**).

3. Drag to perform a rolling edit in the audio without editing the corresponding video, or vice versa.

   The In and Out points in the video track now differ from those in the audio track (**Figure 8.51**).

Figure 8.49 Select the Rolling Edit tool.

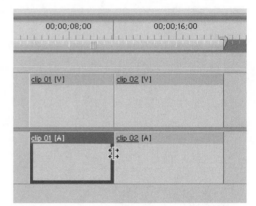

Figure 8.50 Alt+click, and then drag with the Rolling Edit tool...

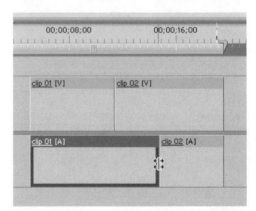

Figure 8.51 ...to create a split edit with linked clips.

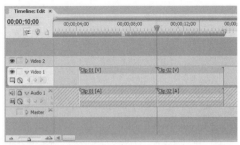

Figure 8.52 In the Timeline panel, target the track that contains the clip you want to trim, and lock the track that contains the linked counterpart.

Figure 8.53 In the Trim panel, perform a rolling edit. This figure shows a rolling edit performed by dragging between the two views.

To split edit clips using the Trim panel:

1. In the Timeline panel, target either a video or an audio track.

2. In the Timeline panel, lock the linked track you don't want to affect (**Figure 8.52**).

   If you targeted video, lock the audio track that contains the linked audio; if you targeted audio, lock the video track that contains the linked video.

3. In the Trim panel, cue the CTI to the cut you want to trim.

4. To use the numerical trim buttons, make sure both views are active by clicking between the views.

   Blue bars appear above and below both views.

5. In the Trim panel, *do one of the following:*

   ▲ Click the Trim Back One Frame button -1 to trim one frame to the left (earlier in time).

   ▲ Click the Trim Back by Large Trim Offset button -5 to trim several frames to the left (earlier in time).

   ▲ Click the Trim Forward One Frame button +1 to trim one frame to the right (later in time).

   ▲ Click the Trim Forward by Large Trim Offset +5 to trim several frames to the right (later in time).

   ▲ Click the Out Shift or In Shift time display, type a relative or absolute time to trim that view, and press Enter.

   ▲ Place the pointer between the two views so that the pointer becomes the rolling-edit icon ‡|‡, and then drag left or right (**Figure 8.53**).

continues on next page

CREATING SPLIT EDITS

▲ Drag the Edit Point Position time display to the left or right.

▲ Drag the center Jog Disk control left or right.

The cut point in the unlocked track changes while the cut point in the locked track remains fixed, creating a split edit (**Figure 8.54**).

✔ Tips

■ Unless you're sure you know what you're doing, don't use a ripple edit to create a split edit. Ripple edits cause clips to shift, and only the selected tracks shift, causing linked clips to lose sync.

■ As you've seen, using the Trim panel to create split edits in linked clips requires what seems to be an unnecessary extra step: locking the track you don't want to trim. Perhaps in future versions, Adobe will streamline the procedure so that specifying a single target track will be sufficient to limit trimming to that track.

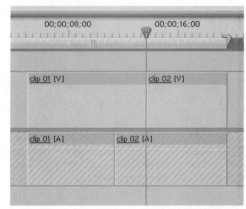

Figure 8.54 In the Timeline panel, you can see that the cut point in the target track changes while the cut point in the locked track remains fixed—creating a split edit.

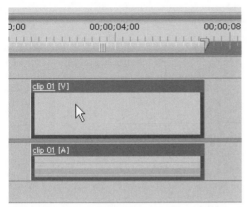

Figure 8.55 Select a linked clip. Note that the name of the video portion contains *[V]* and the name of the audio portion contains *[A]*, and that both names are underlined.

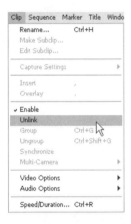

Figure 8.56
Choose Clip > Unlink.

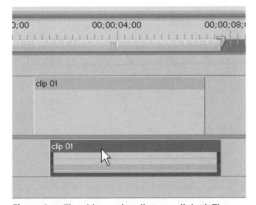

Figure 8.57 The video and audio are unlinked. The names are no longer underlined and don't contain *[V]* or *[A]*.

Breaking and Creating Links

You can break or create links in the timeline, but the links of the source clips and their associated media files on the drive remain unaffected.

To unlink audio and video:

1. In the timeline, select a linked clip.
   Both the video and audio tracks of the linked clip are selected (**Figure 8.55**).

2. Choose Clip > Unlink (**Figure 8.56**).
   The video and audio portions unlink, becoming two independent clips. In the Timeline panel, the names of the clips are no longer underlined, and they don't include *[V]* or *[A]* (**Figure 8.57**).

283

To link a video clip and an audio clip:

1. In the Timeline panel, arrange a video clip and an audio clip to establish their relative positions in time.

2. Select the video clip and the audio clip (**Figure 8.58**).

3. Choose Clip > Link (**Figure 8.59**).

   The video and audio clips behave like a linked clip. In the Timeline panel, the names of the video and audio portions are underlined; [V] is appended to the name of the video portion, and [A] is appended to the name of the audio portion (**Figure 8.60**).

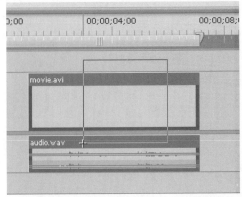

Figure 8.58 Arrange a video clip and an audio clip to establish their synchronized relationship, and then select them.

✔ Tip

- You can use the Link Audio and Video command to sync film footage with audio. Mark the frame in the video where the slate (clapper board) closes, mark the sound of the slate mark in the audio, align the marks, and link the clips. If the shot doesn't contain a slate, you can use some other visible source of a hard, percussive sound as the sync point.

Figure 8.59 Choose Clip > Link.

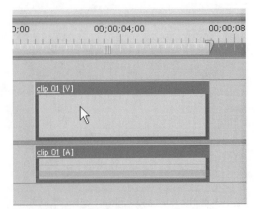

Figure 8.60 In the sequence, the clips look and behave like a single linked clip.

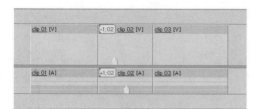

Figure 8. 61 A number indicates the amount that linked video and audio have shifted out of sync.

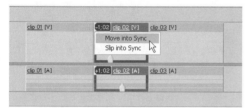

Figure 8.62 Right-click the number, and choose an option.

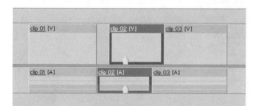

Figure 8.63 When you release the mouse, the clips move into sync.

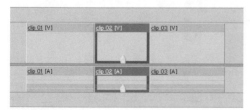

Figure 8.64 When you release the mouse, the clips slip into sync.

Keeping Sync

During the course of editing, you may inadvertently lose sync between linked video and audio. Fortunately, Premiere Pro alerts you when linked clips are out of sync, and it provides a simple way to correct the problem.

To detect loss of sync:

◆ Look at the left edge of linked video and audio.

A timecode number appears at the left edge of linked video and audio that are out of sync (**Figure 8.61**).

To restore sync automatically:

◆ Right-click the out-of-sync time display in either the video or audio portion of the clip, and choose an option (**Figure 8.62**):

▲ **Move into Sync:** Shifts the selected portion of the clip in time to restore sync, overwriting other clips if necessary (**Figure 8.63**).

▲ **Slip into Sync:** Performs a slip edit on the selected portion of the clip to restore sync (**Figure 8.64**).

If the track has space available, the clip shifts in the timeline to resynchronize with the linked portion. If it doesn't, you'll have to create space in the track before resyncing the clips.

For more information about slip edits, see "Making Slip and Slide Edits," earlier in this chapter.

✔ Tip

■ Avoid loss of sync by locking tracks that shouldn't be moved, creating a link between clips that require a synchronized relationship, and using clip markers as sync marks that you can use to check alignment visually. Finally, when you're creating a split edit, use a rolling edit rather than a ripple edit.

Finding Source Clips

As you edit in the timeline, you may want to reexamine the source of a clip in a sequence. The source clip may contain another take of the shot or other footage you want to use, for example. But as you know, trimming the clip in the timeline would disturb your current edit, and double-clicking the clip in question would allow you to view only the clip instance in the Source Monitor, not the source clip (aka master clip). Fortunately, you can view the source clip associated with a sequence clip quickly and easily, without having to search through your project.

To find a sequence clip's source:

◆ Right-click a clip in the timeline, and choose Reveal in Project from the menu (**Figure 8.65**).

The sequence clip's associated source clip is highlighted in the Project panel (**Figure 8.66**).

Figure 8.65 Right-click a clip, and choose Reveal in Project.

Figure 8.66 The sequence clip's associated source clip appears highlighted in the Project panel.

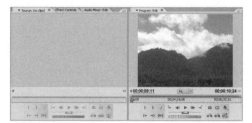

Figure 8.67 Cue the sequence's CTI to the frame you want to match.

Figure 8.68 Pressing T opens the source clip to the matching frame in the Source Monitor.

Finding the Match Frame

Experienced editors may wonder whether Premiere Pro has a *match-frame* feature. This feature not only opens a program clip's associated source clip but also cues the Source Monitor's CTI to the identical frame in the sequence. In other words, by cueing the CTI in the program, you can find the matching frame in the appropriate master clip.

To find a sequence clip's match frame:

1. Cue the sequence to the frame for which you want to find a match frame (**Figure 8.67**).

2. Press T.

   The master clip appears in the Source Monitor (**Figure 8.68**) and is cued to the match frame.

✔ Tip

- After you find the match frame, you can keep the source clip and the sequence synchronized by ganging them together. See "Ganging the Source and Program Monitors," in Chapter 5.

Syncing Up

If clicking the out-of-sync time display isn't a practical way to resynchronize your clips, you can use many other techniques to solve the problem:

- Alt+click to select the video or audio only and then move it into sync.

- Alt+click the video or audio portion of a linked clip with the Slip or Slide tool, and then drag it into sync.

- Use the Track tool to shift all the clips in a track back into sync.

- Insert-edit the proper number of frames, making sure to shift only the out-of-sync track.

- Open the source clip, and edit it into the sequence again

ADDING
TRANSITIONS

In editing, *transition* refers to the way one clip replaces another. Although an instantaneous *cut* is the most basic transition, the term *transition* usually refers to a more gradual change from one clip to another. Adobe Premiere Pro ships with numerous customizable video transitions, including an array of dissolves, wipes, and special effects. You can also transition between audio clips using two types of cross-fade.

You select the transition you want from the *Effects panel*, which lists not only video and audio transitions, but also video and audio filters (including transparency keys) in categorized folders.

Adding a transition is as simple as dragging it to a cut in the Timeline panel. You can even make adjustments to a transition's duration and placement by dragging the transition in the Timeline panel, in much the same way you can move and trim a clip. But to really fine-tune a transition, you use the *Effect Controls panel*. The main area of the Effect Controls panel describes the effect and includes an animated thumbnail demonstration. It also lets you control attributes common to all transitions—duration and placement—as well as settings specific to the particular transition. The Effect Controls panel may also include an area that illustrates the selected transition in an *A/B roll* style of timeline, which depicts the transition between two overlapping clips. This alternative view of a transition can be easier to understand and adjust than the Timeline panel's version.

As you may have guessed, you also use both the Effects panel and Effect Controls panel to add and adjust other types of effects—including motion, transparency, and filters. These techniques are covered in upcoming chapters. This chapter explains how to create and modify transitions, and Chapter 10, "Previewing a Sequence," describes how to render them for playback.

Using the Effects panel

The Effects panel lists and organizes all effects, including audio and video transitions. By default, the Effects panel contains five folders: Presets, Audio Effects, Audio Transitions, Video Effects, and Video Transitions. You can't rename these folders or remove items from them. However, you can add and name custom folders, which can contain copies of your favorite items. You can expand a folder to reveal its contents, but you can't open a folder the way you can open a bin in the Project panel. The Video Transitions folder includes 10 subfolders; the Audio Transitions folder contains 1 subfolder. Video transitions appear as 🗾 icons; audio transitions appear as 🗾 icons.

The number and type of effects and transitions available on the Effects panel are determined by the contents of Premiere Pro's Plug-Ins folder. You can add effects and filters from Adobe and third-party developers by adding plug-in files to the Plug-Ins folder.

To expand and collapse folders:

◆ On the Effects panel, click the triangle next to a folder to expand or collapse it (**Figure 9.1**).

A folder expands to reveal subfolders; a subfolder expands to reveal individual effects or transitions. Double-clicking a folder has no effect.

To create a custom folder:

◆ On the Effects panel, click the New Custom Bin button 🗾 (**Figure 9.2**).

A new custom folder appears on the Effects panel; the folder is named Custom Bin 01 by default (**Figure 9.3**).

Figure 9.1
Click the triangle to expand or collapse a folder.

Figure 9.2
Click the New Custom Bin button.

Figure 9.3
The new bin is named Custom Bin 01 by default.

Figure 9.4
Click the custom folder's name twice to highlight it, and then enter a new name.

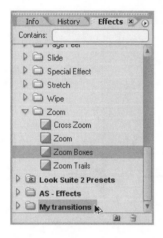

Figure 9.5
Dragging items into a custom folder...

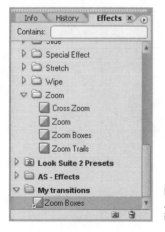

Figure 9.6
...copies them into the folder.

To rename a custom folder:

1. Click the name of the custom folder, and then click again (don't double-click) to highlight the name.

2. Type the name you want (**Figure 9.4**), and press Enter.

   You can rename only custom folders.

To add items to a custom folder:

1. Expand the folders containing the items you want to copy into a custom folder.

2. Select the items you want to copy *by doing one of the following:*

   ▲ Click to select an item.

   ▲ Ctrl+click to add to or subtract from the selection.

   You can't drag a marquee to select items on the Effects panel.

3. Drag the selected items to the custom folder (**Figures 9.5** and **9.6**).

   The selected items appear in the custom folder. Dragging a folder into the custom folder copies all of the folder's contents into the custom folder. A custom folder can contain other custom folders.

USING THE EFFECTS PANEL

To delete custom items:

1. *Do one of the following:*

   ▲ Click to select a custom folder or an item contained in a custom folder.

   ▲ Ctrl+click to add items to or subtract items from your selection.

2. Click the Effects panel's Delete Custom Items button 🗑 (**Figure 9.7**).

   The selected custom items are removed from the Effects panel (**Figure 9.8**).

Finding an item in the Effects panel:

◆ On the Effects panel, in the Contains field, type the name of the item you're looking for (**Figure 9.9**).

   As you type, the panel displays items that match what you type and hides other items. To unsift the list, clear the Contains field.

✔ Tip

■ Even though icons for folders on the Effects panel look like the icons for bins in the Project panel (and the panel includes a Create Custom Bin button), this book refers to effect folders as *folders* rather than *bins*.

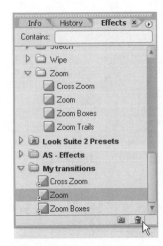

Figure 9.7
Select the items you want to remove from a custom folder, and click the Effects panel's trashcan icon...

Figure 9.8
...to remove the items from the list.

Figure 9.9
As you type the name of the item you're looking for in the Contains field, the list is sifted to show only matching items.

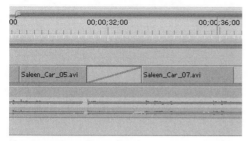

Figure 9.10 In a collapsed track, you can see only the transition's duration...

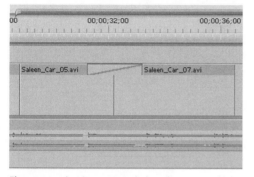

Figure 9.11 ...but in an expanded track, you can also see the transition's position relative to the cut. Neither view shows how much footage each clip has beyond the cut point.

Understanding Transitions

If you're an experienced editor and already know the concepts behind transitions, feel free to skip ahead to the tasks (cut to the chase, as the old editing expression goes). But if you're new to editing—or new to the single-track transition model used in Premiere Pro—the inner workings of transitions can seem a little mysterious at first.

When you cut from one clip to another, the transition is instantaneous. The Out point of the first clip is immediately followed by the In point of the second clip. To switch from one clip to another more gradually, however, transitions must use frames *beyond* the cut point. In other words, the transition must mix some of the frames you previously trimmed away: frames after the first clip's Out point, before the second clip's In point, or, most often, a combination of both. (Remember: because editing in Premiere Pro is nondestructive, the frames you trimmed away are always available for use.)

But in the Timeline panel, these frames are hidden from view. When the track is collapsed, you can see only when the transition begins and ends (**Figure 9.10**). When the track is expanded, you can see the former cut point between the clips and thereby the transition's position relative to the cut (**Figure 9.11**), but you can't tell how much footage lies beyond the cut transition and therefore how much footage is available for making adjustments. For many editors, this layout makes it difficult to plan for the transition beforehand and to adjust it afterward.

Transitions are depicted more explicitly on the Effect Controls panel. In the Effect Controls panel's Timeline view, each clip occupies a separate track—the first in track A, the second in track B. The transition appears between the two clips in its own track (labeled with an effect icon). As usual, the area where the transition overlaps the clips represents the duration of the transition's effect. A vertical line represents the cut point before the transition was applied. But because this view shows each clip in its own track, you can see the otherwise hidden material beyond the cut point—all the available material beyond the first clip's Out point and before the second clip's In point. This view allows you to adjust the transition not only relative to the cut point, but also in terms of the footage available in each clip (**Figure 9.12**).

If there isn't enough footage to create the transition, Premiere Pro repeats the first clip's Out point frame or the second clip's In point frame. Of course, repeating frames results in a freeze-frame effect that you may find unacceptable. You can adjust the transition or trim the clips to avoid repeating frames, which are marked with a pattern of slashes (**Figures 9.13** and **9.14**). (See "Adjusting a Transition's Duration and Alignment," later in this chapter.)

✔ Tip

- Since Premiere Pro 1.5, the Dissolve subfolder has contained a Dip to Black transition. Dip to Black dissolves the first clip to black and then dissolves up from black to reveal the next clip. Previously, you had to apply a Cross Dissolve transition twice or superimpose a black video clip to achieve this common effect.

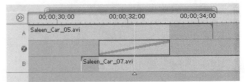

Figure 9.12 Here's the same transition in the Effect Controls panel's timeline view. The A/B roll layout lets you see the footage hidden in the Timeline panel's single-track layout.

Figure 9.13 When there isn't enough footage for the transition, Premiere Pro repeats the edge frames. Premiere Pro marks the area with a pattern of slashes on the transition in the Timeline panel...

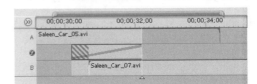

Figure 9.14 ...and in the Effect Controls panel's timeline view.

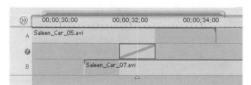

Figure 9.15 When a one-second transition is centered on the cut, it looks like this in the Effect Controls panel.

Figure 9.16 Here's the same transition as in the previous figure, except that it starts on the cut.

Figure 9.17 And here, the transition ends on the cut.

✔ Tip

■ In a typical workflow, transitions and other effects are applied after the main editing tasks are complete. When this is the case, it's a good idea to customize the workspace for the task at hand. Consider rearranging the panels of the interface to emphasize the Program Monitor, Timeline panel, Effects panel, and Effect Controls panel. De-emphasize the Source Monitor and Project panel.

Understanding Transition Duration and Alignment

In the Timeline panel, transitions appear as clip-like objects whose width and position correspond with their duration and alignment (relative to the cut point). Once you add a transition, you can adjust its duration and alignment freely. However, its initial settings are more limited. A transition's initial duration is determined by a default setting you specify; its initial alignment is limited to three options, depending on where you drop it relative to the cut: Center of Cut, Start of Cut, or End of Cut. Understanding these options makes it easier to plan for a transition beforehand and to adjust it afterward:

◆ **Center of Cut:** Centers the transition over the cut so that an equal number of hidden frames on both sides of the edit are used to create the transition. A one-second transition centered on the cut uses 15 frames of footage after the Out point of footage of the first clip and 15 frames before the In point of the second clip (**Figure 9.15**).

◆ **Start of Cut:** Starts the transition at the cut, so that the hidden frames of the first clip are combined with the frames of the second clip that were visible before the transition was applied. Using the same example as before, the transition combines 30 frames of footage after the first clip's Out point (hidden frames) with the first 30 frames of the second clip (**Figure 9.16**).

◆ **End of Cut:** Ends the transition at the cut, so that the hidden frames of the second clip are combined with the frames of the first clip that were visible before you added the transition. Continuing the same example, the transition combines the last 30 frames of the first clip with 30 frames of the footage before the second clip's In point (hidden frames) (**Figure 9.17**).

Setting the Default Transition Duration

Initially, transitions are one second in duration. However, you can specify any default duration for video and audio transitions.

To specify the default duration for transitions:

1. On the Effects panel's menu, choose Default Transition Duration (**Figure 9.18**).

   The General panel of the Preferences dialog box opens.

2. *Do the following* (**Figure 9.19**):

   ▲ For Video Transition Default Duration, enter a value in frames.

   ▲ For Audio Transition Default Duration, enter a value in seconds.

   For audio, you can enter a value to two decimal points.

3. Click OK to close the dialog box.

   From this point on, video and audio transitions will use the durations you specified.

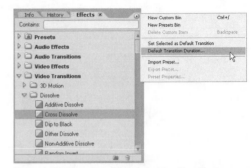

Figure 9.18 Choose Default Transition Duration.

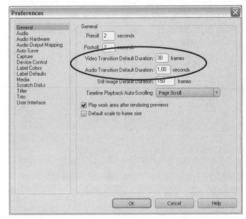

Figure 9.19 On the General panel of the Preferences dialog box, enter a duration for video transitions in frames and a duration for audio transitions in seconds (to two decimal points).

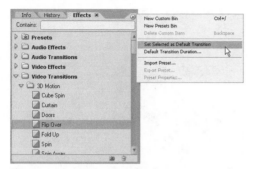

Figure 9.20 Select the transition that you want as the default, and choose Set Selected as Default Transition.

Specifying a Default Transition

If you use a transition frequently, you can set it as the default transition to apply it quickly without having to go to the Effects panel. For more about adding a transition, see the next section, "Applying a Transition."

To specify the default transition:

1. On the Effects panel, select the transition you want to set as the default.

2. On the Effects panel's menu, choose Set Selected as Default Transition (**Figure 9.20**).

   The selected transition becomes the default transition.

✔ Tips

- Although a cross-dissolve transition is the best tool for creating a simple transition from one clip to the next, blending images for longer periods or blending multiple clips is best achieved by using the video fade controls on a superimposed clip. See Chapter 13, "Working with Effects," for more information.

- Most transitions included with Premiere Pro operate along the same lines and use similar settings. However, a few transitions work a little differently from the rest—but they can't all be covered in the limited scope of this book. You should check out the Gradient Map transition and the transitions in the Map and Special Effect subfolders on your own.

Applying a Transition

You can apply a video transition to any cut in a video track, and you can apply any audio transition to any cut in an audio track. Furthermore, video transitions aren't limited to video track 1. Thus, it's possible to layer and composite video tracks, complete with transitions. (See Chapter 13 for more about transparency.)

In addition to adding transitions between clips, you can add a transition to the end of a clip adjacent to an empty area in the track. Doing so automatically aligns the clip using End of Cut and is useful when you want to create an audio fade-out or a video fade-to-black (the empty track acts as silence or black video).

To add a transition:

◆ Drag a transition from the Effects panel to a cut point in the Timeline panel, and position the mouse so that its icon indicates the alignment option you want:

▲ **Center at Cut** ⬚⬚: Centers the transition on the cut so that an equal number of hidden frames from each clip are used (**Figure 9.21**).

▲ **Start at Cut** ⬚⬚ : Aligns the beginning of the transition with the cut (**Figure 9.22**).

▲ **End at Cut** ⬚⬚: Aligns the end of the transition with the cut (**Figure 9.23**).

When you release the mouse, the transition appears over the clips. It uses the alignment you specified and the default duration (**Figure 9.24**).

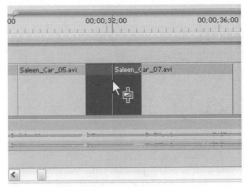

Figure 9.21 You can drop the transition on the center of the cut, as indicated by the icon...

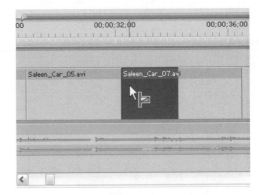

Figure 9.22 ...or at the start of the cut...

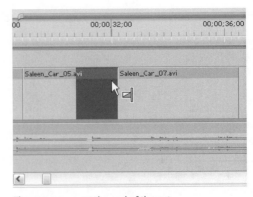

Figure 9.23 ...or at the end of the cut.

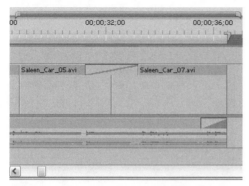

Figure 9.24 In this figure, the new transition is centered on the cut. The cross-dissolve on the audio clip ends on the cut; because the clip is followed by an empty area, the transition functions as an audio fade-out.

To force a Start at Cut or End at Cut transition:

◆ Ctrl+drag a transition from the Effects panel to a cut point in the Timeline panel.

Depending on the side of the cut to which you drag the transition, the icon indicates either of two alignment options: Start at Cut ⌐ or End at Cut ⌐.

To add the default transition:

1. Cue the sequence CTI to a cut point.

The Program Monitor's Go to Previous Edit Point ⌐ and Go to Next Edit Point ⌐ buttons usually offer the quickest way to cue the CTI.

2. With the Monitor panel or the Timeline panel active, press Ctrl+D.

The transition appears over the clips. It uses the alignment you specified and the default duration.

✔ Tips

- You can replace a transition by dropping a new transition on top of the old one.

- The default duration can be applied automatically to a sequence created with the Automate to Timeline feature (explained in Chapter 6, "Creating a Sequence").

- Unlike a clip, a transition in the Timeline panel doesn't include a name, just a diagonal line. Hovering the mouse over a transition reveals the transition's name in a tool tip.

APPLYING A TRANSITION

Using the Effect Controls Panel with Transitions

Although you can adjust a transition directly in the Timeline panel, you need to use the Effect Controls panel to adjust the transition in an A/B layout or to customize the transition's settings. However, because the Effect Controls panel serves many purposes, you must select the transition in the Timeline panel to make its controls appear in the panel.

The Effect Controls panel's main panel contains information about the transition, a thumbnail preview, and controls for adjusting the transition's duration, alignment, and various custom settings. You can also reveal a timeline view, which lets you view and adjust the selected transition in its own timeline using an A/B roll layout. The timeline view's CTI and viewing area bar work just like those in the Monitor panels and in the Timeline panel (see "Using a Monitor's Time Ruler Controls," in Chapter 5, or "Getting Around the Timeline," in Chapter 7).

To view a transition on the Effect Controls panel:

1. *Do either of the following:*
   - ▲ With the Effect Controls panel visible, click a transition in the Timeline panel to select it.
   - ▲ With the Effect Controls panel hidden, double-click a transition in the Timeline panel (**Figure 9.25**).

   The Effect Controls panel displays settings for the selected transition (**Figure 9.26**).

Figure 9.25 Selecting a transition in the Timeline panel...

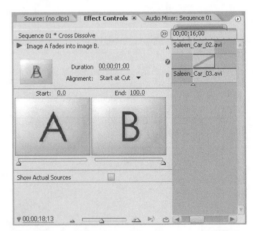

Figure 9.26 ...makes its settings appear on the Effect Controls panel. Double-clicking the transition also opens the Effect Controls panel (or makes the panel the selected tab).

USING EFFECT CONTROLS PANEL W/TRANSITIONS

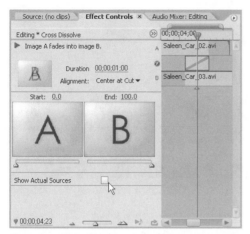

Figure 9.27 Click Show Actual Sources to replace the A and B sample images...

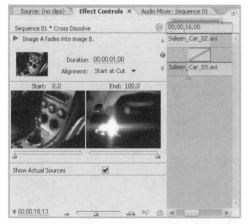

Figure 9.28 ...with the actual footage, including playback.

Figure 9.29 Click the Play button to preview the transition.

2. Adjust the transition *by doing one of the following:*

▲ Use controls on the Effect Controls panel's main panel to adjust the transition's settings.

▲ Use the Effect Controls panel's timeline view to adjust the transition's duration and placement manually or to adjust the cut point between clips.

To show actual sources in thumbnail images:

◆ On the main panel of the Effect Controls panel, select Show Actual Sources (**Figure 9.27**).

When the check box is selected, the A and B sample images are replaced by the clips of the transition, which play back normally (**Figure 9.28**).

To play a thumbnail preview of a transition:

◆ Click the Play button ▶ in the upper-left corner of the Effect Controls panel (next to the transition's description; (**Figure 9.29**).

The Play button toggles to a Stop button. The small thumbnail image demonstrates the transition, including any adjustments you make to the transition's settings. If Show Actual Sources is selected, the A and B sample images are replaced by the clip images.

USING EFFECT CONTROLS PANEL W/TRANSITIONS

To show or hide the Effect Controls panel's timeline view:

◆ In the upper-right corner of the Effect Controls panel's main panel, click the Show/Hide Timeline View button.

When the button's chevrons point left ⊗, the timeline view is concealed (**Figure 9.30**); when the chevrons point right ⊗, the timeline view is visible (**Figure 9.31**).

✔ Tips

■ Typically, you require the Source Monitor primarily during the rough cut; you use the Effect Controls panel in later phases of the editing workflow. Therefore, consider docking the Effect Controls panel into the same frame as the Source Monitor in order to make the most of the workspace.

■ When not all of a transition's customizable settings fit in the available vertical space of the Effect Controls panel, a scrollbar appears. But when the timeline view is visible, the scrollbar appears to the right of the timeline view, not the main panel. If some settings seem to be missing, look for the scrollbar at the far right.

■ As you might expect, you can change the size of the Effects panel's timeline view. Just position the mouse pointer at the border between the panel's main area and the timeline area (so that a width-adjustment tool appears), and then drag left or right.

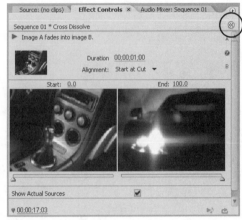

Figure 9.30 Clicking the icon with the chevrons...

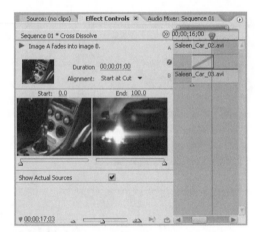

Figure 9.31 ...reveals the Effect Controls panel's timeline view.

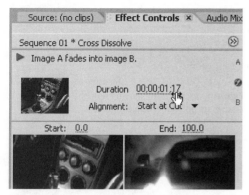

Figure 9.32 You can adjust the transition's duration by changing the Duration value on the Effect Controls panel's main panel.

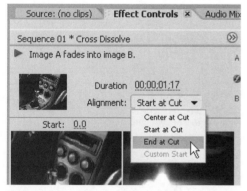

Figure 9.33 You can move the transition by choosing an option from the Alignment drop-down menu.

Adjusting a Transition's Duration and Alignment

Sometimes, a transition's initial duration and alignment work perfectly, and you can move on to other edits. But chances are, you'll want to make small adjustments. You may even need to trim the clips involved in the transition. You can make these adjustments using controls on the Effect Controls panel's main panel. Or you can make manual adjustments by dragging in either the Timeline panel or the Effect Controls panel's timeline view.

To adjust a transition's duration numerically:

◆ On the main panel of the Effect Controls panel, *do one of the following:*

▲ Drag the Duration display to change the value (**Figure 9.32**).

▲ Click the Duration display, type a new duration, and press Enter.

The selected transition reflects the duration you specify in the Timeline panel and in the timeline view of the Effect Controls panel.

To adjust a transition's alignment automatically:

◆ On the main panel of the Effect Controls panel, choose an option from the Alignment drop-down menu (**Figure 9.33**):

▲ **Center at Cut:** Centers the transition on the cut.

▲ **Start at Cut:** Aligns the beginning of the transition with the cut.

▲ **End at Cut:** Aligns the end of the transition with the cut.

Custom Start is dimmed, unless the transition is already positioned at a custom alignment.

To adjust a transition manually:

1. In either the Timeline panel or the Effect Controls panel's timeline view, *do one of the following:*

   ▲ To change the alignment of the transition without changing its duration, position the mouse pointer on the center of the transition, so that the pointer changes into a move transition icon ⊕ (**Figure 9.34**).

   ▲ To change the duration of the transition by changing its starting point, position the mouse on the transition's left edge, so that the pointer changes into the Trim Head tool ⊹ (**Figure 9.35**).

   ▲ To change the duration of the transition by changing where it ends, position the mouse pointer on the transition's right edge, so that the pointer changes into the Trim Tail tool ⊹ (**Figure 9.36**).

   The Trim Head or Trim Tail tool also appears if you position the mouse at the transition's edge in track A or track B.

2. Drag left or right to move or trim the transition.

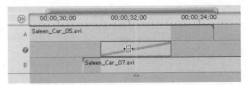

Figure 9.34 Drag the transition from the center to change its position relative to the cut.

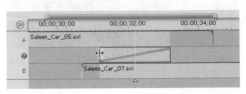

Figure 9.35 You can change the transition's duration by trimming its left edge...

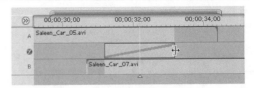

Figure 9.36 ...or by trimming its right edge.

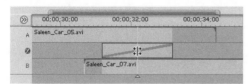

Figure 9.37 You can perform standard edits on the cut point of a transition in the Timeline panel and on the Effect Controls panel. On the Effect Controls panel, drag the white vertical line to apply a rolling edit...

Figure 9.38 ...drag the clip in the A track to ripple-edit its Out point...

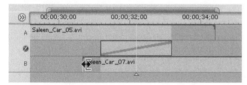

Figure 9.39 ...or drag the clip in the B track to ripple-edit its In point.

To trim clips of a transition in the timeline view:

1. In the Effect Controls panel's timeline view, *do one of the following*:

   ▲ To perform a rolling edit, position the mouse pointer on the white vertical line (that indicates the cut point), so that the pointer becomes the Rolling Edit tool ⁑ (**Figure 9.37**).

   ▲ To ripple-edit the first clip's Out point, position the mouse pointer on the clip in the A track, so that the pointer becomes the Ripple Tail tool ⇥ (**Figure 9.38**).

   ▲ To ripple-edit the first clip's In point, position the mouse pointer on the clip in the B track, so that the pointer becomes the Ripple Head tool ⇤ (**Figure 9.39**).

   If you position the mouse pointer at the edge of the transition, the pointer changes to the Trim Head or Trim Tail tool, which changes the duration of the transition.

2. Drag left or right to trim the clip.

✔ Tip

■ As you make adjustments to a transition, the Program Monitor displays the frames that are affected.

Customizing Transition Settings

Each transition has its own collection of customizable settings. The options available depend on the transition you're modifying. By modifying these settings, you can effectively expand your list of video transitions. You can, for example, set the Wipe transition to wipe in any of eight directions; you can make it hard-edged or soft-edged; and you can add a border of any color or thickness.

As usual, you have to add the transition to a cut first and then select it to modify its settings on the Effect Controls panel.

To set the direction of the transition:

◆ On the Effect Controls panel, click the small arrows, or *edge selectors*, around the transition thumbnail to select the orientation of the transition (**Figure 9.40**).

The movement of the transition, such as the direction of a wipe, progresses in the direction you specify (**Figure 9.41**).

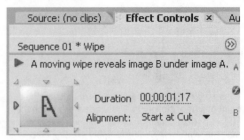

Figure 9.40 Click one of the small arrows to set the direction of a transition. Here, a wipe is set to progress from the right side of the image.

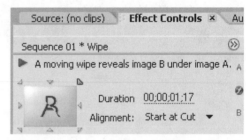

Figure 9.41 Here, the wipe is set to begin from the top-right corner.

To adjust the start and end of the transition:

◆ On the Effect Controls panel, *do one of the following:*

  ▲ Adjust the Start and End values by dragging or by entering a value between 0 and 100.

  ▲ Drag the Start and End sliders under the A and B thumbnail images, respectively (**Figures 9.42** and **9.43**).

  ▲ Shift+drag either slider to set the start and end to the same value.

  A standard transition starts at 0 and ends at 100.

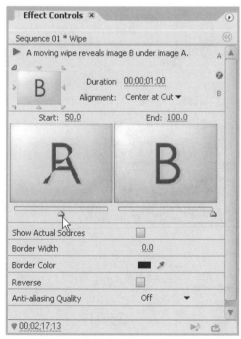

Figure 9.42 Adjust the Start value or drag the corresponding slider to define the initial appearance of the transition.

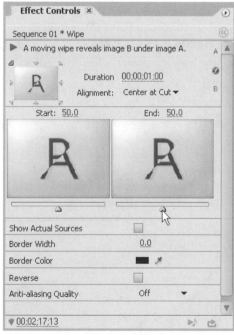

Figure 9.43 Adjust the End value or use the slider to define the transition's final appearance. Instead of wiping from shot A to shot B, this transition is set to show a mix of the two shots for the duration of the transition.

CUSTOMIZING TRANSITION SETTINGS

To reverse a transition:

◆ On the Effect Controls panel, select Reverse.

The transition is reversed. For example, reversing an Iris Round transition makes the iris close to reveal the next shot rather than open (**Figure 9.44**).

✔ Tips

■ You can use the sliders to get a preview of a transition, but make sure you reset the transition to the position you want before you finish.

■ You can't keyframe a transition; you can only set a start state and an end state.

To set the center point of the transition:

◆ On the Effect Controls panel, drag the handle in the Start (A) or End (B) image to set the center point of the transition (**Figures 9.45** and **9.46**).

The handle represents the center of an iris transition, for example.

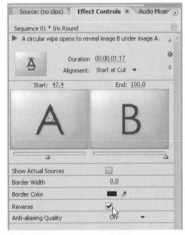

Figure 9.44 Clicking Reverse makes the transition progress in the opposite way. For example, reversing an Iris Round transition makes the iris close to reveal the second shot, rather than open to reveal it.

Figure 9.45 Drag the round handle in the start thumbnail image to set the center point of transitions, such as iris transitions.

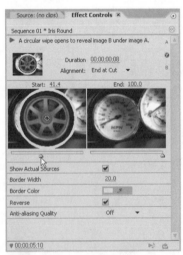

Figure 9.46 Here, the center point, or origin, has been moved slightly to match the center of the wheel. To better illustrate the effect, the Start slider has been moved and a border has been added.

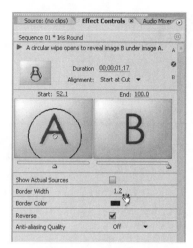

Figure 9.47 When the border width is set to 0, no border appears at the transition's edge (the Start setting has been increased so you can see the edge).

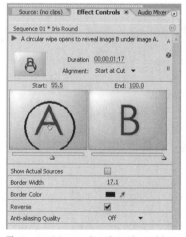

Figure 9.48 Increasing the value adds a border to the transition's edge.

Figure 9.49 Change the color of the border by clicking the color swatch or using the Eyedropper tool.

To set the border thickness:

◆ On the Effect Controls panel, drag the underlined number in the Border Width field, or click it and enter a new value (**Figure 9.47**).

The edges of the transition appear with a border of the thickness you specified (**Figure 9.48**).

To set the border color:

◆ On the Effect Controls panel, in the Border Color field, *do one of the following*:

▲ Click the color swatch to select a color using the color picker (**Figure 9.49**).

▲ Click the Eyedropper tool, and, holding down the mouse button, position the tool over any color on the screen. Release the mouse to set the current color.

The edges of the transition use the border color you specified.

To specify the smoothness of edges:

◆ On the Effect Controls panel, choose an option from the Anti-aliasing Quality drop-down menu (**Figure 9.50**).

Settings range from Off to High. Off applies no anti-aliasing; High applies the maximum amount of smoothing.

✔ Tips

■ To see the border, you have to play the thumbnail preview or the actual transition. You can also set the Start slider to a higher number (such as 50) to help you adjust the border. Make sure you set the Start slider back to 0, though.

■ Border thickness and anti-aliasing can only be approximated in the thumbnail images. The Program Monitor and output television monitor give a much more accurate representation.

To specify custom settings:

◆ On the Effect Controls panel, click the Custom button to define settings specific to that transition (**Figure 9.51**).

You can define the number of slices in the Slash Slide transition, for example (**Figure 9.52**).

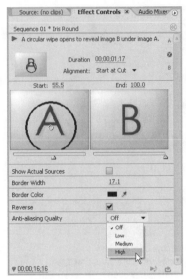

Figure 9.50 Choose an option from the Anti-aliasing Quality drop-down menu.

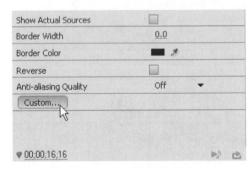

Figure 9.51 Some transitions have additional settings you can access by clicking the Custom button.

Figure 9.52 The Custom button opens a dialog box for the transition's special settings, such as the number of slices in the Slash Slide transition.

CUSTOMIZING TRANSITION SETTINGS

PREVIEWING A SEQUENCE

As you know, you can watch a sequence in the Program Monitor by just clicking its Play button (or the keyboard equivalent). But for the most accurate view, you need to output the video to a television monitor—typically, via a DV camera or deck.

Premiere Pro uses your system's resources to render the frames of a sequence on the fly. Naturally, segments with transitions and other effects require more processing than those without. That's because effects force Premiere Pro to generate new material. To create a cross-dissolve transition, for example, the system must digitally combine the first shot with the next. But with the proper system configuration, Premiere Pro can play back even layered clips, transitions, and other effects in *real time*—that is, right away and at the full frame rate. Even when a complex segment exceeds your system's ability to deliver the effect at the full frame rate, Premiere Pro can still display the effect by reducing the image quality, the frame rate, or both.

To see these segments at the full frame rate, you'll have to forego on-the-fly processing and create a *render file* instead. Initially, rendering takes time—how much time depends on the complexity of the effect and your system's processing speed. But once rendered, the area should play back as easily as any other clip, and at the full frame rate.

In the past, the need to render effects was the Achilles' heel of nonlinear editing systems (NLEs). But technical developments—such as DV's ability to encode high-quality video at modest data rates and ever-increasing storage and processing power—have made real-time editing accessible without the need for special hardware. Even so, special hardware may be required if you want to work with a lot of effects in real time or use formats that have higher data rates.

Using Real-Time Rendering

If your system meets the minimum requirements for DV (listed in the book's introduction), it should be able to render many transitions and effects on the fly and still play them back at the project's full frame rate.

When an effect is too complex for your system to deliver frames at the project's frame rate, you may be able to see the effect in real time by lowering the Program Monitor's Quality setting. Alternatively, you can set the Quality setting to automatically degrade the Program Monitor's image quality as needed.

To set the Program Monitor's image quality:

◆ Click the Program Monitor's Output button , and choose a quality option (**Figure 10.1**):

▲ **Highest Quality:** Displays video in the Monitor at full resolution.

▲ **Draft Quality:** Displays video in the Monitor at one-half resolution.

▲ **Automatic Quality:** Measures playback performance and dynamically adjusts the video quality.

Figure 10.1 Setting the Program Monitor to Automatic Quality lets Premiere Pro dynamically adjust the quality of the image as needed.

✔ Tips

■ Although it's an odd turn of phrase, the term *real time* makes sense to digital video editors, who are necessarily obsessed with rendering times. Rendering times are often measured in multiples of real time. For example, if compressing a movie file to a particular codec on a particular system takes seven times real time, then a 10-second clip will take 70 seconds to compress.

■ If you're considering investing in real-time hardware, make sure you understand what you're getting. Some hardware is designed to process DV footage in real time, and other equipment can handle uncompressed video. And the ability to see real-time previews doesn't necessarily mean you'll get real-time output.

USING REAL-TIME RENDERING

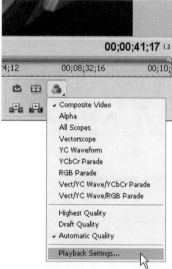

Figure 10.2 Click the Output button, and choose Playback Settings from the menu.

Figure 10.3 Choose the appropriate option in the Realtime Playback area's External Device pull-down menu.

Viewing a Sequence via a DV Device

Even at the Highest Quality setting, the image in the Program Monitor is inferior to video output to a television monitor. When you're editing DV, you can output the video signal through your DV camera or deck to a television monitor. This allows you to see (and evaluate) the video as your audience will see it.

The DV playback settings let you specify whether to play video and audio through your DV device or in the Program Monitor only.

To use these options, your IEEE 1394 interface must be connected to a DV camcorder (set to VTR mode) or DV deck, which in turn must be connected to an NTSC (television) monitor.

To play back via a DV device:

1. Make sure a DV camera or deck is connected to your computer's Premiere Pro–certified IEEE 1394 controller card and to a television monitor. Also make sure the DV device is on and set to receive a signal.

2. Click either view's Output button ⬛, and choose Playback Settings (**Figure 10.2**). The Playback Settings dialog box appears.

3. In the Realtime Playback area, choose the option in the External Device pull-down menu that matches your DV device (**Figure 10.3**).

   If you use DV in the NTSC standard, choose DV 29.97i (720 x 480). Choose None to disable video output to an external device and view video in the Monitor panel only.

   continues on next page

VIEWING A SEQUENCE VIA A DV DEVICE

4. In the Aspect Ratio Conversion pull-down menu, choose whether you want hardware or software to correct distortion caused by differences between the video's and the display's pixel aspect ratio (**Figure 10.4**).

5. *Select either of the following* (**Figure 10.5**):

▲ **Desktop Audio**—Outputs audio through the speakers connected to your computer's audio card.

▲ **External Device Audio**—Outputs audio through the speakers of an external device, such as a connected television.

Because the video and audio output on the computer isn't in synch with the signals output through an external device, it's best to watch and listen to the video on the same device.

6. If you want, select Disable Video Output When Premiere Pro Is in the Background (**Figure 10.6**).

Selecting this option turns off output to the television whenever Premiere Pro is minimized to the Windows taskbar or when another program is active and in the foreground.

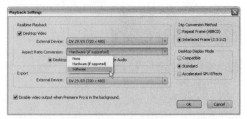

Figure 10.4 Select an Aspect Ratio Conversion method. Software is appropriate for most users.

Figure 10.5 Specify whether audio will be output via your computer's speakers or through an external device.

Figure 10.6 Specify whether you want to disable video output when Premiere is in the background.

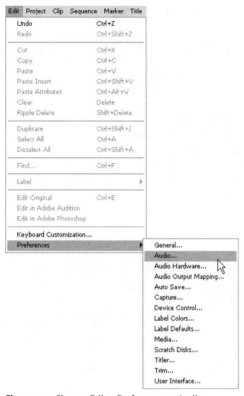

Figure 10.7 Choose Edit > Preferences > Audio.

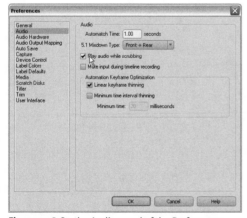

Figure 10.8 On the Audio panel of the Preferences dialog box, select Play Audio While Scrubbing.

To play audio while scrubbing:

1. Choose Edit > Preferences > Audio (**Figure 10.7**).

   The Audio panel of the Preferences dialog box appears.

2. Select Play Audio While Scrubbing (**Figure 10.8**).

   When this option is selected, you can hear audio as you drag the CTI in the time ruler of the Source Monitor, Program Monitor, or Timeline panel.

✔ Tip

■ You can also access the Playback Settings dialog box by choosing Project > Project Settings > General and then clicking the Playback Settings button.

VIEWING A SEQUENCE VIA A DV DEVICE

315

Rendering the Work Area

At the bottom of the Timeline panel's time ruler, a thin red line appears above any frame that requires additional processing, such as the frames involved in a transition or a clip with effects (**Figure 10.9**). Premiere Pro's real-time rendering feature can process and play back most of these areas on the fly at the project's full frame rate, assuming that your system meets the minimum requirements to do so. Otherwise, you can render these areas, creating new media on your hard drive called *render files* or *preview files*.

You specify the area you want to render, called the *work area*, with (appropriately) the *work area bar*. The work area bar is the adjustable bar located near the bottom of the Timeline panel's time ruler (**Figure 10.10**). Premiere Pro automatically sets the work area bar over all the clips in the project, extending it as clips are added. However, you can reset the work area bar manually.

When you render the work area, Premiere Pro generates new media for all the transitions and effects under the work area bar and places them in a Preview Files folder on your hard disk. Once the frames have been rendered, the thin red line indicators become green. By default, Premiere Pro plays back the work area after the render is complete. This setting can be changed to not play the work area, leaving the CTI in place.

Red line indicates frames that require rendering

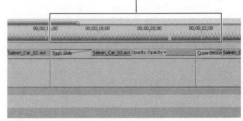

Figure 10.9 Thin red lines appear over frames that require additional processing. Here, a line appears over each transition (the lines are highlighted to make them more visible).

Work area bar

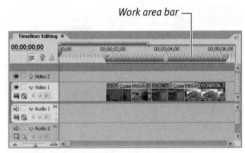

Figure 10.10 The work area bar defines the part of a sequence you can render. In this figure, the work area spans the entire sequence.

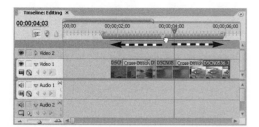

Figure 10.11 Drag the work area bar from the center to move it over the area you want to render...

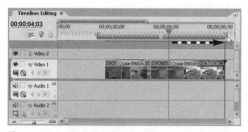

Figure 10.12 ...or drag either end to resize the work area bar. In this figure, snapping is on, so the start of the work area easily aligns with the beginning of the transition.

When you make changes to a previewed area, Premiere Pro tries to use the rendered file as much as possible. However, significant changes will make the preview file obsolete; the green line will turn red, and you'll have to re-render the area or use the standard playback method, which may not be able to play complex effects at the full frame rate (see "Using Real-Time Rendering," earlier in this chapter).

This section explains how to set the work area bar and preview the part of the sequence it includes. However, you can also export the work area, as explained in Chapter 15.

To preview the work area:

1. To set the work area bar over the part of the program that you want to preview, *do one of the following:*

   ▲ Drag the textured area at the center of the work area bar to move the bar without resizing it (**Figure 10.11**).

   ▲ Drag either end of the work area bar to shorten or lengthen it (**Figure 10.12**).

   ▲ Double-click the dark gray area at the bottom of the Timeline panel's time ruler to resize the work area bar over a contiguous series of clips or the current visible area of the time ruler, whichever is shorter.

   continues on next page

2. *Do one of the following:*

▲ Choose Sequence > Render Work Area (**Figure 10.13**).

▲ Press Enter.

The Rendering dialog box appears; a progress bar indicates the approximate time required to process the effects, based on the current operation (**Figure 10.14**). Click the triangle to expand the Render Details section to see additional information (**Figure 10.15**). When processing is complete, the red lines under the work area bar turn green, and the audio and video under the work area bar play back.

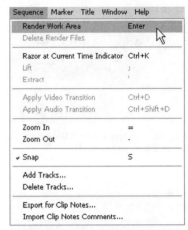

Figure 10.13 Choose Sequence > Render Work Area.

Figure 10.14 A Rendering dialog box estimates the approximate processing time.

Figure 10.15 Clicking the triangle expands the dialog box and provides additional details.

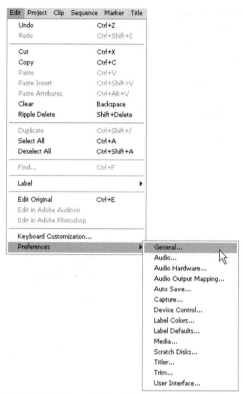

Figure 10.16 Choose Edit > Preferences > General.

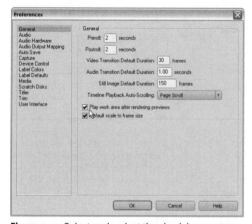

Figure 10.17 Select or deselect the check box next to Play Work Area after Rendering Previews.

To specify whether the work area plays after rendering:

1. Choose Edit > Preferences > General (**Figure 10.16**).

    The General panel of the Preferences dialog box appears.

2. Select or deselect Play Work Area after Rendering Previews (**Figure 10.17**).

    When the option is selected, the part of the sequence under the work area bar plays after rendering. When the option isn't selected, the CTI remains where it was when rendering commenced.

✔ Tips

- If snapping is on, the work area bar snaps to clip and transition edges, markers, and the CTI.

- Hover the mouse pointer over the work area bar to see a tool tip showing the bar's start, end, and duration.

- You can set a preference that specifies whether the timeline scrolls to keep the CTI within the visible area of the Timeline panel and, if so, how smoothly it scrolls. See the task "To specify the timeline scrolling option," in Chapter 7.

Storing Preview Files

By default, Premiere Pro stores rendered effects alongside the project file, in a folder called Adobe Premiere Pro Preview Files. Unless you specify a custom location, you can find this file by following the path My Documents > Adobe > Premiere Pro > 2.0 > Adobe Premiere Pro Preview Files. In this main folder, Premiere Pro stores each project's preview files in separate subfolders; the files use the naming convention *project-name*.prv.

However, by specifying a scratch disk, you can designate any location for the video and audio preview files. This way, you can take a more active role in managing your files or ensure they're being played from a disk with adequate space and speed.

To choose scratch disks for preview files:

1. Choose Edit > Preferences > Scratch Disks (**Figure 10.18**).

   The Scratch Disks panel of the Preferences dialog box appears (**Figure 10.19**).

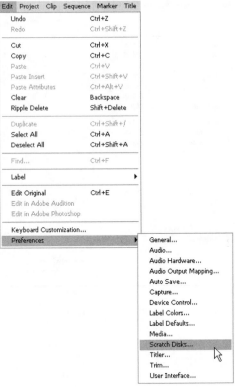

Figure 10.18 Choose Edit > Preferences > Scratch Disks.

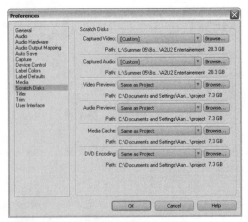

Figure 10.19 The Scratch Disks panel of the Preferences dialog box appears.

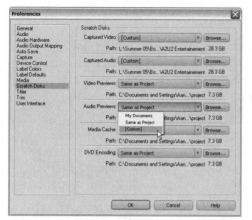

Figure 10.20 Choose a location for the video previews and audio previews from the appropriate drop-down menus, or choose a custom location by clicking the Browse buttons.

2. For the Video Previews and Audio Previews settings, *do one of the following* (**Figure 10.20**):

▲ To store preview files in the My Documents folder, choose My Documents from the drop-down menu.

▲ To store preview files in the same folder as the current project, choose Same as Project from the drop-down menu.

▲ To specify a location for the Preview Files folder, click Browse.

The path for the folder appears for each type of scratch disk.

3. Click OK to close the Preferences dialog box.

✔ Tips

■ Because the scratch disk plays back audio and video files, it should be a relatively large, fast disk. If you have several volumes, consider putting the Premiere Pro application, media files, and preview files on separate volumes.

■ By default, the Adobe Premiere Pro Preview Files folder resides in the user's My Documents folder under \Adobe\ Premiere Pro\2.0\.

Media Cache Files

To enhance playback performance, Premiere Pro creates several types of files, known collectively as *media cache files*. Although files in the media cache assist in playback, they aren't integral to a project. In other words, deleting them won't affect your project or associated media files, and you won't be prompted to find them when you reopen the project (as you would if you deleted preview files using the operating system).

Media cache files reside in the same folder as their associated project, or in a folder you specify by choosing Edit > Preferences > Scratch Disks. Premiere Pro generates these files automatically. If you want to remove them, you must do so manually. There's no command within Premiere Pro to remove media cache files (as there is with preview files).

In general, you don't have to worry about the media cache. You can specify a scratch disk to manage where these files are stored, or you can delete them manually if you need to reclaim a little hard disk space. If you continue to work on the project, Premiere Elements will regenerate the necessary media cache files.

32-Bit Floats (Your Boat)

Premiere Pro processes all internal audio using 32-bit floating-point numbers (32-bit *floats*). In contrast to integers, which are limited in their ability to represent a large range of numbers with precision, 32-bit floating-point calculations are capable of representing very small and very large values with great precision. More precise calculations mean less error accumulation with each succeeding calculation. In terms of audio, this precision introduces less noise and error with each audio adjustment you make. Put simply, 32-bit float audio processes faster and sounds better than, say, audio that uses 16-bit integer processing.

Consequently, audio mixing in Premiere Pro is far superior to that in older versions of Premiere. Because earlier versions worked entirely in 16- (or 8!) bit audio, any audio adjustments (including volume changes) were likely to reduce the effective signal-to-noise ratio. The more you tweaked the signal, the more noise you added. Beginning with Premiere Pro, all audio is maintained at 32-bit float, from import to export.

The cost for all this is disk space. But devoting a relatively small amount of storage to process the audio this way is a small price to pay to make audio sweetening a little bit sweeter.

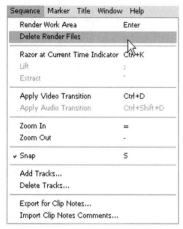

Figure 10.21 Choose Sequence > Delete Render Files.

Figure 10.22 Click OK to confirm that you want to delete all preview files for the project.

Deleting Preview Files

You can delete preview files to free up drive space or for housekeeping purposes (to save a project just prior to archiving it, for example). In contrast to deleting the preview files by using the operating system, using Premiere Pro's Delete Render Files command ensures that the project no longer refers to the preview files and doesn't prompt you for them the next time you open the project.

To delete preview files:

1. Choose Sequence > Delete Render Files (**Figure 10.21**).

   A Confirm Delete dialog box prompts you to confirm your choice and warns you that the operation can't be undone.

2. Click OK (**Figure 10.22**).

   The preview files associated with the current project are deleted from the hard disk. In the Timeline panel, the green lines indicating rendered areas turn red.

✔ Tips

- Premiere Pro keeps track of preview files in much the same way it references source media files. If you move or delete preview files using the operating system instead of from within Premiere Pro, you're prompted to locate the files the next time you open the project. In this case, direct Premiere Pro to the preview file's new location. Or, if you deleted the preview files, choose Skip Preview Files when prompted. See Chapter 2, "Starting a Project," for more about locating missing files.

- Premiere Pro uses the terms *render files* and *preview files* interchangeably.

Mixing Audio

Whether you use numerous audio tracks or just a few, you'll probably need to make subtle adjustments to them to achieve the best overall effect. This process, known as audio mixing, can be accomplished by employing the Audio Mixer panel.

The Audio Mixer resembles a physical audio mixing board, complete with fade and pan controls and volume unit (VU) meters that display audio power in decibels. But unlike a physical mixing board, Premiere Pro's Audio Mixer includes a set of controls for every audio track in a sequence. To create complex mixes, you can route the audio using submixes and sends. You can also apply a wide range of audio effects to correct or enhance the tracks—a process some call *audio sweetening*—right from the Audio Mixer. With the proper hardware, you can even use the mixer to record audio directly into a track of a sequence.

The Audio Mixer works like an automated mixing console. As you mix a track, the Audio Mixer records your adjustments. When you play back the mix, the Audio Mixer reproduces your adjustments, moving the pan and fade controls just as you did.

In the Timeline panel, these adjustments are depicted as specified values, or keyframes, in property graphs. Whereas you use the Audio Mixer to control tracks of audio, you manipulate keyframes to adjust both entire tracks of audio and individual clips in the tracks. But because keyframes work the same for audio properties as they do for other effects—transparency, motion, and filters—a full discussion of keyframes is reserved for Chapter 13, "Working with Effects." This chapter focuses on the use of the Audio Mixer to make track-based audio adjustments.

If you're already familiar with audio mixing principles and practices, feel free to skip to the end of the chapter to start mixing with the Audio Mixer. If there's a step you don't understand, you can turn back to the pertinent section. Otherwise, proceed from the beginning for a detailed explanation of each part of the process.

Planning an Audio Mix

As a rule, you mix a sequence's audio only after you're satisfied with the editing, a stage sometimes referred to as *picture lock*. This workflow helps ensure that you don't waste time and effort repeatedly revising a carefully crafted mix. However, this approach is only part of your overall audio editing strategy. It's possible to make adjustments on several levels: to clips, to the track containing the clips, or to a submix track that includes several tracks. By nesting the sequence, you allow the cycle to start over. To avoid making redundant or conflicting adjustments, it's important to understand your choices at each step in the process.

Specifying the track type

As always, tailor your plans to your output goal. Make sure your final sequence's master track matches the type of audio you want to output: mono, stereo, or 5.1. The master track's channel type is fixed when you create the sequence—so if you need a different type of master track, you'll have to create a new sequence. In contrast, you can add or delete the type of standard or submix tracks you need at will.

Clip-based vs. track-based editing

You can pan, fade, and apply effects both to individual clips and to entire tracks. In general, adjust individual clips first and then mix the tracks. However, don't adjust a clip when it would make more sense to make the same adjustment to the entire track. Similarly, be careful not to let a clip's setting contradict the track's setting, and vice versa. Adjust clips in the Timeline panel and Effect Controls panel (see Chapter 13). Adjust tracks in the Timeline panel or the Audio Mixer.

Audio Processing Order

When you're planning a mix or troubleshooting problems, it's helpful to know the order in which audio adjustments are processed. Premiere Pro processes audio data in the following order:

1. Gain adjustments using the Audio Gain command

2. Effects applied to individual clips

3. Track settings in this order: pre-fader effects, pre-fader sends, mute, fader, meter, post-fader effects, post-fader sends, pan/balance

4. Track output volume, from left to right in the Audio Mixer (or top to bottom in the Timeline panel)

Subtractive Mixing

When you adjust audio levels, follow the principle of *subtractive mixing*. In subtractive mixing, you favor reducing (subtracting) levels over increasing them. First, establish a strong, representative audio level for the sequence (such as the standard level for dialogue). Then, if necessary, decrease the gain of a clip in relation to others. Increasing a level in relation to other clips often leads to successive increases. Adding volume increases not only the signal (the sounds you want) but also the noise (the sounds you don't want, such as buzz and hiss) and can introduce distortion.

Automation vs. keyframing

In the Audio Mixer, you use automation to adjust a track's pan, fade, and effect values as the audio plays; in the Timeline panel, you directly manipulate the values, called *keyframes*, on a graph. Both methods affect the same set of audio track property values. The Audio Mixer offers real-time audio response, whereas keyframing favors graphical control. You can also view and adjust keyframes for individual audio clips (as well as other effects, such as transparency, motion, and filters) in the Timeline panel and the Effect Controls panel.

Routing and nesting

Complex mixes involving multiple tracks can be grouped into submix tracks and output, or *routed*, to other submix tracks or to the master track. You can also use sends to blend processed or *wet* versions of a track or submix with its unprocessed or *dry* signal. And, as you learned in Chapter 6, "Creating a Sequence," you can nest one sequence within another, so that the combined tracks of one sequence appear as a single linked clip in another sequence. This means you mix a sequence's tracks and then make adjustments to the audio track of its nested instance.

Audio Tracks and Channel Types

Recall from Chapter 6 that a sequence can contain any number of standard audio tracks, but it must contain a single master audio track that controls the combined output of all the other tracks in the sequence.

You can also create submix tracks, which you can use to redirect the output of standard tracks and other submix tracks before it reaches the master track. Routing with submix tracks helps you group tracks and control the processing of effects.

You must specify the number of channels each track supports: mono, stereo, or 5.1 surround:

◆ **Mono**, or monophonic, tracks contain a single channel of audio data, which is output equally by all the output speakers.

◆ **Stereo**, or stereophonic, tracks contain two discrete channels of audio. When reproduced on a stereo speaker system, a sound's relative strength in each channel, or balance, gives it an apparent location between stereo speakers.

◆ **5.1**, or 5.1 surround, tracks contain five discrete channels of information, plus a low-frequency effects (LFE) channel that may be decoded either by the main speakers or a separate subwoofer. A surround-sound system uses five or more speakers placed around the listener to give sounds an apparent location anywhere in a 360-degree lateral range.

Standard audio tracks contain audio clips of the same audio type, including audio you record using the Audio Mixer. Once a track is created, you can't change its channel type.

✔ Tip

■ Once you create a sequence, its master track's channel type is fixed. However, you can easily create a new sequence with the type of master track you want. Then you can either paste the contents of the original sequence in the new one or nest the original sequence in the new one.

Specifying Audio Hardware Options

To record, process, and output audio, Premiere Pro uses your system's audio hardware. Although a run-of-the-mill audio card is adequate for stereo input and output, multichannel recording and output require an *ASIO-compliant* audio device. Audio Stream Input/Output (ASIO) is a widely accepted audio transfer protocol that allows software like Premiere Pro to use the multichannel recording and output capabilities of more powerful sound cards. With the proper hardware, you can use the Audio Mixer to record multiple tracks simultaneously and to mix and output audio in 5.1 surround.

You can specify the way Premiere Pro uses your particular device on the Audio panel of the Preferences dialog box. The panel includes various options:

- **Default Device** specifies which audio hardware device Premiere Pro uses, unless you're exporting to an external video device (as specified in the Playback Settings dialog box).

- **ASIO Settings** accesses a separate dialog box for configuring your particular ASIO-compliant audio device.

ASIO

ASIO stands for Audio Stream Input/Output, a multichannel audio transfer protocol developed by Steinberg (the company that produces audio products such as Cubase).

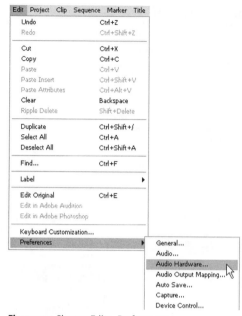

Figure 11.1 Choose Edit > Preferences > Audio Hardware.

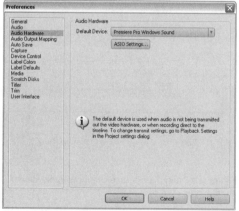

Figure 11.2 The Audio Hardware panel of the Preferences dialog box appears.

Figure 11.3 For Default Device, choose Premiere Pro Windows Sound.

The Audio Output Mapping panel of the Preferences dialog box lets you specify how the output channels of your audio device correspond, or map, to a Premiere Pro output channel. It includes the following options:

◆ **Map Output for** lets you specify the output channels you want to map to your hardware audio device.

◆ **Output Channel Mappings** describes how your device's output channels correspond to a sequence's master track output. The column marked with a stereo icon ⋈ shows the correspondence between each channel of your device and a stereo or mono mix: left speaker ⋈ and right speaker ⋈. (Mono mixes are output to a left and right speaker.) The column labeled 5.1 shows the correspondence between each channel of your device and the channels in a 5.1 surround mix: left ▨, right ▨, center ▨, surround left ▨, and surround right ▨.

To specify audio hardware preferences:

1. Choose Edit > Preferences > Audio Hardware (**Figure 11.1**).

   The Audio Hardware panel of the Preferences dialog box appears (**Figure 11.2**).

2. Select Premiere Pro Windows Sound from the Default Device pull-down menu (**Figure 11.3**).

3. If it's available, click ASIO Settings to access options specific to your particular sound card (**Figure 11.4**).

Figure 11.4 If available, click ASIO Settings to access options specific to your sound card.

To specify audio output mapping:

1. Choose Edit > Preferences > Audio Output Mapping (**Figure 11.5**).

   The Audio Output Mapping panel of the Preferences dialog box appears.

2. In the Map Output For pull-down menu, select Premiere Pro Windows Sound (**Figure 11.6**).

3. To change a source channel's output, drag the source channel's icon from one row to another (**Figure 11.7**).

   The icons rearrange accordingly, and the source channel is assigned to the corresponding output channel (**Figure 11.8**).

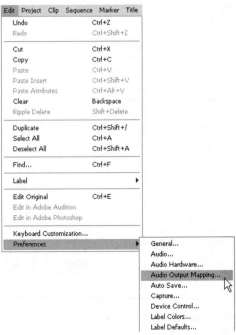

Figure 11.5 Choose Edit > Preferences > Audio Output Mapping.

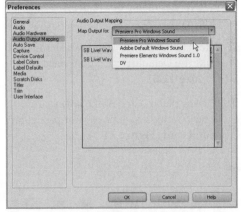

Figure 11.6 In the Map Output For pull-down menu, select Premiere Pro Windows Sound.

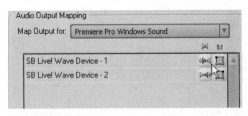

Figure 11.7 Dragging a source channel's audio icon to another row...

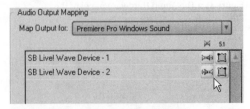

Figure 11.8 ...moves it to that row and assigns it to the corresponding output channel (here, the source left has been assigned to the right output channel).

SPECIFYING AUDIO HARDWARE OPTIONS

Figure 11.9 Select a mono clip.

Converting Mono and Stereo Clips

As discussed previously, audio tracks can contain only clips that use the same channel type. However, you can easily work around this limitation. A few simple commands allow you to treat a mono clip as a stereo clip or, conversely, extract a stereo clip's channels as two mono clips.

To treat a mono clip as stereo:

1. In the Project panel, select a mono audio clip (**Figure 11.9**).

2. Choose Clip > Audio Options > Source Channel Mappings (**Figure 11.10**).

   The Source Channel Mappings dialog box appears. The Track Format reflects how the clip's source tracks are mapped for output—in this case, Mono.

3. Select Mono as Stereo, and then click OK (**Figure 11.11**).

   The selected mono clip is treated as a stereo clip, and you can add the clip to any stereo audio track.

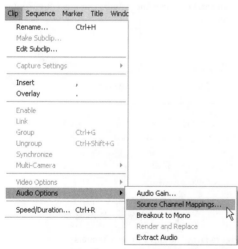

Figure 11.10 Choose Clip > Audio Options > Source Channel Mappings.

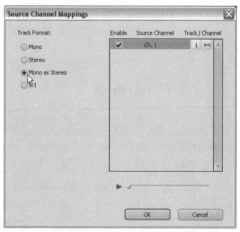

Figure 11.11 In the Source Channel Mappings dialog box, select the Track Format you want the clip to use—in this case, Mono as Stereo. Once you click OK, the clip can be used in stereo tracks.

To break out mono clips from a stereo clip:

1. In the Project panel, select a stereo audio clip (**Figure 11.12**).

2. Choose Clip > Audio Options > Breakout to Mono (**Figure 11.13**).

   Each of the clip's stereo channels becomes a mono clip in the Project panel. *Left* is appended to one clip's name, and *Right* is appended to the other (**Figure 11.14**).

✔ Tips

- The Audio Output Mapping pane of the Preferences dialog box allows you to treat an audio clip using any track format (such as stereo) as another format (such as mono) by selecting the appropriate option. Depending on the format, you can click and drag the speaker icon (or 5.1 stereo icon) to change how the clips tracks correspond to output channels.

- Make sure your audio cabling is correct. It's surprisingly common for the left and right channels to be reversed.

- On stereo equipment, the left channel is synonymous with audio channel 1 and a white connector. The right channel is synonymous with audio channel 2 and a red connector.

Figure 11.12 Select a stereo clip.

Figure 11.13 Choose Clip > Audio Options > Breakout to Mono.

Figure 11.14 The clip's stereo channels appear as two mono clips in the Project panel.

Decibels

A decibel (dB) is the standard measure of acoustical power used by audio professionals everywhere. To double the volume, increase the level by +6 dB.

Technically speaking, a decibel is one-tenth of a bel, which measures the ratio of two audio power levels—usually an audio signal and a reference (such as the threshold of hearing). And yes, it's bel as in Alexander Graham Bell, the telephone guy.

CONVERTING MONO AND STEREO CLIPS

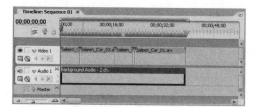

Figure 11.15 In the Timeline panel, select an audio clip.

Figure 11.16 Choose Clip > Audio Options > Audio Gain.

Figure 11.17 In the Clip Gain dialog box, either enter a gain value in dB or click Normalize to have Premiere Pro calculate the gain automatically.

Adjusting a Clip's Gain

You can adjust the overall volume, or *gain*, of a clip in the timeline by using a menu command. You can think of gain as the clip's *input levels*—the volume the clip starts with. The Audio Gain command provides a good way to bring a clip's levels in line with those of other clips before making adjustments to the *output levels*, either for the individual clip or for all the clips in the track. Adjusting gain doesn't affect the initial position of a clip's volume value graph. See "Viewing Audio Data in the Timeline," later in this chapter. To learn about adjusting a value graph, see Chapter 13.

To adjust a clip's gain:

1. In the Timeline panel, select an audio clip (**Figure 11.15**).

2. Choose Clip > Audio Options > Audio Gain (**Figure 11.16**).

   The Clip Gain dialog box appears (**Figure 11.17**).

3. To adjust the gain, *do one of the following*:

   ▲ Enter a value for the gain, in decibels.

   A value of more than 0 amplifies the audio; a value of less than 0 attenuates the audio, making it quieter.

   ▲ Click Normalize to have Premiere Pro calculate the gain value automatically.

   Normalizing audio boosts the volume where it's too quiet and limits it where it's too loud.

4. Click OK.

   The audio clip's overall gain is adjusted by the amount you specified.

✔ Tip

■ Certain audio effects let you boost or attenuate gain in particular frequencies.

Creating Cross-Fades with Audio Transitions

A *cross-fade* occurs when one audio clip fades out (grows silent) while another audio clip fades in (becomes audible). In Premiere Pro, you can fade up, fade out, and cross-fade audio using an audio transition. Although transitions were covered in Chapter 9, "Adding Transitions," it's useful to review them in the context of audio.

To create a cross-fade transition:

1. On the Effects panel, open the Audio Transitions folder to reveal the audio transitions. *Select one of the following* (**Figure 11.18**):

   ▲ **Constant Gain:** Changes the volume using a linear scale, which nonetheless may not sound like a linear, constant change.

   ▲ **Constant Power:** Changes the volume using a logarithmic scale, which emulates the way the human ear perceives volume changes.

2. Drag the audio transition to a cut between audio clips in a track, so that the mouse icon indicates the alignment you want.

   Alignment options include Start at Cut, Centered at Cut, and End at Cut (**Figure 11.19**).

3. Release the mouse to drop the transition.

   The transition appears at the edit using the alignment you specified and the default transition duration (**Figure 11.20**). You can adjust the audio transition's alignment or duration using any of the techniques you learned in Chapter 9.

Figure 11.18 On the Effects panel, open the Audio Transitions folder and drag either Constant Gain or Constant Power...

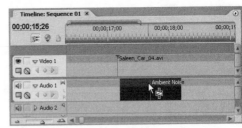

Figure 11.19 ...and drop it at an audio cut in the Timeline panel, aligning it so it starts at the cut, ends at the cut, or is centered on the cut (shown here).

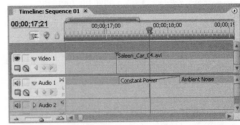

Figure 11.20 The audio transition appears on the cut using the alignment you specified, at the default duration.

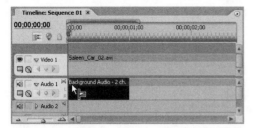

Figure 11.21 To fade in audio, drag an audio transition to start at the cut.

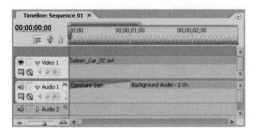

Figure 11.22 The transition appears at the beginning of the clip and uses the default duration.

To create a fade-up or fade-out:

1. On the Effects panel, open the Audio Transitions folder to reveal the audio transitions. Select one of the following:

   ▲ **Constant Gain:** Changes the volume using a linear scale, which nonetheless may not sound like a linear, constant change.

   ▲ **Constant Power:** Changes the volume using a logarithmic scale, which emulates the way the human ear perceives volume changes.

2. *Do one of the following:*

   ▲ Drag the transition to the head of an audio clip so that the Start at Cut icon appears (**Figure 11.21**).

   ▲ Drag the transition to the tail of an audio clip so that the End at Cut icon appears.

   Release the mouse to drop the transition in place.

   The transition appears at the edit, using the default transition duration (**Figure 11.22**). You can adjust the transition's duration using any of the techniques explained in Chapter 9.

Viewing Audio Data in the Timeline

In Chapter 7, "Editing in the Timeline," you learned that you can view audio waveforms for clips in a track by expanding the track and setting its display style to Show Waveforms. An expanded audio track can also display other information, including controls for manipulating levels, panning, balancing, and effects. Each parameter's values appear as a graph, which you can keyframe; that is, you can specify values for particular points in time, thereby changing the graph and altering the values over time. You can view one graph at a time for individual clips in the track or for the entire track.

For now, you'll learn how to view parameter values for tracks, to get visual feedback for adjustments you make using the Audio Mixer. Turn to Chapter 13 to find out how to view audio data for clips and how to make adjustments by manipulating the graph directly in the Timeline panel.

To show track volume in the Timeline panel:

1. If necessary, expand an audio track by clicking the triangle next to the track's name.

2. In the audio track, click the Show/Hide Keyframes button (next to the Show Waveforms button), and choose Show Track Volume (**Figure 11.23**).

   When you specify Show Track Volume, the button's icon reflects your choice. The track display includes a line that graphs the track's volume values over time (**Figure 11.24**). When the line is at the center of the track, the volume is unadjusted; when the line is at the top of the track, the volume is doubled, or +6 dB; when the line is at the bottom of the track, the track is silent, or −~dB.

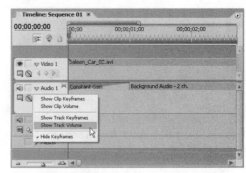

Figure 11.23 In an audio track, click the Show/Hide Keyframes button, and choose Show Track Volume.

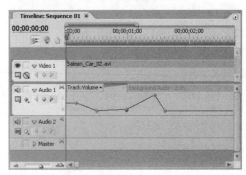

Figure 11.24 A yellow line graphs the audio levels. In this figure, the line reflects the results of automation as keyframes in the graph. Waveforms are hidden so the line is easier to see.

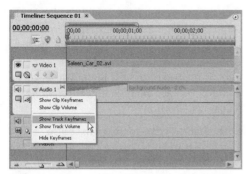

Figure 11.25 In the audio track, click the Show/Hide Keyframes button, and choose Show Track Keyframes.

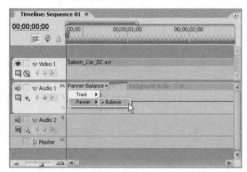

Figure 11.26 In the track's pull-down menu, choose the parameter for which you want to view a value graph—in this case, Balance.

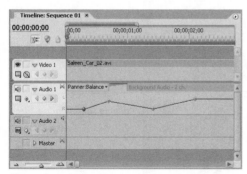

Figure 11.27 A yellow line graphs the selected panning values. In this figure, the line reflects the results of adjusting balance values as keyframes in the graph. Again, waveforms are hidden.

To show track-panning values in the Timeline panel:

1. If necessary, expand an audio track by clicking the triangle next to the track's name.

2. In the audio track, click the Show/Hide Keyframes button, and choose Show Track Keyframes from the menu (**Figure 11.25**).

   When you specify Show Track Keyframes, the button's icon 🔹 reflects your choice. A pull-down menu appears in the track at the beginning of the visible area of the timeline.

3. In the track's pull-down menu, choose Panner, and then choose an option from the submenu (**Figure 11.26**):

   ▲ **Balance:** Shows the balance between left and right channels when outputting to a stereo track.

   ▲ **Left–Right:** Shows the balance between left and right channels when outputting to a 5.1 track.

   ▲ **Front–Rear:** Shows the balance between front and rear channels when outputting to a 5.1 track.

   ▲ **Center:** Shows the percentage value output to the center channel in a 5.1 track.

   ▲ **LFE:** Shows the volume, in dB, output to the LFE channel in a 5.1 track.

   A line in the track graphs the selected value over time (**Figure 11.27**). When the line is at the center of the track, the track is distributed evenly between the channels represented by the graph. When Center or LFE is selected, the line is initially at the bottom of the track, which represents silence (0 percent when Center is selected or −~dB when LFE is selected).

Using the Audio Mixer

The Audio Mixer resembles a conventional mixing board in both form and function (**Figure 11.28**). Just as each channel of a mixing board contains controls to adjust and monitor each audio source, each track in the Audio Mixer corresponds to a track in the sequence. Unlike its physical counterpart, however, the Audio Mixer adds tracks for each track you add to the sequence.

Faders (or fade controls) control the audio levels, expressed in decibels (dB). Alternatively, you can enter a numeric value for the level. Similarly, you can pan audio using the Audio Mixer's pan knobs or by entering a numerical value.

You make these adjustments in each track as the video and audio play back. As you do, Premiere Pro creates keyframes in the corresponding track's fade and pan lines in the timeline.

To help you evaluate the levels, a volume unit (VU) meter graphically represents the levels of each channel, as well as the overall combined, or *master*, level. An indicator light at the top of the VU meter warns you if your levels are too high and are *clipping* (causing distortion).

Each channel of the Audio Mixer also contains standard buttons for selectively *monitoring* (listening to) each track. You can monitor all the channels, *mute* a channel to exclude it from output, or *solo* a channel to monitor it without the others. Each channel also includes a Record button, which you can use to record live audio directly to the track.

As in the Program Monitor and Timeline panel, each sequence of the project can appear as a tab in the Audio Mixer. Clicking a sequence's tab in any panel makes it the current sequence in all panels.

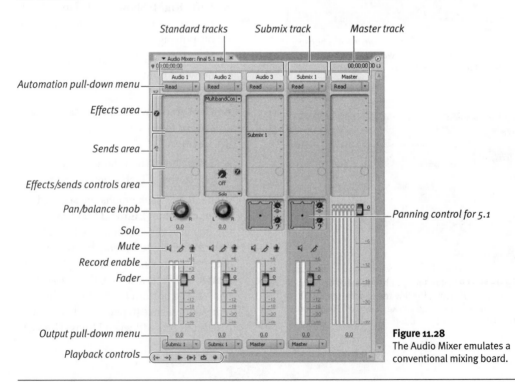

Figure 11.28
The Audio Mixer emulates a conventional mixing board.

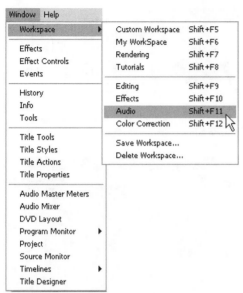

Figure 11.29 Choose Window > Workspace > Audio.

Figure 11.30 The arrangement of panels is optimized for audio mixing. But don't hesitate to modify the configuration and save your own preset.

To optimize the workspace for audio mixing:

◆ Choose Window > Workspace > Audio (**Figure 11.29**).

The arrangement of panels is optimized for audio mixing. You can use the arrangement as a starting point for customizing your workspace (**Figure 11.30**).

✔ Tips

■ You may find that the preset audio workspace is a good start, but it probably needs a little tweaking to get the right arrangement for your screen and personal style.

■ You may hear audio engineers refer to a knob on a mixing console as a *pot*, which is short for potentiometer (it affects electrical potential). In other words, like most volume knobs, a pot controls the amount of electrical current that flows through a circuit.

■ Ordinarily, each source on a mixer is referred to as a channel. (*Channel* also refers to the way audio data is recorded, as in mono, stereo, and 5.1 channels.) But for the sake of convenience, and to remain consistent with the terminology used in the Premiere Pro interface, this book refers to *tracks* in the timeline and in the Audio Mixer.

USING THE AUDIO MIXER

Customizing the Audio Mixer

Like the Program Monitor and the Timeline panel, the Audio Mixer lets you toggle the current sequence's time ruler between frames and audio samples. Depending on whether your mix requires effects, you can expand or collapse an area that includes effects and sends (later sections explain how to use effects and sends). When the number of tracks in a complex mix makes the Audio Mixer consume too much screen space, you can hide the tracks you're not using. On the other hand, when you're concentrating on video editing, you can reduce the Audio Mixer to show only the master meters, so you can keep an eye on the output levels.

To toggle between frames and audio units:

◆ In the Audio Mixer's pull-down menu, choose Audio Units (**Figure 11.31**).

The time displays in the Audio Mixer and in the Timeline panel switch to audio samples. Select the option again to switch the time displays back to frames. The Audio Mixer and the Timeline panel always display the same units, and you can toggle between frames and samples from either panel's pull-down menu.

To show or hide effects and sends:

◆ Click the triangle at the upper left in the Audio Mixer to expand and collapse the Audio Mixer's effects and sends area (**Figures 11.32** and **11.33**).

Effects and sends are explained in detail later in this chapter.

Figure 11.31 In the Audio Mixer's pull-down menu, choose Audio Units.

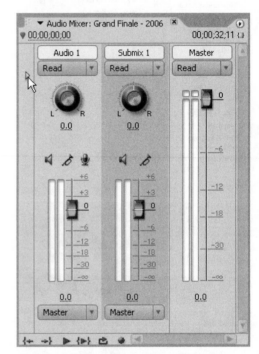

Figure 11.32 Clicking the triangle toggles between hiding the effects and sends...

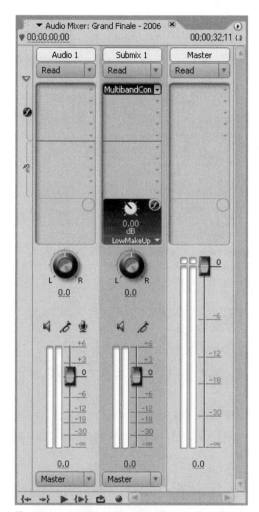

Figure 11.33 ...and revealing the effects and sends.

To show or hide tracks in the Audio Mixer:

1. In the Audio Mixer's pull-down menu, choose Show/Hide Tracks (**Figure 11.34**). The Show/Hide Tracks dialog box appears.

2. *Do one of the following* (**Figure 11.35**):
   - ▲ Select a track to make a check appear next to its name and to include the track's controls in the Audio Mixer panel.
   - ▲ Deselect a track to make the check mark disappear and exclude the track's controls from the Audio Mixer.
   - ▲ Click Show All to include all tracks' controls in the Audio Mixer.
   - ▲ Click Hide All to exclude all tracks' controls from the Audio Mixer (leaving only the master track's controls visible).

3. Click OK.
   Only the tracks you selected appear in the Audio Mixer. The tracks still appear in the Timeline panel, and their clip contents continue to play (provided the tracks aren't muted).

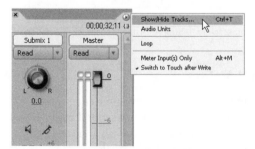

Figure 11.34 In the Audio Mixer's pull-down menu, choose Show/Hide Tracks.

Figure 11.35 In the Show/Hide Tracks dialog box, select the tracks you want to appear in the Audio Mixer.

Monitoring Tracks in the Audio Mixer

Although mixing audio is about making all the tracks sound good together, one way to do this is to listen to them separately. Buttons above each track's fader allow you to control which track you listen to, or monitor. If you don't want to monitor a track, click the Mute button. Conversely, click the Solo button to monitor a track without hearing the others. Monitor buttons don't affect the levels—just whether you hear the audio during the mixing process.

To mute a track:

◆ In the Audio Mixer, click the Mute button ◄ for the track you want to exclude from playback (**Figure 11.36**).

 Deselect the Mute button to include the track's audio in playback.

To solo a track:

◆ In the Audio Mixer, click the Solo button ♪ for the track you want to hear exclusively (**Figure 11.37**).

 Deselect the Solo button to include the audio of other tracks in playback.

✔ Tip

■ Musicians who amplify their instruments use the term *monitor* to refer to a speaker directed toward the band. These monitors help the musicians hear (and therefore modulate) their own performance better.

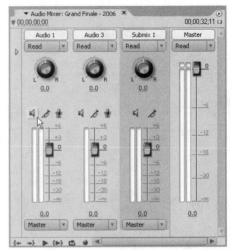

Figure 11.36 Click a track's Mute button to exclude its output from playback.

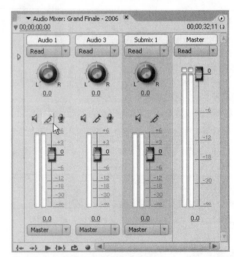

Figure 11.37 Clicking a track's Solo button mutes all other tracks, letting you listen to the track in isolation.

Reading the VU Meters

As you monitor audio, watch the levels in the VU meters. Your speaker volume can provide only a relative, changeable indication of levels. You can rely on the VU meters for a more objective measure. The loudest sounds should reach their highest levels, or *peak*, near the top of the meters, at 0 dB. If a sound is too loud to be accurately reproduced, it clips and will sound distorted. When clipping occurs, the indicator light above a VU meter comes on. Click the lights to turn them off. Readjust the levels to avoid clipping.

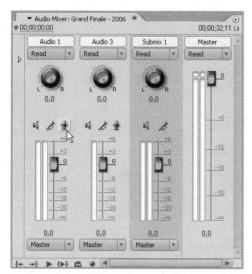

Figure 11.38 Click the Enable Record button to enable the track for recording.

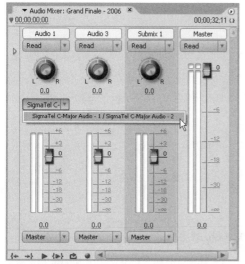

Figure 11.39 In the pull-down menu, select the recording device you want to use.

Recording with the Audio Mixer

With the proper sound card, you can connect a microphone, an instrument, or a MIDI device to your system and record audio directly to a track of the sequence. The types of devices you can connect and the number of tracks you can record simultaneously depend on your sound card's features.

Submix tracks don't contain audio clips; they serve to route the audio of other tracks. Therefore, you can't record audio to a submix track, and in the Audio Mixer, submix tracks don't include a Record button.

To record with the Audio Mixer:

1. Make sure your sound card is configured and that a microphone or other device is connected properly.

2. In the Audio Mixer, click the Enable Record button 🎤 for the tracks to which you want to record audio (**Figure 11.38**).

   A pull-down menu appears above the Mute, Solo, and Record buttons listing the recording devices (sound cards) connected to your system.

3. Choose the proper recording device from the track's pull-down menu (**Figure 11.39**).

4. Monitor the tracks you want to hear during recording, and mute tracks you don't want to hear.

   In some circumstances, it's best to monitor the audio using headphones instead of speakers. For example, you should prevent a microphone from picking up audio from the speakers. If a microphone picks up its own audio, the result will be audio feedback.

continues on next page

5. Cue the sequence's CTI to the point at which you want to start recording.

If you want, set sequence In and Out points to more easily cue and repeat the section of the sequence you're recording.

6. In the Audio Mixer, click the Record button 🔴 to activate record mode, and then click the Play button ▶ to begin recording. When you've finished recording, click the Audio Mixer's Stop button ■ (**Figure 11.40**).

7. To review your recording, make sure to monitor the tracks you want to hear. If necessary, repeat steps 5 and 6. When you're satisfied with your recording, deselect the Record button.

✔ Tips

■ The Audio pane of the Preferences dialog box includes a setting to mute input during timeline recording.

■ Recording audio to a track is unrelated to its automation settings. Mixing automation options are for automating output settings, such as pan and fade adjustments.

Figure 11.40 Cue the sequence's CTI, and then click the track's Record and Play buttons. When you've finished recording, click Stop or press the spacebar.

Controlling Audio Quality

You must maintain audio quality at every step of the production process: recording, digitizing, processing, and exporting. At each step, your goal is to capture and maintain a strong audio signal without distorting it. At the same time, you want to minimize noise: any extraneous sounds, including electronic hum and hiss. Audio engineers like to call achieving these goals *maintaining a good signal-to-noise ratio*; you might think of it as keeping the sound loud and clear.

If you use good recording and digitizing techniques, preserving audio quality in the editing and export process will be much easier.

Fading, Panning, and Balancing

Two tasks are basic to audio mixing: fading and panning. *Fading* adjusts the volume, or level, that the track outputs. Over the course of a sequence, chances are you'll need to control the relative levels of the audio tracks. You may need to match the levels of dialogue recorded in different takes. Or you may need to gradually change the level of a sound effect track. For example, you might fade down the sound of a car to make it seem as though the car is driving away.

You can also control how a track's audio channels are distributed when they're output to a track with stereo or 5.1 channels. Distributing a mono track's single channel of audio between a stereo track's two channels or among a 5.1 track's multiple channels is called *panning*. When you output a stereo or 5.1 track to another stereo or 5.1 track, the process is called *balancing*. But because both methods are ways of controlling the distribution of audio output to channels in a submix or master track, it's common to refer to both as panning and to the control as a *pan control*, or *panner*. (For the sake of convenience, this book uses the term *pan* for both pan and balance, unless it's useful to make a distinction.)

Panning/balancing audio can imply an apparent position for a sound. Using the example of a car sound effect, panning can make a car sound as though it's moving from the listener's right to the left when played on a stereo system. Panning a 5.1 mix can make the car seem to drive right past or run circles around the listener (when reproduced on a 5.1 surround system).

With the Audio Mixer, you can adjust each track's fading and panning settings as the sequence plays, using controls that resemble those found on physical mixing consoles.

Mixing 5.1 Audio

Whereas a stereo track includes two discrete channels, a 5.1 audio track includes five discrete channels: left, right, center, surround left, and surround right. Just as sounds reproduced on a stereophonic system can seem to emanate from anywhere between the right and left speakers, sounds on a 5.1 audio system can seem to originate from anywhere in a 360-degree field created by (at least) five speakers.

The .1 in 5.1 refers to an optional LFE channel. In contrast to the five main channels—which deliver a full range of frequencies—the LFE channel delivers bass information only.

To balance audio in 5.1:

1. In a track's output pull-down menu, select a 5.1 audio track (**Figure 11.41**).

   A 5.1 control panel appears above the track's Mute, Solo, and Record buttons (in place of a pan/balance knob when the output is set to a stereo track).

2. To balance the audio, drag the black dot, or *puck*, to any position within the tray, which represents the 5.1 channels graphically (**Figure 11.42**).

   Rounded pockets along the edge of the tray correspond to the left, center, right, left surround, and right surround channels.

3. To adjust the center percentage value, drag the top-right knob in the 5.1 control panel, labeled with the icon 🎙.

4. To adjust the LFE volume, drag the lower-right knob in the 5.1 control panel, labeled with a bass clef icon 🎼.

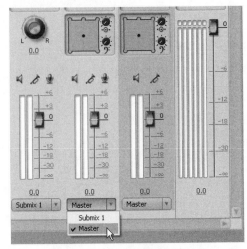

Figure 11.41 In the track's output pull-down menu, select a 5.1 submix or master track.

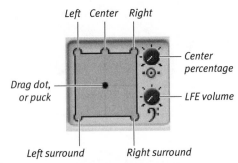

Figure 11.42 To distribute the track's audio among the five main channels, drag the black dot in the panning tray.

✔ Tip

■ Hovering the mouse pointer over the 5.1 tray reveals a tool tip describing the puck's position expressed as coordinates on a grid, where Left/Right axis and Front/Rear axis range from −100 to +100. Therefore, positioning the puck in the left channel places it at −100, −100; the right surround channel is at +100, +100.

Figure 11.43 Choose Edit > Preferences > Audio.

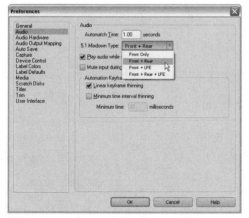

Figure 11.44 In the 5.1 Mixdown Type pull-down menu, choose the channels you want mixed down.

To specify how 5.1 audio is mixed down:

1. Choose Edit > Preferences > Audio (**Figure 11.43**).

   The Audio panel of the Preferences dialog box appears.

2. For 5.1 Mixdown Type, choose the channels you want mixed down from the pull-down menu (**Figure 11.44**).

5.1, 6.1, 7.1

When you're comparing sound cards and speaker systems that support 5.1 surround sound, you may find that some manufacturers boast that their equipment can support 6.1 and even 7.1 surround sound. All these systems decode 5.1 channels but can output them to different numbers of speakers: 6.1 outputs five main channels to six speakers, and 7.1 outputs five main channels to seven speakers. Plus, the optional LFE channel can be output to a subwoofer.

The LFE Channel and Subwoofer Output

Although the LFE channel provides additional bass, it isn't necessarily output to a subwoofer speaker. The system used to decode the 5.1 signal may not output to a subwoofer if the main speakers are capable of reproducing the LFE signal instead. Conversely, if the main speakers can't reproduce the soundtrack's bass content, the system may output it to a subwoofer—even when an LFE channel isn't present.

Selecting an Automation Mode

Using the Audio Mixer is comparable to using a physical mixing console that can automate fade and pan adjustments. In other words, the Audio Mixer can record, or *write*, the adjustments you make as the sequence plays. Afterward, you can set the track to play back, or *read*, the adjustments you made—making the pan knobs and faders move as if controlled by some unseen hand. Alternatively, you can set the Audio Mixer to ignore the adjustments during playback, without deleting them.

Figure 11.45 Choose an option in each track's automation pull-down menu.

Although only one automation option is called Write, three modes record your adjustments: Touch, Latch, and Write. Depending on the mode you choose, a track's pan knob and fader remain in place or snap back to the 0 position when you release the mouse during a mix, or when you stop playback and resume mixing. You can specify the amount of time it takes for a control to snap back to 0 during a mix by setting the automatch time. Switching between the automation modes allows you to make careful adjustments in multiple passes.

To set a track's automation mode:

◆ For each track in the Audio Mixer, choose an option from the automation pull-down menu (under the track's name) (**Figure 11.45**):

  ▲ **Off:** Ignores the adjustments you made to a track when using the Audio Mixer for playback, but doesn't delete the settings (which appear as keyframes in the timeline).

  ▲ **Read:** Reproduces the adjustments you made to a track during playback.

Figure 11.46 In the Audio Mixer's menu, choose Switch to Touch after Write.

Figure 11.47 Choose Edit > Preferences > Audio.

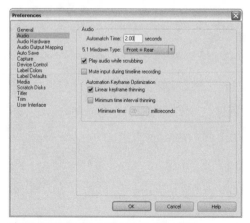

Figure 11.48 On the Audio panel of the Preferences dialog box, enter a value for Automatch Time.

▲ **Latch:** Releasing the mouse button leaves the fade/pan control at the current position. When playback is stopped and restarted, the fade/pan control resumes from 0.

▲ **Touch:** Releasing the mouse button automatically returns the fade/pan control to 0. How quickly it returns to 0 is determined by the Automatch Time setting (see the task "To specify the automatch time").

▲ **Write:** Releasing the mouse button leaves the fade/pan control at the current position. When playback is stopped and restarted, the fade/pan control resumes from the current position.

To switch from Write to Touch automatically:

◆ In the Audio Mixer's pull-down menu, choose Switch to Touch after Write (**Figure 11.46**).

When this option is selected, tracks' automation mode switches from Write to Touch automatically. When the option is deselected, tracks remain in Write mode after a mixing pass.

To specify the automatch time:

1. Choose Edit > Preferences > Audio (**Figure 11.47**).

The Audio panel of the Preferences dialog box appears.

2. For Automatch Time, enter a value in seconds, and click OK (**Figure 11.48**).

The value you enter determines the time it takes for a track's controls to return to 0 when the track's automation mode is set to Touch.

Routing Track Output

By default, each audio track is output, or *routed*, to the master audio track. However, you can route any number of tracks to a submix track. The submix track combines the signals routed to it, enabling you to process multiple tracks together. In turn, the output of the submix can be routed to yet another submix track or to the master track.

Submixing allows you to work with multiple tracks more efficiently. For example, by applying an effect to a submix, you avoid applying the effect to each track separately, thereby sparing your system from processing the effect multiple times.

In the Audio Mixer, submix tracks always appear to the right of the standard audio tracks. To help further distinguish them from the standard tracks (which, unlike submix tracks, can contain audio clips), submix tracks appear slightly darker. To prevent feedback, a submix track can be routed only to a submix track to the right of it or to the master track.

To route a track's output:

◆ At the bottom of a track's controls in the Audio Mixer, choose a track from the output pull-down menu (**Figure 11.49**):

▲ **Master:** Outputs the track's audio to the sequence's master track.

▲ **Submix:** Outputs the track's audio to the submix track you specify.

The track's audio is output to the track you specify. The output pull-down menu of a submix track contains only the names of submix tracks to the right and the master track.

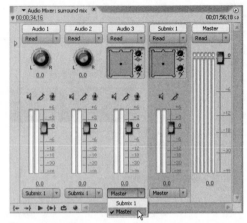

Figure 11.49 Route each track's output by choosing an option from its output pull-down menu.

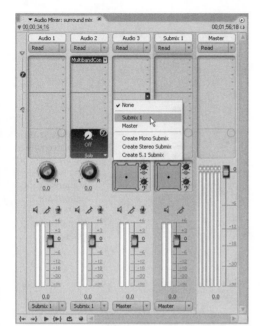

Figure 11.50 To assign a send, click a triangle in the sends list, and choose a track from the pull-down menu.

Working with Sends

Some mixes call for blending the processed version of an audio signal with its unprocessed signal. However, routing the signal to a sub-mix track using the output pull-down menu won't retain an unprocessed signal. Instead, you need to use a *send*.

You assign a send by selecting an option from any of the five pull-down menus indicated by the sends icon ⊛ (grouped under the track effects). Each send includes a volume knob, which you use to control the volume of the processed (wet) signal produced by the submix relative to the unprocessed (dry) signal sent by the track. This process is known as *adjusting the wet/dry mix*.

In addition, you can specify whether the send is applied pre-fader or post-fader. A pre-fader send routes the audio before the track's fader settings are applied; a post-fader send routes the audio after. Therefore, a pre-fader send's output level isn't affected by adjustments you make to the track's fader. In contrast, a post-fader send's output changes according to the track's fader level.

Typically, you use a pre-fader send and set the wet/dry mix to maximize the wet signal. This allows you to control the dry signal with the track's fader and to control the wet signal with the submix's fader.

To assign a send:

1. In the Audio Mixer, make sure the effects/sends area is visible.

2. In the sends area, click one of the five triangles, and choose a track from the pull-down menu (**Figure 11.50**).

   The track's audio is output to the selected track, either pre-fader or post-fader, depending on your choice (see the task "To specify whether a send is pre-fader or post-fader").

To create a submix and assign a send simultaneously:

◆ In a track's sends area (indicated by a sends icon ⊙), click one of the five triangles, and choose an option from the pull-down menu (**Figure 11.51**).

A submix track of the channel type you specified is added to the sequence and appears in its timeline and its Audio Mixer panel. Make sure to specify whether the send is pre-fader or post-fader (see the next task).

To specify whether a send is pre-fader or post-fader:

◆ Right-click a track's send area, and choose an option from the menu (**Figure 11.52**):

▲ **Pre-Fader:** Sends the track's signal to the specified submix before the track's fade settings are applied.

▲ **Post-Fader:** Sends the signal to the specified submix after the track's fade settings are applied.

Figure 11.51 You can also create a submix and send simultaneously by choosing the appropriate create option in the pull-down menu.

Figure 11.52 Right-click a track's send, and select either Pre-Fader or Post-Fader.

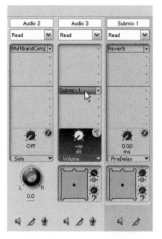

Figure 11.53
Selecting the name of a send makes its controls appear at the bottom of the effects/sends area.

Figure 11.54
Choose the send parameter you want to view from the pull-down menu below the control.

Sends enabled
Sends disabled

Figure 11.55
Click the Sends button to toggle it on and off. A crossed-out icon means the send is disabled, or muted.

To view volume and panning controls for a send:

1. In a track of the Audio Mixer, select a send.

   Controls for one of the send's parameters appear at the bottom of the track's effects/sends area (**Figure 11.53**).

2. From the pull-down menu below the send's parameter controls, select the parameter you want to control (**Figure 11.54**).

   A control appears for the selected parameter.

To mute a send:

1. In a track of the Audio Mixer, select a send.

   Controls for one of the send's parameters appear at the bottom of the track's effects/sends area.

2. In the send's controls, click the Sends button ⑫ to toggle it off, so that it appears crossed out ⑬ (**Figure 11.55**).

   When the send is off, it's excluded from output until you toggle it back on.

✔ Tips

■ During automation, remember to protect effects and sends from inadvertent changes by right-clicking the effect or send and selecting Safe during Write.

■ Older versions of Premiere allowed you to gang pan and fader controls. Submix tracks make that feature obsolete, and Premiere Pro doesn't include it.

Adding Track Effects

You can apply up to five effects to each track and submix track. There are many effects to choose from, but you can add VST plug-ins to expand your choices. (See the sidebar "What Is VST?") You can specify whether each effect is pre-fader or post-fader—that is, whether the effect is applied before or after the track's volume settings take effect.

As is the case with other settings, you can automate effect settings to change them over time. As with fade and pan controls, you can protect effect settings during mixing by choosing Safe during Write from the effect's context menu. And as with other effects, your automated changes can be viewed as keyframed values in the Timeline panel.

When an effect has multiple parameters, you can view and adjust each parameter's values by selecting it from the effect's pull-down menu. Some effects also allow you to view the effect's controls in a separate panel, which often contains special graphical controls to help you visualize the adjustments you're making.

You can also add effects to individual audio clips. Effects for audio clips, like those for video clips, are listed on the Effects panel. You adjust their settings over time by manipulating keyframes in the Timeline panel and Effect Controls panel. These techniques are covered in Chapter 13.

What Is VST?

Virtual Studio Technology (VST) generally refers to a widely accepted audio plug-in format developed by Steinberg (the same company that introduced the ASIO standard). Third-party VST plug-ins often include controls in a dialog box separate from the Audio Mixer.

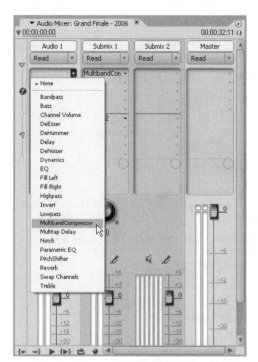

Figure 11.56 Click one of the five triangles in the effects area, and choose a track effect from the pull-down menu.

To apply a track effect:

1. If the effects/sends area of the Audio Mixer isn't visible, click the triangle at the upper left of the panel (below and to the left of the first track's automation pull-down menu) to make the area visible.

2. At the right side of the effects area, indicated by an effects icon 🕙, click one of the five triangles, and choose an effect from the pull-down menu (**Figure 11.56**). The effect's name appears in the list of effects, and the effect is applied to the track at the default settings. If the effect has adjustable parameter values, the first parameter's controls appear at the bottom of the track's effect/sends area.

3. Specify whether the effect is applied before or after the track's volume settings by right-clicking the effect's name and choosing one of the following (**Figure 11.57**):

   ▲ **Pre-Fader:** Applies the effect before volume adjustments.

   ▲ **Post-Fader:** Applies the effect after volume adjustments.

Figure 11.57 Right-click the effect name, and select either Pre-Fader or Post-Fader.

355

To view and adjust effect parameters:

1. Select a track effect.

   The controls for the effect's first parameter appear at the bottom of the track's effects/sends panel.

2. At the bottom of the track's effects/sends panel (below the parameter's value control), choose a parameter from the pull-down menu (**Figure 11.58**).

   The selected parameter's value control appears at the bottom of the track's effects/sends panel.

3. Adjust the selected parameter's values for the entire track, or during automation.

   To adjust effect parameters over time, follow the instructions in the task "To mix with automation," later in this chapter.

4. To protect the effect's parameters from changes during mixing, right-click the effect's name, and choose Safe during Write (**Figure 11.59**).

To select an effect preset:

◆ To select settings presets, right-click the effect's name, and choose a parameter from the menu (**Figure 11.60**).

Figure 11.58 Choose the parameter from the pull-down menu below the current control.

Figure 11.59 To protect effect settings from being changed during automation, right-click the effect's name and choose Safe during Write.

Figure 11.60 If the effect has preset settings, you can right-click the effect and select the preset name from the pull-down menu.

ADDING TRACK EFFECTS

Figure 11.61 You can view the controls for many effects in a separate dialog box, which you access by double-clicking the effect's name or by right-clicking the effect and choosing Edit.

Figure 11.62 This dialog box provides more graphical controls for the Reverb effect.

Figure 11.63 To disable the selected effect, click its effect icon so that it appears crossed out. Click the icon again to re-enable the effect.

To adjust a track effect's values using a separate dialog box:

1. *Do one of the following:*

   ▲ Double-click the effect's name.

   ▲ Right-click an effect's name, and choose Edit from the menu (**Figure 11.61**).

   A dialog box for the effect's parameter controls opens. This option isn't available for all effects (**Figure 11.62**).

2. Adjust the effect's parameters in the dialog box either for the entire track or during automation.

   When you're finished, close the dialog box.

To disable a track effect:

1. Select a track effect.

   The effect's parameter controls appear at the bottom of the track's effects/sends panel.

2. In the effect's parameter controls, click the effect icon 🎛 to toggle it off 🎛 (**Figure 11.63**).

   The effect is disabled and won't alter the track's audio. Click the icon again to toggle it on and enable the effect.

✔ Tip

■ You can also apply effects to individual clips. To learn about clip-based effects and how to make a clip's effect parameters change over time, see Chapter 13.

Specifying Audio Keyframe Optimization

Using the Audio Mixer to automate audio changes can create many more keyframes than are needed in the audio track and so slow down the performance of your system. Also, an overabundance of keyframes makes it much more difficult to edit them individually.

To avoid creating too many keyframes, you can set the Automation Keyframe Optimization preference. You have a choice between Linear Keyframe Thinning and Minimal Time Interval Thinning:

◆ **Linear Keyframe Thinning:** Removes any superfluous keyframes between two perfectly straight keyframes so that only the start and end keyframes of the segment remain. This option is selected by default.

◆ **Minimal Time Interval Thinning:** Removes any keyframes within a specified time interval. The default is 20 milliseconds. Choosing this option can result in incremental keyframes of equal value. The slower the change in the effect, the more superfluous keyframes.

To set the Automation Keyframe Optimization preference:

1. Choose Edit > Preferences > Audio (**Figure 11.64**).

   The Audio panel of the Preferences dialog box appears.

2. In the Automation Keyframe Optimization area, select one of the following, and click OK (**Figure 11.65**):

   ▲ **Linear Keyframe Thinning:** Eliminates adjacent keyframes of identical value.

   ▲ **Minimal Time Interval Thinning:** Eliminates keyframes within a specified interval. Enter a time interval between 1 and 30 milliseconds (20 ms is the default).

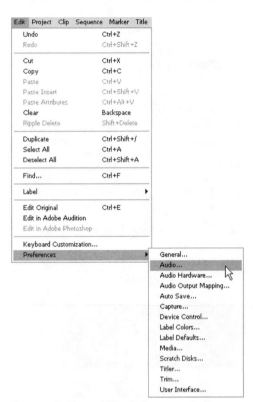

Figure 11.64 Choose Edit > Preferences > Audio.

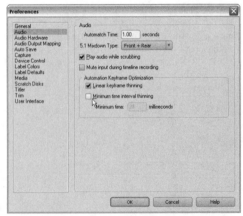

Figure 11.65 In the Automation Keyframe Optimization area, set your preferences.

Figure 11.66 Set sequence In and Out points to define the area you want to mix. To see your adjustments in the timeline, set the tracks to show the appropriate audio data.

Figure 11.67 In the Audio Mixer, monitor the tracks you want to hear during the mix and make sure the controls you need are visible. In this figure, audio 2 is muted.

Mixing with the Audio Mixer

Now that you understand all your options, you're ready to mix. Mixing can involve many tracks and encompass the entire length of a sequence. For this reason, you break the process into smaller, more manageable units by defining In and Out points in the sequence. Controls in the Audio Mixer let you play the selected area for mixing and evaluation.

Because your computer's mouse allows you to adjust only one thing at a time (and because doing so is an efficient strategy), you make adjustments to a single parameter in a single track and then adjust other parameters and tracks in separate passes.

To prepare to mix:

1. To define the part of the sequence you want to mix, set sequence In and Out points (**Figure 11.66**).

2. To view the track volume or pan keyframes in the Timeline panel, expand the audio tracks you want to adjust, and then click the track's Show/Hide Keyframes button and *do one of the following:*

   ▲ Choose Show Track Keyframes > Panner; then, choose the Panning option.

   ▲ Choose Show Track Volume.

3. In the Audio Mixer, choose monitoring options for each channel (**Figure 11.67**). You can monitor and mute any track or solo a track.

continues on next page

4. Make sure the controls for the parameters you want to adjust are visible.

Remember: You must select the effect or send parameter you want to adjust to view its controls.

5. Route each track's signal using its output pull-down menu and by assigning sends (**Figure 11.68**).

Routing doesn't affect automated settings directly, but it does influence the way the final mix sounds.

To mix with automation:

1. In the Audio Mixer, set each channel's automation option (**Figure 11.69**).

Choose Touch, Latch, or Write for the channels you want to adjust. Generally, you adjust each channel in a separate pass.

2. To protect particular settings from being overwritten (in Touch, Latch, or Write mode), right-click the appropriate control, and choose Safe during Write (**Figure 11.70**).

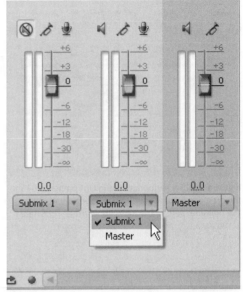

Figure 11.68 Route each track's signal by choosing a destination in the output pull-down menu (shown here). You can also use sends to control signal flow and to blend wet and dry signals.

Figure 11.69 In the Audio Mixer, use the automation pull-down menus to specify which tracks will write automated adjustments and which will read or ignore track settings.

Figure 11.70 To protect a setting from being affected during automation, right-click the setting's controls, and choose Safe during Write. Here, the pan/balance control is being set to Safe during Write.

Figure 11.71 Play the sequence, and make adjustments to settings in tracks you set to an automation write mode (Latch, Touch, or Write). Here, the fader (output level) is being adjusted.

3. Cue the sequence's CTI to the point at which you want to start mixing, and then play back the sequence.

4. As the sequence plays, make adjustments to any parameters of the tracks set to record automation (Latch, Touch, or Write) (**Figure 11.71**).

5. To stop playback and finish the mixing pass, click the Stop button ■ in the Audio Mixer or Program Monitor, or press the spacebar.

   In the Timeline panel, changes appear as a value graph with keyframes (when the appropriate property is visible).

6. To review your adjustments, set all tracks' automation mode to Read (**Figure 11.72**), and then monitor and play back the mix.

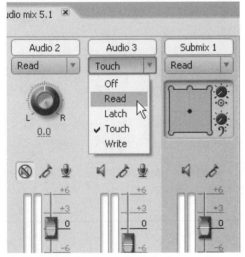

Figure 11.72 Reset the tracks' automation mode to Read so you can review your changes.

12

CREATING TITLES

Although Premiere Pro can accept graphic files created with other applications, no editing system would be complete without a title-creation tool of its own. At the very least, most videos require an opening title and end credits. But titles and graphics are far more pervasive than that. Titles can identify the onscreen speaker in a documentary, show the company logo in a commercial, list important concepts in a business presentation, or subtitle foreign-language footage. Even narrative projects may use titles within the program—for example, to identify a change of scene or time, like this: "Orlando, Florida, 1970" or "36 Years Later."

Premiere Pro's Titler includes tools for creating text and graphics, title rolls, and crawls. It also includes an extensive list of templates and preset styles, path text, pen tools, stroke and fill controls, and precise controls over a host of object attributes.

The Titler

Whenever you create or change a title clip, you invoke a "suite" of panels collectively known as the Titler(**Figure 12.1**). The Titler's main panel, called the Title Designer, consists of a large drawing area that corresponds to the television screen. It also includes a strip of buttons for creating a new title and for various typesetting tasks. The Titler includes several secondary panels:

◆ **Title Tools panel:** Includes buttons to help you create and modify text, shapes, and images.

◆ **Title Actions panel:** Helps you align and distribute selected items in a title.

◆ **Styles panel:** A collection of preset and custom settings you can apply to objects in a title quickly and easily.

◆ **Title Properties panel:** Lets you control a multitude of attributes categorized under Transform, Properties, Fill, Strokes, and Shadow headings.

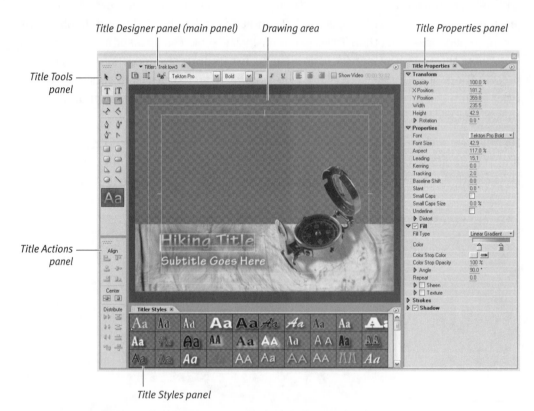

Title Designer panel (main panel)   Drawing area   Title Properties panel

Title Tools panel

Title Actions panel

Title Styles panel

Figure 12.1 The Title Designer panel is divided into several sections.

THE TITLER

Figure 12.2 . You can view different titles by choosing the title's name in the Title Designer tab's pull-down menu.

When it comes to viewing titles, they're comparable to sequences; they're listed in the Window menu only when they're open, under Window > Titler Designer > *titlename*. And just as you can access a different sequence by selecting its name in the Program Monitor's tab, you can reopen a title by choosing its name in the Title Designer tab's pull-down menu (**Figure 12.2**).

When the panel is active, a Title menu appears in the menu bar, and the Preferences dialog box includes Titler settings.

✔ Tips

- If you've used previous versions of Premiere Pro (or its predecessor, Premiere), keep an eye out for a number of subtle but important enhancements, such as the Align and Distribute buttons; a Current Style swatch; a revised Font menu; reorganized and renamed areas; Titler tab pull-down menu; and of course, the panel-based interface. In addition, titles are no longer saved as separate files, but as part of the project.

- This chapter concentrates on the core features of the Titler. To find out how to convert titles created in older versions of Premiere, consult the help system and user guide.

THE TITLER

Creating a Title

The Titler comes with an extensive list of preset templates—ready-made designs with generic text that you can replace with your own messages. Templates are organized into categories, and many contain photographic images that pertain to the selected topic.

You can also create a new title from scratch by choosing a menu command or by clicking the New Item button in the Project panel.

When the title is added to the timeline's video track 2 or higher, empty areas in the title appear transparent, revealing the image contained by the track below. To help you visualize the final effect, you can set the Titler to show the current frame of the sequence in the Timeline. Otherwise, transparent areas appear as a checkerboard pattern in the Title Designer panel. For more information, see the section "Viewing the Video in the Background," later in this chapter.

In contrast to the previous version of Premiere Pro, the current version saves all titles as part of the project—not as separate files. This way, saving your titles is as easy as saving your project, and you won't have to worry about losing track of your title files.

To create a new title with a menu command:

1. Choose File > New > Title (**Figure 12.3**). A New Title dialog box appears.

2. Enter a name for the title, and then click OK.

   The five panels that make up the Titler appear in a floating window. Titles match the image size you selected in the project settings.

Figure 12.3 Choose File > New > Title...

Figure 12.4 ...or click the New Item button, and choose Title from the menu.

Figure 12.5 Enter a name for the title in the New Title dialog box.

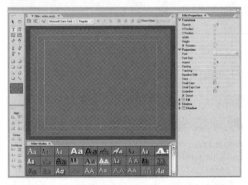

Figure 12.6 The Titler appears, with an untitled Title Designer panel.

To create a new title with the New Item button:

1. In the Project panel, click the New Item button , and choose Title from the menu (**Figure 12.4**).

   A New Title dialog box appears (**Figure 12.5**).

2. Enter a name for the title, and then click OK.

   The five panels that make up the Titler appear in a floating window (**Figure 12.6**). Titles match the image size you selected in the project settings.

To create a title based on the current title:

1. In the Title Designer panel, click the New Title Based on Current Title button ⓣ (**Figure 12.7**).

   A New Title dialog box appears.

2. Type a name for the new title, and then click OK (**Figure 12.8**).

   The objects contained in the former title are copied into the current title. The Title Designer panel's tab indicates the new title name you entered, and the title is listed in the Project panel.

3. Modify the title's objects. For example, select text and type the appropriate message in its place (**Figure 12.9**).

4. When you're finished modifying the title, you can create other titles or switch to the workspace best suited to the task at hand.

   The new title is added to the Project panel automatically and saved with the project whenever you save the project.

✔ Tips

■ Although titles are saved as part of the project, you can still export a title as a separate file. This way, you can import the title into another project and share a title with Premiere Pro users.

■ You can use traditional keyboard shortcuts to copy and paste objects in the Title Designer: Ctrl+C to copy; Ctrl+V to paste.

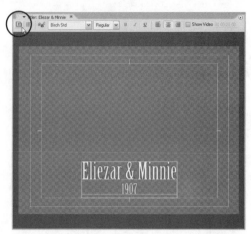

Figure 12.7 In the Title Designer panel, click the New Title Based on Current Title button.

Figure 12.8 Enter a name for the title in the New Title dialog box, and then click OK.

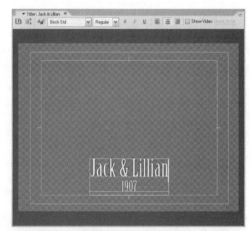

Figure 12.9 The new title includes the objects contained by the previous title, which you can modify as necessary. Here, the names have been changed to match the photo.

Figure 12.10 With the Titler active, choose Title > Templates.

Figure 12.11 A preview of the selected template appears in the dialog box.

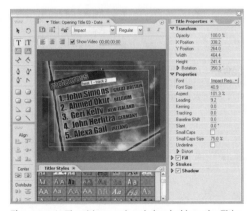

Figure 12.12 The title template is loaded into the Title Designer panel.

Using Title Templates

Premiere Pro comes with an extensive list of preset title templates—ready-made designs with generic text that you can replace with your own. Templates are organized into categories, such as Celebrations, Sports, and Travel. Many contain photographic images that pertain to the topic at hand. There's also a long list of *lower third*, *upper third*, and *over the shoulder* titles (common designs in broadcast video). In addition, you'll find informational lists, which are perfect for business presentations on video.

To load a title template:

1. With the Titler active, choose Title > Templates (**Figure 12.10**).

   The Templates dialog box appears.

2. Select the title template you want to use.

   If necessary, click the triangle next to a folder or subfolder to reveal the templates it contains. A preview of the selected template appears in the Templates dialog box (**Figure 12.11**).

3. Click Apply.

   The title template is loaded into the Title Designer panel (**Figure 12.12**). Modify the text or other objects (using methods described later in the chapter), and save the title.

✔ Tips

■ You can use options in the Templates dialog box to create, rename, or delete title templates.

■ A few templates don't include titles per se but are designed to mask off areas of the video with black borders. You'll find them in the Mattes category of templates. For example, the *letterbox* template simulates a common motion-picture film aspect ratio.

■ A *lower third* title is aligned with the bottom of the title-safe zone, where a title that identifies an onscreen subject is typically placed.

Viewing the Video Safe Zones

As you learned in Chapter 5, "Viewing Clips in the Monitor Panels, in the section "Viewing Video Safe Zones," standard television monitors *overscan* the image, cropping off the outer edges. For this reason, the Monitor panels can display NTSC safe zones: reference marks indicating the areas of the screen that are considered to be action safe and title safe. It's only logical that the Title Designer panel also displays guides to help you keep the titles you create within the safe zones (**Figure 12.13**). As you may recall, the inner 90 percent of the screen is considered action safe; the inner 80 percent of the screen is considered title safe.

To view safe zones:

◆ With the Title Designer panel selected, choose Title > View, and select an option (**Figure 12.14**):

▲ **Safe Title Margin:** Displays guides for the inner 80 percent of the title panel.

▲ **Safe Action Margin:** Displays guides for the inner 90 percent of the panel.

Deselect an option to hide the safe-zone marks in the Title Designer panel.

Title-safe zone ⎯ ⎯ Action-safe zone

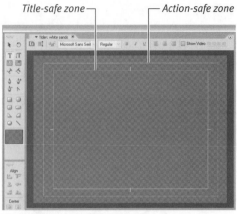

Figure 12.13 You can display reference marks to indicate the action-safe and title-safe zones.

Figure 12.14 With the Title Designer panel active, choose Title > View, and choose the safe zone you want to display.

Figure 12.15 Click Show Video to display a frame of the program video as the background in the drawing area.

Figure 12.16 Change the background frame by scrubbing the current time display...

Figure 12.17 ...or clicking the time display, and entering a frame number.

Viewing the Video in the Background

Because most titles are keyed over video (see Chapter 13, "Working with Effects"), the background of a title is transparent. In the drawing area, a checkerboard pattern represents the transparent areas. However, you can fill the background with a representative frame of video from the program so you can adjust the colors and elements of the title to match.

The background frame isn't saved as part of the title; it's merely a helpful reference.

To toggle background video:

◆ In the Title Designer panel, click Show Video to display a frame of the program as the background of the drawing area (**Figure 12.15**).

Deselect Show Video to view a checkerboard background in the drawing area.

To cue the background video frame:

◆ Do one of the following:

▲ In the Title Designer panel, scrub the current frame display to change the frame number (**Figure 12.16**).

▲ In the Title Designer panel, click the current frame display, and enter a valid frame number (**Figure 12.17**).

▲ Use controls in the Program Monitor or Timeline panel to cue the CTI.

The background video frame corresponds to the frame number you select.

✔ Tips

■ When you're selecting colors for objects you create in the Titler, you can use the Eyedropper tool to sample colors from the background video.

■ If the composition of the background video changes over the course of a title, be sure to spot-check the title against several representative frames.

Adjusting Values

Each object you create has its own set of attributes—font, fill color, stroke color, opacity, drop shadow, and so on. Although many of an object's attributes (its position, for example) are apparent in the drawing area, the values of all attributes are listed in detail in the Title Properties panel. Select an object, and its properties appear in the Title Properties panel (**Figures 12.18** and **12.19**).

The operation of most property controls should be familiar to the experienced computer user. This chapter assumes that you know how to pick a color using a color picker or eyedropper, how to set an angle using a graphical control, and how to click a triangle to view hidden options. And by now you should be familiar with the ways to change a numerical value: either by clicking it and entering a number or by dragging it. As in other areas of Premiere Pro (and throughout Adobe programs), you can change a numerical value in the Titler by dragging, or *scrubbing*, the value.

This section explains how to temporarily disable certain properties of objects in a title. Later sections explain properties in greater detail: first the properties unique to each kind of object—text and graphics—and then the properties common to both text and graphics.

Figure 12.18 Selecting an object...

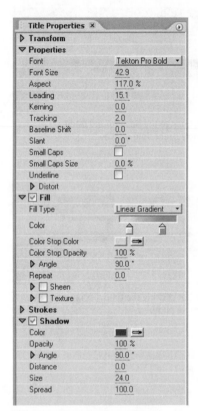

Figure 12.19 ...makes its attributes appear in the Title Properties panel.

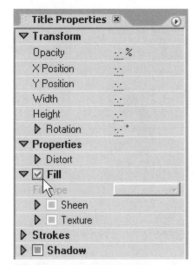

Figure 12.20 Click the box next to a property value to enable it; deselect the box to disable the property.

To enable or disable an option:

1. Select an object in the Title Designer panel.

2. *Do one of the following:*

   ▲ Click the box next to a property to enable it and the options associated with it (**Figure 12.20**).

   ▲ Deselect the box to temporarily disable the property.

   Reselecting a property restores the most recent settings associated with it.

✔ Tip

■ Although the Title Properties panel has a Properties category, this book uses the term *properties* more generically, to refer to any attribute.

ADJUSTING VALUES

Creating Text Objects

The Titler includes tools for creating two types of text: text confined only by the drawing area, and text confined to a text box that you define. In each method, you can create either horizontally oriented or vertically oriented text (**Figure 12.21**).

At first glance, there seems to be little difference between using the type tools and using the text-box tools (**Figure 12.22**). But a big practical difference emerges after you create the text. Whereas changing a text box reflows the text it contains, changing the bounding box of text created with a type tool *transforms* the text—that is, doing so resizes or stretches it (**Figure 12.23**). Therefore, it's best to use a text box to create larger blocks of text that may require tabs or margin changes. Use a type tool to create shorter messages that lend themselves to more expressive modifications such as distortion or rotation.

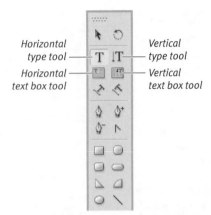

Horizontal type tool — Vertical type tool
Horizontal text box tool — Vertical text box tool

Figure 12.21 The Titler includes tools for creating type bounded by the drawing area or by a text box.

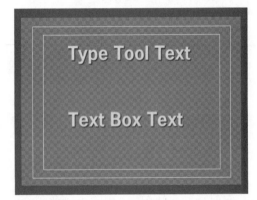

Figure 12.22 At first glance, creating text with the type tools and the text-box tools yields similar results.

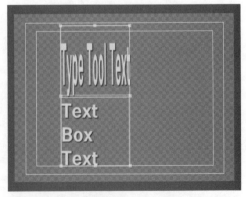

Figure 12.23 Changing the size of a text box reflows the text it contains; changing the bounding box of text created with a type tool transforms the text.

Figure 12.24 Select either the Horizontal (shown here) or Vertical Type tool.

Figure 12.25 Click in the drawing area to set the insertion point, and then type.

To create text within the drawing area:

1. In the Title Tools panel, select one of the type tools (**Figure 12.24**):

   ▲ **Horizontal Type tool** T: Creates horizontal text.

   ▲ **Vertical Type tool** ⏐T: Creates vertical text.

2. Click the mouse pointer in the drawing area where you want to begin typing.

   A blinking insertion point appears.

3. Type the text you want (**Figure 12.25**).

4. When you've finished typing, click the Selection tool ⬧ in the Title Tools panel.

5. With the title object still selected, modify any of its attributes, such as position, alignment, font, or color.

   You can use options on the Title menu or controls on the Title Properties panel, or you can select a style from the Title Styles panel (see the following sections).

To create text within a text box:

1. In the Title Tools panel, select one of the text box tools (**Figure 12.26**):

   ▲ **Horizontal Text Box tool** 🖺:
   Creates horizontal text constrained by a text box.

   ▲ **Vertical Text Box tool** 🖺:
   Creates vertical text constrained by a text box.

2. Drag the mouse pointer diagonally in the drawing area to define a text box (**Figure 12.27**).

   When you release the mouse, a text box appears, with a blinking insertion point in the upper-left corner.

3. Type the text you want (**Figure 12.28**).

   You can type more than the text box can contain. To view the hidden text, resize the text box after you've finished typing.

4. When you've finished typing, click the Selection tool ▶ in the Title Tools panel.

   With the title object still selected, modify any of its attributes, such as position, alignment, font, or color.

✔ Tip

■ Stretching type by changing the size of the bounding box doesn't affect the Distort values in the Properties section of the Title Properties panel.

Figure 12.26 Select either the Horizontal (shown here) or Vertical Text Box tool.

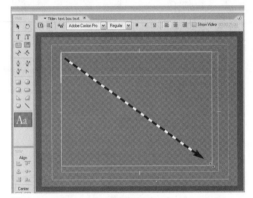

Figure 12.27 Drag diagonally in the drawing area to set the boundaries of the text box.

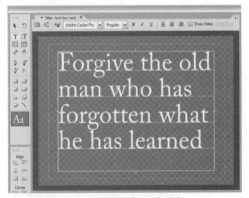

Figure 12.28 Type in the text box. If all the text doesn't fit in the box, you can resize the text later.

Figure 12.29 Choose Title > Word Wrap.

Setting Word Wrap

You can use the *word wrap* setting to control how text reflows within a text box. When word wrap is on, text automatically starts a new line when it reaches the edge of the text box or drawing area (depending on the kind of text you're using; see the previous sections). If you turn off word wrap, a line of text will continue offscreen if created with a type tool or beyond the confines of its text box if created with a text box tool. To see the hidden text, reposition or resize the text, or resize the text box so that more text fits inside.

To toggle word wrap:

◆ With a text object selected, choose Title > Word Wrap (**Figure 12.29**).

Click Word Wrap to turn it on; deselect Word Wrap to turn it off. The word wrap setting you choose affects selected text objects.

✔ Tip

■ Resizing the bounding box reflows only lines of text created with soft returns—new lines created by word wrap. Hard returns—new lines created by pressing Enter—are not affected by resizing the bounding box.

SETTING WORD WRAP

Setting Tabs

Larger blocks of text may also use tabs. You can set tab stops much as you would in a word-processing program and view them in a text box.

To set tabs:

1. Using a text-box tool, create a text box.

2. With a text box object selected, choose Title > Tab Stops (**Figure 12.30**).

   The Tab Stops dialog box opens (**Figure 12.31**).

3. Select the type of tab you want to set (**Figure 12.32**):

   ⌊ Left-aligned tab

   ↓ Center-aligned tab

   ⌋ Right-aligned tab

4. Click above the ruler where you want to set the tab (**Figure 12.33**).

5. To delete a tab stop, drag it away from the ruler.

6. Click OK to close the Tab Stops dialog box.

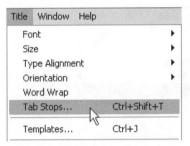

Figure 12.30 Choose Title > Tab Stops.

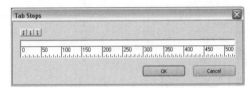

Figure 12.31 The Tab Stops dialog box opens.

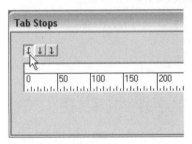

Figure 12.32 Select the kind of tab you want to use.

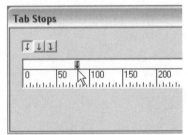

Figure 12.33 Click above the ruler to set the tab's position.

Figure 12.34 Choose Title > View > Tab Markers.

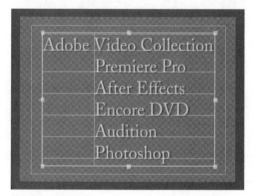

Figure 12.35 A yellow reference line corresponds to each tab you set.

To toggle tab reference marks:

1. Select a text box.

2. Choose Title > View > Tab Markers (**Figure 12.34**).

   A yellow line appears, corresponding to each tab (**Figure 12.35**). Deselect Tab Markers to hide the reference lines.

✔ Tip

■ Remember that it's hard to fit large amounts of text into the confines of a television screen—and still have it be legible, that is. Consider cutting the amount of copy to the bare essentials or using a title roll instead (see "Creating Rolls and Crawls," later in this chapter).

Creating Path Text

Rather than following a ramrod-straight baseline, path text follows a curved path that you create.

To create path text:

1. In the Title Tools panel, select one of the path text tools (**Figure 12.36**):

   ▲ **Horizontal Path Text tool** ✎: Creates text horizontally aligned to the path.

   ▲ **Vertical Path Text tool** ✎: Creates text vertically aligned to the path.

2. Create a Bézier curve in the drawing area (**Figure 12.37**).

   The mouse becomes the Pen tool ✎. To learn more about creating Bézier curves, see "Using the Pen Tools," later in this chapter.

3. After you've finished creating the curve, choose the Selection tool ▶ in the Title Tools panel.

   The Bézier curve's bounding box appears.

Figure 12.36 Select either the Vertical or Horizontal (shown here) Path Text tool.

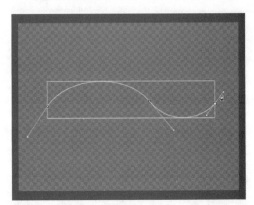

Figure 12.37 Create a Bézier curve in the drawing area.

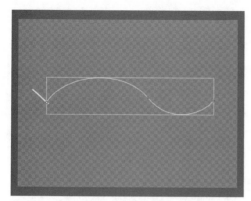

Figure 12.38 Using the Selection tool, double-click the curve to make the insertion point appear.

Figure 12.39 The text follows the curve.

4. Double-click inside the curve's bounding box.

   A blinking insertion point appears at the beginning of the curve (**Figure 12.38**).

5. Type the text you want.

   Each character's baseline is tangent to the curve (**Figure 12.39**).

✔ Tips

- Path text is prone to problems with *kerning*, the spacing between letters. Use the kerning controls as explained later in this chapter.

- You can edit path text just like you would text created with the type or text-box tools.

- You can reshape the path text's curve at any time by double-clicking the path text object with the Selection tool and then clicking a control point.

Selecting Text

Whenever you want to edit or modify any of a text object's attributes, you must first select all or part of the object.

To select text for editing:

1. *Do one of the following:*

   ▲ To select the entire text object, click the text with the Selection tool (**Figure 12.40**).

   ▲ To set an insertion point, double-click the text object with the Selection tool (**Figure 12.41**).

   ▲ To select a range of text, drag across the text with the insertion-point cursor (**Figure 12.42**).

2. Type to change the selected text or to insert text at the insertion point.

   You can also adjust other attributes of selected text, such as font, size, and fill color. (See the following sections to find out more about adjusting text attributes.)

3. When you finish making changes to the text, choose the Selection tool.

   Click an empty part of the drawing area to deselect the text, or select another object-creation tool.

✔ Tip

■ You can use the arrow keys to move the insertion point.

Figure 12.40 To select an entire text object, click it with the Selection tool.

Figure 12.41 Double-click to set a blinking insertion point.

Figure 12.42 Drag the insertion-point cursor to select a contiguous range of text.

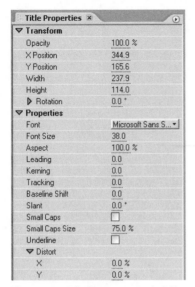

Figure 12.43 Edit the text as needed. Use the Object Style section of the Title Designer to adjust properties.

Setting Text Properties

You can assign numerous properties—color, drop shadow, and so on—to any object in the drawing area. However, some properties are exclusive to text. (See the next section, "Using the Font Browser," to learn how to select a font.)

To set text properties:

1. Select all or part of a text object.

2. In the Properties section of the Title Properties panel, set any of the following (**Figure 12.43**):

   ▲ **Font:** Lists fonts in a pull-down menu.

   ▲ **Font Size:** Sets the size of the text, in points.

   ▲ **Aspect:** Sets the horizontal (x) and vertical (y) scale of the selected font.

   ▲ **Leading:** Sets the spacing between lines of text.

   ▲ **Kerning:** Sets the spacing between character pairs; position the cursor between the characters you want to adjust.

   ▲ **Tracking:** Sets the spacing between a range of characters.

   ▲ **Baseline Shift:** Sets the distance of text characters from the baseline; use Baseline Shift to create superscripts and subscripts.

   ▲ **Slant:** Sets the slant of text, in degrees.

   ▲ **Small Caps:** When selected, makes selected characters appear as upper-case; all characters except the leading character (the first letter of each word) become small caps.

continues on next page

SETTING TEXT PROPERTIES

▲ **Small Caps Size:** When the All Caps check box is selected, sets the size of small caps as a percentage of the ordinary capital letter's height.

▲ **Underline:** When selected, underlines selected characters.

▲ **Distort (*x, y*):** Distorts the selected characters; adjust the *x* value to distort the selection along its horizontal axis; adjust the *y* value to distort it along the vertical axis.

✔ Tips

■ You can avoid scrolling through long lists of fonts by selecting More from the font list. Fonts are now grouped in categories, such as Japanese fonts and Latin fonts.

■ Like most text-editing or layout programs, the Titler allows you to *justify*, or align, the text within its text box. (There are positioning commands to move the box itself.) To align text within its text box, choose Title > Type Alignment, and choose the alignment option you want: Left, Center, or Right. Better yet, use the corresponding alignment buttons at the top of the Title Designer panel: ▤, ▤, and ▤.

Figure 12.44 In the Title Designer panel, click the Browse button.

Using the Font Browser

Choosing a font from a long pull-down menu works great if you're already familiar with the font you want. But if you could use a little help selecting a font, use the Font Browser feature. It not only lists fonts—it also shows what they look like and instantly changes the font of the selected text. This allows you to preview various fonts before you settle on one.

To select a font using the Font Browser:

1. *Do one of the following:*

   ▲ Select one or more text objects.

   ▲ Select a range of text.

   ▲ Set an insertion point using one of the text tools.

2. In the Title Designer panel, click the Browse button ᵃ_ᴮᶜ (**Figure 12.44**).

   The Font Browser dialog box appears.

   continues on next page

3. Select a font you want to consider (**Figure 12.45**).

The selected text reflects the font you choose in the Font Browser (**Figure 12.46**).

4. When you find the font you want, click OK.

✔ Tips

■ Not all fonts look like letters. Special fonts—often called symbols, ornaments, and dingbats—let you create useful graphic elements easily (**Figure 12.47**). You use these fonts just like other fonts, and you don't have to draw a thing.

■ By default, the font browser presents a sample of each font consisting of six letters: *AaegZz*. You can change the letters by choosing Edit > Preferences > Titler and typing any other six letters you want.

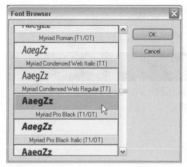

Figure 12.45 Select a font in the Font Browser.

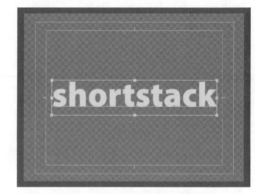

Figure 12.46 The selected text reflects your choice.

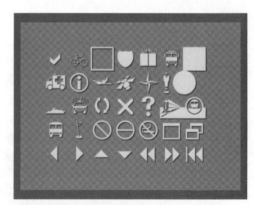

Figure 12.47 The font Webdings creates symbols instead of letters.

USING THE FONT BROWSER

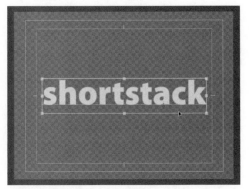

Figure 12.48 Select a text object or range of text.

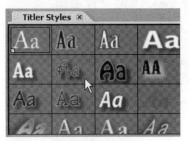

Figure 12.49 Click a style swatch in the Titler Styles area of the Title Designer panel.

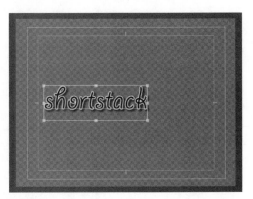

Figure 12.50 The style is applied to the selection.

Using Styles

Besides conveying raw information, titles also contribute to the overall look of a project. So, it's common for all the titles in a project to share similar characteristics. Using the Styles feature, you can reapply your favorite attributes quickly, without adjusting attributes time and time again.

The Current Style swatch always reflects the current style of the text. Any modifications you make to the style of the text updates the Current Style swatch.

To assign a style to text:

1. Select a text object or a range of text (**Figure 12.48**).

2. In the Titler Styles panel, click a style swatch. (**Figure 12.49**).

   The selected text uses the style you selected (**Figure 12.50**).

To set a style as the default:

1. Make sure no text objects in the drawing area are selected, and then click the style swatch you want to set as the default.

   A thin square outline indicates that the style is selected (**Figure 12.51**). If a text object is selected, it takes on the attributes of the style you choose.

2. *Do one of the following:*

   ▲ From the Styles panel's menu, choose Set Style as Default.

   ▲ Right-click the style swatch, and choose Set Style as Default from the context menu (**Figure 12.52**).

   The swatch moves to the upper-left corner of the Styles panel. A small icon appears in the corner of the selected style swatch (**Figure 12.53**).

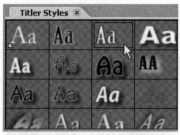

Figure 12.51 Click a style swatch to select it. The swatch should display a thin square.

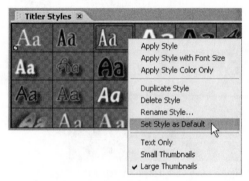

Figure 12.52 Choose Set Style as Default in the Styles panel's menu or in a context menu.

Figure 12.53 The default swatch always appears in the upper-left corner, with a small icon.

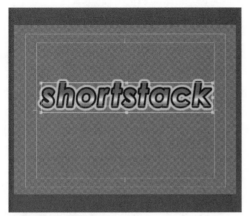

Figure 12.54 Select text that uses the attributes you want to save as a style.

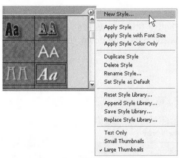

Figure 12.55 From the Styles panel's menu, choose New Style.

Figure 12.56 Name the style in the New Style dialog box, and click OK.

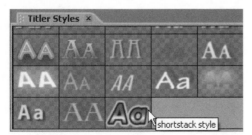

Figure 12.57 The new style appears among the style swatches.

To save a custom style:

1. Select a text object or range of text that has the attributes you want to save as a style (**Figure 12.54**).

2. In the Styles panel's menu, choose New Style (**Figure 12.55**).

    A New Style dialog box appears.

3. Enter the name of the style, and click OK (**Figure 12.56**).

    The style is added to the style swatches (**Figure 12.57**).

4. To view the styles by name, choose Text Only from the Styles panel's menu.

✔ Tips

■ Commands in the Styles panel's menu also allow you to delete and rename styles and change the way the style swatches look.

■ By default, style swatches show the way an uppercase and lowercase letter *A* look in the style. If you want to, you can choose Edit > Preferences > Titler and specify other letters.

USING STYLES

389

Creating Rolls and Crawls

In a title roll, text appears to move from beyond the bottom of the screen to beyond the top of the screen. Title rolls are frequently used in a final credit sequence or to present lengthy text onscreen.

A title crawl moves across the screen horizontally, typically from right to left. An emergency news bulletin is a classic example of a title crawl.

To create a roll or crawl:

1. Choose Title > New Title, and select an option from the submenu (**Figure 12.58**):
   - ▲ **Default Still:** Creates stationary text.
   - ▲ **Default Roll:** Creates rolling text.
   - ▲ **Default Crawl:** Creates crawling text.

   A New Title dialog box appears.

2. Enter a name for the title, and then click OK (**Figure 12.59**).

   The Titler appears.

3. Select the Horizontal Text Box tool ▣.

   To create vertically oriented text, choose the Vertical Text Box tool ▣.

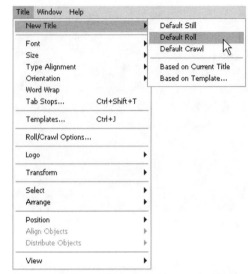

Figure 12.58 Choose Title > New Title >, and select an option from the submenu pull-down. Here, a title roll is selected.

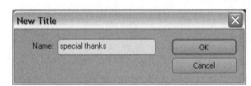

Figure 12.59 Name the title, and click OK.

Figure 12.60 Using a text-box tool (the Horizontal Text Box tool is selected here), drag in the drawing area to create a text box.

4. Drag in the drawing area to create a text box (**Figure 12.60**).

   You should drag beyond the bottom edge for a roll, or beyond the right edge for a crawl. Typically, you should keep title rolls between the left and right edges of the title-safe zone (see "Viewing the Video Safe Zones," earlier in this chapter).

5. Type the text you want (**Figure 12.61**).

6. *Do one of the following:*

   ▲ To make the text box larger, switch to the Selection tool, and drag one of the text box's control handles to resize the box.

   ▲ To view other parts of the text box, drag the scroll bar (**Figure 12.62**).

7. Set the roll/crawl options, as explained in the next task.

   When you add the title clip to the timeline, it rolls or crawls, according to your selections. The duration of the clip helps determine the speed of the roll or crawl.

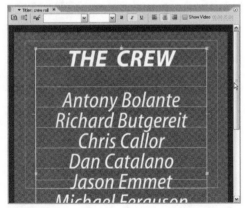

Figure 12.61 Type the text you want to scroll or crawl. Note that the drawing area includes a scroll bar.

Figure 12.62 To make the text box larger, resize it with the Selection tool; use the scroll bar to view different parts of the box.

CREATING ROLLS AND CRAWLS

To set roll and crawl options:

1. With a rolling or crawling text object selected, choose Title > Roll/Crawl Options (**Figure 12.63**).

   The Roll/Crawl Options dialog box appears (**Figure 12.64**).

2. In the Roll/Crawl Options dialog box, choose one or more of the following options:

   ▲ **Start Off Screen:** Positions the text box offscreen at the beginning of the roll or crawl.

   ▲ **End Off Screen:** Positions the text box offscreen at the end of the roll or crawl.

   ▲ **Preroll:** Sets the number of frames to hold the title in its starting position before the roll or crawl begins (not available when Start Off Screen is selected).

   ▲ **Ease-In:** Sets the number of frames during which the roll or crawl slowly accelerates before reaching full speed.

   ▲ **Ease-Out:** Sets the number of frames during which the roll or crawl slowly decelerates before stopping.

   ▲ **Postroll:** Sets the number of frames to hold the title in its ending position after the roll or crawl ends (not available when End Off Screen is selected).

3. Click OK to close the dialog box.

   The roll or crawl obeys the settings you selected.

✔ Tip

■ Although you can hold a title roll in its ending position by setting a Postroll value, getting the last lines to stop where you want may take some practice. For example, to get the text *copyright 2004* to end up alone in the center of the screen, you may have to experiment with adding blank lines or resizing the text box.

Figure 12.63 With the rolling or crawling object selected, choose Title > Roll/Crawl Options.

Figure 12.64 Choose the options you want in the Roll/Crawl Options dialog box.

Figure 12.65 Select one of the shape tools. In this example, the Ellipse tool is selected.

Creating Shape Objects

When you create a shape, you define its dimensions by defining the size of an invisible, rectangular box called a *bounding box.* Whereas a rectangle fits exactly inside its bounding box, other shapes are circumscribed within theirs. When you select a shape, its bounding box appears with six *handles,* small squares that you can grab and drag to change the dimensions of the box—and thereby the shape it contains.

You can also create open and closed polygons and Bézier shapes. These techniques are covered in later sections.

To create a shape:

1. In the Title Tools panel, select a shape tool (**Figure 12.65**):
   - Rectangle
   - Clipped-Corner Rectangle
   - Rounded-Corner Rectangle
   - Rounded Rectangle
   - Wedge
   - Arc
   - Ellipse

continues on next page

2. *Do one of the following:*

▲ Drag in the drawing area to define the size of the shape (**Figure 12.66**).

▲ Shift+drag in the drawing area to make the shape's horizontal and vertical aspects the same (to create perfect circles and squares or wedges and arcs with two equal sides).

▲ Alt+drag in the drawing area to define the shape from its center rather than its corners.

✔ Tips

■ You can change the dimensions of a shape (or text created with a type tool) by selecting it and dragging a handle of its bounding box.

■ You can change an existing shape into another shape with the same dimensions by selecting it and choosing an option from the Graphic Type pull-down menu.

■ Rounded-corner and clipped-corner rectangles have a Fillet Size setting, which specifies how much of the corner is rounded or clipped, respectively.

Figure 12.66 Drag in the drawing area to define the size of the shape. Hold down Shift to constrain the aspect of the shape, and hold down Alt to draw the shape from its center.

Figure 12.67 Anchor points have no direction lines extending from them.

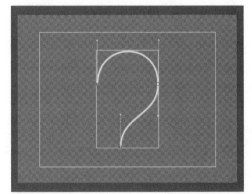

Figure 12.68 Smooth points have two opposite direction lines.

Understanding Control Points and Segments

You can use pen tools to create more complex shapes—the same kind of Bézier curves you can build in programs like Adobe Illustrator. But if you've never used a pen tool or heard of Bézier curves, it's time to review some basics.

Bézier paths consist of control points connected by line segments. *Control points* define each end of a segment; *direction lines* define the curve of the segment.

Direction lines and handles extend from control points to define and control the curve of a path segment. The length and angle of a direction line influence the shape of the curve. (Imagine that direction lines exert a gravitational pull on the line that enters and exits a control point.) Dragging the end of a direction line alters the line and thus its corresponding curve. When a point has two direction lines, the incoming direction line influences the preceding curve; the outgoing direction line influences the following curve.

It's helpful to categorize control points by how they use, or don't use, direction lines:

◆ **Anchor point:** Click with the Pen tool ✎ to create an anchor point. Anchor points have no control handles extending from them (**Figure 12.67**).

◆ **Smooth point:** Drag with the Pen tool ✎ to create a smooth point. Dragging extends two equal and opposite direction lines from a smooth point. Path segments connected by a smooth point result in a continuous curve (**Figure 12.68**).

continues on next page

- ◆ **Corner point:** A corner point's direction lines operate independently. You can convert a smooth point into a corner point by dragging a direction handle with the Convert Point tool ▷. Path segments connected by a corner point result in a discontinuous curve, or *cusp* (**Figure 12.69**).

✔ Tips

- ■ Although the concepts that underlie the creation of Bézier curves are constant, terminology and practice differ slightly from one program to another. Even among well-integrated programs—Illustrator, Photoshop, After Effects, and Premiere Pro—the pen tools and keyboard shortcuts differ.

- ■ You'll apply what you learn about Bézier curves to adjusting the spatial and temporal interpolation used when animating a clip's position and other effects. In other words, you can use Bézier curves to set a clip's motion path and to accelerate or decelerate changes in an animated effect. Learn all about it in Chapter 13.

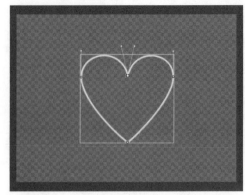

Figure 12.69 Corner points, or cusps, result from two discontinuous direction lines.

Qu'est-ce Que C'est Bézier? *Qui Est* Bézier?

In case your French is rusty, Bézier is pronounced *bay-zee-yay*, after the late Pierre Etienne Bézier, who developed the math behind his namesake curve in the 1970s for use in computer-aided design and manufacture. This same math became the basis for Adobe Postscript fonts, path-based drawing, and—yes—the interpolation methods used in computer animation. Bézier died in 1999. Merci, Monsieur Bézier.

Figure 12.70 Select the Pen tool.

Using the Pen Tools

In contrast to the title feature found in older versions of Premiere, the Title Designer comes with the powerful Pen tool. Now the kinds of shapes you can create are practically limitless. You can create an open Bézier path—anything from a simple straight line to a complex squiggle—or you can join the ends to form a closed Bézier path.

To create a Bézier curve:

1. In the Title Tools panel, select the Pen tool ◊ (**Figure 12.70**).

2. *Do one of the following:*

   ▲ To create an anchor point, click in the drawing area (**Figure 12.71**).

   ▲ To create a smooth point, drag the cursor around in the drawing area (**Figure 12.72**). If you want, drag a control handle to adjust the curve before continuing.

   continues on next page

Figure 12.71 Click to create an anchor point with no control handles...

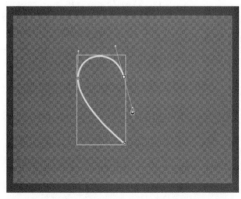

Figure 12.72 ...or drag to create a smooth point and define its control handles.

USING THE PEN TOOLS

3. To create a corner point, select the Convert Point tool, and drag a control handle (**Figure 12.73**).

Afterward, you must reselect the Pen tool and click the corner point. Otherwise, the next point you create will begin a new path.

4. Repeat steps 2 and 3 to create straight and curved segments between points (**Figure 12.74**).

5. *Do one of the following:*

▲ To close the path, position the Pen tool over the first control point so a circle icon appears 🖋, and then click (**Figure 12.75**).

▲ To leave the path open, choose the Selection tool ➤.

✔ Tips

■ Don't let all the options confuse you; creating simple shapes with the Pen tool is easy. To create a line with the Pen tool, just click where you want one end of the line, and then click to set the other end. To create a polygon, keep clicking to create more anchor points, and then click the first point to close the shape.

■ Because the Pen tool can do everything the Line tool can and more, the Line tool isn't covered here. Besides, a line appears as an open Bézier object in the Graphic Type pull-down menu (in the Title Properties panel).

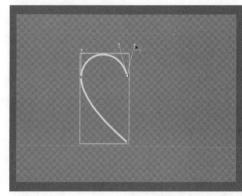

Figure 12.73 Select the Convert Point tool, and drag a smooth point's control handle independently.

Figure 12.74 Continue to create control points to build the path.

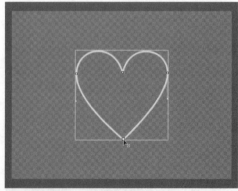

Figure 12.75 To close the path, position the Pen tool over the first control point (a circle icon appears), and then click.

Figure 12.76 To reshape a Bézier object, select it. Then, position the Pen tool over the object.

Figure 12.77 To move a control point, drag with the Pen tool.

Reshaping a Bézier Curve

You can change the shape of a Bézier path at any time by moving, adding, or deleting control points or direction lines.

To move a control point:

1. Select a Bézier object.

2. Select the Pen tool 🖊, and position it over the object.

   The object's control points appear (**Figure 12.76**).

3. Drag a control point (**Figure 12.77**).

To remove a control point:

1. Select a Bézier object.

2. Select the Remove Point tool 🖊.

3. Click a control point (**Figure 12.78**).

   The point is removed, and the path adjusts (**Figure 12.79**).

Figure 12.78 Position the Remove Point tool over a control point...

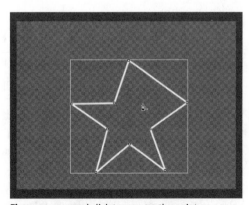

Figure 12.79 ...and click to remove the point.

RESHAPING A BÉZIER CURVE

To add a control point:

1. Select a Bézier object.

2. Select the Add Point tool .

3. *Do one of the following:*
   - ▲ To add a point without changing the path, click the path (**Figure 12.80**).
   - ▲ To add a point and change the path, drag the path (**Figure 12.81**).

Figure 12.80 To create a new control point, click a line segment with the Add Point tool...

Figure 12.81 ...or click and drag to move the new control point.

Pen Pointers

If your goal is to create smooth and shapely Bézier curves, here are a few tips.

The most pleasing curves use direction handles that are about one-third the size of the curve.

As a rule, any line segment should use two direction lines or none at all. When only a single direction line influences a curve, one end of the curve flattens out, which looks awkward.

Use a minimal number of control points to achieve the curve you want. The curve will be smoother and easier to control.

Creating a smooth point always extends two equal and opposite direction lines. However, drag in the direction of the curve to follow.

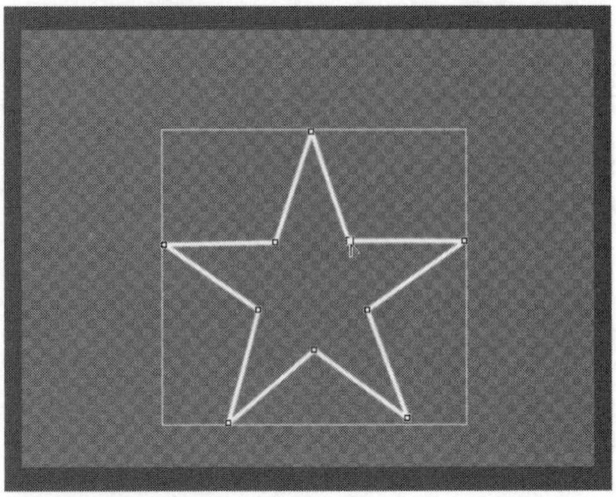

Figure 12.82 Click a smooth point or corner point to convert it to an anchor point.

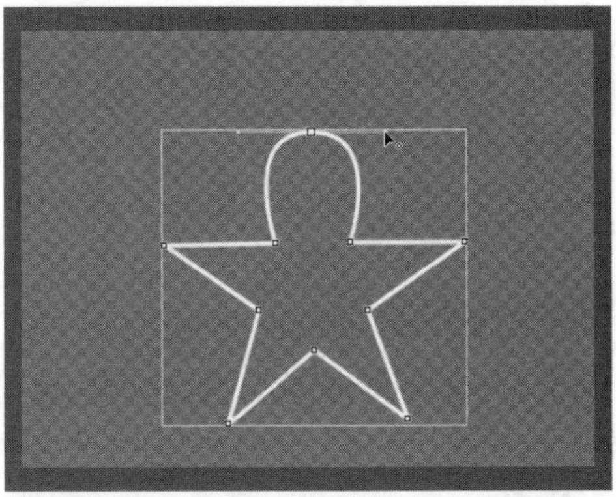

Figure 12.83 Drag an anchor point or corner point to convert it into a smooth point.

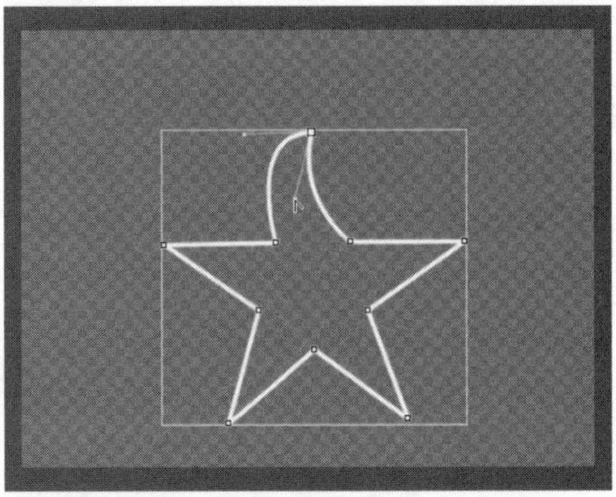

Figure 12.84 Drag the control handle of a smooth point to convert it to a corner point.

To convert a control point:

1. Select a Bézier object.
2. Select the Convert Point tool.
3. *Do one of the following:*
   - ▲ Click a smooth point or corner point to convert it to an anchor point (**Figure 12.82**).
   - ▲ Drag an anchor point or corner point to convert it to a smooth point (**Figure 12.83**).
   - ▲ Drag the control handle of a smooth point to convert it to a corner point (**Figure 12.84**).

Specifying Line and Path Properties

In addition to adjusting the angle and curves of line segments, you can control the appearance of the corners and ends. The *cap type* determines how the ends of a path look. You can choose butt, square, or round caps (**Figure 12.85**). The type of join determines whether a corner is mitered, rounded, or beveled (**Figure 12.86**). Framed Bézier shapes and lines have both join and cap options; filled Bézier shapes have only join options.

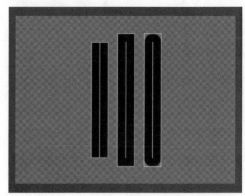

Figure 12.85 These three thick lines have exactly the same length but use different caps: butt, square, and round (left to right).

Figure 12.86 These Bézier shapes are exact copies, but they use different joins: rounded, mitered, and beveled. The lower star's miter limit is set to make the joins pointed rather than beveled.

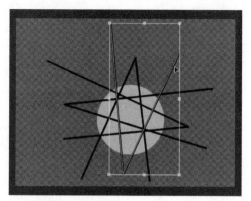

Figure 12.87 Select a Bézier shape, including lines.

To specify the attributes of open Bézier objects or lines:

1. Select an open Bézier object or line (**Figure 12.87**).

2. In the Title Properties panel, adjust the Line Width value (under the Properties category) (**Figure 12.88**).

3. For Cap Type, choose an option from the pull-down menu (**Figure 12.89**).

4. For Join Type, choose an option from the pull-down menu (**Figure 12.90**).

5. If you selected Miter as the join type, adjust the Miter Limit value.

   This value specifies when the miter switches to a bevel, expressed as a multiple of the line's stroke weight. Therefore, a miter limit of 1 results in a bevel. At the default value of 4, the miter switches to a bevel when the length of the point reaches 4 times the stroke weight.

   The object uses the properties you specified.

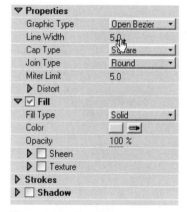

Figure 12.88 Adjust the Line Width value.

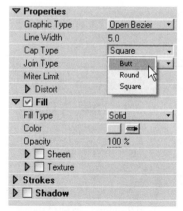

Figure 12.89 Choose an option from the Cap Type pull-down menu.

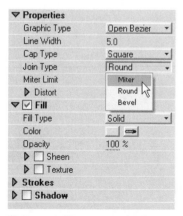

Figure 12.90 Choose an option from the Join Type pull-down menu.

SPECIFYING LINE AND PATH PROPERTIES

Converting Shapes to Filled Bézier Shapes

When you create a closed Bézier shape, it's framed by default—that is, empty in the middle. However, you can convert it to a filled Bézier shape by using a simple menu command.

To convert to a filled Bézier shape:

1. Select a Bézier object or other shape (**Figure 12.91**).

2. In the Title Properties, choose Filled Bézier from the Graphic Type pull-down menu (**Figure 12.92**).

   The object fills with the current fill color. If the object was an open Bézier shape, it closes and fills (**Figure 12.93**).

✔ Tip

■ You can open a closed Bézier shape (and vice versa) by selecting the appropriate option from the Graphic Type pull-down menu. Closed shapes such as those created with the Rectangle tool can also be opened this way. However, you won't be able to see that the shape has been opened until you drag the appropriate control point.

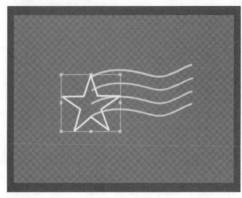

Figure 12.91 Select a Bézier object.

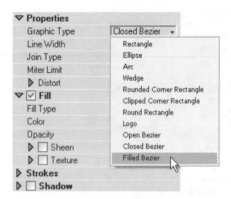

Figure 12.92 Choose Filled Bézier from the Graphic Type pull-down menu...

Figure 12.93 ...to convert the object to a filled shape.

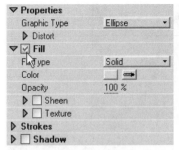

Figure 12.94 Click the Fill option in the Object Style area. If necessary, click the triangle to expand the fill options.

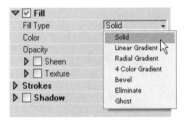

Figure 12.95 Select a fill type from the pull-down menu.

✔ Tips

■ A color that looks great on your computer screen may not be *NTSC safe* and may look noisy or bleed on a television.

■ Naturally, choosing Eliminate as the fill type is useful only if you add a stroke to the object. See "Setting Stroke Options" later in this chapter.

Setting Fill Options

Both text and shapes can be filled with a color. In addition to color, there are numerous other fill options.

To set fill options:

1. Select an object in the drawing area.

2. In the Title Properties, make sure Fill is selected (**Figure 12.94**).

   You may need to click the triangle next to Fill to view its properties.

3. Select an option from the Fill Type pull-down menu (**Figure 12.95**):

   ▲ **Solid:** Sets a uniform color fill.

   ▲ **Linear Gradient:** Sets a fill that gradually changes from one color to another in a linear pattern.

   ▲ **Radial Gradient:** Sets a fill that gradually changes from one color to another in a circular pattern.

   ▲ **4 Color Gradient:** Sets a gradient composed of four colors, each starting from a different corner of the object's bounding box.

   ▲ **Bevel:** Gives the object's edges a beveled appearance.

   ▲ **Eliminate:** Makes the fill transparent and unable to cast a shadow.

   ▲ **Ghost:** Makes the fill transparent yet capable of casting a shadow.

4. Set other Fill property values:

   ▲ **Color:** Use either a color swatch to select a color from a color picker or the Eyedropper tool to sample a color from the drawing area.

   ▲ **Opacity:** 100% is completely opaque, and 0% is completely transparent.

Setting Gradient Options

As you saw in the previous section, three of the seven fill types are gradients: linear gradient, radial gradient, and four-color gradient (**Figure 12.96**). All the gradients change from one color to another. However, gradients can also change from one opacity level to another. For this reason, gradients use special controls to define color and transparency.

Under the Fill property heading, each color used in a gradient is represented by a *color stop*—a small box alongside a sample image of the gradient. For linear and radial gradients, the left color stop shows the starting color; the right color stop shows the ending color (**Figure 12.97**). Four-color gradients have a color box for each corner of the object (**Figure 12.98**).

Figure 12.96 In this example, the circle uses a linear gradient.

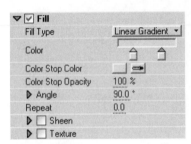

Figure 12.97 Color stops represent the starting and ending colors of a linear or radial gradient.

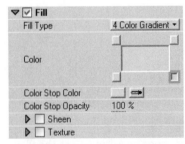

Figure 12.98 Four-color gradients have a color stop in each corner of the gradient sample.

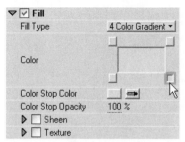

Figure 12.99 Select a color stop, and then set its color by clicking the Color Stop Color swatch or eyedropper. Double-clicking a color stop also opens a color picker.

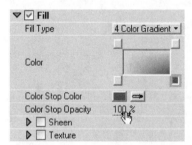

Figure 12.100 Adjust the selected color stop by picking a color or adjusting the Color Stop Opacity value.

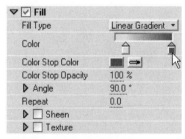

Figure 12.101 Drag the color swatches left or right. Their relative positions affect the gradient ramp—the transition between the colors.

To set gradient options:

1. Select an object that uses a linear, radial, or four-color gradient fill.

2. Click the color stop you want to adjust (**Figure 12.99**).

3. To set the color stop's color, *do one of the following*:

   ▲ Click the color swatch next to Color Stop Color to use a color picker.

   ▲ Click the Eyedropper tool ⇒ to sample a color from the screen.

   You can also double-click a color stop to open a color picker.

4. To set the opacity of the selected color stop, adjust the Color Stop Opacity value (**Figure 12.100**).

5. Repeat steps 2 through 4 for other color stops, as needed.

6. To adjust a linear or radial gradient's *ramp*, drag the color swatches along the gradient sample (**Figure 12.101**).

   The relative spacing of the color swatches along the gradient sample affects the transition between colors.

7. To adjust the angle of a linear gradient, adjust the Angle value.

8. To repeat a linear or radial gradient, increase the Repeat value.

✔ Tips

■ Double-clicking a color stop also opens a color picker.

■ The Render category of the Video Effects folder on the Effects panel includes an After Effects filter called Ramp. You can apply this filter to a clip to create a full-screen linear or radial gradient. The Ramp effect has Scatter and Blend with Original parameters, but no Repeat parameter.

SETTING GRADIENT OPTIONS

Setting Sheen Options

Both fill and stroke options include a parameter called Sheen. Sheen makes an object seem smooth and shiny by simulating light reflecting from the object's surface.

To apply a sheen:

1. Select an object in the drawing area.

2. Apply a fill to the object, if it doesn't already have one.

   Be sure to expand the Fill property heading in the Title Properties panel.

3. Under the Fill property heading, click the Sheen subheading.

   A sheen appears on the object, using the default settings.

4. Click the triangle next to Sheen to reveal its properties.

5. Under Sheen, set the following options (**Figure 12.102**):

   ▲ **Color:** Sets the color of the sheen; white is the default.

   ▲ **Opacity:** Sets the opacity of the sheen.

   ▲ **Size:** Sets the width of the sheen.

   ▲ **Angle:** Sets the angle of the sheen, in degrees.

   ▲ **Offset:** Shifts the position of the sheen.

   The object's sheen uses the settings you specified (**Figure 12.103**).

✔ Tip

■ The Basic 3D video effect has a parameter called *specular highlight* that also gives an object a subtle sheen.

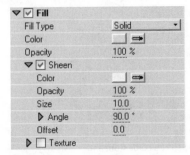

Figure 12.102 Click the Sheen option and set its color, opacity, size, angle, and offset.

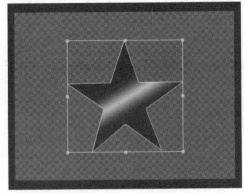

Figure 12.103 In this example, the object's sheen implies a polished surface.

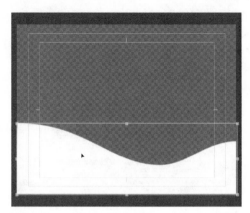

Figure 12.104 Select a filled object.

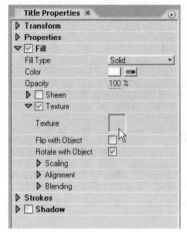

Figure 12.105 Click Texture, and then click the Texture swatch to open the Choose a Texture Image dialog box.

Applying a Texture

Both the fill and stroke options include a parameter called Texture. As the name suggests, a texture gives the impression that an object has a surface composed of a given material. But you can use the Texture property to fill an object with any image.

To apply a texture:

1. Select an object (**Figure 12.104**).

   If necessary, expand the Fill property heading in the Title Properties panel.

2. Click Texture.

3. Click the Texture swatch (**Figure 12.105**).

   A Choose a Texture Image dialog box appears.

continues on next page

APPLYING A TEXTURE

4. Select an image to serve as the object's texture fill, and then click Open (**Figure 12.106**).

   The image you chose fills the selected object (**Figure 12.107**).

5. Under the Texture property heading, set the texture's scaling, placement, tiling, and compositing options.

✔ Tips

■ The Texture property includes a lot of parameters, so experiment with them.

■ Sheens and textures tend to work better with shapes than with text objects. Letters don't always have a lot of surface area or space to fill. A sheen or fill can be hard to see within the contours of the letters and can even make words hard to read. And although you apply a sheen or texture to an entire text object, the actual image appears within each letter.

■ A texture can help you create an effect similar to the image-matte key (see Chapter 14, "Advanced Effects"). Each technique has its advantages and disadvantages. For example, applying a texture within the title can be more convenient than applying an image matte effect. An image matte, on the other hand, might get the result you want when filling text with an image (see the previous tip).

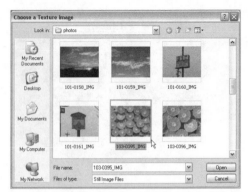

Figure 12.106 Select the texture you want, and click Open.

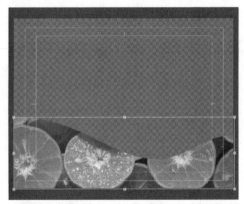

Figure 12.107 The object is filled with the texture you specified.

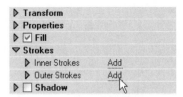

Figure 12.108 Click the Add button next to the kind of stroke you want.

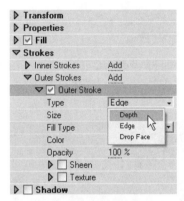

Figure 12.109 Choose an option from the Type pull-down menu.

Setting Stroke Options

The Titler has full-fledged stroke options for objects, much like the ones found in dedicated graphics applications.

You can add up to 12 strokes to each object. The Title Properties panel lists and renders strokes in the order you create them. Each successive stroke is considered subordinate to the last stroke, in a kind of hierarchy. As a result, resizing a stroke higher in the hierarchy resizes all the strokes beneath it. At any time, you can change the hierarchy, disable strokes, or delete strokes.

To add strokes:

1. Select one or more objects in the drawing area.

2. In the Title Properties panel, expand the Strokes property controls.

3. Click Add next to the type of stroke you want (**Figure 12.108**).

4. Choose an option from the Type pull-down menu (**Figure 12.109**):

   ▲ **Depth:** Creates a stroke that makes the object appear extruded and three-dimensional.

   ▲ **Edge:** Strokes the entire inner or outer edge of the object (depending on whether the stroke is an inner or outer stroke).

   ▲ **Drop Face:** Creates a stroke identical to the object, but behind the object and with its own attributes. Drop face is similar to a drop shadow, except it doesn't have a Spread property.

continues on next page

5. Set other attributes of the stroke (**Figure 12.110**):

▲ **Size:** Sets the thickness of the stroke in pixels (not available for drop-face strokes).

▲ **Angle:** Sets the angle of the stroke in degrees (not available for edge strokes).

6. Set the fill options, including Fill Type, Color, Opacity, Sheen, and Texture.

The stroke takes on the attributes you specified (**Figure 12.111**). For more information on using fill options, see "Setting Fill Options," earlier in this chapter.

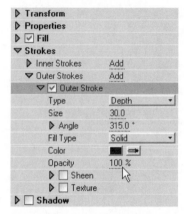

Figure 12.110 Set the stroke's size, angle, and fill options.

Figure 12.111 This example shows all three stroke types: depth (top), edge (center), and drop face (bottom).

Figure 12.112 This object has three outer strokes. The first is transparent (Eliminate fill), followed by a black stroke and then a yellow stroke.

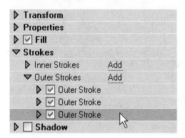

Figure 12.113 In the Title Properties panel, select the stroke you want to move in the hierarchy.

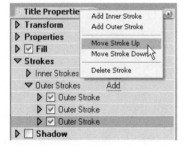

Figure 12.114 Choose an option from the Title Properties panel's pull-down menu. In this example, the black stroke is being promoted.

To change the hierarchy of strokes:

1. Select an object that contains multiple strokes (**Figure 12.112**).

2. In the Title Properties panel, select the stroke you want to move in the hierarchy (**Figure 12.113**).

3. Choose an option from the Title Properties panel menu (**Figure 12.114**):

   ▲ **Move Stroke Up:** Moves the stroke higher in the hierarchy.

   ▲ **Move Stroke Down:** Moves the stroke lower in the hierarchy.

   The stroke is shifted in the hierarchy according to your choice (**Figure 12.115**).

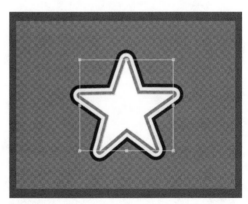

Figure 12.115 The stroke is reordered. In this example, the black stroke becomes the outermost stroke.

To delete a stroke:

1. Select an object that contains a stroke.

2. In the Title Properties panel, select the name of the stroke you want to delete.

3. From the Title Properties panel menu, choose Delete Stroke (**Figure 12.116**).

✔ Tips

■ You can't specify a join type for strokes (as you can with Bézier objects, which themselves can be stroked). However, you may notice that the outer edges of outer strokes have curved obtuse angles and sharp acute angles. The inner edges of inner strokes have sharp obtuse angles, and acute angles have what might be called a *faceted* corner. If you don't like the way strokes handle joins, use Bézier objects instead (**Figure 12.117**).

■ Experiment with strokes to create an object that looks like several concentric shapes with transparent gaps in between.

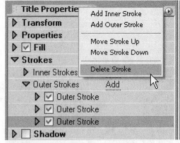

Figure 12.116 You can also choose to delete the stroke.

Figure 12.117 The first object uses an inner stroke, the second uses an outer stroke, and the third is actually two shapes: a Bézier object with miter joins and a filled Bézier object behind it.

Figure 12.118 Select an object to which you want to add a shadow.

▷ Transform	
▷ Properties	
▷ ☑ Fill	
▽ Strokes	
▷ Inner Strokes	Add
▷ Outer Strokes	Add
▽ ☑ Shadow	
Color	◼ ⟹
Opacity	60 %
▷ Angle	45.0 °
Distance	10.0
Size	0.0
Spread	10.0

Figure 12.119 Click the Shadow option, and choose the properties you want.

Figure 12.120 This shadow's property settings are Opacity = 60%, Angle = 45 degrees, Distance = 10, Size = 0, Spread = 10.

Adding Drop Shadows

A drop shadow can set an object apart from the background or impart a sense of depth. You can apply a drop shadow to any object.

To apply a shadow:

1. Select an object to which you want to add a shadow (**Figure 12.118**).

2. In the Title Properties panel, click Shadow.

3. Set the shadow's properties (**Figure 12.119**):

   ▲ **Color:** Use a color swatch to open a color picker or the Eyedropper tool to sample a color from the drawing area.

   ▲ **Opacity:** 100% is completely opaque, and 0% is completely transparent.

   ▲ **Angle:** The direction, in degrees, from the object in which the shadow falls.

   ▲ **Distance:** The distance, in pixels, that the shadow falls from the object.

   ▲ **Size:** The shadow's size; 0 creates a shadow of the same size as the object that casts it.

   ▲ **Spread:** Blurs the shadow; 0 creates a sharp-edged shadow.

   The shadow uses the settings you specified (**Figure 12.120**).

✔ Tips

■ You can see a shadow through a semi-transparent object (as long as the fill type isn't set to Eliminate). If a stroke or fill seems darker than it should be, the drop shadow may be showing through.

■ Typically, a convincing drop shadow is anywhere from 50 to 75 percent opaque.

■ A fill or stroke set to Ghost is transparent, but it can still cast a shadow.

Inserting Logos

Titles often feature a company or brand logo. With the Title Designer, you can place a logo directly in the drawing area along with the other objects you create. This makes it simple to incorporate the logo—or any bitmapped graphic—into the design.

To insert a logo:

1. Make sure no objects are selected, and then choose Title > Logo > Insert Logo (**Figure 12.121**).

    The Load Logo dialog box appears. By default, it opens the Logos folder, which is located in Premiere Pro's Presets folder.

2. Locate the logo you want to use, and click Open (**Figure 12.122**).

    The logo appears in the drawing area at full size (**Figure 12.123**).

3. If necessary, adjust the logo's properties, such as Position, Opacity, and Scale.

Figure 12.121 Make sure no objects are selected, and choose Title > Logo > Insert Logo.

Figure 12.122 In the Load Logo dialog box, locate the logo you want to use, and click Open.

Figure 12.123 The logo appears in the drawing area at the size it was originally created.

Figure 12.124 Select a text box, and choose Title > Logo > Insert Logo in to Text.

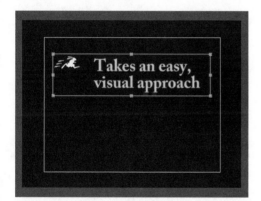

Figure 12.125 Here, a slightly different version of the logo is inserted as a character in a text box. (Note that Show Video is selected, so the black video in the timeline serves as the background.)

To insert a logo in a text box:

1. Select a text box and position the insertion point where you want the logo.

2. Choose Title > Logo > Insert Logo into Text (**Figure 12.124**).

3. A Load Logo dialog box appears. By default, it opens the Logos folder.

4. Locate the logo you want to use, and click Open.

   The logo appears at the insertion point, scaled to fit into the line of text. Changing the font size also scales the inserted logo (**Figure 12.125**).

✔ Tips

- Adjusting the Slant property of text containing a logo distorts the logo, as well—probably with undesirable results. If you need to slant text, insert a logo as a separate object.

- The graphic you insert doesn't have to be a logo per se. The Insert Logo into Text command can be a great way to create a special character that you can't get with a font.

Transforming Objects

An object's *Transform properties* include its position, scale, rotation, and opacity. With the exception of opacity, you can control these properties by dragging the object in the drawing area. However, you can also adjust them using controls in the Transform area of the Title Properties panel. Even if you do transform an object by dragging, look in the Transform area to view the exact values.

You can also access Transform properties from the Title menu, but there's no need to cover that procedure here. The next sections will describe how to use menu commands to automatically position, arrange, and distribute objects.

To transform an object from the Transform area:

1. Select an object in the drawing area.

2. In the Transform area of the Title Properties panel, adjust any of the following values (**Figure 12.126**):

   ▲ **Opacity:** Sets the overall opacity. This setting works in combination with the object's other opacity settings.

   ▲ **X Position:** Sets the horizontal position, measured from the object's upper-left corner.

   ▲ **Y Position:** Sets the vertical position, measured from the object's upper-left corner.

   ▲ **Width:** Sets the horizontal aspect.

   ▲ **Height:** Sets the vertical aspect.

   ▲ **Rotation:** Sets the object's angle, measured from its vertical edge.

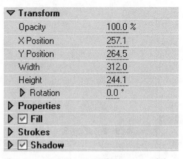

Figure 12.126 The Transform area of the Title Properties panel allows you to view and adjust a selected object's Transform properties.

✔ Tips

- Fill, stroke, and shadow properties each have their own opacity controls. Use these to set opacity levels relative to one another. The Opacity control in the Transform area adjusts the selected object's *overall* opacity. It controls the opacity of the entire object, but it doesn't override the relative opacity levels you set for its fill, strokes, and shadow.

- The Transform area's Opacity control doesn't affect the opacity of Texture fills. To adjust the opacity of textures, use the controls under the Texture property.

Figure 12.127 Select the Rotation tool.

To rotate an object using the Rotation tool:

1. Select an object in the drawing area.

2. In the Title Tools panel, select the Rotation tool ⟳ (**Figure 12.127**).

3. Drag the selected item to rotate it freely. The object rotates around the center of the bounding box (**Figure 12.128**).

✔ Tip

■ Transformations—such as scaling and rotation—are calculated from the center of an object's bounding box. There's no way to change an object's center point (called an *anchor point* in other programs) in the Title Designer.

Figure 12.128 Drag an object with the Rotation tool to adjust its angle. Here, multiple objects are selected and rotated as a group.

Positioning Objects Automatically

You can move selected objects by dragging them with the mouse, pressing the arrow keys, or entering coordinates in the Transform area of the Title Properties panel. But menu commands can quickly center objects or align objects with the bottom edge of the title-safe zone.

To position objects using menu commands:

1. Select one or more objects in the drawing area.

2. Choose Title > Position, and then choose an option from the submenu (**Figure 12.129**).

   The selected objects are positioned according to your choice (**Figure 12.130**).

✔ Tips

- The position commands place the bounding box, not the object within the box. If a text object doesn't look centered even after you've used the Horizontal Center command, make sure you've centered the text within the box using the Type Alignment command.

- You can copy a selected object by Alt+dragging it. A double arrow icon ![arrow] (like the one you'd see in Adobe Illustrator) appears when you use this keyboard shortcut.

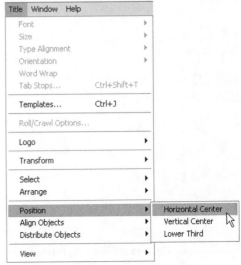

Figure 12.129 Choose Title > Position, and then choose an option from the submenu.

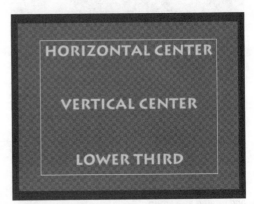

Figure 12.130 These three text objects illustrate the Position command options. All of them are centered horizontally.

Figure 12.131 Select the object you want to move in the stacking order.

Arranging Objects

In addition to controlling the position of objects, you can control the way they're layered. Initially, the most recently created object appears in front of the others, but you can change the stacking order at any time.

To change the stacking order:

1. Select an object in the drawing area (**Figure 12.131**).

2. Choose Title > Arrange, and select one of the following options (**Figure 12.132**):

   ▲ **Bring to Front:** Makes the selected object first in the stack.

   ▲ **Bring Forward:** Moves the selected object one step up in the stack.

   ▲ **Send to Back:** Makes the selected object last in the stack.

   ▲ **Send Backward:** Moves the selected object back one step in the stack.

   The object's placement in the stacking order changes according to your selection (**Figure 12.133**).

Title	Window	Help	
New Title			▶
Font			▶
Size			▶
Type Alignment			▶
Orientation			▶
Word Wrap			
Tab Stops...		Ctrl+Shift+T	
Templates...		Ctrl+J	
Roll/Crawl Options...			
Logo			▶
Transform			▶
Select			▶
Arrange			▶
Position			▶
Align Objects			▶
Distribute Objects			▶
View			▶

Bring to Front	Ctrl+Shift+]
Bring Forward	Ctrl+]
Send to Back	Ctrl+Shift+[
Send Backward	Ctrl+[

Figure 12.132 Choose Title > Arrange, and select the appropriate option...

Figure 12.133 ...to change the object's relative position in the stacking order. Here, Send to Back makes the rectangle last in the stacking order, so it appears behind the text.

421

Aligning Objects

Other menu commands allow you to align multiple objects with one another.

To align objects:

1. Select two or more objects in the drawing area (**Figure 12.134**).

2. *Do one of the following:*

   ▲ Choose Title > Align Objects, and select one of the alignment options from the submenu.

   ▲ In the Title Actions panel, select the button that corresponds to the alignment you want (**Figure 12.135**).

   The objects are aligned according to your choice (**Figure 12.136**).

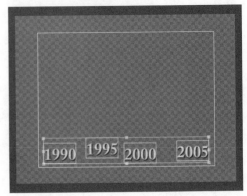

Figure 12.134 Select two or more objects in the drawing area.

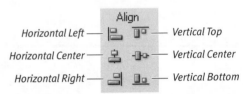

Figure 12.135 Each alignment option has a tool in the Title Actions panel.

Figure 12.136 The objects are aligned according to your choice. Here, the bottom edges of several dates are aligned using Vertical Bottom.

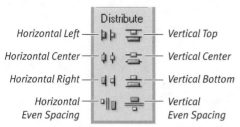

Figure 12.137 Each distribution option has a tool in the Title Actions panel.

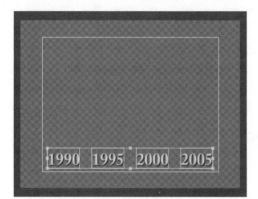

Figure 12.138 The objects are spaced according to your selection. Here, the dates from Figure 12.136 are evenly spaced horizontally.

Distributing Objects

Other menu items allow you to evenly distribute multiple objects, saving you from meticulous placement or—*gulp!*—even math.

To distribute objects:

1. Select multiple objects in the drawing area.

2. *Do one of the following:*

   ▲ Choose Title > Distribute Objects, and select an option from the submenu.

   ▲ In the Title Actions panel, select the button that corresponds to the distribution option you want (**Figure 12.137**).

   The objects are spaced according to your selection (**Figure 12.138**).

WORKING WITH EFFECTS

Although it's possible that the clips in your sequence require no alteration, chances are you need to modify them in some way, using effects. In Premiere Pro, the rubric *effects* encompasses any means by which you adjust a clip's audio or video characteristics, or properties.

Effects are categorized by function: motion, opacity, volume, and filters. By changing a clip's spatial properties, for example, you can resize the clip for use as a picture-in-picture effect or simulate a camera move over a large image. Altering a clip's opacity lets you superimpose one clip over another. You can also apply any combination of audio and video filters. Apply an equalizer (EQ) filter to enhance a voice-over or use reverb to imply certain acoustics. Similarly, video filters can alter an image in countless ways, from subtle color correction, to fantastic distortions, to an image composited with a background.

Befitting moving media, nearly all effect settings can change over time, using a technique called *keyframing*. This allows you to animate motion, fade a clip's opacity or volume, or vary the character or intensity of any video or audio filter. You can even specify whether the change is constant, accelerates, or decelerates. For example, you can simulate the way the camera starts to move slowly, comes up to full speed, and then slows to a stop. When animating a clip's position, you can determine whether the image takes a straight or curved path, using a feature common to many graphics programs: Bézier curves.

Despite their diversity, you apply, adjust, and animate effects using only a few methods. This chapter reflects Premiere Pro's unified approach. First, you'll learn to distinguish effects not only by function, but by methodology. Then, you'll learn methods to view and adjust effect properties. You'll find that by first focusing on techniques common to *all* effects, you'll be prepared to tackle *any* effect.

Summarizing the Chapter

On one hand, Premiere Pro streamlines its approach to effects by applying a small set of methods to a wide range of effects: opacity, volume, motion, and a multitude of filters. On the other hand, it takes a little time to show how to apply the techniques in various situations. But don't be misled by the length of this chapter or the number of tasks it includes. In reality, it covers effects in just a handful of sections. As usual, you can progress through the chapter from beginning to end or jump to the sections you need. (More advanced animation techniques and keying effects are reserved for the next chapter.)

Understanding effects

Comparing Effect Types explains the difference between inherent effects and standard effects.

Setting and Animating Effect Properties explains how you can specify whether an effect is constant or changes over time.

Viewing Effect Properties explains how you can view and adjust an effect's properties in the Timeline panel, Effect Controls panel, and Program Monitor.

Choosing a Keyframing Method explains the relative advantages of animating an effect in an expanded clip's property graph and in the Effect Controls panel.

Viewing and setting property values

Viewing Properties in the Timeline Panel shows you how to reveal an effect's property graph in the timeline.

Viewing Properties in the Effect Controls Panel shows how to view all of a selected clip's effect properties in the Effect Controls panel.

Viewing Motion Effects shows how to reveal a clip's position keyframes and motion path in the Program Monitor.

Viewing and Setting Spatial Properties shows how you can directly manipulate a clip's spatial properties in the Program Monitor.

Working with effects

Adding Standard Effects explains how to apply standard effects, or filters, to a clip.

Disabling and Resetting Effects explains how to temporarily exclude an effect, or reset it to its default values.

Using Multiple Effects illustrates how multiple effects interact and explains how the order in which they're rendered influences the final result.

Basic animation

Changing Property Values in the Timeline explains how to keyframe a specified property using an expanded clip's value graph, a method known as *rubberbanding*.

Animating Opacity and Volume applies the keyframing techniques covered in the previous section to the effects most commonly animated using the rubberbanding method.

Animating with the Effect Controls Panel explains how to keyframe any effect using controls in the Effect Controls panel.

Editing Keyframes in the Effect Controls Panel explains how to modify keyframes for an animated property using the Effect Controls panel.

Working with Effect Presets

This section includes tasks that cover how to apply effect presets—ready-to-use combinations of effects and animated effects—and how to save your own.

SUMMARIZING THE CHAPTER

Comparing Effect Types

Although we describe effects by what they do, it's just as useful to classify them by how they're applied. In Premiere Pro, effects fall into two major categories: fixed effects and standard effects.

Fixed/inherent effects

Motion effects, opacity, and volume are called *fixed effects*. This isn't meant to imply that you can't adjust or animate the settings over time; you can. *Fixed* refers to the fact that these effects let you control attributes that are inherent to the clip: its position on the screen, its level of opacity, and its volume. Better terms might be *inherent effects* or *intrinsic effects*. The upshot is that you don't have to actively apply these effects to a clip; they're always listed in the Effect Controls panel (which you'll learn more about soon) (**Figure 13.1**). Naturally, the clip must contain video to have motion or opacity; it must include an audio track to have volume.

Standard effects/filters

Effects that you actively apply to clips are known as *standard effects*. Standard effects are also called *filters*, after the filters you place in front of a camera lens to filter light or distort an image. Of course, digital filters can modify both images and sound in countless ways. You can make subtle adjustments—such as color correction or audio equalization—or create more dramatic distortions and stylizations. Standard effects are listed in categorized folders in the Effects panel (**Figure 13.2**). (You learned about the Effects panel in the context of transitions, back in Chapter 9, "Adding Transitions.")

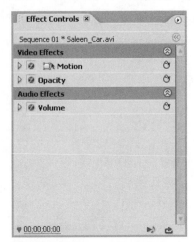

Figure 13.1 Motion, opacity, and volume are inherent to clips and are always listed in the Effect Controls panel.

Figure 13.2 The Effects panel lists audio and video effects in categorized folders. Note that it also includes a folder of preset effects.

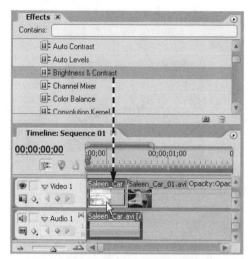

Figure 13.3 You add standard effects by dragging them from the Effect Controls panel to a clip in the Timeline panel.

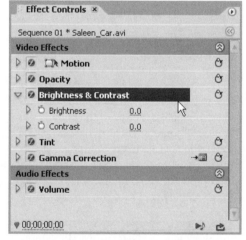

Figure 13.4 Once standard effects are applied, they appear in the Effect Controls panel in the order they were added.

You apply a standard effect by dragging it from the Effects panel to a clip in the timeline (**Figure 13.3**). Once the effect has been applied, you can view and adjust its parameters using the same methods you use for fixed effects (**Figure 13.4**).

Note that standard effects include *keying effects*, which are used to composite layers of images. On the other hand, standard effects are listed separately from transitions (which operate differently and are explained in Chapter 9).

✔ Tips

- Standard effects are stored in Premiere Pro's Plug-Ins folder. You can add compatible filters created by other software developers to expand your collection.

- If you have Adobe After Effects installed, launching Premiere Pro loads compatible filters from the After Effects directory.

Obsolete Effects

Some of the effects present in the initial release of Premiere Pro have become obsolete and are omitted from the current version: Crystallize, Pinch, Pointillize, Shear, Tiles, Wind, and Zig Zag. Nevertheless, the current version of Premiere Pro will recognize the obsolete versions if you import older projects that use them.

Setting and Animating Effect Properties

A *property* refers to any effect parameter to which you can assign a value. For example, you can specify a clip's Opacity property value from 0 percent (completely transparent) to 100 percent (completely opaque), or you can determine the intensity of the Gaussian Blur filter by adjusting its blur value.

Static / Global property values

You can set any property to a single *global* value for the duration of the clip. For example, you might apply the Black & White effect to a clip to give it a vintage feel, or resize a clip (using the Motion effect's scale property) so that it's inset for a picture-in-picture effect. Such static effects are achieved by setting only one, unchanging set of property values (the Black & White filter has no parameters to adjust).

Animated / Keyframed property values

On the other hand, you can animate a property, varying its values over time—for example, you create motion by changing a clip's position over time. In Premiere Pro (as in other programs), you define and control these changes using keyframes.

A *keyframe* defines a property's value at a specific point in time. When you create at least two keyframes with different values, Premiere Pro *interpolates* the value for each frame in between. In other words, Premiere Pro calculates how to progress smoothly from one keyframe value to another—or, in terms of motion, how to get from Point A to Point B (**Figures 13.5** and **13.6**).

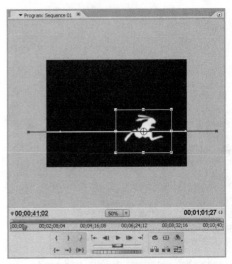

Figure 13.5 You can vary any property's value over time using keyframes. In this example, Premiere Pro calculates the position of a clip between two position keyframes...

Keyframes

Keyframe is a term borrowed from traditional animation. In a traditional animation studio, a senior animator might draw only the keyframes—what the character looked like at key moments in the animation. The junior animators then drew the in-betweens (a process sometimes called *tweening*). The same principle applies to animating effects in Premiere Pro: If you supply the keyframes for a property, the program calculates the values in between. And you can keyframe any property, not just movement.

In Premiere Pro, you're always the senior animator, so you should supply only the keyframes—just enough to define the animation. Premiere Pro does the tedious tweening. Setting too many keyframes defeats the purpose of this division of labor. (Hence, it's even useful to thin out, or *optimize*, the keyframes created by the audio mixing process, as you learned in Chapter 11, "Mixing Audio.")

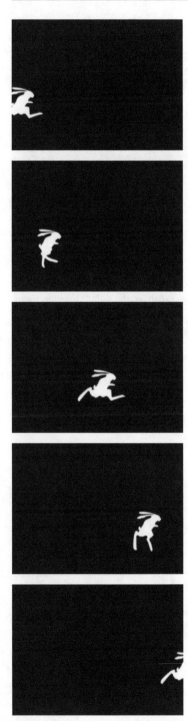

But of course, the property you animate doesn't have to be spatial in nature; you can, for example, change a clip's opacity over time, or make it progressively blurry (**Figure 13.7**).

As you adjust any effect, you can view it right away in the Program Monitor. But as you learned in Chapter 10, "Previewing a Sequence," whether you can play it at the project's full frame rate depends on both the complexity of the effect and your system's resources.

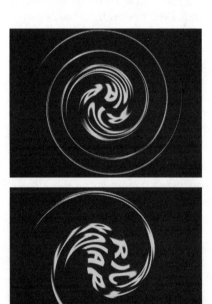

Figure 13.6 ...to create movement.

Figure 13.7 However, you can keyframe any effect property. Here, a twirl effect is animated.

Viewing Effect Properties

You can view and adjust an effect's property values in several ways: in an expanded track of the Timeline panel, in the Effect Controls panel, or (in the case of motion effect properties) in the Program Monitor.

Timeline panel

In the Timeline panel, expanding a track reveals additional clip data not visible when the track is collapsed. (In Chapter 7, "Editing in the Timeline," you learned how expanding a track allows you to view thumbnails and audio waveforms.) In an expanded track, you can view a selected effect's property values as a graph (**Figure 13.8**). Diamond-shaped icons on the graph represent values you specify (keyframes). The line connecting the keyframes represents the values between keyframes that Premiere Pro calculates automatically (interpolated values).

In the expanded clip's property graph—particularly when it represents a value like opacity or volume—keyframes are also known as *handles*. The graph itself is often referred to as a *rubberband* view, and the keyframing process is called *rubberbanding*.

✔ Tip

■ Strictly speaking, the graph in the expanded clip represents either the selected property's values or its *velocity* (the property value's rate of change)—whichever is most appropriate. You'll learn all about that distinction in Chapter 14, "Advanced Effects."

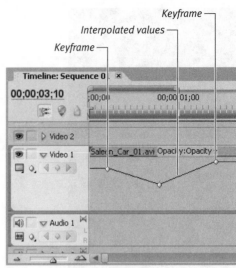

Figure 13.8 You can view any effect's property values as a graph in an expanded track of the timeline. Here, the Opacity property's value graph is selected.

Property track   Timeline view   Keyframe

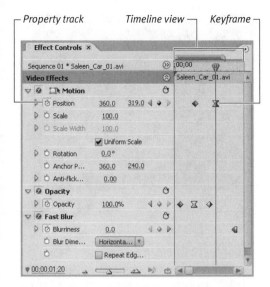

Figure 13.9 You can view multiple effect property values at once in the Effect Controls panel.

Expanded property   Velocity graph

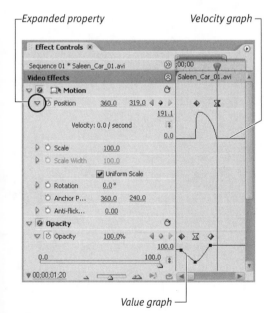

Value graph

Figure 13.10 You can expand any property to view it in the form of an editable graph. These graphs are particularly useful in adjusting how values between keyframes—interpolated values—are calculated.

Effect Controls panel

You can also view and control effect property values in the Effect Controls panel (**Figure 13.9**). Whereas an expanded clip in the timeline can show only one property's value at a time, the Effect Controls panel lists all of the clip's effects and displays their values at the current frame. You can expand effect headings to reveal effects in that category and, in turn, expand each effect to reveal its property controls—which appear in vertically stacked rows, or *property tracks*.

To vary values over time, you can reveal the Effect Controls panel's *timeline view*. The timeline view corresponds to the sequence's timeline and includes familiar controls, such as a CTI and viewing area bar. Just under its time ruler, a duration bar representing the selected clip appears. Under the clip, keyframe icons for each animated property appear in the corresponding property track.

Instead of manipulating a graph to change the keyframed (and hence, the interpolated) values, you can use numeric controls. But if you want to use a graph, you can expand its property's track yet another level. This way, you can adjust the way values progress from one keyframe to the next (the interpolated values) (**Figure 13.10**). (Interpolation options are fully explained in Chapter 14.)

✔ Tip

■ For each effect property, both the Timeline panel and the Effect Controls panel include a set of buttons for navigating, adding, and removing keyframes. More about that later in the chapter.

Spatial controls in the Program Monitor

Because they're spatial in nature, Premiere Pro lets you view and control motion effect properties—position, rotation, scale, and anchor point—by dragging in the Program Monitor, a method Adobe likes to call *direct manipulation* (**Figure 13.11**). In the Program Monitor, an animated position property appears as keyframe icons connected by a *motion path*. Direct manipulation controls complement the Effect Controls panel's controls. You use the former to control the spatial properties at a keyframe; you use the latter to control the timing. Certain filters also offer direct manipulation controls, including crop, corner pin, lightning, mirror, ramp, and transform.

Figure 13.11 Spatial properties—position, scale, rotation, and anchor point—can also be viewed and controlled in the Program Monitor.

✔ Tip

■ After reading Chapter 9, you may wonder how the Effect Controls panel can be optimized for adjusting both transitions and a clip's effects. The answer is simple: The content of the Effect Controls panel changes according to the item you select in the Timeline panel.

Graph Types

There are two types of property graphs: a value graph and a velocity graph.

A *value graph* represents the property's values over time. Therefore, its slope corresponds directly with the value: When the graph goes up, so does the value.

A *velocity graph* depicts the property value's *rate of change*. Its slope represents speed, not the value itself. When the graph goes up, the value's rate of change—its speed—is increasing; the value may be increasing or decreasing.

The type of graph displayed in an expanded clip depends on the property. Properties that consist of a single value invoke a value graph. For example, opacity is defined by a single value range (0 percent to 100 percent opaque) and so is represented by a value graph. Properties like position—which include both an x and a y value—invoke a velocity graph.

The Effect Controls panel displays both types of graphs for properties with single values. Other properties (like position) include a velocity graph only.

For now, you'll concentrate on using value graphs only, in order to animate opacity and clip volume in the timeline. A more thorough discussion of each graph type is reserved for Chapter 14.

VIEWING EFFECT PROPERTIES

Choosing a Keyframing Method

Although you can switch among keyframing methods freely, you'll find that each is better suited for certain tasks.

Opacity and volume in the Timeline panel

As you learned in the section, "Viewing Property Values,"the Timeline panel allows you to reveal a clip's property values as a graph; the graph is sometimes called a rubberband, and adjusting the keyframed values in the graph is referred to as rubberbanding. Rubberbanding in the timeline is ideal for making adjustments to opacity and volume— not only because this approach is time-tested and familiar to many users, but also because these properties are particularly easy to understand in the form of a value graph (**Figure 13.12**). When a value graph goes up, the opacity or volume value increases; when the graph goes down, the value decreases. Properties like rotation, for instance, don't translate as well to a value graph (and properties like position don't translate at all). Moreover, adjusting opacity and volume requires only a single property graph, whereas motion effects and many filters include several parameters you need to adjust.

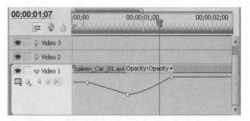

Figure 13.12 Keyframing in the timeline—sometimes called *rubberbanding*—is best suited for controlling clip volume and opacity (shown here).

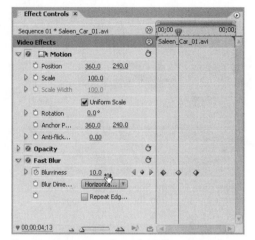

Figure 13.13 Motion and standard effects are more easily controlled in the Effect Controls panel.

Standard effects and motion in the Effect Controls panel

For all other effects, focus on the Effect Controls panel. It lets you adjust both the value and timing of several properties at once with numerical precision (**Figure 13.13**).

For motion effects, use the Effect Controls panel to activate the direct manipulation tools in the Program Monitor and to control the timing of keyframes for the various spatial properties: position, rotation, scale, and anchor point.

✔ Tip

■ The recommendations made in this section are reinforced by Premiere Pro's interface. In the timeline, the display of keyframes for opacity and volume can be accessed through a menu separate from other properties.

Viewing Properties in the Timeline Panel

In an expanded track of the Timeline panel, you can view a graph of any effect property. However, each clip can show only one property graph at a time.

Audio tracks can show property values either for individual clips or for the entire track. The same audio track property values can be adjusted using the audio mixer, covered in Chapter 11.

Premiere Pro selects the type of graph automatically. Properties that consist of a single value invoke a value graph; properties that include more than one value (such as x and y coordinates) invoke a velocity graph. (See the sidebar "Graph Types." Chapter 14 covers each graph type in detail.)

To view property values for video clips in the timeline:

1. Click the triangle next to a track's name to expand the track.

   The track expands, revealing additional track controls.

2. Click the expanded track's Show Keyframes button, and choose an option (**Figure 13.14**):

   ▲ **Show Keyframes:** Displays keyframes for any video effect property.

   ▲ **Show Opacity Handles:** Display keyframes for each clip's inherent Opacity property (not an opacity property included in a standard effect, such as the transform filter).

   The Show Keyframe button's icon reflects your choice. If you choose Show Keyframes, each clip in the track includes a pull-down menu of its fixed and standard effect properties.

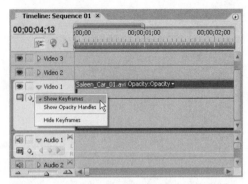

Figure 13.14 Click the Show Keyframes button, and choose an option from the menu that appears.

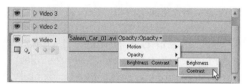

Figure 13.15 When Show Keyframes is selected, choose the property you want to view from the clip's pull-down menu.

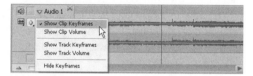

Figure 13.16 Click the audio track's Show Keyframes button, and choose an option from the menu that appears.

Figure 13.17 When Show Clip Keyframes is selected, choose the property you want to view from the audio clip's pull-down menu.

✔ Tips

■ An audio track's Show Keyframes button also includes options for viewing a value graph for Track Keyframes and Track Volume. These graphs correspond to changes you make using the audio mixer, covered in Chapter 11.

■ Remember that you can resize the height of any track to make it easier to see and manipulate a property graph.

3. If you chose Show Keyframes in step 2, choose the effect property you want to view from the clip's effect pull-down menu (**Figure 13.15**).

You may have to use submenus to find the property you want. The selected property's value graph or velocity graph appears in the expanded area of the clip.

To view property values for audio clips in the timeline:

1. Click the triangle next to a track's name to expand the track.

The track expands, revealing additional track controls.

2. Click the expanded track's Show Keyframes button, and choose an option (**Figure 13.16**):

▲ **Show Clip Keyframes:** Displays a value graph for any audio clip's effect property.

▲ **Show Clip Volume:** Displays a value graph for each clip's inherent Volume property (not a volume property included in a standard effect, such as the volume filter).

The Show Keyframe button's icon reflects your choice. If you choose Show Clip Keyframes, each clip in the track includes a pull-down menu of its fixed and standard effect properties.

3. If you chose Show Clip Keyframes in step 2, choose the effect property you want to view from the clip's effect pull-down menu (**Figure 13.17**).

You may have to use submenus to find the property you want. The selected property's value graph appears in the expanded area of the clip. The range of values represented by the vertical position of the graph depends on the particular parameter.

Viewing Properties in the Effect Controls Panel

The Effect Controls panel lists all the effects for a selected clip and provides controls for adjusting each property's value (**Figure 13.18**). Fixed (aka inherent) video and audio effects are listed separately; standard effects (aka filters) are listed in the order they're applied (see the section "Adding Standard Effects").

You can control each effect property using familiar numerical controls that you set by dragging or by selecting and entering a value. Most property value controls can also be expanded to reveal a slider control, knob, or color picker.

To see and adjust the timing of keyframes, you can expand the Effect Controls panel to reveal a *timeline view*. Naturally, the timeline view includes a time ruler. Under the ruler, each effect property occupies a horizontal track where you set keyframes; expanding a track reveals a graph of the property's values over time. The Effect Controls' timeline view includes a CTI and viewing area bar, and you can toggle the time count to audio samples. At the bottom of the panel, you'll find playback and zoom controls. By now, all these controls should be familiar to you, and they won't be reviewed here.

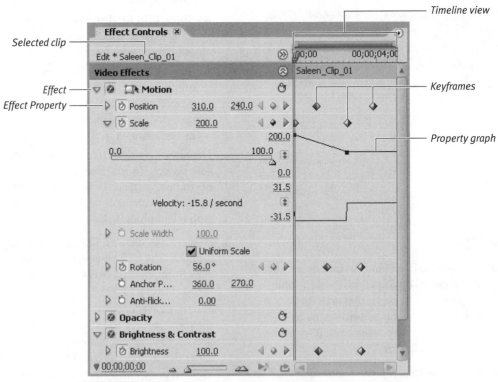

Figure 13.18 The Effect Controls panel lists all the effects for the selected clip and provides controls for adjusting their values over time.

VIEWING PROPERTIES IN EFFECT CONTROLS PANEL

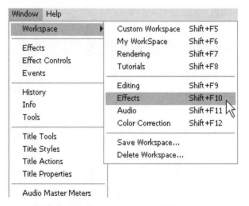

Figure 13.19 Choose Window > Workspace > Effects.

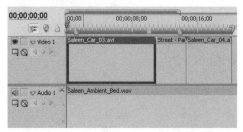

Figure 13.20 In the Timeline panel, select the clip that contains the effect properties you want to adjust.

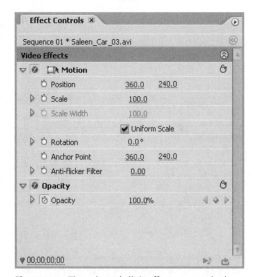

Figure 13.21 The selected clip's effects appear in the Effect Controls panel.

But unlike its counterparts in the timeline or Program Monitor, you can set the total range of the Effect Controls panel's time ruler. Selecting Pin to Clip makes the maximum visible area of the ruler correspond to the selected clip. This can make it easier for you to focus on the selected clip and prevent you from setting keyframes beyond the limits of the clip's duration. If you prefer, you can deselect the Pin to Clip option so that the time ruler corresponds to the duration of the sequence. This allows you to see the selected clip in a wider context or set keyframes beyond the clip's duration.

To set the Effects workspace:

◆ Choose Window > Workspace > Effects (**Figure 13.19**).

The default Effects workspace resembles the editing workspace, but it replaces the Source Monitor with the Effect Controls panel and the Info panel with the Effects panel. If you want, you can customize the relative size or arrangement of panels, as described in Chapter 1, "Premiere Pro Basics."

To view effect properties in the Effect Controls panel:

1. Make sure the Effect Controls panel is open.

2. In the Timeline panel, select the clip that contains the effect properties you want to adjust (**Figure 13.20**).

The selected clip's effects appear in the Effect Controls panel (**Figure 13.21**).

To show and hide effect categories:

◆ In the Effect Controls panel, click the double-chevron icon for the effect category you want to show or hide.

Effect category headings are set against a dark gray background. When the chevrons point down 🗸, the effects under the heading are hidden from view (**Figure 13.22**); when the chevrons point up 🗸 the effects in that category are visible (**Figure 13.23**).

To show and hide the Effect Controls panel's timeline area:

◆ In the Effect Controls panel, click the double-chevron icon in the upper-right corner of the effects list area.

When the chevrons point to the left 🗸, the timeline area is hidden (**Figure 13.24**); when the chevrons point to the right 🗸, the timeline area is visible (**Figure 13.25**).

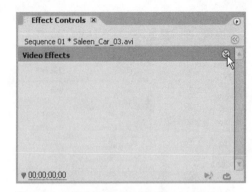

Figure 13.22 Clicking the double-chevrons button toggles it between pointing down to hide effects...

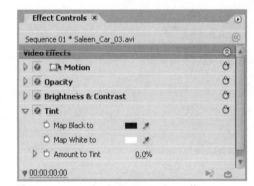

Figure 13.23 ...and pointing up to show effects.

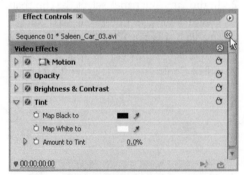

Figure 13.24 Clicking this double-chevrons button toggles between hiding the timeline view...

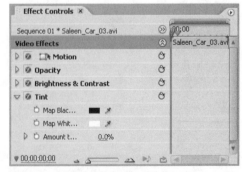

Figure 13.25 ...and showing the timeline view.

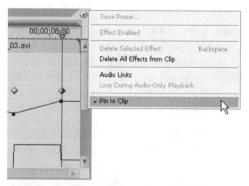

Figure 13.26 In the Effect Controls panel's menu, choose Pin to Clip.

To set the zoom range of the Effect Controls panel's time ruler:

◆ In the Effect Controls panel's menu, *do one of the following:*

▲ Select Pin to Clip to make the maximum visible area of the time ruler correspond to the duration of the selected clip (**Figures 13.26** and **13.27**).

▲ Deselect Pin to Clip to make the maximum visible area of the time ruler correspond to the duration of the sequence (**Figure 13.28**).

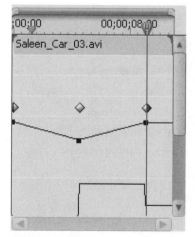

Figure 13.27 When Pin to Clip is selected, the maximum visible area of the time ruler corresponds to the selected clip.

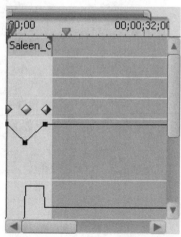

Figure 13.28 When Pin to Clip is deselected, the maximum visible area of the time ruler corresponds to the sequence's duration.

Viewing Motion Effects

Motion effects include the inherent spatial properties of a video clip: position, scale, rotation, and anchor point. You can adjust these properties as you would any other property, using controls in the Effect Controls panel.

But because these properties are spatial in nature, it's more convenient to change them by dragging the clip in the Program Monitor, using what are called *direct manipulation controls* (**Figure 13.29**). When these controls are enabled, the selected clip appears with a bounding box and control handles. A circle with an X indicates the clip's anchor point. Dragging the clip changes its position, whereas dragging the control handles can alter the clip's scale or rotation. When you animate the clip's position, the keyframed positions appear as small x icons in the Program Monitor. The clip's route (its interpolated position values) is represented by a dotted line, or *motion path,* connecting the x icons.

The spacing of the motion path's dots indicates speed: Closely spaced dots correspond to slower movement, and widely spaced dots correspond to faster movement. You can change a clip's position at a keyframe by dragging the keyframe's X icon in the Program Monitor.

Whereas you can control position, scale, and rotation using direct manipulation controls, you must set the clip's anchor point using controls in the Effect Controls panel. You must also use the Effect Controls panel (or, if you prefer, the property graph) to adjust the timing of keyframes.

✔ Tip

■ Certain filters also offer direct manipulation controls. You can identify them by the direct manipulation icon ▨ next to the effect's name in the Effect Controls panel. Select the effect's name to activate the controls.

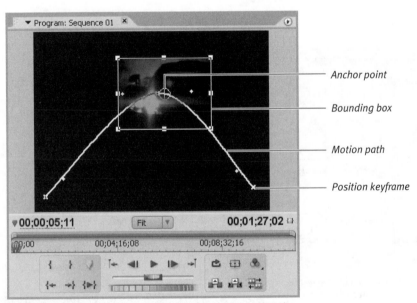

Figure 13.29 Selecting the frame in the Program Monitor makes the direct manipulation controls appear.

VIEWING MOTION EFFECTS

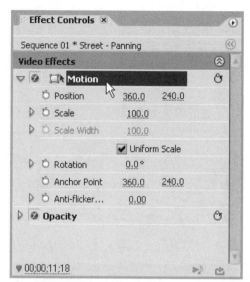

Figure 13.30 In the Effect Controls panel, select the Motion category.

Figure 13.31 In the Program Monitor, the selected clip's spatial controls become visible.

To view spatial controls in the Program Monitor:

1. Select a clip in the timeline so that its effects appear in the Effect Controls panel.

2. Cue the sequence time to anywhere within the selected clip's duration, so that it appears in the Program Monitor.

3. In the Effect Controls panel, select the Motion category (**Figure 13.30**).

   In the Program Monitor, the selected clip appears with a bounding box and handles, and its anchor point is represented by a circle with an X. When the clip's position is animated, keyframes and a motion path also become visible (**Figure 13.31**).

✔ Tip

- All effects with direct manipulation capability are activated by selecting the effect's name in the Effect Controls panel and then directly manipulating the frame in the Program Monitor. Because it's the most commonly used effect, the Motion control's direct manipulation can also be activated by clicking directly on the frame in the Program Monitor.

Viewing and Setting Spatial Properties

Once you enable the selected clip's direct manipulation controls, you can adjust its position, scale, and rotation by dragging in the Program Monitor.

Be aware that Premiere Pro calculates the position, scale, and rotation of a clip by its anchor point. In other words, the anchor point defines the position of a layer, the point around which a layer is scaled, and the pivot point of the layer's rotation. By default, a layer's anchor point is positioned in the center of the layer. In the Program Monitor, a clip's anchor point is represented by a circle with an X.

✔ Tip

■ Adjusting and keyframing effects in Premiere Pro works much the same as in the program's sibling, After Effects. However, there are differences, including variations in terminology. In After Effects, spatial properties (position, scale, rotation, and anchor point) are referred to as *transform* properties. And in After Effects, transform properties also include opacity. However, both programs include a Transform filter, which emulates these properties.

Setting the position

Setting a layer's position places its anchor point anywhere inside or outside the viewable area of the Program Monitor (which corresponds to the screen). The exact position of a layer is expressed in x, y coordinates, where the upper-left corner of the Program Monitor is 0, 0. When the clip image doesn't fill the screen, the empty areas of the screen reveal either clips in lower tracks or (when there is no video in lower tracks) black video.

Figure 13.32 With the direct manipulation controls active, you can drag the selected clip in the Program Monitor to change its position.

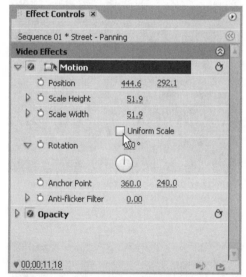

Figure 13.33 In the Effect Controls panel, deselect Uniform Scale to scale the clip's vertical and horizontal aspects separately.

To position a clip in the Program Monitor:

◆ In the Program Monitor, drag the clip to the position you want (**Figure 13.32**).

The Position property values in the Effect Controls panel change accordingly. If the property's stopwatch icon is selected 🖉, then changing the position creates a keyframe at the current time.

✔ Tip

■ When you change the anchor point, it may appear as if you've also changed the clip's position. Actually, the layer's Position property remains the same; you simply changed the spot in the clip's image that determines its position on the screen.

Setting the scale

By default, a layer is set to 100 percent of its original size, or scale. You scale a layer around its anchor point. In other words, the anchor point serves as the mathematical center of a change in size. When you scale a layer by dragging, you'll notice that the handles of the layer seem to stretch from the anchor point.

Remember that bitmapped images look blocky and pixelated when they're scaled much beyond 100 percent.

To scale a clip in the Program Monitor:

1. In the Effect Controls panel, deselect Uniform Scale under the Scale property (**Figure 13.33**).

If you select Uniform Scale, dragging any handle maintains the clip's proportions, or *aspect ratio*.

continues on next page

2. In the Program Monitor, *do one of the following:*

▲ To scale the clip's horizontal aspect, drag the center-left or center-right handle (**Figure 13.34**).

▲ To scale the clip's vertical aspect, drag the center-top or center-bottom handle (**Figure 13.35**).

▲ To scale the clip horizontally and vertically, drag a corner handle (**Figure 13.36**).

▲ To scale the layer while maintaining its proportions, press Shift as you drag a corner handle (or click Uniform Scale in the Effect Controls panel).

Figure 13.34 Drag the center-left or center-right handle to scale horizontally.

Figure 13.35 Drag the center-top or center-bottom handle to scale vertically.

Figure 13.36 Drag a corner handle to scale both aspects, or Shift+drag a corner handle to maintain the clip's aspect ratio as you scale.

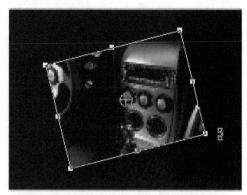

Figure 13.37 Position the mouse just off the clip's corner handle, so that the rotation icon appears, and then drag to rotate.

Setting the rotation

When you rotate a clip, it pivots around the clip's anchor point. Therefore, make sure the anchor point is where you want it before you adjust rotation.

To rotate a clip in the Program Monitor:

1. Position the mouse pointer near, but not on, a corner handle, so that the mouse becomes the rotation icon ↰.

2. With the rotate icon visible, drag to rotate the clip (**Figure 13.37**).

✔ Tips

■ You can't flip a clip's image by changing its horizontal or vertical scale. However, you can achieve this effect with the Horizontal Flip or Vertical Flip filter. You can animate a flipping movement with the Transform filter or the Basic 3D filter.

■ You can't use the Shift key to constrain rotational movement to 45-degree angles. To rotate the clip to exact angles, use the Rotation property controls in the Effect Controls panel.

■ Unlike After Effects, Premiere Pro includes no auto-orient option that orients a clip tangential to its motion path automatically. You'll have to do it manually by setting rotation keyframes.

Rotational Values

Rotation is expressed as an absolute, not relative, value. You might even think of it as a rotational position. A clip's default rotation is 0 degrees; setting its rotation to 0 degrees always restores it to its original upright angle. This is true when you keyframe rotational values as well. For example, if you want to rotate a layer 180 degrees clockwise (upside down) and back again, the rotation values at each keyframe are 0, 180, and 0. Mistakenly setting values of 0, 180, and −180 will cause the layer to turn clockwise 180 degrees and then turn counterclockwise—past its original position—until it's upside down again.

Adding Standard Effects

The procedure for adding a standard effect, or filter, to a clip is nearly self-explanatory: You drag a filter from the Effects panel directly to a compatible clip in the timeline. Clips with effects applied appear with a thin blue line under their name.

On the Effects panel, video and audio are contained in separate folders and are further organized into categorized subfolders. Audio filters are sorted by channel type and must match the channel type of the clip to which they're added—after all, you can't filter a channel that isn't there (**Figure 13.38**). (You already learned how to organize and find items on the Effects panel in Chapter 9, so that information won't be repeated here.)

Figure 13.38 On the Effects panel, video filters are sorted by function, and audio filters are organized by channel type.

Nearly all filters have one or more properties that you can adjust either by using a value graph in the Timeline panel or by using the Effect Controls panel. But as explained in "Choosing a Keyframing Method" earlier in this chapter, using the Effect Controls panel is the most appropriate method for most filters. Some filters also include a settings dialog box that opens automatically when you apply the filter. You can also reopen the dialog box from the Effect Controls panel.

This task summarizes the basic process of adding an effect to a clip. You'll discover that each effect has a unique set of parameters, or *properties,* that you can customize. In the following sections, you'll first learn how to apply an effect and specify *global* property values—a single set of property values for the duration of the clip. Then you'll learn how to animate any effect—fixed or standard—using the Effect Controls panel.

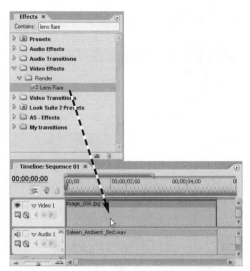

Figure 13.39 Drag a filter from the Effects panel to the appropriate clip in the Timeline.

Figure 13.40 If a settings dialog box opens automatically, specify values for the effect's properties, and click OK.

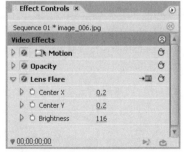

Figure 13.41 You can select the clip in the timeline to view its properties in the Effect Controls panel.

To add an effect to a clip:

1. On the Effects panel, *do one of the following:*

   ▲ Select a video effect.

   ▲ Select an audio effect that matches the audio clip's channel type (mono, stereo, or 5.1).

   For more about organizing and locating effects, see Chapter 9.

2. Drag the effect to the appropriate clip in the Timeline panel (**Figure 13.39**).

   The effect is applied to the clip and is listed on the Effect Controls panel when the clip is selected. Clips with effects applied appear with a thin blue line under their name.

3. To adjust the effect's settings, *do one of the following* (depending on the particular effect):

   ▲ If a settings dialog box appears automatically, specify values for the effect's parameters, and click OK (**Figure 13.40**).

   ▲ Select the clip in the timeline, and adjust its effect properties in the Effect Controls panel (**Figure 13.41**).

4. To vary effect properties over time, specify keyframes as explained in the task "To set keyframes in the Effect Controls panel," later in this chapter.

✔ Tip

■ You can add audio effects to entire tracks of clips using the audio mixer. See Chapter 11 for details.

Disabling and Resetting Effects

Whereas you can view effect values in either the Timeline panel or the Effect Controls panel, you can disable effects or reset their values to the default settings only in the Effect Controls panel. Disabling an effect doesn't delete your settings; it merely turns off the effect until you toggle it back on. Resetting an effect, on the other hand, removes your adjustments, replacing them with the default property values.

To disable or enable an effect:

◆ In the Effect Controls panel, click the effects icon ⊘ next to the effect you want to disable (**Figure 13.42**).

The icon disappears, and the effect is disabled (**Figure 13.43**). Clicking the empty box makes the icon reappear and enables the effect.

To reset any effect to its default settings:

◆ In the Effect Controls panel, click the reset icon ♻ for the effect you want to reset to its default property values (**Figure 13.44**).

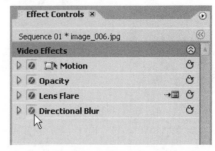

Figure 13.42 Clicking an effect's effects icon...

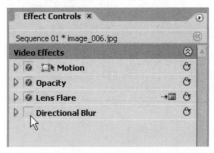

Figure 13.43 ...makes the icon disappear and disables the effect. Click again to make the icon reappear and enable the effect.

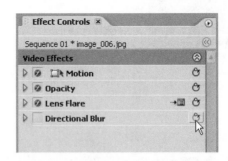

Figure 13.44 Clicking the reset icon resets the effect property values to their default settings.

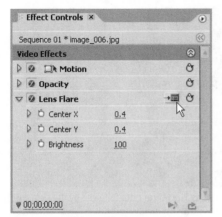

Figure 13.45 Click an effect's Setup button...

Figure 13.46 ...to access custom options for that effect. In this example, the Setup button reopens the Lens Flare Settings dialog box.

To use a standard effect's custom settings:

◆ In the Effect Controls panel, click a standard effect's Setup button ➡▦ (**Figure 13.45**).

Depending on the effect, a settings dialog box may open, or (in the case of effects like the Image Matte filter) a dialog box for choosing a file to serve as an effect source may appear (**Figure 13.46**).

✔ Tip

■ If you selected the option Default Scale to Frame Size on the General panel of the Preferences dialog box, Premiere Pro may have scaled some of your clips automatically. See Chapter 3, "Capturing and Importing Footage."

Using Multiple Effects

You can add any number of effects to a clip. You can layer different effects onto a single clip or apply the same effect more than once, specifying different settings each time.

Because each filter adds to the effect of the preceding one, the order of the filters determines the cumulative effect. Changing the order of filters can change the final appearance of the clip (**Figures 13.47** and **13.48**).

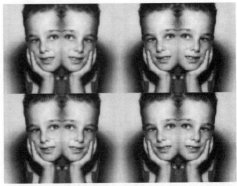

Figure 13.47 The Mirror filter followed by the Replicate filter results in this image.

Figure 13.48 Reversing the order of the filters in Figure 13.47 results in this image.

Rendering Order

When Premiere Pro renders frames for playback or export, it calculates each clip's attributes in a particular sequence, referred to as the *rendering order*.

Having interpreted your source footage according to your specifications and conformed the video frame rate and audio sample rate to match your project, Premiere Pro processes each frame. Rendering proceeds from lower-numbered tracks to higher-numbered tracks, and from nested sequences up through the hierarchy of sequences. Filters are applied in the order in which they're added—or, in terms of how they're listed in the Effect Controls panel, from the top to the bottom. Then fixed effects are applied: motion effects followed by opacity.

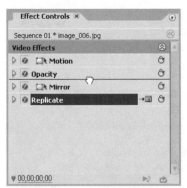

Figure 13.49 In the Effect Controls panel, drag a filter's name up or down to change the filter's position in the list.

Figure 13.50 The filter appears in the new position, and the filters are rendered accordingly.

To set the order of standard effects:

◆ In the Effect Controls panel, drag an effect up or down to change its position in the list (**Figure 13.49**).

The effect name appears in the new position (**Figure 13.50**). You can't drag a standard effect (filter) above the fixed effects (motion and opacity for video, or volume for audio effects).

Subverting the Render Order

At times, the rendering order prevents you from achieving the result you want. For example, you may want to use the Replicate filter to create numerous copies of a rotating image. However, the rendering order dictates that the Replicate filter is applied before rotation. This causes the image to be replicated before it's rotated, making it appear as though all the images are rotated as a group—*not* the effect you desire. To solve the problem, you need to defy the rendering order so that the effect is applied after rotation.

Although you can't alter the rendering order, you can subvert it by using standard effects that emulate fixed effects. One such effect is the Transform filter. Its properties match those of fixed effects: anchor point, position, scale, rotation, and opacity. It also includes skew and shutter angle. By applying the Transform filter after the Replicate filter, you can adjust the properties in the order you want.

Changing Property Values in the Timeline

Figure 13.51 Select the Pen tool.

In the Timeline panel, you can add, delete, move, and change the value of keyframes using the Pen tool. You can also add, delete, and cue the CTI to keyframes using a set of buttons in the track header area, called the *keyframe navigator.*

To add keyframes with the pen:

1. In the Timeline panel, expand the track that contains the clips with effect properties you want to adjust, and view the appropriate property graph.

    For detailed instructions, see "Viewing Properties in the Timeline Panel" earlier in this chapter.

2. In the Tools panel, select the Pen tool  (**Figure 13.51**).

    Position the pen on the property graph (the thin black line) where you want to add a keyframe, and Ctrl+click the line.

    Pressing Ctrl makes the pen appear with a plus sign 🖋₊ (**Figure 13.52**); Ctrl+clicking adds a keyframe at that point (**Figure 13.53**).

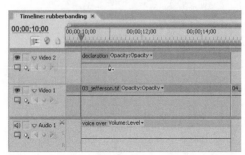

Figure 13.52 Ctrl+clicking the graph with the Pen tool...

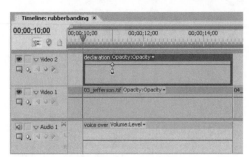

Figure 13.53 ...adds a keyframe.

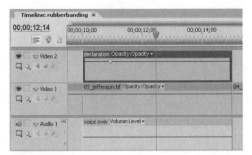

Figure 13.54 You can also add a keyframe by setting the CTI...

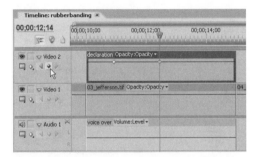

Figure 13.55 ...and clicking the diamond icon in the keyframe navigator.

To add keyframes with the timeline's keyframe navigator:

1. In the Timeline panel, expand the track that contains the clips with effect properties you want to adjust, and view the appropriate property graph.

   For detailed instructions, see "Viewing Properties in the Timeline Panel" earlier in this chapter.

2. Position the CTI at the point where you want to add a keyframe to the visible property graph (**Figure 13.54**).

3. In the track's keyframe navigator (under the track's name), click the Add/Remove Keyframe button (the diamond-shaped icon between the Previous and Next Keyframe arrows) 🔘.

   A keyframe appears on the property graph at the CTI (**Figure 13.55**).

To select keyframes:

1. Make sure the Pen tool 🖉 is selected.

2. In a property graph of a clip in the time-line, *do one of the following:*

   ▲ To select a keyframe, click it with the Pen tool (**Figure 13.56**).

   ▲ To add keyframes to and subtract them from your selection, Shift+click them with the Pen tool.

   ▲ To select one or more keyframes, drag a marquee around them (**Figure 13.57**).

   Selected keyframes appear yellow; unselected keyframes appear gray.

To move keyframes in time:

1. Select one or more keyframes.

2. Drag any of the selected keyframes left or right (**Figure 13.58**).

3. To constrain the mouse to horizontal movement only, press Shift after you begin dragging horizontally.

   Shift+dragging constrains the movement so you can't drag the keyframes vertically and thereby change their values. As you drag, a tool tip shows the sequence time of the keyframe you grabbed before you started dragging.

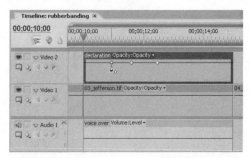

Figure 13.56 To select a keyframe, click with the Pen tool; Shift+click to add to or subtract from the selection.

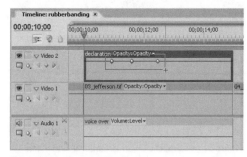

Figure 13.57 You can also drag a marquee to select several consecutive keyframes.

Figure 13.58 Drag selected keyframes right or left to move them in time.

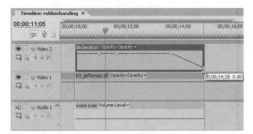

Figure 13.59 Drag selected keyframes up to increase their value or down to decrease their value.

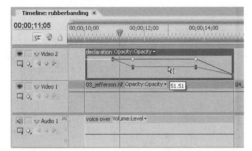

Figure 13.60 With the Pen tool, drag the line between keyframes to shift both keyframe values by the same amount.

To change keyframe values with the pen:

1. With the Pen tool ![pen icon], select one or more keyframes.

2. Drag any of the selected keyframes up or down (**Figure 13.59**).

3. To constrain the mouse to vertical movement only, press Shift after you begin dragging vertically.

   Shift+dragging constrains the movement so you can't drag the keyframes horizontally and thereby change their position in time. As you drag, a tool tip shows the property's value at the keyframe you grabbed before you started dragging. Interpolated values (the slope of the graph) change accordingly.

To change two keyframes simultaneously:

1. Position the Pen tool on the line between two keyframes in the property graph.

   The Pen tool appears with a vertical adjustment icon ![icon].

2. Drag up or down (**Figure 13.60**).

   Keyframe icons on either side of the Pen tool move up or down by the same amount. The slope of the property graph's line (interpolated values) adjusts accordingly.

To cue the CTI to keyframes:

◆ In the track's keyframe navigator, *do one of the following:*

▲ To cue the CTI to the previous keyframe, click the Left Arrow button ◀.

▲ To cue the CTI to the next keyframe, click the Right Arrow button ▶ (**Figure 13.61**).

The sequence's CTI moves to the keyframe you specify (**Figure 13.62**). The sequence's CTI moves in any panel that shows the sequence, including the Timeline panel and the Program Monitor.

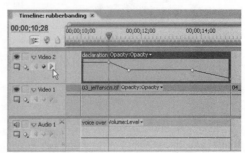

Figure 13.61 In the track's keyframe navigator, clicking the left arrow or the right arrow (shown here)...

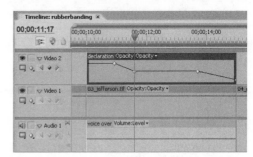

Figure 13.62 ...cues the sequence's CTI to the previous or next keyframe, respectively.

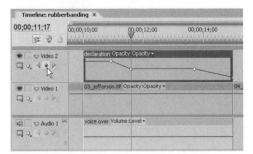

Figure 13.63 Cue the CTI to the keyframe you want to remove.

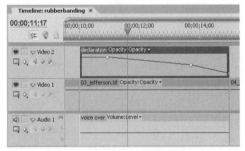

Figure 13.64 Clicking the keyframe navigator's diamond icon removes the keyframe at the CTI.

To remove keyframes in the timeline:

1. In a track's keyframe navigator, click the Left or Right Arrow button (◀ or ▶) to cue the CTI to the keyframe you want to remove.

   You can use any playback control to cue the CTI, but the keyframe navigator offers the easiest method.

2. Click the keyframe navigator's Add/Remove Keyframe button (the diamond between the left and right arrows) ◈ (**Figure 13.63**).

   The keyframe at the CTI is removed from the property graph. Interpolated values (the line between keyframes) adjust accordingly (**Figure 13.64**).

✔ Tips

■ In the property graph, the thin black line connecting keyframes represents interpolated property values. By default, values are interpolated using a linear scale. You can change the interpolation method. For more about interpolation, see chapter 14, "Advanced Effects."

■ To temporarily disable an effect, you must use the Effect Controls panel (as explained earlier in the chapter).

CHANGING PROPERTY VALUES IN THE TIMELINE

Animating Opacity and Volume

As explained in "Choosing a Keyframing Method," earlier in this chapter, keyframing in the timeline, or rubberbanding, is ideally suited to controlling opacity and volume. The Show Keyframes button's pull-down menu, opacity and volume are listed separately from other property keyframes. Even though the previous sections covered rubberbanding techniques, it's worthwhile to review the process in terms of opacity and volume.

But remember: To create simple video dissolves and audio fades, use a video or audio transition instead of keyframes (see Chapter 9).

✔ Tip

■ You can also apply opacity changes using the Transform filter and volume changes using a Volume filter. Because Premiere Pro renders filters after fixed effects, using the filter version may allow you to achieve a result you couldn't get otherwise.

Keying

In contrast to fading, *keying* makes only certain parts of a clip transparent. You encountered one form of keying in Chapter 12, "Creating Titles," where you learned that empty areas in a title become transparent automatically. Similarly, any areas of the screen left empty when you move a clip using a motion effect also become transparent automatically. This way, it's easy to create a picture-in-picture or split-screen effect. In both cases, Premiere Pro generates an alpha channel for the empty areas and applies an *alpha key* to make areas corresponding with the alpha channel transparent. Premiere Pro also applies an alpha key to imported clips that contain an alpha channel.

Other key types—listed in the Key subfolder of the Effects panel—must be added manually. These keying filters make parts of an image transparent based on other factors, such as brightness or color.

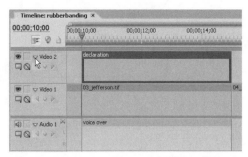

Figure 13.65 Arrange a clip you want to superimpose in a higher layer, and expand its track.

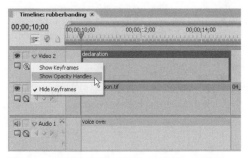

Figure 13.66 Click the track's Show Keyframes button, and choose Show Opacity Handles from the menu that appears.

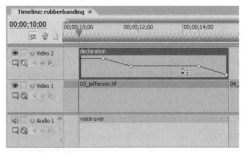

Figure 13.67 Use the track's keyframe navigator and the Pen tool to add keyframes and adjust them in the opacity graph. In this example, the opacity starts at 100 percent, drops to 50 percent, holds at 50 percent, and then ends at 0 percent.

Rubberbanding opacity

You can keyframe the opacity of clips in video track 2 and higher to blend them with clips in lower tracks. Lowering the opacity of clips in track 1 blends the image with black. If you want to make only parts of the clip transparent, apply a keying effect. Of course, you can combine keying with fading—for example, when you want to make a superimposed title semitransparent.

To rubberband opacity:

1. Arrange clips in the timeline so that the clip you want to superimpose is in a higher video track than the clip (or clips) that serve as the underlying image.

2. Expand the track that contains the clip you want to adjust (**Figure 13.65**).

3. Click the track's Show Keyframes button, and choose Show Opacity Handles (**Figure 13.66**).

   An opacity property graph appears for the clips in the track. The property graph's vertical position corresponds to clip opacity levels, so that near the top of the clip is 100 percent opaque, and near the bottom of the clip is 0 percent opaque (completely transparent).

4. Using keyframing techniques described in the previous sections, adjust the clip's opacity over time (**Figure 13.67**).

   Opacity levels affect the entire clip's overall opacity. To make certain parts of an image transparent, use a keying filter.

Rubberbanding volume

When you're keyframing audio, remember that you can adjust levels for individual clips or for the entire track of clips. But in general, you should use the rubberbanding method to adjust individual clips and the audio mixer to mix the tracks. Make only the adjustments you need to prepare the clips for track mixing, and be sure to avoid making redundant or conflicting adjustments.

To rubberband clip volume:

1. To monitor the audio level output, make sure the Audio Master Meters panel is visible, or choose Window > Audio Master Meters.

   The Audio Master Meters panel's VU meter shows the output levels.

2. Expand the track containing the audio clip you want to adjust (**Figure 13.68**).

3. Click the track's Show Keyframes button, and choose Show Clip Volume (**Figure 13.69**).

   A volume property graph appears for the clips in the track (not for the track as a whole). The property graph's vertical position corresponds to clip volume levels, so that levels are adjusted 0 dB when the graph is in the center of the clip, +6 dB near the top of the clip, and −6 dB near the bottom.

4. Using keyframing techniques described in the previous sections, adjust the clip's volume over time (**Figure 13.70**).

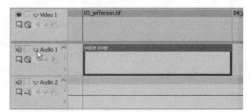

Figure 13.68 Expand the track that contains audio clips you want to adjust.

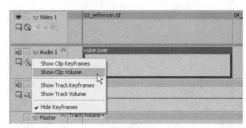

Figure 13.69 Click the track's Show Keyframes button, and choose Show Clip Volume from the menu that appears.

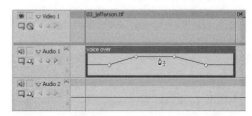

Figure 13.70 Using the keyframe navigator and Pen tool, add keyframes and adjust them in the clip's Volume property graph. In this example, the volume starts at the normal level, or changes by 0 dB. Then the volume is boosted by +3 dB and brought back to its normal level.

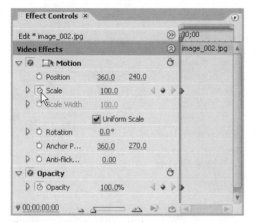

Figure 13.71 Set the CTI to the frame where you want to specify a property value, and then click the stopwatch icon to set the first keyframe at the CTI and initiate the keyframing process.

Animating with the Effect Controls Panel

Essentially, keyframing is nothing more than repeating a two-step process: setting the current frame and setting the property value for that frame. The specific steps are outlined in this section.

If you're new to animating with keyframes, you may want to start with a simple effect property that yields results that are easy to see. For starters, try the Scale property (under the Motion category) or add a standard effect such as Fast Blur.

In later sections, you'll learn to gain greater control over your animations by manipulating the interpolation method used between keyframes.

One more thing: Keyframing involves using the Effect Controls panel's timeline area. Make sure you know how to view it and how to set the Pin to Clip option before you proceed. If you need to, review the section "Viewing Properties in the Effect Controls Panel," earlier in this chapter.

To set keyframes in the Effect Controls panel:

1. In the Timeline panel, select the clip that contains effect properties you want to adjust.

   The selected clip's effect properties appear in the Effect Controls panel.

2. In the Effect Controls panel, make sure the timeline view is visible.

3. Set the sequence CTI to the frame where you want to specify a keyframed property value.

4. Click the stopwatch icon ⏱ next to the layer property you want to keyframe, to activate the icon and the keyframing process (**Figure 13.71**).

continues on next page

ANIMATING WITH THE EFFECT CONTROLS PANEL

The property's stopwatch icon appears selected ⏱. To the right of the property name, a keyframe navigator appears; a selected diamond indicates that the CTI is cued to a keyframe. In the property's track in the timeline view, a keyframe icon appears at the CTI.

5. Set the value for the keyframe (**Figure 13.72**).

6. Set the CTI to another frame.

7. *Do one of the following:*

   ▲ To create a keyframe with a new value, change the property's value (**Figure 13.73**).

   In the property's track of the timeline view, a new keyframe appears, and the diamond at the center of the keyframe navigator is highlighted.

   ▲ To create a keyframe without changing the property's value at that frame, click the center diamond of the keyframe navigator (**Figure 13.74**).

   If the new keyframe becomes the last keyframe for the property, it has the same value as the previous keyframe. Otherwise, the new keyframe's value is based on the previously interpolated value for that frame.

8. To create additional keyframes, repeat steps 6 and 7.

   To modify the keyframe values or to change the keyframes' position in time, use the methods explained in the following sections.

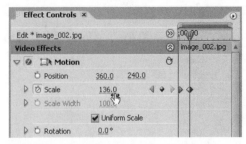

Figure 13.72 Use the property value controls to set the keyframe's value.

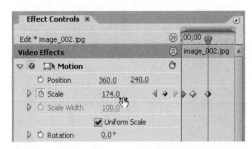

Figure 13.73 Set the CTI to a new frame, and change the property's value to set a keyframe with a new value...

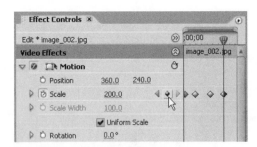

Figure 13.74 ...or click the keyframe navigator's diamond icon to set a keyframe using the value already calculated for that frame.

Figure 13.75 Use the playback controls or render a preview file to see the effect in motion.

9. To see the effect property values vary over time in the Program Monitor, use the playback controls in the Effect Controls panel or any of the sequence playback controls you've learned about so far. You may need to render a preview file to see the effect play back at the project's full frame rate (see Chapter 10) (**Figure 13.75**).

✔ Tips

■ Although it's possible to set a keyframe beyond the duration of the clip, doing so is usually unnecessary and will prevent you from seeing the keyframe in the timeline view of the Effects Control panel when Pin to Clip is selected.

■ There's more than one way to make a property pause, or hold, at a certain value. You can create two consecutive keyframes that use the same value, or you can apply a hold interpolation method to a keyframe (explained later in this chapter). And naturally, a value is also maintained after the last keyframe.

■ Property values before the first keyframe use the first keyframe's values; values after the last keyframe use the last keyframe's values. Therefore, setting the first keyframe after the beginning of the clip delays the animation, and setting the last keyframe before the end of the clip makes the value hold until the clip's Out point.

Keyframes with Interpolated Property Values

When you select the diamond in the keyframe navigator, the keyframe you create uses *interpolated* property values: values determined by calculating the progression between the keyframed values that come immediately before and after it. The mathematical term *interpolation* is the equivalent of the animation term *tweening*. For more about interpolation, see Chapter 14.

You usually create keyframes with interpolated values to modify an animation or, when no animation exists yet, to repeat a value. For example, adding a keyframe with interpolated values between two position keyframes lets you modify the existing motion path. When there's no difference between keyframed values, a new interpolated keyframe uses the same value. Likewise, when you make the last keyframe an interpolated keyframe, it uses the same value as the previous one.

By comparison, all keyframes you add to a value graph in the Timeline panel initially use interpolated values. After all, you can add a keyframe only to the line of the value graph, which represents interpolated values.

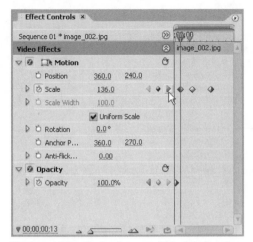

Figure 13.76 Use the keyframe navigator's Left and Right Arrow buttons to cue the CTI. In this example, clicking the right button...

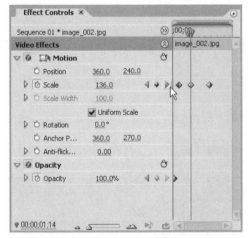

Figure 13.77 ...cues the CTI to the next keyframe.

Editing Keyframes in the Effect Controls Panel

As in the value graph, you can change the timing of keyframes by dragging them in the Effect Controls panel's timeline view. However, to change the property value at a keyframe, you must cue the sequence CTI to the keyframe and then change the value using controls in the left side of the panel. In the case of the position, you can also drag the keyframe's x icon in the motion path of the Program Monitor. In addition, you can copy and paste keyframes within a property, or from a property in one clip to the same property in another clip.

To cue the CTI to keyframes:

1. Make sure the property with the keyframes you want to see is visible in the Effect Controls panel.

2. In the keyframe navigator for the property, *do one of the following:*

   ▲ To cue the current time to the previous keyframe, click the left arrow ◀.

   ▲ To cue the current time to the next keyframe, click the right arrow ▶ (**Figure 13.76**).

   The sequence's CTI moves to the keyframe you specify (**Figure 13.77**). If no keyframe exists beyond the current keyframe, the appropriate arrow appears dimmed.

To change a property's value at a keyframe:

1. Cue the sequence CTI to the keyframe whose value you want to adjust.

2. Adjust the property's value by using controls at the left side of the Effect Controls panel or, in the case of motion properties, by dragging in the Program Monitor (**Figure 13.78**).

   Remember that changing a property value when the current time isn't cued to a keyframe creates a new keyframe at that point.

To select keyframes:

◆ *Do one of the following:*

   ▲ To select a keyframe, click it in the timeline view (**Figure 13.79**).

   ▲ To add to or subtract from your selection, Shift+click a keyframe.

   ▲ To select all the keyframes for a property, click the name of the property (**Figure 13.80**).

   Selected keyframes appear blue.

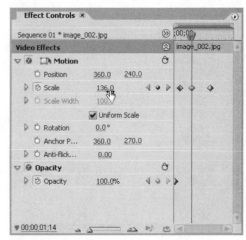

Figure 13.78 To change the property value at a keyframe, make sure the CTI is cued to the keyframe, and then change the property's value. If the CTI isn't cued to a keyframe, changing the value creates a new keyframe at that point.

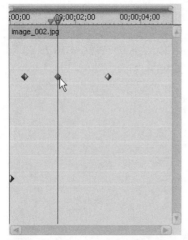

Figure 13.79 In the Effect Controls panel's timeline view, click a keyframe to select it, or Shift+click to add to or subtract from the selection.

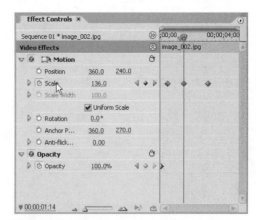

Figure 13.80 Click the property's name to select all of its keyframes.

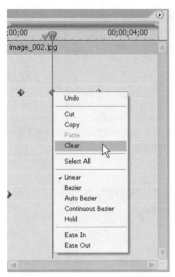

Figure 13.81 To delete a keyframe, select it and press Delete, or right-click it and choose Clear from the menu.

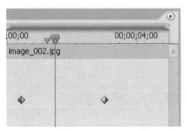

Figure 13.82 The keyframe is removed, and the property's values between the remaining keyframes are recalculated.

To delete keyframes:

◆ In the Effect Controls panel's timeline view, *do one of the following:*

▲ Select one or more keyframes, and press Delete.

▲ Right-click a keyframe, and choose Clear from the menu (**Figure 13.81**).

The keyframes are removed, and the property's interpolated values are recalculated accordingly (**Figure 13.82**).

To delete all keyframes for a property:

◆ Deactivate the stopwatch icon ⏱ for the property (**Figure 13.83**), and confirm your choice when prompted.

All keyframes disappear (**Figure 13.84**). You can't restore the keyframes by reactivating the stopwatch (doing this only starts a new keyframe process).

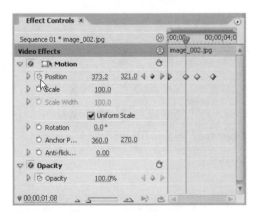

Figure 13.83 Click the stopwatch to deactivate it...

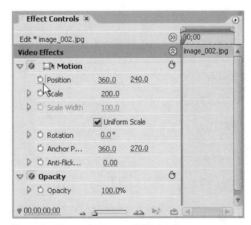

Figure 13.84 ...and remove all the keyframes.

To move keyframes in time:

1. Select one or more keyframes (as explained earlier in this chapter).

2. Drag the selected keyframes left or right to a new position in time (**Figure 13.85**).

To copy and paste keyframed values:

1. Select one or more keyframes (as explained earlier in this chapter) (**Figure 13.86**).

2. Choose Edit > Copy, or press Ctrl+C (**Figure 13.87**).

3. Set the CTI to the time at which you want the pasted keyframes to begin (**Figure 13.88**).

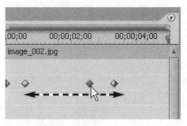

Figure 13.85 Drag keyframes right or left to change their positions in time.

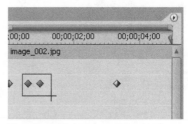

Figure 13.86 Select one or more keyframes.

Figure 13.87 Choose Edit > Copy.

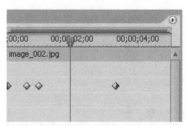

Figure 13.88 Set the CTI to the frame at which you want the pasted keyframes to start...

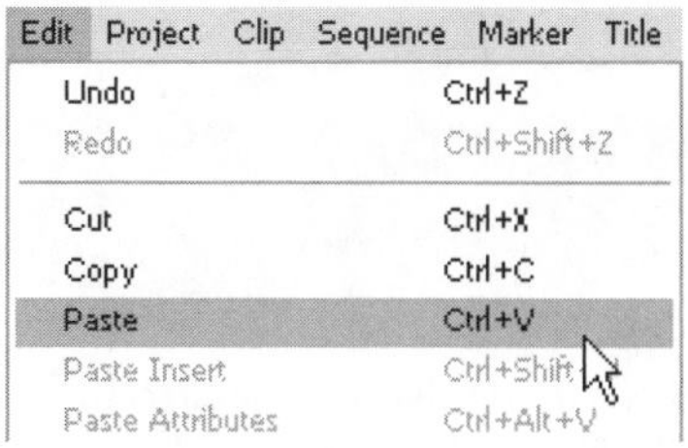

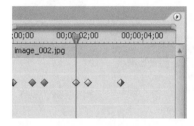

Figure 13.89 ...and choose Edit > Paste or press Ctrl+V.

Figure 13.90 The keyframes are pasted into the property, starting at the CTI.

4. Choose Edit > Paste, or press Ctrl+V (**Figure 13.89**).

The keyframes are pasted into the property, starting at the CTI (**Figure 13.90**).

✔ Tips

■ You can select multiple keyframes by dragging a marquee around them, just as you can with keyframes in the Timeline panel.

■ You can paste keyframes from a property in one clip to the same property in another clip. To do this, select the new clip and set the CTI before you use the Paste command.

Keyframe Icons

A property's keyframes appear in its corresponding row, or *property track*, in the timeline view. When the property heading is expanded, its keyframes appear as large icons (**Figure 13.91**). When the property heading is collapsed, the keyframes of the properties in that category appear as smaller circles and can't be modified (**Figure 13.92**).

The full-size keyframe icons vary according to the interpolation method used by the keyframe (for more about temporal interpolation, see Chapter 14). Regardless of method, shading indicates that the property value either before or after the keyframe hasn't been interpolated.

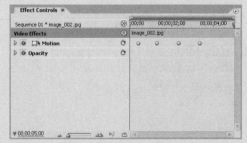

Figure 13.91 When the property heading is expanded, its keyframe icons appear full-sized and reflect interpolation methods.

Figure 13.92 When the property heading is collapsed, the keyframes of the properties in that category appear as smaller circles and can't be modified.

Working with Effect Presets

Earlier in this chapter, you learned how to drag an effect to a clip in the timeline and modify its parameters in the Effect Control panel.

It can take a lot of time and effort to get the effect you want. Luckily, you can save any combination of effects and their settings as a *preset*.

Adobe has supplied a number of presets to get you started. Many of the most common tasks, such as creating a beveled border for a picture-in-picture effect and using different effects to transition into and out of a clip, are already available in the new Presets bins. You can use an existing preset, as well as modify, save, and import a preset. And because presets are saved as small files on your hard disk, it's easy to share presets with other editors. When you change the parameters of an effect in the Effect Controls panel, you have the option of saving the effect as a preset in the Effect Controls panel's pull-down menu. Premiere Pro stores the new preset in the root preset directory, but as you'll learn later in this section, you can create custom preset bins and drag the new presets into the new bins.

To create and save an effect preset:

1. In the Timeline panel, select the clip that uses the effect you want to save as a preset (**Figure 13.93**).

2. In the Effect Controls panel, select the effect that you want to save (**Figure 13.94**).

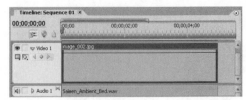

Figure 13.93 Select the clip that uses the effect you want to save as a preset.

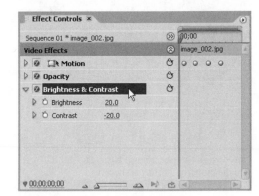

Figure 13.94 Select the effect that you want to save.

WORKING WITH EFFECT PRESETS

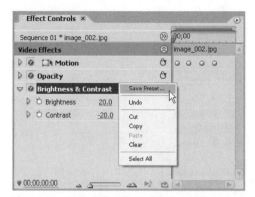

Figure 13.95 In the Effect Controls panel menu, choose Save Preset.

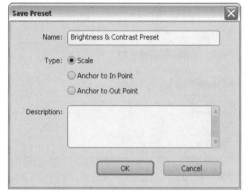

Figure 13.96 Enter a new name for the preset, and select a keyframe option.

3. In the Effect Controls panel menu, choose Save Preset (**Figure 13.95**).

The Save Preset dialog box appears (**Figure 13.96**).

4. Enter a name for the preset.

Premiere Pro provides a name based on the effect that was modified. Keep the default name, or enter a name that will help you remember what the preset does.

5. Determine the way the effect preset's keyframes will be applied to other clips by *selecting one of the following:*

▲ **Scale:** The keyframes scale proportionally to the duration of the clips.

▲ **Anchor to In Point:** The first keyframe's distance from the In point of the target clip will be the same as it was from the In point of the source clip. All other keyframes follow without scaling for the duration of the target clip.

▲ **Anchor to Out Point:** The last keyframe's distance from the Out point of the target clip will be the same as it was from the Out point of the source clip. All other keyframes precede the last keyframe without scaling for the duration of the target clip.

6. If you want, type a description of the preset in the Description field.

A description can be helpful in identifying the origin or purpose of the preset at a later time.

7. Click OK.

To apply an effect preset:

1. On the Effects panel, expand the Presets bin (**Figure 13.97**).

2. Select a preset, and drag it to a clip on the timeline (**Figure 13.98**).

Figure 13.97 Expand the Presets bin to expose the presets.

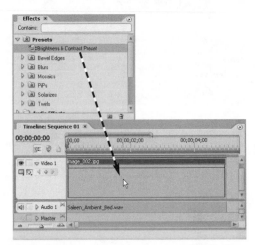

Figure 13.98 Drag the preset to a clip on the timeline.

Figure 13.99 Choose New Presets Bin from the menu.

Figure 13.100 Enter a name for the new presets bin.

To create and rename a preset bin:

1. Click the Effects tab to display the Effects panel.

2. Choose New Presets Bin from the Effects panel's menu (**Figure 13.99**).

   Premiere Pro names the new bin Preset Bin followed by a number.

3. Click the name of the new preset bin on the Effects panel; then, click again (don't double-click), and enter a new name (**Figure 13.100**).

To move effect presets into custom preset bins:

1. Make sure the presets you want to move and the destination bin are both visible on the Effects panel.

2. Select one or more presets (**Figure 13.101**).

3. Drag the selected items to the destination bin (**Figure 13.102**).

   The items are moved into the destination bin (**Figure 13.103**).

✔ Tip

■ When you save an effect as a preset, give it a good, descriptive name that will make sense to you in the future. Otherwise, all your hard work may become lost or forgotten, never to grace your later projects.

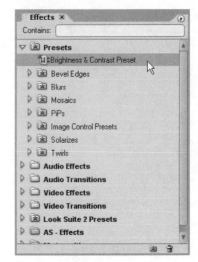

Figure 13.101 Select one or more presets.

Figure 13.102 Drag the selected items to the destination bin.

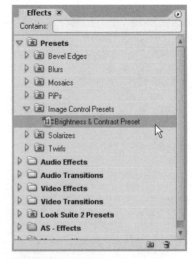

Figure 13.103 The items are moved into the destination bin.

14

Advanced Effects

In the previous chapter, you learned how to add and adjust a wide range of effects using a relatively small number of techniques. This chapter explores a few techniques more deeply, enhancing your command over animation and compositing.

Whereas the last chapter focused on setting keyframes, this chapter concentrates on influencing the values between keyframes, the *interpolation*. So far, you've allowed Premiere Pro to calculate the interpolation using the default scheme. But fortunately, you can instruct Premiere Pro to use a range of interpolation methods. Some methods create steady changes from one keyframe to the next; others vary the rate of change. Movement can take a direct path or a curved route; an action can glide in for a soft landing or blast off in a burst of speed. This chapter explains how you can assign various interpolation methods to keyframes to impart nuance and variation to your animations.

In addition to covering advanced animation technique, this chapter also pays special attention to a category of effects of particular interest to many users: keying. As you recall, keying effects (or simply, *keys*) make parts of an image transparent based on a specified factor, such as brightness, color, or even another image. For the most part, you apply keying effects like other effects. However, they're distinguished both by their usefulness and by their specialized controls, and therefore they merit a more thorough treatment.

Understanding Interpolation

The beauty of keyframes is that they save you work. If you set the keyframes, Premiere Pro calculates the values for the frames in between, a process known as *interpolation*. But interpolation by itself wouldn't be the labor-saving scheme it is if you couldn't also specify different ways to calculate it. Some methods create steady changes from one keyframe to the next; others vary the rate of change. This way, you can add nuance without adding keyframes. Interpolation affects the animation in terms of both space and time.

Spatial interpolation

Spatial interpolation refers to the way that Premiere Pro calculates changes in position—in other words, how a layer moves through the visible area of the screen. Does it proceed directly from one keyframe to the next, or does it take a curved route (**Figures 14.1** and **14.2**)?

By default, Premiere Pro calculates the values between position keyframes—the motion path—using a curved progression, called an *auto* Bézier curve. In spatial terms, this means there is a smooth rate of change through the keyframe, with no sharp changes in direction.

Figure 14.1 Spatial interpolation determines the path between position keyframes. Does the clip proceed directly from one keyframe to the next...

Figure 14.2 ...or does it take a curved route?

UNDERSTANDING INTERPOLATION

Figure 14.3 Temporal interpolation influences the rate of change between keyframes. Here, both rabbits run the same distance in the same amount of time. The top rabbit moves at a steady pace, whereas the bottom rabbit accelerates as it nears the final position.

Temporal interpolation

Temporal interpolation refers to any property value's rate of change between keyframes. Does the value change at a constant rate from one keyframe to the next, or does it accelerate or decelerate?

For example, **Figure 14.3** shows two familiar rabbits (the logo of Peachpit Press's Visual QuickStart and QuickPro series of books). They both travel the same distance in the same amount of time. However, one proceeds from the first keyframe to the last keyframe at a constant rate. The other gradually accelerates, starting slowly and then speeding up. As a result, the second rabbit falls behind at first and then gradually catches up. Both reach their destination simultaneously.

By default, Premiere Pro calculates temporal interpolation using a linear progression, or *Linear interpolation* method. This means property values change at a constant rate, or speed. However, you can set the rate of change to accelerate or decelerate (either manually or by choosing an automated option). You can even specify no interpolation, so that a keyframe value holds until the next keyframe value is reached (in terms of the example, this rabbit would magically appear at the finish line at the moment the others reach it by foot).

Incoming and outgoing interpolation

Although *interpolation* refers to values *between* keyframes, it's important to understand that you assign an interpolation type to keyframes themselves. The interpolation type, in turn, determines how values are calculated before the keyframe and after the keyframe—the *incoming* and *outgoing interpolation*. Therefore, the values between any two keyframes are determined by the first keyframe's outgoing interpolation type and the next keyframe's incoming interpolation type.

The concept is most easily understood in spatial terms. Just as a direction handle in a path shape influences the preceding curve, a motion keyframe's tangent affects the path preceding the keyframe. Similarly, the opposite tangent influences the motion path after the keyframe (**Figure 14.4**).

Temporal interpolation also affects a property value's rate of change before and after the keyframe. In a speed or value graph, ease handles work a lot like tangents in a motion path. But because the graph lines don't trace a spatial path, they can be a little more difficult to interpret and adjust (**Figure 14.5**).

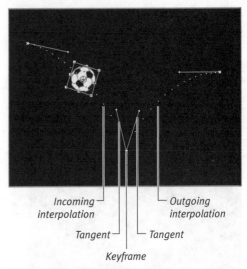

Incoming interpolation — Outgoing interpolation
Tangent — Tangent
Keyframe

Figure 14.4 In a motion path, keyframe tangents define the outgoing and incoming interpolation and hence, the curve of the motion path.

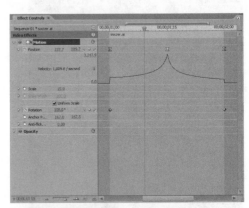

Figure 14.5 A value graph's direction lines and a speed graph's ease handles (shown here) define the incoming and outgoing interpolation. Here, the rate of change gradually accelerates after the first keyframe and then decelerates into the second keyframe.

Viewing and adjusting spatial interpolation

You can adjust the motion path—the spatial interpolation—directly in the Program Monitor by using the mouse (**Figure 14.6**). You'll find that editing motion paths works in much the same way as drawing shapes with the Pen tool in the Titler (see Chapter 12, "Creating Titles"), or as in a path-based drawing program, such as Adobe Illustrator. That's because a motion path is also defined by an editable line known as a Bézier curve (see the sidebar "Bézier Curves and the Motion Path"). Although the spacing of dots in a motion path provides a rough indication of speed, it doesn't give you direct control over the speed or the temporal interpolation.

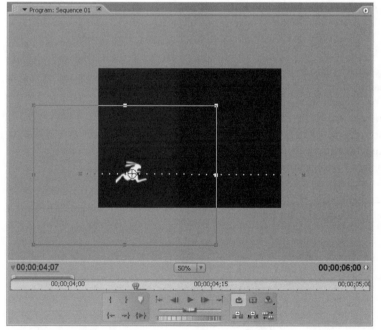

Figure 14.6 Interpolated values for spatial properties appear as a motion path connecting keyframes in the Program Monitor. You can shape the path as you would any Bézier curve.

Viewing and adjusting temporal interpolation

Temporal interpolation is represented by a property graph that you can view by expanding the property's heading in either the clip in the timeline or the Effect Controls panel. You can adjust the curve in much the same way as you would adjust a motion path, except that you control the rate of change between any property's keyframed values (**Figure 14.7**).

Despite its similarity to a motion path, however, temporal interpolation is more difficult to understand visually. Instead of tracing a physical path, the line connecting keyframes is like a mathematical graph. In a value graph, a straight line represents a constant speed, whereas a curved line shows acceleration or deceleration. But as in a motion path, a sharp corner in the graph represents an abrupt shift in the rate of change, and a smooth curve indicates a gradual change.

✔ Tip

■ You can expand a clip in the timeline and reveal an effect property graph, or expand the property in the Effect Controls panel. But whereas a clip in the timeline limits your view to a single property, the Effect Controls panel can show the graph in the context of other properties and effects. For this reason, this chapter favors viewing and adjusting temporal interpolation in the Effect Controls panel.

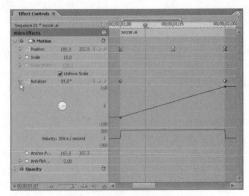

Figure 14.7 An expanded clip in the timeline or in the Effect Controls panel (shown here) represents property values as a graph. The curve of the graph corresponds to how the values are interpolated between keyframes.

Figure 14.8 Spatially, Linear interpolation defines a corner at each keyframe and a straight path between keyframes.

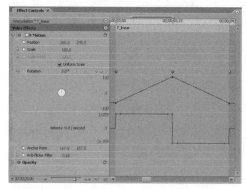

Figure 14.9 Temporally, Linear interpolation results in a constant rate of change between keyframes (and a straight line in a velocity graph). When speed differs between pairs of keyframes, the change is instantaneous.

Interpolation Types

Although their default settings differ, Premiere Pro calculates both spatial and temporal interpolation using a similar set of methods, or interpolation types. You can apply the following interpolation methods to calculate both spatial and temporal interpolation. (Later, you'll learn about methods unique to temporal interpolation: Hold interpolation and the Ease In and Ease Out options.)

The following figures illustrate each interpolation type spatially (in a motion path) and temporally (using a velocity graph).

Linear interpolation dictates a constant rate of change from one keyframe to the next. Spatially, Linear interpolation defines a straight path from one keyframe to the next (**Figure 14.8**); temporally, Linear interpolation results in a constant speed between keyframes (**Figure 14.9**).

Auto Bézier interpolation automatically reduces the rate of change equally on both sides of a keyframe. Spatially, a keyframe set to Auto Bézier is comparable to a smooth point, with two equal direction lines extending from it. It results in a smooth, symmetrical curve in a motion path (**Figure 14.10**). Temporally, Auto Bézier interpolation reduces the rate of change equally before and after a keyframe, creating a gradual deceleration that eases into and out of the keyframe (**Figure 14.11**).

Adjusting an Auto Bézier keyframe's direction handles manually make it a Continuous Bézier keyframe.

Continuous Bézier interpolation, like Auto Bézier, reduces the rate of change on both sides of a keyframe. However, Continuous Bézier interpolation is set manually, so it doesn't affect the incoming and outgoing rates of change equally. In the motion path, Continuous Bézier interpolation results in a smooth and continuous, but asymmetrical, curve (**Figure 14.12**). Temporally, Continuous Bézier interpolation reduces the rate of change both before and after a keyframe unequally (**Figure 14.13**).

Ctrl+clicking a Continuous Bézier keyframe's handles make it a Bézier keyframe.

Figure 14.10 Auto Bézier interpolation creates a curved path with equal incoming and outgoing interpolation.

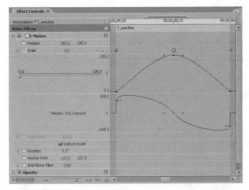

Figure 14.11 Temporally, Auto Bézier interpolation yields gradual, even speed changes and a curved graph.

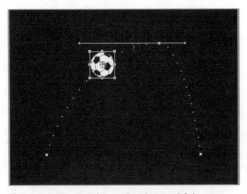

Figure 14.12 You might use Continuous Bézier interpolation to trace the asymmetrically arced path of a thrown ball.

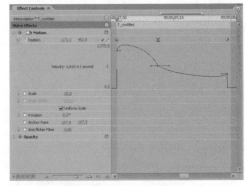

Figure 14.13 Temporally, rate of change is reduced smoothly—but unevenly—on either side of a Continuous Bézier keyframe. A rolling ball may decelerate gradually as it crests a hill but accelerate more sharply on its descent.

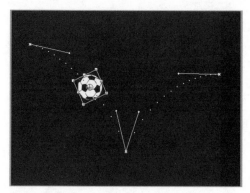

Figure 14.14 Bézier interpolation can allow the motion path to follow discontinuous curves, such as the one that describes the path of a ball's bounce.

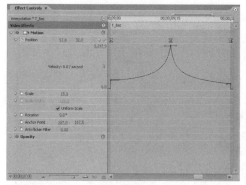

Figure 14.15 Temporally, Bézier interpolation can create sudden acceleration and deceleration. The bouncing ball accelerates until the moment of impact and then suddenly decelerates as it ascends.

Bézier interpolation is set manually, like Continuous Bézier. Bézier interpolation can either decrease or increase the rate of change on either or both sides of a keyframe. Spatially, Bézier keyframes are comparable to a corner point in a motion path. As in a corner point, the direction lines extending from the keyframe are unequal and discontinuous. In a motion path, Bézier interpolation creates a discontinuous curve, or *cusp*, at the keyframe (**Figure 14.14**). Temporally, Bézier interpolation can alter the rate of change abruptly before and after a keyframe (**Figure 14.15**).

✔ Tip

■ Don't worry if the velocity graph doesn't make sense to you yet. Just get a feel for the differences between smooth and abrupt changes, and between acceleration and steady speed. Over the course of the chapter, you'll learn to recognize how each interpolation type translates into a graph.

Bézier Curves and the Motion Path

Motion paths work like Bézier curves you find in other programs—particularly programs that include drawing tools, such as Photoshop, Illustrator, and After Effects.

Instead of drawing a shape freehand, you can define a shape using a *Bézier curve*. In a Bézier curve, you define control points, which are connected by line segments automatically. (It already sounds a lot like keyframes and interpolation, doesn't it?)

The curves of the line segments are defined and controlled by *direction lines*. Two direction lines can extend from each control point. The length and angle of one direction line influences the shape of the curve preceding the control point; the other influences the curve following the control point. (Imagine that the direction lines exert a gravitational pull on the line that enters and exits a control point.) Dragging the end of a direction line alters the line and thus its corresponding curve (**Figure 14.16**).

Figure 14.16 Bézier curves in a drawing program...

Just as a Bézier curve consists of control points connected by line segments, a *motion path* consists of position keyframes connected by line segments (albeit dotted lines). The same techniques you use to draw shapes in a drawing program can be applied to creating motion paths in Premiere Pro (**Figure 14.17**).

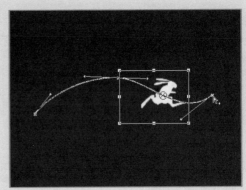

Figure 14.17 ...work essentially the same as motion paths in Premiere Pro.

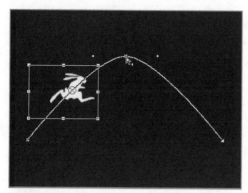

Figure 14.18 Position the mouse over a position keyframe so the pointer becomes a Move Keyframe icon...

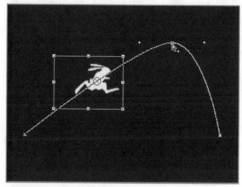

Figure 14.19 ...and drag the keyframe to the position you want.

Reshaping a Motion Path

When you make adjustments to a motion path, you alter either a clip's position keyframes or the spatially interpolated values between them. Like the keyframed position values, you can alter the interpolated values by dragging in the Program Monitor. Reshaping a motion path works just like reshaping a Bézier curve in a drawing program (see the sidebar "Bézier Curves and the Motion Path").

To move a position keyframe:

1. In a clip's motion path, position the mouse pointer over a position keyframe (an x in the path) so that the pointer changes into a Move Keyframe icon ⬚ (**Figure 14.18**).

2. Drag the keyframe to a new position (**Figure 14.19**).

   The clip's Position property value at the keyframe changes accordingly.

To convert Auto Bézier to Continuous Bézier:

◆ In a clip's motion path, drag the end handle of any keyframe's direction line.

   If the keyframe's direction lines are continuous (Auto Bézier or Continuous Bézier), dragging changes the angle of both direction lines, but it changes the length of only the line you grab (Continuous Bézier) (**Figures 14.20** and **14.21**). If the direction lines are split (Bézier), dragging moves the line you grab independently.

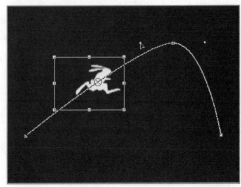

Figure 14.20 Dragging the direction line of an Auto Bézier keyframe...

To toggle between Continuous Bézier and Bézier (and vice versa):

◆ In a clip's motion path, Ctrl+drag the end handle of any keyframe's direction line.

   The mouse pointer becomes a Convert Keyframe icon ▷ (**Figure 14.22**). If the keyframe's direction lines are continuous (Auto Bézier or Continuous Bézier), the line's length and angle change independently of the other direction line (**Figure 14.23**).

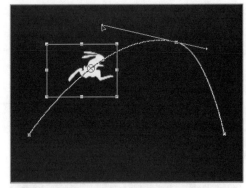

Figure 14.21 ...converts it to a Continuous Bézier keyframe, allowing you to change the angle of both lines but the length of only one.

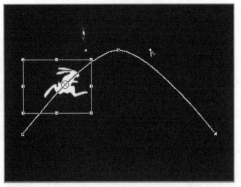

Figure 14.22 Ctrl+dragging changes the mouse into a Convert icon...

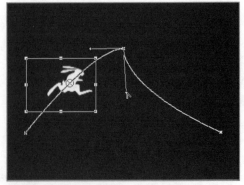

Figure 14.23 ...converting the keyframe (in this case) from Continuous Bezier to Bezier, breaking the relationship between direction lines.

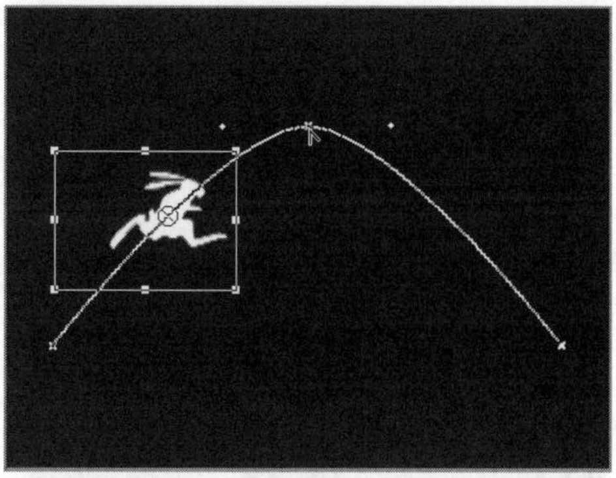

Figure 14.24 Pressing Ctrl as you position the mouse over a position keyframe changes the mouse into a Convert Keyframe icon...

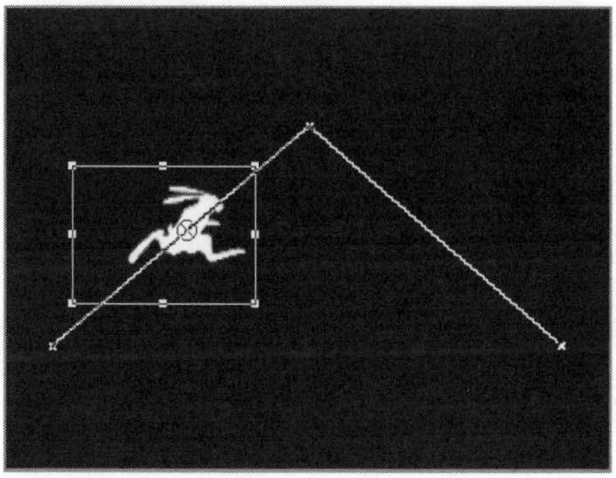

Figure 14.25 ...and clicking toggles the keyframe from (in this case) Auto Bézier to Linear.

To toggle between Auto Bezier and Linear interpolation:

1. In a clip's motion path, press Ctrl, and position the mouse pointer over a position keyframe (an x in the path) so that the pointer changes into a Convert Keyframe icon (**Figure 14.24**).
2. Click the keyframe.

   The keyframe toggles from having two equal and continuous direction lines and a curved path (Auto Bézier interpolation) to having no direction lines and a straight path (Linear interpolation) (**Figure 14.25**).

✔ Tip

- Technically speaking, direction lines define the spatial interpolation between position keyframes. See the section "Understanding Interpolation," earlier in this chapter, for more information.

Specifying a Spatial Interpolation Method

As you've seen, you can reshape a motion path—in effect, its spatial interpolation—by dragging. You can also use commands to set a keyframe's interpolation type.

To specify a spatial interpolation method:

1. In either the Effect Controls panel or the Program Monitor, right-click a keyframe for a spatial property; in the context menu, choose Spatial Interpolation, and select an option (**Figure 14.26**):

   ▲ Linear

   ▲ Bézier

   ▲ Auto Bézier

   ▲ Continuous Bézier

2. Drag the Bézier handles in the Program Monitor.

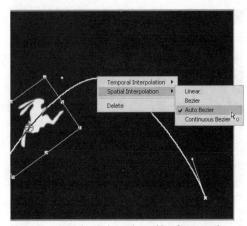

Figure 14.26 Right-click a selected keyframe and choose an option from the context menu.

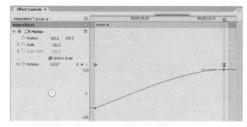

Figure 14.27 The value graph measures value vertically and time horizontally. This is a value graph for rotation (the rate of rotation gradually decelerates as it reaches the second keyframe).

Understanding Value and Speed Graphs

In the following sections, you'll learn to adjust a property's graph, either in an expanded clip in the timeline, or in the Effect Controls panel (generally, this book depicts the Effect Controls panel). But first, let's take a moment to examine the two types of graphs you'll encounter: the value graph and speed graph.

Value graph

A *value graph* measures a property's value vertically and its time horizontally (**Figure 14.27**). The units in which values are expressed depend on the type of property: Rotation is measured in rotations and degrees, Opacity in percentages, and so on. The slope of the line between keyframes represents the rate of change in units/second. Straight lines indicate a constant rate; curved lines indicate a changing rate, or acceleration.

Value graphs tend to be easy to understand: When the value increases, the graph goes up; when the value decreases, the graph slopes down. A value graph is particularly well suited to properties such as opacity and audio levels, because these properties correspond well with the "up and down" or "high and low" nature of the graph. (Recall your experience in the previous chapter, in which you learned that adjusting a value graph in the timeline is also called *rubberbanding*.)

Velocity graph

The velocity graph corresponds with the rate of change, not the value itself (**Figure 14.28**). The units measured by a velocity graph depend on the property type: degrees of rotation/sec, percentage opacity/sec, and so on. Regardless of the specific property, the rate of change (units/sec) is measured vertically, and time (sec) is measured horizontally in both graphs. Therefore, the slope of the graph represents acceleration (units/sec/sec), which is dictated by the temporal interpolation method.

Velocity graphs can take some getting used to. A horizontal graph indicates a constant speed; a sloped graph indicates changing speed (acceleration or deceleration). But the slope's angle can be deceptive. For example, a velocity graph that slopes up indicates acceleration—but the property's value may be increasing or decreasing.

Graph types in the timeline

Because an expanded clip is designed to show only a single property graph at a time, Premiere Pro selects the most appropriate type of graph automatically. Many properties are defined by a single value, or *dimension*. Opacity, for example, contains a single property, which is defined by a single value. Selecting a single-dimensional, quantitative property from a clip's effect pull-down menu reveals a value graph (**Figure 14.29**).

However, other properties consist of more than one value. For example, a Position property includes values for both *x* and *y* coordinates. Hence, a value graph for position must include two lines: one representing the *x* coordinate value and the other representing the *y* coordinate value. Rather than clutter the expanded clip with two value graphs, Premiere Pro displays a velocity graph (**Figure 14.30**).

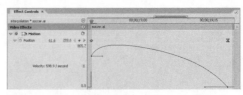

Figure 14.28 A velocity graph measure rates of change vertically and time horizontally. Therefore, it represents acceleration in terms of units/sec/sec.

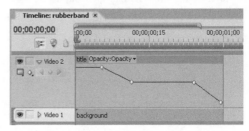

Figure 14.29 A property defined by a single value is also called *single-dimensional*. When you select such a property an expanded clip's pull-down menu, it invokes a value graph.

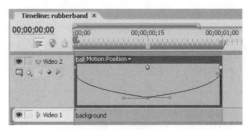

Figure 14.30 By contrast, a property with more than one dimension (such as Position) always invokes a velocity graph.

Graph types in the Effect Controls panel

As you know, the Effect Controls panel lists all the effects contained in the selected clip; the panel's timeline view lets you view and set keyframes. In addition, you can expand any effect property to reveal value and velocity graphs. Single-dimensional property values always include both graphs, whereas properties that have more than one dimension reveal a velocity graph only (**Figure 14.31**).

✔ Tip

■ For effect properties that can't be graphed—such as a color choice—you must turn to other controls in the Effect Controls panel. For example, see "To use a standard effect's custom settings," in Chapter 13.

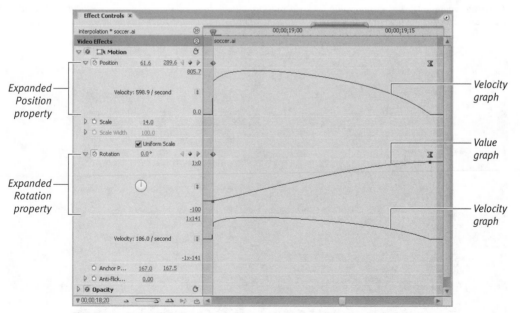

Expanded Position property

Expanded Rotation property

Velocity graph

Value graph

Velocity graph

Figure 14.31 In the Effect Controls panel, a single-dimensional property (such as Rotation) reveals both a value and velocity graph. A property with more than one dimension reveals a velocity graph only.

Analyzing Value and Velocity Graphs

Table 14.1 and **Figures 14.32** and **14.33** summarize how an animation corresponds to the shape of a value graph or velocity graph. (These examples are exaggerated for the purpose of illustration; your property graphs will be more subtle.)

Note that the slope and curve of the value graph and the speed graph can differ. For example, an increasing value results in a value graph with a positive, upward slope; however, the rate of change may also be decreasing (even as it approaches a higher value), resulting in a speed graph that slopes down.

Table 14.1

Recognizing Temporal Interpolation		
TEMPORAL INTERPOLATION	IN THE VALUE GRAPH	IN THE SPEED/VELOCITY GRAPH
No speed change	Horizontal line	Horizontal line
Constant speed	Straight line with any slope	Horizontal line
Sudden speed change	Sharp corner	Disconnected line/ease handles
Acceleration	Curve with steep slope	Upward-sloping curve
Deceleration	Curve with shallow slope	Downward-sloping curve
Holding	Horizontal line, unconnected	Horizontal line, where current speed = 0

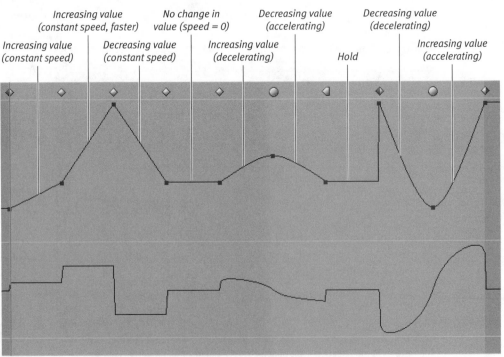

Figure 14.32 A value graph shows changes in a property's value (in this case, Rotation). Examine how the slope or shape of the graph corresponds with interpolation.

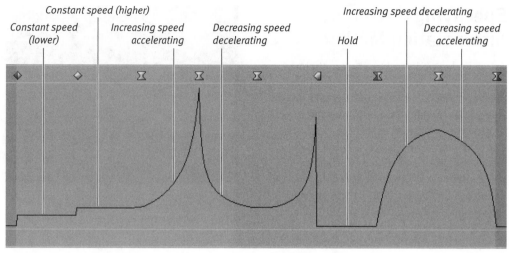

Constant speed (higher)

Constant speed (lower)

Increasing speed accelerating

Decreasing speed decelerating

Increasing speed decelerating

Hold

Decreasing speed accelerating

Figure 14.33 A velocity graph shows changes in a property's speed (here, Position).

Keyframe Icons and Interpolation

The Effect Controls panel's timeline view shows interpolation explicitly in the form of a value and/or velocity graph.

In a graph, keyframe icons appear as small boxes, or *control points*—regardless of the interpolation type. However, the shape of large keyframe icons reflects the incoming and outgoing interpolation (**Figure 14.34**). If you collapse an effect containing multiple properties to show just its main heading, all of its properties' keyframes appear as small dots, or *summary keyframes*, that indicate their presence and position only.

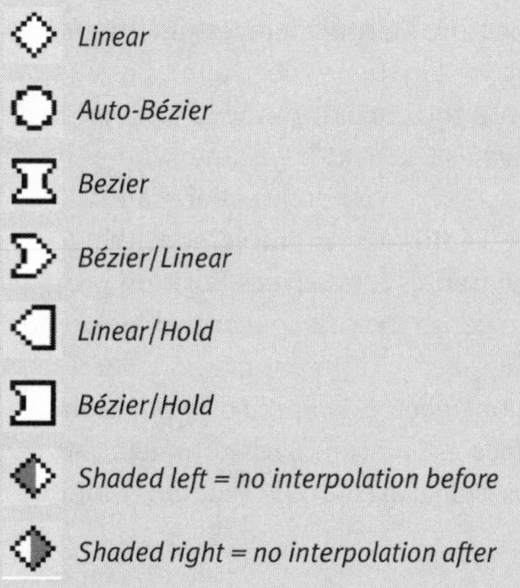

◇ *Linear*

◯ *Auto-Bézier*

⏳ *Bezier*

⟫ *Bézier/Linear*

◁ *Linear/Hold*

⏳ *Bézier/Hold*

◈ *Shaded left = no interpolation before*

◈ *Shaded right = no interpolation after*

Figure 14.34 In the Effect Controls panel, the shape of each keyframe's large icon indicates the type of interpolation.

497

Specifying a Temporal Interpolation Method

As you've learned, temporal interpolation affects not the change between positions, but the rate of change between any keyframed value, and you adjust it not by altering the motion path in the Program Monitor, but by altering a clip's property graph in the timeline or in the Effect Controls panel. Apart from these differences, temporal interpolation is analogous to spatial interpolation. All the spatial interpolation types (linear, auto-Bézier, and so on) have a corresponding temporal interpolation type. (See "Interpolation Methods" earlier in this chapter.)

You can also specify an interpolation method unique to temporal interpolation: Hold interpolation. In addition, you can quickly ease the incoming or outgoing interpolation of a keyframe using the Ease In and Ease Out options. These options let you achieve these common effects without having to adjust the interpolation manually.

Hold: Although you can observe its effects both spatially and temporally, Hold interpolation is a strictly temporal type of interpolation, halting changes in a property's value at the keyframe. The value remains fixed until the current frame of the composition reaches the next keyframe, where the property is set to a new value instantly (**Figure 14.35**). For example, specifying Hold keyframes for a layer's Position property can cause it to disappear suddenly and then reappear in different places. When Hold interpolation is applied to position keyframes, no motion path connects the keyframes displayed in the Program Monitor.

Figure 14.35 Hold interpolation suspends calculations, retaining the current keyframe's property values until the next keyframe is reached. Here, the title clip "GO!" will appear instantly at each keyframe (x in the Monitor panel).

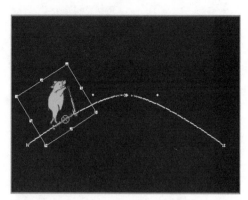

Figure 14.36 Ease In smoothes the incoming rate of change. You can use it to simulate gradual deceleration into a keyframe. Setting the second keyframe to Ease In makes the pig decelerate as it approaches the keyframe.

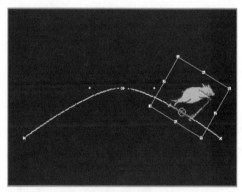

Figure 14.37 Ease Out smoothes the outgoing rate of change. You can use it to simulate gradual acceleration out of a keyframe. Setting the second keyframe to Ease Out makes the pig gradually accelerate as it leaves the keyframe.

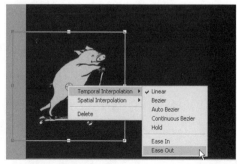

Figure 14.38 Right-click a selected keyframe, and choose an option from the context menu.

Ease In: The property value's rate of change accelerates from, or eases out of, the previous keyframe and then decelerates into, or eases into, the selected keyframe (**Figure 14.36**). Contrast this to the Auto or Continuous Bézier option, which affects both the incoming and outgoing interpolation.

Ease Out: The property value's rate of change accelerates from, or eases out of, the selected keyframe and then decelerates into, or eases into, the following keyframe (**Figure 14.37**). Contrast this to the Auto or Continuous Bézier option, which affects both the incoming and outgoing interpolation.

To set a keyframe's temporal interpolation method:

1. View a clip's keyframed properties in an expanded track of the Timeline panel.

   By default, interpolated temporal values are calculated using a linear progression.

2. Right-click the keyframe you want to adjust, and in the context menu, choose Temporal Interpolation, and then choose an option from the submenu (**Figure 14.38**):

   ▲ Linear

   ▲ Bézier

   ▲ Auto Bézier

   ▲ Continuous Bézier

   ▲ Hold

   ▲ Ease In

   ▲ Ease Out

   ▲ Delete

Adjusting Temporal Interpolation Manually

As you've seen, many of the principles of adjusting a motion path apply to adjusting a property graph. Both are described by Bézier curves, although the terminology can differ. And whereas a motion path traces a literal course through space, the line of a graph corresponds to a property's value or velocity. But although the techniques you use to edit Bézier curves resemble one another in principle, they differ in practice. The main difference lies in how you adjust the curves manually: dragging direction lines in a value graph, or ease handles in a velocity graph.

In a value graph, you can drag direction lines 180 degrees to influence the graph's curve—and, hence, its incoming and outgoing interpolation. Bézier curves closely resemble their counterparts in a motion path.

In a velocity graph, *ease handles* influence the shape of the curve and, thereby, the interpolation. However, ease handles always extend horizontally from a keyframe; their length but not their angle helps shape the curve. Whereas a sudden change in a value plots a cusp in a value graph, a sudden change in speed splits the keyframe so that it occupies two different vertical positions on the velocity graph.

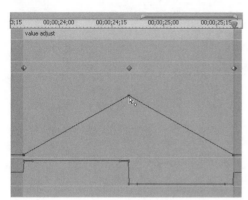

Figure 14.39 Drag a keyframe up to increase...

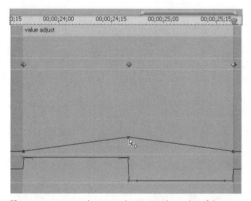

Figure 14.40 ...or down to decrease the value (shown here) or speed.

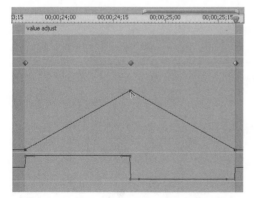

Figure 14.41 With the Pen tool, Ctrl+click the dot under the keyframe to convert it from Linear...

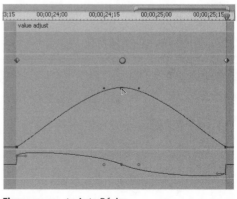

Figure 14.42 ...to Auto Bézier.

To adjust a value graph manually:

1. *Do either of the following:*
   - ▲ In the Timeline panel, expand the track containing the clip you want to adjust, and select the effect property name from its pull-down menu.
   - ▲ Select a clip, and, in the Effect Controls panel, expand the property you want to adjust so that its property graph appears in the timeline view.

   Property values with a single dimension reveal a value graph.

2. In the value graph, select the keyframes you want to adjust.

3. *Do any of the following* to the incoming or outgoing direction lines:
   - ▲ Drag the handle under the keyframe up to increase the value or down to decrease the value (**Figures 14.39** and **14.40**)
   - ▲ To convert Linear to Auto Bézier, Ctrl+click the handle under the keyframe with the Pen tool (**Figures 14.41** and **14.42**)

   continues on next page

ADJUSTING TEMPORAL INTERPOLATION MANUALLY

▲ To convert Auto Bézier to Continuous Bézier, drag one direction line so that the direction lines are unequal but retain their continuous relationship (**Figure 14.43**).

▲ To toggle between Continuous Bézier and Bézier, Option+drag (Mac) or Alt+drag (Windows) a direction handle (**Figure 14.44**).

The Selection tool becomes the Convert Vertex tool when you position it over a direction handle. Dragging a direction handle of a Bézier keyframe converts it to Continuous Bézier with two related direction handles; dragging a direction handle of a Continuous Bézier keyframe splits the direction handles, converting it to Bézier (**Figure 14.45**).

✔ Tip

■ As usual, avoid converting a keyframe unintentionally: Invoke the Convert Vertex tool only when you want to convert a keyframe; otherwise, use the Selection tool.

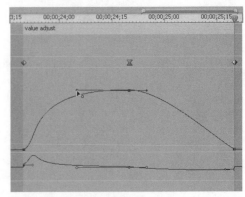

Figure 14.43 In the value graph, extend an Auto Bézier's direction line manually to change it to Continuous Bézier interpolation.

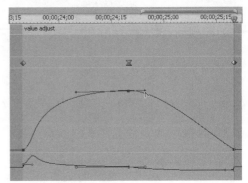

Figure 14.44 In the value graph, Opt+drag (Mac) or Alt+drag (Windows) a direction handle.

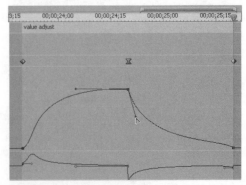

Figure 14.45 Dragging a direction handle of a Continuous Bézier keyframe splits the direction handles, converting it to Bézier.

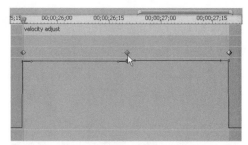

Figure 14.46 Select the keyframes you want to adjust.

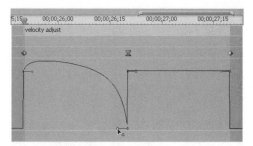

Figure 14.47 Drag an ease handle down to decrease the incoming or outgoing speed at a keyframe.

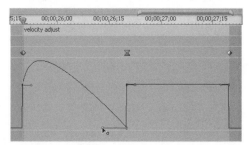

Figure 14.48 Drag an incoming ease handle to the left to increase the influence of the previous keyframe's value.

To adjust a velocity graph manually:

1. *Do either of the following:*

   ▲ In the Timeline panel, expand the track containing the clip you want to adjust, and select the effect property name from its pull-down menu.

   ▲ Select a clip, and, in the Effect Controls panel, expand the property you want to adjust so that its property graph appears in the timeline view.

   Property values with more than one dimension reveal a velocity graph.

2. In the velocity graph, select the keyframes you want to adjust (**Figure 14.46**).

3. *Do any of the following* to the incoming or outgoing ease handles:

   ▲ Drag an ease handle up to increase the incoming or outgoing speed at a keyframe.

   ▲ Drag an ease handle down to decrease the incoming or outgoing speed at a keyframe (**Figure 14.47**).

   ▲ Drag the left ease handle to change its length and influence on the preceding curve (**Figure 14.48**).

   continues on next page

▲ Drag the right ease handle to adjust its length and influence on the following curve.

▲ Option+click (Mac) or Alt+click (Windows) a keyframe to toggle it between Linear and Auto Bézier.

The shape of the graph and the corresponding property's speed change according to your adjustments (**Figures 14.49** and **14.50**). When the incoming and outgoing speeds differ, a keyframe's icon splits, occupying two different vertical positions on the graph.

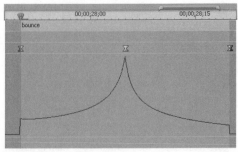

Figure 14.49 An abrupt shift from acceleration to deceleration, or *bounce*, looks like this in a speed graph.

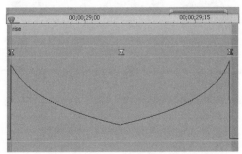

Figure 14.50 A gradual deceleration followed by a gradual acceleration (as when a rising object slows at its apex) looks like this in a speed graph.

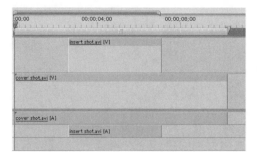

Figure 14.51 Placing a clip in a higher track (and retaining its full opacity)...

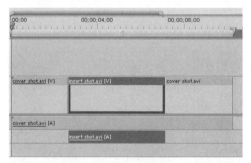

Figure 14.52 ...has the same result as an overlay edit.

Figure 14.53 Most often, you use the higher tracks to blend and key clips. Here, a title is keyed over video.

Superimposing Images

One of the major techniques covered in this chapter is the use of keying filters to superimpose images. But before you learn how to use keying filters, take a moment to review how opacity works in general, and in Premiere Pro in particular.

About track hierarchy

Video tracks 2 and higher are also referred to as *superimpose tracks*. If video clips are playing simultaneously in different tracks (and the monitor buttons are active), only the clip in the highest track is visible in the program view of the Monitor panel, provided that you don't alter the clips' opacity levels. In other words, the superimpose tracks in Premiere Pro work much like layers in Adobe Photoshop (or Illustrator or After Effects).

It's possible to take advantage of track hierarchy for basic editing purposes. By placing a clip in a higher track, you can achieve an effect that looks like an overlay edit in the program view without recording over a clip in the timeline (**Figures 14.51** and **14.52**).

But in general, you use superimpose tracks as their name suggests: to superimpose the clips they contain. By layering clips in superimpose tracks, you can blend and composite images (**Figure 14.53**).

About fading and keying

Previous chapters already introduced you to the two principal methods for superimposing clips: fading and keying.

Fading blends an entire clip with the clips in lower tracks. In Chapter 13, you learned that you can control a clip's overall opacity levels in much the same way that you fade audio levels. Although fading can look similar to a cross-dissolve transition, fading is generally used to blend clips for more sustained periods, not just to transition between them. And unlike with a cross-dissolve (which occurs between two adjacent clips), you can fade multiple layers of clips together (**Figure 14.54**).

In contrast to fading, *keying* makes only certain parts of a clip transparent. You encountered one form of keying in Chapter 12, where you learned that empty areas in a title become transparent automatically (**Figure 14.55**). Similarly, any areas of the screen left empty when you move a clip using a motion effect also become transparent automatically (as you discovered in Chapter 13). This behavior makes creating a picture-in-picture or split-screen effect easy (**Figure 14.56**).

Figure 14.54 Fading blends an entire clip with the underlying image. Here, opacity has been faded to superimpose one clip over another.

Figure 14.55 Keying makes certain parts of a clip transparent. Here, filters have been applied to the document and then the document paper has been keyed out.

Figure 14.56 Areas of the screen left empty as a result of a motion effect are also keyed out automatically, as in this picture-in-picture effect.

Gaspar "Tony" Bolante

Figure 14.57 In addition to automatically keying out an alpha channel generated by Premiere Pro, you can key out parts of an image based on other factors. Here, areas are keyed out based on a matte in the shape of a cameo.

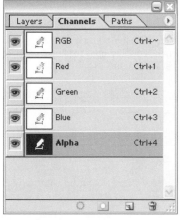

Figure 14.58 You may be familiar with channels from Photoshop, which shows you the R, G, B, and alpha channels on the Channels panel.

As you'll see, you can also *key out,* or remove, parts of an image based on other factors, such as a clip's brightness or color. A keying effect can also utilize a clip's preexisting alpha channel or one you define using another image (**Figure 14.57**).

Naturally, you can combine the effects of fading and keying, such as when you fade up a title over a video.

About the alpha channel

Regardless of the method you use to change a clip's opacity, what you're really modifying is its *alpha channel.*

In 8-bit RGB color images, each channel—red, green, and blue—uses 8 bits (for a total of 24 bits), yielding millions of colors. A 32-bit file contains a fourth 8-bit channel, known as an *alpha channel* (**Figure 14.58**). Whereas the RGB channels define the amount of visible color for each pixel in the image, the alpha channel defines each pixel's level of opacity. Even when a footage file doesn't contain an alpha channel, as is often the case with video, Premiere Pro processes it as a 32-bit file.

The alpha channel is usually depicted as a grayscale matte in which the range from white to black corresponds to the range from opaque to transparent. You can see a clip's alpha channel as a grayscale by setting the source or program view's display mode to Alpha (see "Choosing a Display Mode," in Chapter 5) (**Figure 14.59**).

You already know several ways to modify a clip's alpha channel. Fading adjusts a clip's alpha channel's values for all of its pixels—or, in terms of the matte, changes their grayscale values anywhere from white to black. In the case of titles and motion effects, Premiere Pro automatically generates an alpha channel for empty areas and keys them out. The following sections cover numerous other keying methods.

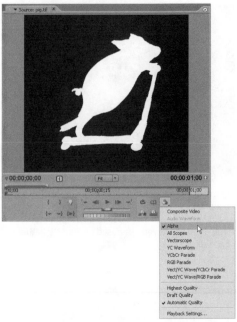

Figure 14.59 In Premiere Pro, you can set the Source or Program Monitor's display mode to show the alpha channel as a grayscale matte.

Figure 14.60 Keying effects are listed in a folder alongside folders for other video effect categories.

Using Keying Filters

In addition to using a clip's opacity property to make the entire image transparent, you can restrict transparency to particular areas—a technique called *keying*. Keying effects are listed among the other standard effects, and you adjust them using the methods you learned in Chapter 13 (**Figure 14.60**). But because keying effects (or simply *keys*) constitute such a useful class of techniques, they merit special attention.

Although Premiere Pro provides many keying filters, all fall into four basic categories. You can *key out*, or make parts of an image transparent, based on the clip's existing alpha channel, luminance, or chrominance, or on a separate image that defines the alpha channel's matte. You can also make these keying filters more effective by employing a *garbage matte*—a filter that crops out extraneous edges of an image.

This chapter assumes that you know how to apply a filter from the Effects panel and how to use the Effect Controls panel to adjust and animate effect properties. (To review those techniques, refer to Chapter 13.) The following sections cover the key types by category, explaining the most commonly used keying filters in detail and summarizing the others.

Keying

Keying makes only certain parts of a clip transparent. The terms *key* and *keying* refer to their physical counterpart, the *keyhole*. Essentially, keying cuts a keyhole in an image, making that part of the image transparent. The hole is then filled with another image—in this case, clips in lower tracks of the timeline. You can *key out*, or remove, parts of an image based on brightness or color. You can also base a key on a clip's alpha channel or even on a separate image.

✔ Tip

■ Strictly speaking, a few of the keying filters may be more accurately described as *blending modes*, like the ones found in Photoshop and After Effects. Whereas keys adjust transparency, blending modes (also called *layer modes*) blend images by comparing the corresponding pixels of two images and applying a formula to get a new result. For the sake of simplicity, however, this book draws a distinction only between adjusting a clip's opacity property and applying keying filters and doesn't refer to these keying filters in terms of blending modes.

Using Alpha-Based Keys

Technically, a clip's opacity is always defined by its alpha channel. The term *alpha-based keys* refers to keying methods that use either the alpha channel included in a clip or one generated by Premiere Pro.

Some footage items already contain an alpha channel. For example, you might create an image in Photoshop and define its alpha channel using that program's suite of tools. Or Premiere Pro can generate an alpha channel for a clip, for empty areas of a title or areas of the screen left uncovered by clips that have been moved with motion effects. By now, you know that adding a clip to a superimpose track automatically keys out areas based on the clip's alpha channel.

Premiere Pro applies an alpha key automatically because that's usually what you want to happen. However, sometimes you want to override the setting and ignore the alpha channel. Other times, opaque and transparent areas need to be reversed. You can also use the alpha channel as a grayscale matte. Doing so can be helpful when you want to evaluate and correct the effectiveness of a key; or you can use the matte as the source of a track matte key (see "Using Matte-Based Keys" later in this chapter). Finally, you can use a filter to adjust the clip's opacity level without using its fixed (or inherent) opacity property. This allows you to work around Premiere Pro's rendering order (see the sidebar "Subverting the Render Order" in Chapter 13).

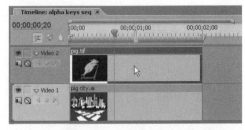

Figure 14.61 Select the clip that contains the Alpha Adjust filter, and set the CTI to a representative frame.

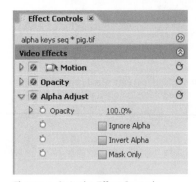

Figure 14.62 In the Effect Controls panel, specify the options you want.

Figure 14.63 Opacity adjusts the clip's overall opacity (after the alpha key is applied). Here, the pig image is set to 75 percent opaque.

Figure 14.64 Ignore Alpha prevents Premiere Pro from keying out the alpha channel.

Figure 14.65 Invert Alpha reverses the opaque and transparent areas of the clip.

Figure 14.66 Mask Only replaces opaque areas with white.

To use the Alpha Adjust filter:

1. In the Effects panel, drag the Alpha Adjust filter, and *do one of the following:*

   ▲ Drop the effect on a clip in a super-impose track of the timeline.

   ▲ Drop the effect on to the Effect Controls panel while the appropriate clip is selected.

   Make sure the clip is selected so the effect appears in the Effect Controls panel, and that the CTI is on a frame that will help you evaluate your adjustments (**Figure 14.61**).

2. In the Effect Controls panel, adjust any of the filter's properties (**Figure 14.62**):

   ▲ **Opacity:** Adjusts the overall opacity levels of the clip (**Figure 14.63**).

   ▲ **Ignore Alpha:** Prevents Premiere Pro from using the alpha channel included in the clip. However, this option doesn't prevent you from fading a clip or applying other keying filters (**Figure 14.64**).

   ▲ **Invert Alpha:** Reverses the opaque and transparent areas of the clip (**Figure 14.65**).

   ▲ **Mask Only:** Ignores the RGB information included in the clip, and instead shows the clip's opacity as white areas (**Figure 14.66**).

✔ Tip

■ Scaling or repositioning a clip using the motion effects may produce unwanted results. Inverting a resized clip's alpha channel, for example, can reveal the clip's edges. To solve problems caused by motion effects, resize the clip in a separate sequence and then use a nested version. Or resize the clip using the Transform filter.

Using Luminance-Based Keys

Luminance-based keys use luminance (brightness) levels to define transparent areas. You can choose to key out either the brightest or the darkest pixels contained in the image. Luminance-based key types include Luminance, Multiply, and Screen.

The Luminance key isn't the only key type that uses luminance to define transparency, but it's probably the most commonly used (both in Premiere Pro and in traditional editing suites). You may hear luminance keys generically referred to as *luma keys*.

To adjust the Luminance key:

◆ In the Effect Controls panel, adjust the Luminance filter's property settings until the image in the program view looks the way you want (**Figure 14.67**):

  ▲ **Threshold:** Sets the range of darker pixels that become transparent.

  ▲ **Cutoff:** Sets the transparency of the areas defined by the Threshold value.

  Areas of the clip are keyed out based on luminance levels (**Figures 14.68 and 14.69**).

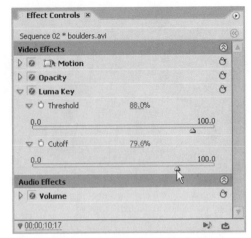

Figure 14.67 Adjust the luma key's Threshold and Cutoff values.

Figure 14.68 In this example, the luma key is applied to the rocks image; the sand dunes on the right serve as the background.

Figure 14.69 Here, brighter areas of the clip are keyed out, revealing the underlying image.

Figure 14.70 Reversing the relative positions of the Cutoff and Threshold values inverts the key.

Figure 14.71 Multiply makes the clip more transparent where the bright areas of the clip and the underlying image correspond. Here, the dunes show through more where the bright areas of both images correspond.

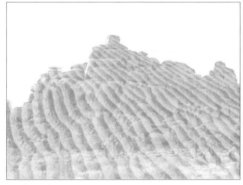

Figure 14.72 Screen makes the clip more transparent where the dark areas of the clip and the underlying image correspond.

When the relative positions of the threshold and cutoff are reversed, the key is reversed, and lighter areas become transparent (**Figure 14.70**).

✔ Tip

■ To better judge the transparency settings, use a bright color (such as a bright yellow or green) as a temporary background for the keyed clip. You can do this by temporarily placing a color matte (see Chapter 2, "Starting a Project") in the track below the clip you're keying. Then the color will show through when you preview in the program view. When you've finished, remove the color matte from the timeline (or disable it).

Using Multiply and Screen keys

The Multiply and Screen options blend a clip with a clip in a lower track based on luminance values taken from both clips. Multiply averages the product of the pixel values of the clip and the underlying image. The resulting image is darker than both and never brighter than the original. Multiply preserves the black areas of the clip while allowing the underlying image to show through the brighter areas (**Figure 14.71**).

Screen uses inverse luminance values in its calculations. Therefore, the resulting image is brighter than either original image and never darker than the clip to which it's applied. Screen preserves white areas of the clip and allows the underlying image to show through darker areas (**Figure 14.72**).

The best way to understand these keys is to compare them.

To adjust a Multiply or Screen filter:

◆ In the Effect Controls panel, adjust the
Multiply or Screen filter's property values
(**Figure 14.73**):

▲ **Opacity:** Sets the overall opacity,
regardless of luminance values.

▲ **Cutoff:** Sets the amount of blending,
based on luminance values.

✔ Tip

■ Multiply and Screen keys aren't just for
blending two different clips—they can
also combine two copies of the same clip.
For example, you can use a Screen key to
quickly brighten underexposed areas of
a clip.

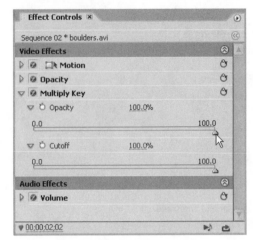

Figure 14.73 Multiply and Screen keys allow you to
adjust Opacity and Cutoff values.

Figure 14.74 Chrominance-based keys are typically used to composite bluescreen or greenscreen footage.

Using Chrominance-Based Keys

Chrominance-based keys use *chrominance* (color) to define the transparent areas of a clip. Chrominance-based keys are commonly used to composite moving subjects that were shot against a colored background, usually a blue or green backdrop called a *bluescreen* or *greenscreen,* respectively. Provided that the subject doesn't contain the key color, a chrominance-based key can remove the background while leaving the subject opaque.

Blue and green are standard key colors because they're relatively absent from human skin tones. Without the key color to differentiate the background from the subject, it would be difficult, if not impossible, to perfectly separate a moving subject from the background (**Figure 14.74**).

Chrominance-based key types include Chroma, Blue Screen, Green Screen, RGB Difference, and Non-Red. The following sections explain in detail how to apply the Chroma key and summarize the other color-based keys.

To use the Chroma key:

1. In the Effect Controls dialog box, choose a key color by doing *one of the following:*

   ▲ To choose a color from the color picker, click the color swatch. In the color picker that appears, select a color, and then click OK to set the key color and return to the Transparency Settings dialog box.

   ▲ To select a color from the image in the program view, click the Eyedropper tool 🖋, and then click the eyedropper on the color you want to use (**Figures 14.75** and **14.76**).

2. To modify the key, adjust the filter's property values (**Figure 14.77**):

   ▲ **Similarity:** Increases or decreases the range of colors similar to the key color that are keyed out.

   ▲ **Blend:** Blends the clip with the underlying clip.

   ▲ **Threshold:** Controls the amount of shadow that you keep in the range of key colors.

   ▲ **Cutoff:** Darkens or lightens shadows. Don't drag the cutoff beyond the threshold, or you'll invert the gray and transparent pixels.

   ▲ **Smoothing:** Anti-aliases (smoothes) the edges of the opaque areas. You can choose Low, Medium, or High.

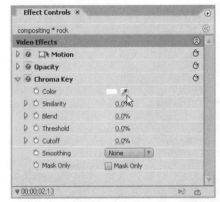

Figure 14.75 To select the key color, click the mouse on the Eyedropper tool...

Figure 14.76 ...and then click the eyedropper on the color you want to sample.

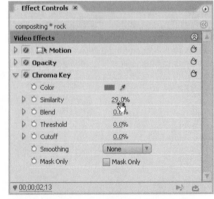

Figure 14.77 You can adjust the Chroma key using a number of parameters.

USING CHROMINANCE-BASED KEYS

Figure 14.78 The color is keyed out, revealing the underlying background image. In this example, a clear blue sky is replaced with a more dramatic one.

3. To see the opaque areas as white, click Mask Only.

You can use this option to see the effectiveness of the key more easily; deselect it when you're satisfied with the results. When you've finished making adjustments, the key color is transparent and reveals the underlying image (**Figure 14.78**).

✔ Tips

■ If you want to take another color sample, you can temporarily disable the Chroma key effect and still sample a color from the unmodified clip.

■ In some areas of Premiere Pro—including the controls for selecting a key color— the color picker works a little differently than in other programs. Rather than selecting the eyedropper and then selecting a color, you must keep the mouse button down after you select the eyedropper and then release it only after you position the eyedropper over the color you want to use.

■ Before you begin adjusting a Chroma key, crop out extraneous portions of the image using a garbage matte, as explained in "Using Garbage Mattes," later in this chapter. This way, you don't waste effort adjusting for parts of the background that can be eliminated at the outset.

■ If your shot uses a good blue or green background, you may get better results with the Blue Screen or Green Screen key than with the Chroma key (see the next section, "Other chrominance-based keys").

■ Temporarily switch on the Mask Only option to better evaluate the effectiveness of your keying adjustments. White areas represent opaque parts of the clip, whereas black areas will be transparent. Check for unwanted holes or gray areas in the matte.

Other chrominance-based keys

The following list summarizes the other chrominance-based keys:

◆ **RGB Difference key:** Works like a simpler version of the Chroma key. It provides only the Similarity and Smoothing properties. You can also use the Drop Shadow option, which adds a 50 percent gray, 50 percent opaque shadow, offset four pixels to the right and four pixels down.

◆ **Blue Screen and Green Screen keys:** Optimized for use with true chroma blue and true chroma green, respectively. However, these keys don't provide as many controls as the Chroma key.

◆ **Non-Red key:** Makes blue and green areas (nonred) transparent. This key type also provides a Blend property.

Keys to the Kingdom

The results you get from chroma keying depend a great deal on the quality of your footage. Here are a few things to consider if you plan to do bluescreen work:

◆ Shoot using the best format possible. For video, choose a format with the least compression and the greatest color depth.

◆ Use a high-quality bluescreen. A good bluescreen should be painted with paint specially formulated for bluescreen work. If possible, use a shadow-free *cyclorama*, a background constructed from hard materials with rounded corners, to prevent shadows.

◆ Use good lighting techniques on the set. Preferably, work with someone experienced in lighting an evenly lit, shadow-free bluescreen. Use lighting to help separate the subject from the background and reduce spill (blue light reflected on the subject).

◆ Use a high-quality capture device. If possible, transfer the footage uncompressed, using a high-quality transfer method, such as SDI.

◆ Doing good bluescreen compositing is harder than it sounds. You may need to use software dedicated to the job, such as plug-ins like Ultimatte's Primatte keyer or the Keylight plug-in found in After Effects' Professional.

Figure 14.79 This matte's edges perfectly match the statue in the beauty.

Using Matte-Based Keys

Matte-based keys use an external image to define transparent areas of a clip. A typical matte is a high-contrast grayscale image (sometimes called a *high-con*). You can think of it as an external stand-in for a clip's alpha channel.

As in an alpha channel's grayscale, brightness in the matte corresponds to opacity in the foreground clip, so that white areas specify opacity, and black areas define transparency. The matte itself never appears in the final output; it only defines the opaque and transparent areas of the foreground clip, sometimes called the *beauty*. Sometimes the matte perfectly matches the shape of the beauty; other times, the matte cuts a shape out of the beauty (**Figures 14.79**, **14.80**, and **14.81**). However, the image size of the matte should match the sequence's image size. Otherwise, the matte's relative size may not be what you expect, and the edges of the matte may be apparent.

Figure 14.80 This matte is designed to retain some of the beauty's background color along with the text.

Figure 14.81 This matte is intended as a stencil.

Matte-based key types include Image Matte and Track Matte. The Difference Matte key also falls into this category, although it creates its own matte by comparing two clips.

Using the Image Matte key

The Image Matte key can use any grayscale still image as the matte. Alternatively, you can use a still image that contains an alpha channel, effectively borrowing its alpha channel to define opacity in another clip. You choose the image matte from the Effect Controls panel; the matte doesn't have to be used in the timeline or even imported into the project. However, once you specify a file as a matte, the project refers to the file just as it does other clips.

You can't specify a title you created in Premiere Pro as an image matte. However, a title can serve as a matte if you use the Track Matte key (see "Using the Track Matte key," later in this chapter).

To adjust the Image Matte key:

1. In the Effect Controls panel, click the Image Matte key's Setup button **⊶▤** (**Figure 14.82**).

   The Select a Matte Image dialog box appears.

2. Locate the still image you want to use as the matte, and click Open (**Figure 14.83**).

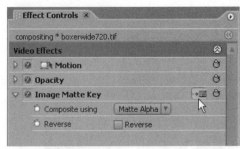

Figure 14.82 In the Effect Controls panel, click the Image Matte key's Setup button.

Figure 14.83 In the Select a Matte Image dialog box, locate the still image you want to use as the matte, and click Open.

Figure 14.84 In the Composite Using pull-down menu, select the appropriate option.

Figure 14.85 Here, a soft-edged cameo makes the boxer opaque. Areas outside the matte become transparent, revealing a duplicate of the clip that has been filtered to appear darker and blurred.

Figure 14.86 Selecting Reverse exchanges the opaque and transparent areas.

3. In the Effect Controls panel, choose an option from the Composite Using pull-down menu (**Figure 14.84**):

▲ **Matte Alpha:** Uses the matte image file's alpha channel to define opacity.

▲ **Matte Luma:** Uses the matte image file's luminance values to define opacity.

The specified value of the matte (alpha or luma) corresponds to opacity in the clip to which you applied the Image Matte filter (**Figure 14.85**).

4. To invert the opaque and transparent areas, select Reverse (**Figure 14.86**).

✔ Tip

■ Resizing a clip using motion effects also affects its matte. To avoid this, use nesting to work around the rendering order, or resize using the Transform filter.

Using the Track Matte key

The Track Matte key uses a moving matte, often called a *traveling matte*. As with the Image Matte key, the matte can be a high-contrast, grayscale video clip or an image that you animate with motion settings, a filter, or a title roll. Or you can use a clip's alpha channel as the matte. But unlike a still-image matte that you specify with the Image Matte key, the clip that serves as the traveling matte must be arranged in the sequence with the foreground and background clips. This allows you to control the relative timing of all the elements.

As with the Image Matte effect, the clip you designate as the track matte doesn't appear in the final output; it defines which parts of the clip containing the effect remain opaque and which reveal the underlying image. Premiere Pro disables the video output of the track containing the matte clip for the duration of the clip containing the track matte effect. But beyond the area occupied by the clip containing the track matte, the track and the clips it contains behave normally.

Track Matte filter applied to foreground

Figure 14.87 Layer the clips in separate tracks. Apply the Track Matte filter to the clip that will serve as the foreground.

Figure 14.88 Specify the track that contains the matte clip from the Matte pull-down menu.

To use the Track Matte key:

1. In the Timeline panel, arrange the clips so that each is in a different track. The following is a typical configuration:

   ▲ Position the background clip in the lowest track among the three clips.

   ▲ Position the foreground clip in the track above the background clip.

   ▲ Position the moving matte in the track above the foreground clip.

   Because you can specify both the track that contains the matte and whether the key is reversed, each clip can occupy any track. Be aware that the track containing the matte clip won't output video for the duration of the clip containing the track matte effect.

2. Turn off the output of the track that contains the matte clip.

   Clicking the track's Monitor button, or eye icon 👁, makes the icon disappear and excludes the contents of the track from output.

3. Apply the Track Matte filter to the foreground clip (**Figure 14.87**).

4. In the Effect Controls panel, select the track that contains the matte clip from the Track Matte key's Matte pull-down menu (**Figure 14.88**).

   continues on next page

USING MATTE-BASED KEYS

523

5. In the Effect Controls panel, choose an option in the Composite Using pull-down menu (**Figure 14.89**):

▲ **Matte Alpha:** Uses the matte image clip's alpha channel to define opacity.

▲ **Matte Luma:** Uses the matte image clip's luminance values to define opacity.

The specified value of the matte (alpha or luma) corresponds to opacity in the clip to which you applied the Track Matte filter (**Figure 14.90**).

6. To invert the opaque and transparent areas, select Reverse (**Figure 14.91**).

The matte image defines the opaque and transparent areas of the foreground clip. As the matte image moves, the foreground clip's opaque and transparent areas change accordingly.

Figure 14.89 In the Composite Using pull-down menu, specify whether the matte's alpha channel or luminance values will define transparency.

Figure 14.90 The matte defines the opaque and transparent parts of the clip that contain the Track Matte filter.

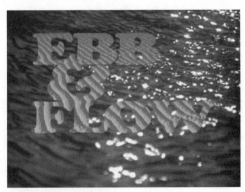

Figure 14.91 Selecting Reverse exchanges the opaque and transparent areas.

✔ Tips

- The Track Matte effect works differently in Premiere Pro 2.0 than in previous versions. You don't have to disable the output (eye icon) of the track containing the matte; its output is disabled for the duration of the clip containing the Track Matte effect automatically. This way, using a Track Matte effect doesn't disable a track's output for the entire sequence.

- Sometimes you can generate a useful matte by applying one or more effects to a clip. For example, you can remove color from a clip using the Black and White filter, control the range and contrast of the matte using the Levels filter, and add motion by animating the clip's motion properties.

- When you're creating effects like a track matte, consider arranging the elements in a separate sequence and then using the sequence as a clip in the main sequence. (To review nesting sequences, see Chapter 6, "Creating a Sequence.")

About the Difference Matte key

The Difference Matte key creates the transparent areas of a clip by comparing the clip with another still image and keying out the areas where the two clips match. The Difference Matte key is designed to remove a static background from behind a moving subject. By using a frame of a static background as the matte, you can key out the existing background and replace it with another. This key works only if the subject keeps moving and the camera remains static, however. This key type also provides a drop-shadow option.

Using Garbage Mattes

Garbage mattes earned their name because they're generally used to throw out extraneous areas of the frame.

You can use a garbage matte in conjunction with other keys to eliminate unnecessary elements. For example, use a garbage matte to crop out the extraneous areas of the frame before you apply a Chroma key. This way, you won't waste time adjusting the key for parts of the image you can exclude right away (**Figure 14.92**). You can also use a garbage matte to create a simple split-screen effect (**Figure 14.93**).

Beginning with Premiere Pro 1.5, the Effects panel contains 4-point, 8-point, and 16-point garbage mattes.

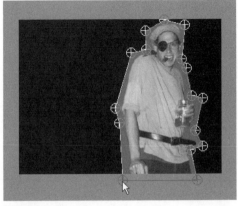

Figure 14.92 Use a garbage matte to crop out extraneous areas of an image before you apply another key.

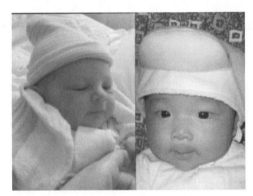

Figure 14.93 You can also use a garbage matte to create a split-screen effect.

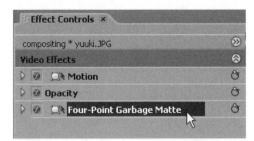

Figure 14.94 In the Effect Controls panel, select one of the garbage mattes.

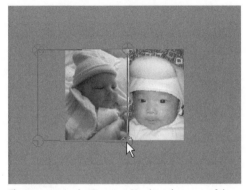

Figure 14.95 In the Program Monitor, drag one of the garbage matte's four handles to crop out unwanted areas.

To adjust the Garbage Matte filter:

1. In the Effect Controls panel, select one of the Garbage Matte filters by clicking its name (**Figure 14.94**).

   A direct manipulation icon indicates that selecting the effect activates controls in the program view. In the program view, handles appear at each corner of the selected clip.

2. Drag the handles of the image to key out unwanted areas of the clip (**Figure 14.95**).

3. If necessary, apply other key types and adjust the clip's opacity levels.

15

CREATING OUTPUT

At the beginning of the editing process, you asked yourself, "What is my final output goal?" Now it's time to deliver.

If your computer can capture video (via IEEE 1394, USB 2, or other device), you can also output the completed sequence directly from the timeline to a video camera or videotape recorder. But for many, DVD has become the viewing format of choice. With Premiere Pro's DVD Layout feature and a DVD burner, you can create a DVD complete with a navigational menu and animated scene buttons.

Alternatively, you may want to create a stand-alone movie file to present over the Web, burn to a CD-ROM, or transfer to an even more full-featured DVD authoring program (like Adobe's own Encore DVD). However, the number of export options can be daunting, and the minutiae of issues such as compression and video standards can be difficult to grasp—and boring. Luckily, Premiere Pro's Adobe Media Encoder spares you from setting a multitude of arcane parameters by providing presets tailored to particular output goals.

But export isn't necessarily the final step in a project. An exported movie may also serve as source material for a PowerPoint presentation, an After Effects composition, or even another Premiere Pro project. If you're using Premiere Pro as an offline editing tool, you can export an Advanced Authoring Format (AAF) file or edit-decision list (EDL) to transfer your work to another system.

Finally, exporting may be part of a collaborative workflow. With the new Clip Notes feature, you can export a work-in-progress for review—and even have it uploaded to a shared server automatically. Reviewers' comments are attached to the appropriate point in the sequence so that you can more easily view and incorporate their suggestions (or challenge them, as the case may be).

Considering Output Goals

Your output goal helps determine the settings you choose. Although you've thought about it from the beginning of your project (right?), the considerations are worth reviewing.

DVD

If you have a DVD burner attached to or installed in your computer, you can record your project to a DVD that plays on any standard DVD player. Premiere Pro's DVD Layout panel lets you create a bare-bones DVD or a more full-featured DVD based on a choice of templates. You can even customize the template with your own images, audio, and motion menu buttons.

Whether you produce a simple or more complex DVD, Premiere Pro utilizes a preset included in its specialized export mechanism, the Adobe Media Encoder.

Videotape

You should be able to record footage to videotape even more easily than you captured it (way back in Chapter 3, "Capturing and Importing Footage"). Using IEEE 1394 or USB 2, the same cable that delivered video and audio to your computer will send it from your computer to a recording device. Other setups may require you to configure separate output and input cables (but you know that). Whatever the case, the requirements for capture and export are almost always identical. However, if you're preparing your videotape for television broadcast, be sure to check with the presenter or a post-production facility to learn their requirements. They may accept only certain formats or require your tapes to meet strict technical standards or include specified content (such as a leader).

Movie files

If you want to export a movie file, your choices become more varied and complex. You choose the combination of options best suited for the purpose you have in mind. Do you want to play the movie from a CD-ROM, present it on the Web, import it into a full-fledged DVD authoring program (like Encore DVD), or use it in another program (such as a presentation or multimedia program)?

Many formats include a multitude of variables —which often require advanced technical knowledge to adjust intelligently. Fortunately, Premiere Pro's Adobe Media Encoder includes numerous presets tailored to the most common output goals. Or if you if you're so inclined, you can fine-tune the export settings yourself.

Still images and audio-only files

In addition to exporting the entire edited sequence to DVD or tape, users commonly use a few other export options.

You can export a still image from any frame of the video—for use as a freeze frame in the sequence, for printed materials, or to post on the Web.

You can also export an audio-only file. For example, you may want just the audio track of an interview to use as a voiceover; an audio file without the video track is significantly smaller than with the video.

Exporting for the Web

When you optimize movies for Web delivery, file size (and its conjoined twin, data rate) is the primary concern. To stream a movie, you need to limit the movie's data rate to the slowest anticipated connection speed. Even for fast Internet connections, that's a big limitation. You'll have to decide whether the loss in quality is worth the immediate playback capability.

The limitations are more forgiving for movies that can be downloaded. In this case, file size influences how long the viewer has to wait before watching your movie. Although a *progressive download* format begins playing before the movie is fully downloaded to the viewer's hard drive, file size remains an impediment—especially if the movie is more than, say, one minute in duration.

Exporting for CD-ROM

When you optimize a movie to play from a CD-ROM, your primary goal is compatibility. You also should answer the following questions:

- Does the movie need to be cross-platform compatible?

- What movie-player software will be used?

- What is the slowest possible CD drive that will be playing the movie?

- Will the movie be copied from CD to play back from a hard drive? If so, what is the slowest hard drive that will be playing back the movie?

- What image quality do you require?

- What is the total running time of the movie, and can you reduce the file size to fit onto a typical CD-ROM?

Export for Other Programs

If you're exporting footage from Premiere Pro to use in another program, the factors you should consider depend on the format and the program. Nevertheless, you should bear in mind several common issues.

Make sure you know the file formats and compression types the program accepts. If you want to retain transparency, choose a codec that supports an alpha channel (such as Uncompressed in Windows Media, or None or Animation when exporting QuickTime). When you're exporting still frames acquired on video, be aware that video resolution translates into a mere 72 dpi, which is appropriate only for relatively small, low-quality printouts. You should also know how to deal with other aspects of translating video to other formats: color, interlacing, and image and pixel aspect ratios.

About Creating DVDs

Using Premiere Pro and a DVD burner, you can create DVDs that play in just about any DVD player. Before getting to the tasks, let's overview the process.

Autoplay and menus

The DVDs you create in Premiere Pro can work in either of two ways, depending on the choice you specify:

◆ **AutoPlay DVD** creates a DVD that plays from the beginning when you insert the DVD into the player. It contains no navigational menus for cuing to scenes; but, naturally, you can use your player's standard playback controls, such as Play, Stop, Rewind, and Fast Forward.

◆ **DVD with Menus** creates a more full-featured DVD, including a menu with buttons that cue to the scenes you specify. In Premiere Pro, you specify scenes (also called *chapters*) by setting DVD markers in the timeline; you create the DVD menu by customizing one of the numerous DVD menu templates in the DVD Layout panel.

DVD menus

Making a DVD that includes a scene menu involves two simple procedures, which you can perform in any order:

◆ **Add DVD markers**—DVD markers work a lot like timeline markers (see Chapter 7, "Editing in the Timeline"). But rather than designate important points in the sequence for editing, they specify points in the sequence used in the DVD's menu. Specifically, they assign the location of the main menu, scenes (chapters), or points at which the DVD returns to the main menu. You can specify DVD markers manually in the Timeline panel. Or, you can have Premiere Pro set scene markers automatically, either from the main menu bar or from the DVD Layout panel.

◆ **Customize a DVD template**—Using Premiere Pro's DVD Layout panel, you can select from DVD menu layouts designed with themes in mind: Corporate, Entertainment, and so on. DVD scene markers are translated into DVD menu buttons automatically, but you can adjust them as needed. Before burning, you can test-drive the DVD using the Preview DVD panel, to ensure that everything looks and works just right.

✔ Tip

■ You must register your copy of Premiere Pro with Adobe in order to gain access to the full selection of DVD motion menu templates.

Figure 15.1 You can set, clear, and cue to DVD markers using menu commands comparable to those for timeline markers.

DVD marker   Timeline marker

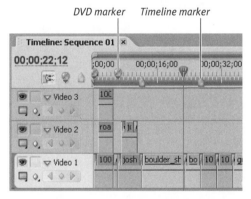

Figure 15.2 DVD markers are similar in appearance to timeline markers, but they're lower in the timeline's time ruler and are color coded according to function. They don't appear in the Monitor panel's time ruler.

DVD Markers

DVD markers work something like the timeline markers you learned about in Chapter 7. You can set, clear, and cue to them using comparable menu commands (**Figure 15.1**). Therefore, those procedures won't be reviewed here.

Unlike timeline markers, DVD markers don't appear in the time ruler of the Program Monitor; they're only displayed in the Timeline panel's time ruler. Instead of appearing in the lower half of the Timeline panel's time ruler, they're in the upper half, and they use a distinctive DVD marker icon 🌚 (**Figure 15.2**).

In contrast to timeline markers, DVD markers create links to buttons in a DVD menu you create using Premiere Pro' DVD Layout panel. The color of a DVD marker corresponds to its function:

◆ **Blue**—Scene marker

◆ **Green**—Main menu marker

◆ **Red**—Stop marker

Setting DVD markers

You can add DVD markers in the Timeline panel manually, using the DVD Marker button. Alternatively, Premiere Pro can set scene markers automatically, placing them at points that correspond to cuts in the sequence, or at the interval you specify. The Auto-Generate DVD Scene Markers command is available in the Timeline panel and in the DVD Layout panel.

To add DVD markers manually:

1. Set the timeline's CTI to the frame you want to mark.

2. In the Timeline panel, click the DVD Marker button ▓ (**Figure 15.3**).

   The DVD Marker dialog box appears. The video frame at the marker appears as a thumbnail image in the dialog box.

3. Enter a name for the marker.

   DVD scene marker's names are transferred to chapter button names automatically.

4. In the Marker Type pull-down menu, specify the type of marker you want to set (**Figure 15.4**):

   ▲ **Scene Marker**—Creates a Scene button in the DVD's scene menu, and appears as a blue marker in the Timeline panel.

   ▲ **Main Menu Marker**—Creates a button on the DVD's main menu, and appears as a green marker in the Timeline panel.

   ▲ **Stop Marker**—Causes the DVD to return to the main menu at the specified time, and appears as a red marker in the Timeline panel.

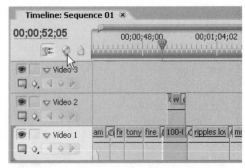

Figure 15.3 Position the timeline's CTI, and click the DVD Marker button.

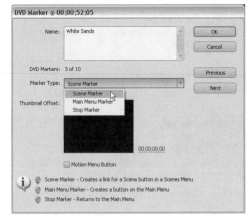

Figure 15.4 In the DVD Marker dialog box, name the marker, and specify its type.

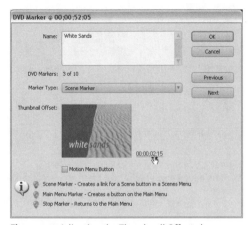

Figure 15.5 Adjusting the Thumbnail Offset changes the image used for the scene marker in the DVD menu.

Figure 15.6 You can set DVD scene markers automatically by selecting the timeline and choosing Marker > Auto-Generate DVD Markers...

Figure 15.7 ...or by choosing the same command in the DVD Layout panel's pull-down menu.

5. If the video frame at the marker isn't representative of the scene it's meant to designate, adjust the value for Thumbnail Offset.

You can scrub the value under the thumbnail image or select it and enter a new value, so that the thumbnail image shows the frame you want (**Figure 15.5**).

6. Click OK to close the dialog box.

The specified type of marker appears at the CTI in the timeline.

To add DVD scene markers automatically:

1. *Do either of the following:*

▲ With the Timeline panel selected, choose Marker > Auto-Generate DVD Markers (**Figure 15.6**).

▲ In the DVD Layout panel's pull-down menu, choose Auto-Generate DVD Markers (**Figure 15.7**).

The Automatically Set DVD Scene Markers dialog box appears.

continues on next page

DVD MARKERS

2. *Select one of the following* (**Figure 15.8**):

▲ **At Each Scene**—Sets a scene marker at each cut in the sequence.

▲ **Every *x* Minutes**—Sets a scene marker at intervals of the number of minutes you specify.

▲ **Total Markers**—Sets the number of scene markers you specify, spacing them evenly over the total duration of the sequence.

3. To remove scene markers already in the timeline, check Clear Existing DVD Markers (**Figure 15.9**).

4. Click OK to close the dialog box.

The DVD scene markers appear in the timeline according to the options you specified and dictate chapter breaks when you use the DVD Layout panel.

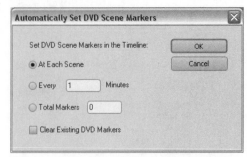

Figure 15.8 In the Automatically Set DVD Scene Markers dialog box, specify how often scene markers appear.

Figure 15.9 Check Clear Existing DVD Markers to remove DVD markers already in the timeline.

Figure 15.10 When creating a DVD, you'll focus much of your attention on the DVD Layout panel.

Figure 15.11 The Effect Controls panel toggles to the tools you need to modify a DVD template.

Setting the Workspace for DVD Authoring

Before you start using Premiere Pro to create a DVD, take a moment to review the tools you need: the DVD Layout panel and the Effect Controls panel.

Primarily, you'll require the DVD Layout panel (**Figure 15.10**). It lets you specify whether you want to produce a simple autoplay DVD or one based on a template. It's the access point for other panels related to each step in the process: selecting templates, previewing the DVD's functionality, and burning the DVD. And as its name suggests, it's where you view and modify elements of the main and menu pages.

As usual, the Effect Controls panel toggles to show the controls for the task at hand—in this case, formatting the items in the DVD Layout panel (**Figure 15.11**).

Naturally, you may also consult the Program Monitor or go back to the Timeline panel to fix problems with the sequence or reset DVD Markers.

✔ Tips

- Premiere Pro doesn't include a preset workspace. But as you learned in Chapter 1, "Premiere Pro Basics," you can create your own custom workspaces. Consider arranging the Effect Controls panel, DVD Layout panel, and Program Monitor along the top of your workspace.

- The DVD Layout panel's tab works as a pull-down menu, listing the sequences that have a DVD template associated with them. Like the Program Monitor tab's pull-down menu, you can use the DVD Layout panel tab's pull-down to switch sequences. Similarly, the Window > DVD Layout menu includes a submenu of the sequences associated with a DVD template.

Selecting a DVD Template

In Premiere Pro, you base your DVD menu on one of any number of templates, much like the title templates you use to create titles in the Titler (see Chapter 12, "Creating Titles"). Some DVD menu templates even include moving elements, animated backgrounds, and buttons.

Each template includes a layout for the DVD's main menu page and for the pages that contain buttons for skipping to scenes (aka *chapters*).

You can switch to another DVD menu template any time before you burn the DVD. Or, if you want to depart from the template's preset designs, you can customize it completely, as explained in later sections.

Figure 15.12 Choose Window > DVD Layout.

To select a DVD template:

1. Select the sequence you want to export as a DVD.

2. Choose Window > DVD Layout (**Figure 15.12**).
   The DVD Layout panel appears.

3. Click Change Template (**Figure 15.13**).
   The DVD Templates dialog box appears.

4. Select Apply a Template for a DVD with Menus.

Figure 15.13 In the DVD Layout panel, click Change Template

SELECTING A DVD TEMPLATE

Figure 15.14 In the DVD Templates panel, select Apply a Template for a DVD with Menus, and choose a category in the Theme pull-down menu.

Figure 15.15 Select the particular template you want from among the templates in the theme category.

Figure 15.16 The Template you select appears in the DVD Layout panel, and controls appear in the Effect Controls panel.

5. In the Theme pull-down menu, select a category of templates to choose from (**Figure 15.14**).

Templates in the selected category appear in the main panel of the DVD Templates dialog box.

6. Use the scroll bar to review the templates in the selected category.

The thumbnail image on the left shows the template's main menu; the image on the right depicts a Scenes menu.

7. Select the menu template you want (**Figure 15.15**).

The Template Details area of the dialog box describes the number of buttons on each page of the template.

8. Click OK to close the dialog box.

The DVD Layout panel appears, and controls appear in the Effect Controls panel (**Figure 15.16**). Scenes in the Scenes Menu pages of the template use the name and thumbnail images of DVD scene markers in the sequence. Otherwise, they use generic scene names, such as scene 1, scene 2, and so on.

✔ Tips

■ If you set DVD scene markers ahead of time, they'll be linked to the scene buttons once you select the template you want. Otherwise, you can use the Auto-Generate DVD Scene Marker command and name the buttons in the DVD Layout panel.

■ To switch to a different template, click the DVD Layout panel's Change Template button.

SELECTING A DVD TEMPLATE

Customizing a DVD Menu

Premiere Pro creates a DVD menu according to the template you select, using the DVD scene markers you set to name the buttons and create corresponding thumbnail images. If you like the template, and if you named the buttons ahead of time, then you're ready to preview and burn a DVD (and you can skip this section). But if you want to customize the DVD menu, read on.

The DVD Layout panel allows you to select and modify text and images in much the same way the Titler does. And as usual, the Effect Controls panel automatically switches to the controls you need for the task at hand—in this case, setting a DVD menu's background image, audio, and text attributes.

You can specify a still image or video clip as the background image. The menu can use a video background's linked audio or no audio, or you can specify a separate audio file. Video and audio loops for the duration you specify, up to a maximum of 30 seconds. You can even specify whether menu buttons use a static thumbnail image or play a video loop at the scene marker.

To view DVD menu pages:

◆ In the DVD Layout panel, click the page in the DVD Menus area (**Figure 15.17**).

If necessary, use the scroll bars to make later pages visible.

To edit text in DVD menu pages:

1. In the DVD Menus area of the DVD Layout panel, select the page you want to view.

The selected page appears in the main image area of the DVD Layout panel.

2. Double-click the text you want to edit (**Figure 15.18**).

A Change Text dialog box appears; in it, the current text message is highlighted.

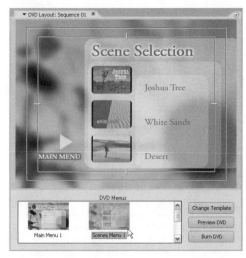

Figure 15.17 Clicking the thumbnail of a menu page makes the page appear in the panel's large image area.

Figure 15.18 In the large image area, double-click the text you want to edit.

Figure 15.19 In the Change Text dialog box, enter the text you want, and click OK.

Figure 15.20 In the DVD Layout panel, the selected text reflects the changes you entered .

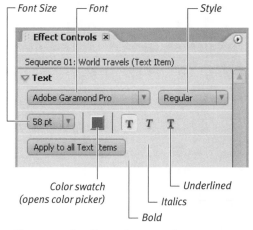

Figure 15.21 Specify any changes to the text attributes you want.

3. Enter the text you want, and click OK (**Figure 15.19**).

The edited text appears in the DVD Layout panel (**Figure 15.20**).

4. To change text attributes, such as font, font size, color, and so on, specify the options you want in the Text area of the Effect Controls panel(**Figure 15.21**).

✔ Tips

- You can reopen a DVD scene marker's dialog box and edit its settings by double-clicking the marker's icon in the Timeline panel.

- Generally, DVD menu buttons can only accommodate relatively short labels. Long labels tend to overlap with other objects on screen (and prevent buttons from operating properly); reducing the text size can render it illegible. Instead of labeling a DVD scene, say, "Traveling Around Europe," try "Europe" or "Eurotrip."

To specify a custom menu background:

1. Set DVD markers, and select a DVD template.

   For detailed instructions, consult the tasks in the sections "DVD Markers," "Using a DVD Template," and "Using the DVD Layout Menu," earlier in this chapter.

2. In the DVD Layout panel, select the menu you want to customize (**Figure 15.22**).

3. In the Effect Controls panel, *do any of the following:*

   ▲ To specify a background image, click the Browse button in the Video or Still area (**Figure 15.23**).

   ▲ To specify an audio loop, click the Browse button in the Audio area.

   A Select Background Media dialog box appears.

Figure 15.22 Select the menu page you want to modify in the DVD Layout panel.

Figure 15.23 In the Effect Controls panel, click the Browse button for the type of file you want.

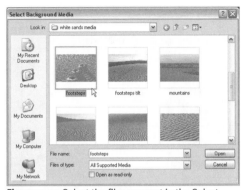

Figure 15.24 Select the file you want in the Select Background Media dialog box.

4. Select the media file you want to use, and then click Open (**Figure 15.24**).

The selected file's image or audio is applied to the selected menu page. Selecting a video file with a linked audio track adds both tracks to the menu page (**Figure 15.25**).

5. To apply the custom file to all menus, click the Apply to All Menus button in the Effect Controls panel (**Figure 15.26**).

Video or still images appear as the menu background for all menus in the DVD Layout, and when you preview or burn the DVD.

6. If you select a video or audio file (or a file with linked video and audio), specify options explained in the task "To set video and audio menu background options."

Figure 15.25 The selected file replaces the template's background image or audio for the selected menu page. A linked file inserts both video and audio into the template (shown here).

Figure 15.26 Click Apply to All Menus to make the background appear in all menu pages.

To reset the menu background to the default:

1. Choose a DVD template, and specify a custom background image.

2. In the Effect Controls panel, *do any of the following:*

   ▲ To reset a custom image background, click Reset in the panel's Video or Still area (**Figure 15.27**).

   ▲ To reset a custom audio file, click Reset in the panel's Audio area.

   Depending on your choice, the menu's reverts to the template's initial image background or audio loop.

To set video and audio menu background options:

1. Select a DVD menu template, and specify a custom video or audio file for a menu background.

2. To set the video or audio file's starting point, *do any of the following* in the corresponding area of the Effect Controls panel:

   ▲ Set a value for the media file's In point.

   ▲ Click the Play button ▷ to play the video thumbnail or audio file, and then click the Pause button ▮▮ when the file reaches the starting point you want (**Figure 15.28**).

   The button toggles between Play and Pause. Setting a starting point for a video file with linked audio sets the linked audio's starting point.

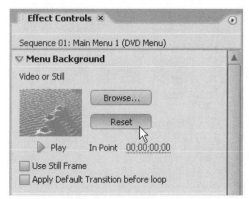

Figure 15.27 Click Reset to revert to the template's original image background or audio.

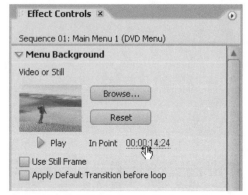

Figure 15.28 Set a video or audio background's starting point by setting the In point or by using the Play / Pause button.

Figure 15.29 Selecting Apply Default Transition before Loop can make a video or audio loop seem less abrupt.

Figure 15.30 For Duration, set the duration of the looping background, up to 30 seconds.

3. To add a transition at the beginning of the video or audio background, select Apply Default Transition before Loop (**Figure 15.29**).

See the task, "To specify the default transition," in Chapter 9.

4. Specify a value for Duration (**Figure 15.30**).

The video and audio loop after playing for the duration you specified. The maximum value is 30 seconds.

To use a single video frame as a menu background:

1. Select a DVD menu template, and specify a custom video file for a menu background.

2. In the Video or Still area of the Effect Controls panel, *do any of the following:*

   ▲ Set a value for the media file's In point.

   ▲ Click the Play button ▷ to play the video thumbnail or audio file, and then click the Pause button ⏸ when the file reaches the starting point you want.

   The button toggles between Play and Pause. Setting a starting point for a video file with linked audio sets the linked audio's starting point.

3. Select Use Still Frame (**Figure 15.31**).

   The frame at the In point you specified is used as the menu background.

4. To use the specified frame for all menu backgrounds, click Apply to All Menus.

To customize DVD menu buttons:

1. Set DVD markers, and select a DVD template.

   For detailed instructions, consult the tasks in the sections "DVD Markers," "Using a DVD Template," and "Using the DVD Layout Menu," earlier in this chapter.

2. In the DVD Layout panel, select the menu containing the menu you want to customize, and then select the menu button (**Figure 15.32**).

   The Effect Controls panel includes controls for customizing menu buttons.

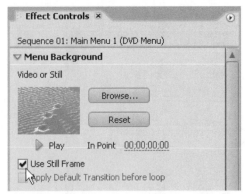

Figure 15.31 To use a single frame of a video clip as the background image, set the In point, and select Use Still Frame.

Figure 15.32 In the DVD Layout panel, select the menu containing the buttons you want to customize, and then select the button.

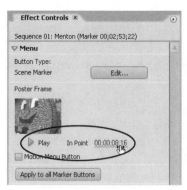

Figure 15.33 Set the button's starting point by setting an In point value or by using the Play / Pause button.

Figure 15.34 Select Motion Menu Button to have the menu button's thumbnail play as a video loop.

Figure 15.35 With no buttons selected, specify a Duration for Motion Menu Buttons in the Effect Controls panel.

3. Specify the button's thumbnail image or starting frame by *doing either of the following* (**Figure 15.33**):

   ▲ Set a value for the media file's In point.

   ▲ Click the Play button ▷ to play the video thumbnail or audio file, and then click the Pause button ❚❚ when the file reaches the frame you want.

   The frame becomes the button thumbnail (for still menu buttons) or the starting frame (for motion menu buttons).

4. To make the thumbnail play as a video loop, select Motion Menu Button (**Figure 15.34**).

5. To apply the same In point and Motion Menu Button setting to all buttons in the DVD menus, click Apply to All Marker Buttons.

   The In point setting is expressed as an offset from each button's initial frame, as determined by the position of its corresponding DVD Marker.

6. To deselect the menu button, click an empty area in the DVD Layout panel.

7. If you specified a motion menu in step 4, specify a Duration value in the Motion Menu Buttons area of the Effect Controls panel (**Figure 15.35**).

   The button's thumbnail video plays for duration you specify (up to 30 seconds) before looping.

CUSTOMIZING A DVD MENU

547

To modify menu-button text attributes:

1. Set DVD markers, and select a DVD template.

   For detailed instructions, consult the tasks in the sections "DVD Markers," "Using a DVD Template," and "Using the DVD Layout Menu," earlier in this chapter.

2. In the DVD Layout panel, select the menu containing the menu you want to customize, and then select the menu button (**Figure 15.36**).

   The Effect Controls panel includes controls for customizing menu buttons.

3. To modify the text attributes of marker buttons, *do any of the following* (**Figure 15.37**):

   ▲ Specify a font in the font pull-down menu.

   ▲ Specify a style in the type style pull-down menu.

   ▲ Specify a font size in the font size pull-down menu.

   ▲ Specify a font color by clicking the color swatch to open a color picker dialog box.

   ▲ Make the text bold, italic, or underlined by selecting the corresponding button.

4. To apply the text attributes you specified to all marker buttons, click Apply to All Marker Buttons.

   The options you specified in step 3 are applied to all menu buttons (**Figure 15.38**).

✔ Tips

■ Consider editing video or audio especially for a motion menu background or audio loop.

■ Like other kinds of stock footage, seamless video and audio loops are also available through third-party vendors.

Figure 15.36 Select the menu page and menu button you want to modify.

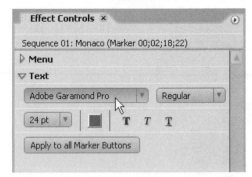

Figure 15.37 Specify the text attributes you want in the Effect Controls panel.

Figure 15.38 The text attributes you selected are reflected in the DVD Layout panel.

CUSTOMIZING A DVD MENU

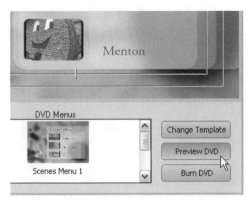

Figure 15.39 In the DVD Layout panel, click the Preview DVD button.

Figure 15.40 The Preview DVD panel appears.

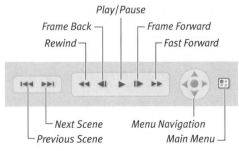

Figure 15.41 The Preview DVD panel's controls emulate those on a standard DVD player.

Previewing a DVD

Before you record, or *burn*, a DVD, you should confirm that the menu is working the way you want: Scene buttons are named correctly, use the proper name, and jump to the proper point in the sequence when you click them. The Preview DVD panel emulates how the finished DVD will play on a standard DVD player and includes a comparable set of playback and navigational controls.

To preview a DVD:

1. In the DVD Layout panel, click the Preview DVD button (**Figure 15.39**).

   The Preview DVD panel appears (**Figure 15.40**).

2. Use the controls to test the menu's operation before creating the DVD (**Figure 15.41**).

3. Close the Preview DVD panel to return to the DVD Layout panel.

   In the DVD Layout panel, you can edit the button names or the placement of markers, change the template, or continue to burn the sequence to DVD (as explained in the following section).

Burning to DVD

If your system is equipped with a DVD burner, you can export your sequence to DVD much as you'd export to tape.

As you learned in the section "About Creating DVDs," earlier in this chapter, you can burn a no-frills DVD that plays when you insert it into a DVD player, or a DVD complete with a navigational menu. Either way, the process is the same when burning from the DVD Layout panel.

This section covers how to burn to DVD recordable media directly, using a connected DVD burner. You can also "burn" to a folder, creating a DVD-compatible file (in the MPEG-2 format) that can be burned to a DVD using any DVD authoring software (say, Adobe Encore DVD). But this chapter sticks to using the simple, preset method—which, after all, is one of the nice things about using Premiere Pro.

To burn a DVD:

1. In the DVD Layout panel, click the Burn DVD button (**Figure 15.42**).

   The Burn DVD dialog box appears.

2. Choose the appropriate Burn To option (**Figure 15.43**):

   ▲ **Disc**—Records the DVD to blank DVD recordable media, using a connected burner.

   ▲ **Folder**—Creates a DVD-compatible MPEG-2 file on your hard disk.

3. Enter a name for the DVD.

4. For Burner Location, choose the DVD burner you want to use (**Figure 15.44**).

   If your DVD burner doesn't appear in the pull-down menu, click the Rescan button.

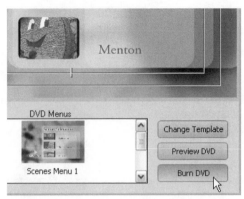

Figure 15.42 In the DVD Layout panel, click the Burn DVD button.

Figure 15.43 In the Burn DVD dialog box, select Disc to burn to a connected DVD burner. Otherwise, you can select Folder to create a file on your hard drive.

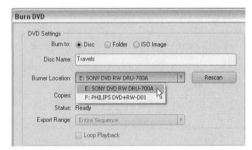

Figure 15.44 Choose the DVD burner you want to use in the Burner Location pull-down menu.

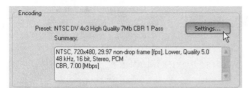

Figure 15.45 Confirm that the current preset meets your output requirements. If it doesn't, click the Settings button to open the Adobe Media Encoder's Export dialog box and modify the settings.

Figure 15.46 Click Burn to start.

5. For Copies, specify the number of DVDs you want to record during this export session.

Premiere Pro will prompt you to insert a new, blank DVD when necessary.

6. In the Encoding area of the Burn DVD dialog box, confirm that the preset meets your requirements.

7. To change the current encoding settings, click Settings (**Figure 15.45**).

The Adobe Media Encoder's Export Settings dialog box opens, in which you can specify a different preset or specify settings manually.

8. Click the Burn button to record the DVD (**Figure 15.46**).

If you're burning to a DVD, first make sure there is a blank recordable DVD in the burner.

✔ Tips

■ To retain quality, consider splitting an extremely long sequence into two projects and burning two DVDs instead of one.

■ The File > Export menu also contains DVD and other export options not covered in this chapter. This method doesn't employ presets, requiring you to specify numerous settings. As relatively advanced options, they won't be covered here.

■ As with capture, preview, and media cache files, you can specify a scratch disk for DVD Encoding. As usual, choose Edit > Preferences > Scratch Disks, and specify a relatively fast, capacious hard disk.

BURNING TO DVD

Selecting a DVD Preset

Without presets, exporting to DVD would force you to slog through numerous and often cryptic settings. However, don't be embarrassed if you find even a handful of presets too numerous, or you can't quite decipher their descriptive names. You probably recognize the distinction between video standards: National Television Standards Committee (NTSC) and Phase Alternation Line (PAL). However, other terms may not be so familiar. A quick rundown of the terms should help you choose the best preset for your needs:

4Mb and 7Mb: Represents the target bit rate in megabits per second (Mbps). A lower bit rate yields a smaller file (enabling you to store more on the DVD) at the expense of quality; a higher bit rate yields higher quality but a larger file (limiting the amount of content you can store).

CBR: Constant bit rate. Maintains a specified bit rate for every frame. This is a relatively inefficient but fast encoding method.

VBR: Variable bit rate. Varies the bit rate according to the content of each frame. This is a relatively efficient scheme, but one that requires more processing time.

1 Pass: Encodes the video in a single pass. This option is faster than two-pass encoding, but it's also a cruder compression method.

2 Pass: First analyzes the video's image content and then encodes the video, tailoring the compression according to the result of the analysis. Two passes yield higher quality video but take much longer than single-pass encoding.

SurCode for Dolby Digital 5.1: A format for encoding multichannel audio for DVD. Other preset options use either MainConcept MPEG Audio or pulse-code modulation (PCM) audio. Because PCM audio is a lossless format with a 48 kHz sample rate, it yields large files compared to the MainConcept MPEG Audio format.

BURNING TO DVD

Figure 15.47 Choose File > Export > Export to Tape.

Figure 15.48 The Export to Tape dialog box appears.

Exporting to Tape

Using the Export to Tape command, you can output video to a connected camera or deck through your IEEE 1394, USB 2, or other capture device. You can export any clip you open in the Source Monitor or, more likely, the selected sequence in the program view and Timeline panel. Using built-in or add-on device control, Premiere Pro can activate your deck automatically (see "Using Device Control" in Chapter 3). You can even choose where on the tape to start recording, if you can provide a timecode number at the start time. Typically, you use a *black and coded* tape—a tape with a black video signal and timecode. (For more about timecode, see "Understanding Capture Options" in Chapter 3 .)

The following task uses a DV camera as the recording device. Options may vary according to your hardware.

To export to tape:

1. *Do one of the following:*

    ▲ To export a sequence, select the sequence's tab in the Timeline panel or the program view of the Monitor panel.

    ▲ To export a clip, open a clip in the source view.

2. Choose File > Export > Export to Tape (**Figure 15.47**).

    The Export to Tape dialog box appears (**Figure 15.48**).

    continues on next page

EXPORTING TO TAPE

3. To have Premiere Pro automatically trigger recording using device control, select Activate Recording Device, and then specify the options you want (**Figure 15.49**):

▲ **Assemble at Timecode:** The time-code number on the tape where you want recording to start. To use Assemble at Timecode, the tape must already have a timecode signal. Therefore, you can't use a blank tape.

▲ **Delay Movie Start by *x* Frames:** The number of frames by which to delay playback after you click the OK button. Some recording devices require time between receiving the record command and the video playback from the computer.

▲ **Preroll *x* Frames:** The number of frames the camera or deck will rewind before the start time (the timecode you specified for the Assemble at Timecode setting, or the tape's current position), to ensure that the tape is up to speed when recording begins.

4. In the Options area of the Export to Tape dialog box, specify the options you want (**Figure 15.50**):

▲ **Abort after *x* Dropped Frames:** Allows you to set the minimum number of frames that must fail to record before Premiere Pro halts recording. For most users, even one dropped frame is unacceptable.

▲ **Report Dropped Frames:** Generates a report if frames are dropped during export.

▲ **Render Audio before Export:** Renders audio prior to exporting the clip or sequence. This can ease the on-the-fly processing demands on Premiere Pro and help prevent dropped frames; however, you must wait for audio to render before export begins.

Figure 15.49 Select Activate Recording Device to have Premiere Pro trigger recording automatically; then, specify related options.

Figure 15.50 In the Options area, specify how Premiere Pro deals with dropped frames during export and whether you want the program to render audio before exporting to tape.

EXPORTING TO TAPE

Figure 15.51 Click Record to start the export to tape and monitor the export progress in the Export Status area.

5. Click Record.

If you're controlling the recording device manually, make sure you trigger record mode. If you clicked Activate Recording Device, Premiere Pro triggers the recording device automatically. You can monitor the progress of the export in the Export Status area of the Export to Tape dialog box (**Figure 15.51**).

✔ Tips

■ Your options may vary according to the device-control plug-in you're using.

■ You don't need to adjust the Delay Movie Start by x Frames setting with most device controllers and decks. If you do need to adjust these settings, follow the recommendations that came with your device and device-control plug-in. Otherwise, you may need to experiment to find the optimal settings.

■ Even though you can leave the export process unattended, it's wise to keep an eye on it. This way, you can spot problems as they occur and export again if necessary. In addition to problems with the export, you may notice issues in the sequence itself. For example, you may have inadvertently left a clip or track disabled, excluding it from the exported video. (Yes, it can happen to you.) In any case, always double-check the tape after export, especially if you're going to hand it off to a client or duplication facility.

Exporting a Movie File

You can create a single, independent file from all or part of the sequence in the timeline. You can also create a movie from a clip. This technique is useful if you want to make a movie from only one portion of a clip or create a version that uses a different format or compression type.

Just as you specify capture and project settings, you must specify the characteristics of the exported movie, such as frame size, frame rate, compression, and audio quality. The settings you choose are determined not only by your output goal but also by the capabilities of your playback device.

This chapter concentrates on the settings that are unique to output.

To export a video file:

1. *Do one of the following:*

   ▲ To export the program from the timeline, select the sequence's tab in the Timeline panel or the program view of the Monitor panel.

   ▲ To export a clip, open a video clip in the source view.

2. To define the footage you want to export, *do one of the following:*

   ▲ In the sequence, set the work area bar over the range in the timeline that you want to export.

   ▲ In a clip, set the In and Out points to define the frames that you want to export.

3. Choose File > Export > Movie (**Figure 15.52**).

   The Export Movie dialog box appears. The bottom of the dialog box summarizes the current export settings.

Figure 15.52 Choose File > Export > Movie.

Figure 15.53 In the Export Movie dialog box, click the Settings button.

Figure 15.54 The Export Movie Settings dialog box appears.

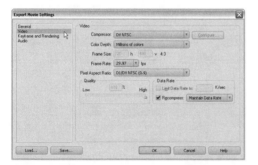

Figure 15.55 Clicking a category on the left allows you to view and adjust the settings on the right.

Figure 15.56 Specify a name and destination for the movie file, and click Save.

4. To change the current export settings, click the Settings button (**Figure 15.53**).

The General panel of the Export Movie Settings dialog box appears (**Figure 15.54**).

5. To change the current export settings, specify settings in the other panels of the Export Movie Settings dialog box by selecting a category on the left side of the dialog box (**Figure 15.55**):

▲ **General:** Specifies the movie's file type, the range of the timeline to export, which tracks to include, and whether to embed the project link.

▲ **Video:** Specifies settings that control aspects of the video image, such as frame size and frame rate.

▲ **Keyframe and Rendering:** Specifies keyframe options (which control how a codec uses frame differencing) and rendering options (which control the elements that are included in the export, as well as video field dominance).

▲ **Audio:** Specifies settings that control aspects of the audio, such as sample rate and bit depth.

6. Click OK to exit the Export Movie Settings dialog box.

You return to the Export Movie dialog box.

7. Specify a name and destination for your file, and click Save (**Figure 15.56**).

A progress bar appears, indicating the processing time required to make the movie.

EXPORTING A MOVIE FILE

Specifying the General Export Settings

In the General panel of the Export Movie Settings dialog box, you can specify the range of the timeline that you want to export, which tracks to include, and whether to open the movie when it's finished. And yes, you can have Premiere Pro beep when the movie's done.

You can also embed a *project link*. Choosing this option links the movie with the project from which it was exported. When you use the movie in After Effects or Premiere Pro, you can use the Edit Original command to open the project that originated the movie to make any needed changes. All the project references must be available on the hard drive, of course, and you'll have to re-render any changes. Nevertheless, this feature does improve workflow when changes must be made.

To specify general export settings:

1. In the Export Movie dialog box, click the Settings button to change the current settings (**Figure 15.57**).

   The General panel of the Export Movie Settings dialog box opens (**Figure 15.58**).

2. To specify a video file format, such as Microsoft DV AVI or QuickTime, choose an option from the File Type pull-down menu (**Figure 15.59**).

   The available options depend on your platform as well as on the plug-ins installed on your system.

3. Specify how much of the program you want to export by *choosing one of the following options* from the Range pull-down menu (**Figure 15.60**):

   ▲ **Entire Sequence:** Exports the entire program from the timeline.

   ▲ **Work Area Bar:** Exports only the part of the program below the work area bar.

Figure 15.57 Click the Settings button to change the current settings.

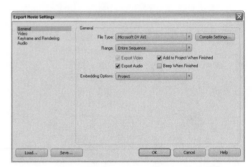

Figure 15.58 The General panel of the Export Movie Settings dialog box opens.

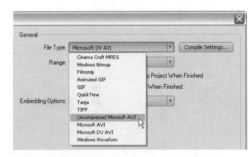

Figure 15.59 In the File Type pull-down menu, choose a video file format.

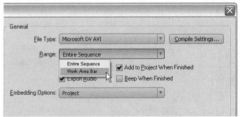

Figure 15.60 In the Range pull-down menu, choose whether you want to export the entire sequence or just the area under the work area bar.

Figure 15.61 In the Embedding Options pull-down menu, specify whether you want the exported movie to include a link to the project that created it.

4. Specify the tracks you want to export by *selecting one or both of the following options:*

- ▲ **Export Video:** Includes video tracks in the exported file.
- ▲ **Export Audio:** Includes audio tracks in the exported file.

Leave an option unselected to exclude the video or audio from the exported file.

5. Set the following options:

- ▲ **Add to Project When Finished:** Imports the rendered movie into the current project automatically.
- ▲ **Beep When Finished:** Alerts you when the rendering process is complete by making your computer beep.

If you don't want to use these options, leave them unselected.

6. Make a selection from the Embedding Options pull-down menu (**Figure 15.61**):

- ▲ **None:** Doesn't link the movie to the project from which it was exported.
- ▲ **Project:** Embeds a link in the movie to the project from which it was exported.

When you play a linked movie in After Effects or Premiere Pro, you can choose the Edit Original command to open the original project.

7. *Do one of the following:*

- ▲ To close the Export Movie Settings dialog box and return to the Export Movie dialog box, click OK.
- ▲ To specify settings in another category, select a category on the left side of the Export Movie Settings dialog box.

Keyframe and Rendering Settings and Audio Settings

In addition to the General settings covered in the previous section, the Export Movie Settings dialog box also includes panels for Video, Keyframe and Rendering, and Audio settings. Although the scope of this book doesn't allow for a detailed explanation of every possible setting, the following overview provides enough information to guide your choices..

Video settings include options that determine the characteristics of the exported video, such as the compressor (or codec), color bit depth, frame size, and so on (**Figure 15.62**). Certain codecs also allow you to control the data rate manually or set the compression's quality setting.

Keyframe and rendering options allow you to control two special aspects of the video (**Figure 15.63**). Rendering options control how video fields are processed. The keyframe options refer to *compression keyframes*—the frames of video a codec uses to track changes in the image. Some output options let you specify the frequency and placement of the keyframes and thereby influence compression quality.

Audio settings define the characteristics of the exported audio, such as the audio codec, bit depth, and sample rate (**Figure 15.64**). As you'd expect, audio settings help determine the quality of the exported audio and, hence, the file's overall data rate. As with other settings, you may need to specify audio settings at several points in the post-production process.

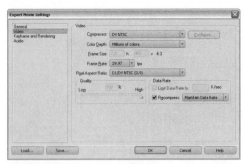

Figure 15.62 Video settings determine the basic characteristics of the exported video.

Figure 15.63 Keyframe and rendering options let you control compression keyframes and field processing.

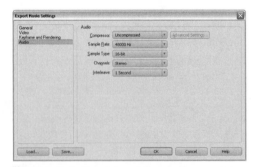

Figure 15.64 Audio settings define the characteristics of the exported audio.

Figure 15.65 In the Export Movie dialog box, click the Settings button.

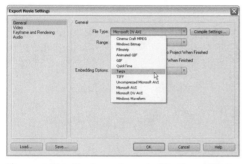

Figure 15.66 In the General panel of the Export Movie Settings dialog box, choose a format that supports still-image sequences.

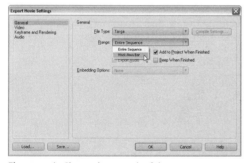

Figure 15.67 Choose how much of the sequence you want to export from the Range pull-down menu.

Exporting Still-Image Sequences

You can export a program or clip as a sequence of still images. Premiere Pro numbers the frames automatically. Many animation and 3D programs can import video images only as a numbered sequence of still-image files.

To export a still-image sequence:

1. In the Export Movie dialog box, click the Settings button (**Figure 15.65**).

   The General panel of the Export Movie Settings dialog box opens.

2. From the File Type pull-down menu, choose a still-image sequence format (**Figure 15.66**).

   GIF, TIFF, Targa, and Windows Bitmap formats support sequences.

3. Using the Range pull-down menu, specify how much of the program you want to export (**Figure 15.67**):

   ▲ **Entire Sequence:** Exports the entire selected sequence.

   ▲ **Work Area Bar:** Exports only the part of the sequence below the work area bar.

4. Set the following options:

   ▲ **Add to Project When Finished:** Add the rendered movie to the current project automatically upon completion.

   ▲ **Beep When Finished:** Alerts you when the rendering process is complete by making your computer beep.

   If you don't want to use these options, leave them unselected.

   continues on next page

5. If you're exporting a GIF sequence (also called a GIF sequence), you click the Compile Settings button in the Export Movie Settings dialog box to access additional options.

6. On the left side of the dialog box, click Video, and specify the options you want, such as color depth, frame size, and frame rate.

7. On the left side of the dialog box, click Keyframe and Rendering to access these options.

8. Specify the following options:

▲ **Fields:** Choose how to export video fields from the pull-down menu. For most DV projects, choose Lower Field First.

▲ **Deinterlace Video Footage:** Select this option to remove interlacing from each frame before exporting. This option reduces resolution but may be desirable to remove field artifacts.

9. In the Export Movie Settings dialog box, click OK.

The Export Movie Settings dialog box closes, and you return to the Export Movie dialog box.

10. Specify a destination and filename, and click Save (**Figure 15.68**).

A Rendering dialog box appears. Premiere Pro exports the range of frames as a sequence of still image files in the format you specified.

Figure 15.68 Specify a destination and filename, and click Save.

Figure 15.69 Cue the clip or sequence's CTI to the frame you want to export.

Figure 15.70 Choose File > Export > Frame.

Figure 15.71 Click the Settings button.

Exporting Single Still Images

You can export the current frame of video from the sequence or source clip as a single still-image file.

To export a single frame:

1. *Do one of the following:*

   ▲ To export a frame from the sequence, cue the sequence's CTI to the frame you want to export.

   ▲ To export a frame from a clip, open a clip in the source view and cue the source view's CTI to the frame you want to export (**Figure 15.69**).

2. Choose File > Export > Frame (**Figure 15.70**).

   The Export Frame dialog box appears.

3. Click Settings (**Figure 15.71**).

   The General panel of the Export Frame Settings dialog box appears.

   continues on next page

4. From the File Type pull-down menu, choose a still-image format (**Figure 15.72**).

5. *Do one of the following:*

▲ To add the exported still image to the current project automatically, click Add to Project When Finished.

▲ To specify options for GIF images, click Compile Settings.

6. To specify Video options, select Video on the left side of the Export Frame Settings dialog box.

Usually, you don't need to change these settings. However, if you want to retain alpha channel information in the still image, choose Millions+ of Colors from the Color Depth pull-down menu (**Figure 15.73**).

7. To deinterlace the exported frame, select Keyframe and Rendering from the left side of the Export Frame Settings dialog box, and then select Deinterlace Video Footage (**Figure 15.74**).

This option removes one field from an interlaced image, which can remove the combing effect sometimes apparent in still frames taken from video that contains objects in motion.

8. Click OK.

The Export Frame Settings dialog box closes, and you return to the Export Frame dialog box.

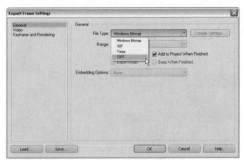

Figure 15.72 Choose a still-image format from the File Type pull-down menu.

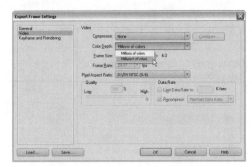

Figure 15.73 If you want to retain alpha channel information, choose Millions+ of Colors from the Color Depth pull-down menu.

Figure 15.74 To deinterlace the exported frame, select Keyframe and Rendering from the left side of the Export Frame Settings dialog box, and then select Deinterlace Video Footage.

Figure 15.75 Specify a name and destination for the still image, and click Save.

9. Specify a name and destination for the still image, and click Save (**Figure 15.75**).

   The frame you specified is exported as a still-frame file in the format and location you set.

✔ Tips

- If you plan to print the still image, you should know that standard-resolution video always translates to 72 dpi, regardless of the camera's tape format. This is fine for small, low-resolution printouts. But if you want to create a press kit or other printed materials, be sure to take production stills with a film camera or a high-quality digital still camera.

- If you plan to use the image in a still-image editing program (such as Photoshop), export the highest image quality possible. Don't resize the image or even deinterlace it. Photoshop's tool set is superior for any image editing you want to do.

- Most stills taken from DV or other video capture cards must be deinterlaced to remove field artifacts and resized to compensate for differences in pixel aspect ratios.

- You can also export all or part of a clip or program as a *filmstrip* file. Appropriately enough, a filmstrip file in Photoshop looks like a filmstrip: a single still image that contains the frames of video arranged in a long column. You manipulate the frames of video using Photoshop's tools, using a technique similar to *rotoscoping* in traditional film.

EXPORTING SINGLE STILL IMAGES

Exporting Audio-Only Files

The process for exporting audio is similar to
that for exporting a movie with video and
audio, except that you're limited to audio-
only file formats.

To export a video file:

1. *Do one of the following:*

    ▲ To export audio from the timeline,
    select the sequence's tab in the
    Timeline panel or the program view
    of the Monitor panel.

    ▲ To export a clip's audio, open a clip in
    the source view.

2. To define the footage you want to export,
do one of the following:

    ▲ In the sequence, set the work area bar
    over the range in the timeline that
    you want to export.

    ▲ In a clip, set the In and Out points to
    define the frames that you want to
    export.

3. Choose File > Export > Audio
(**Figure 15.76**).

    The Export Audio dialog box appears.
    The current export settings are summa-
    rized at the bottom of the dialog box.

4. To change the current export settings,
click the Settings button (**Figure 15.77**).

    The General panel of the Export Audio
    Settings dialog box appears.

Figure 15.76 Choose File > Export > Audio.

Figure 15.77 To change the current export settings,
click the Settings button.

EXPORTING AUDIO-ONLY FILES

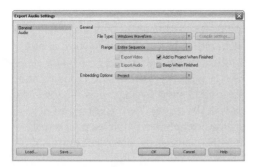

Figure 15.78 Specify the General settings.

Figure 15.79 Specify the Audio settings.

Figure 15.80 Specify a name and location for your file, and click Save.

5. To change the current export settings, specify settings in the other panels of the Export Audio Settings dialog box by choosing a category from the left side of the dialog box:

▲ **General:** Specifies the audio file's file type, the range of the timeline to export, and whether to embed a project link (**Figure 15.78**).

▲ **Audio:** Specifies settings that control aspects of the audio, such as sample rate and bit depth (**Figure 15.79**)

6. Click OK to exit the Export Audio Settings dialog box.

You return to the Export Audio dialog box.

7. Specify a name and destination for your file, and click Save (**Figure 15.80**).

A progress bar appears, indicating the processing time required to make the movie.

Using the Adobe Media Encoder

Several movie formats—particularly those designed for encoding video for DVD or Web delivery—include numerous settings that merit a specialized export dialog box, generally referred to as the *Adobe Media Encoder*.

Although it's labeled Export Settings, the Adobe Media Encoder's interface is far more elaborate than a typical dialog box. A large image area lets you preview the image as well as perform tasks such as cropping and filtering. General settings appear in the upper part of the dialog box; the lower part of the dialog box consists of tabbed panels that organize settings by category (**Figure 15.81**).

Source Image tab

Output Image tab

Pull-down menu button

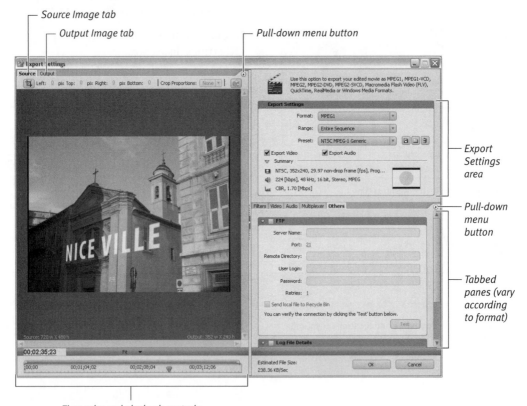

Export Settings area

Pull-down menu button

Tabbed panes (vary according to format)

Time ruler and playback controls

Figure 15.81 The Adobe Media Encoder's Export dialog box is a full-featured tool for exporting movie files, particularly to formats with extensive settings.

USING THE ADOBE MEDIA ENCODER

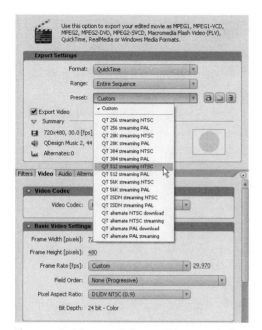

These settings are extensive and can require an in-depth understanding of file compression. Fortunately, you can select from a list of presets designed for particular delivery media (**Figure 15.82**). (You can also save custom presets or delete ones you don't need.)

Regrettably, the scope of this book doesn't permit a detailed discussion of all of the Adobe Media Encoder's features or each format's many settings. You'll find that the Premiere Pro Help system includes some of the technical details omitted from the printed user guide. For more in-depth information, you may have to turn to documentation made available by the format's developer.

✔ Tip

■ Strictly speaking, *Adobe Media Encoder* refers to the output mechanism, not the name of the dialog box. After Effects and Encore DVD also employ the Adobe Media Encoder, although the corresponding dialog boxes differ in appearance and in the way you access them. In spite of the differences, you can still think of these export settings dialog boxes as incarnations of the Adobe Media Encoder and as consistent in most ways.

Figure 15.82 A Preset pull-down menu automatically optimizes extensive settings for a particular output goal.

Adobe Media Encoder Formats

MPEG1: A set of compression standards (developed by the Moving Picture Experts Group) designed to yield results comparable to VHS tape quality at relatively low data rates. This format is typically used for Web download, CD-ROM, or VCD.

MPEG1-VCD: Preset MPEG-1 settings that conform to VCD (also called video CD) specifications. The VCD format supports lower quality than DVD but can be played using a standard CD-ROM player and appropriate software.

MPEG2: Another set of standards developed by the Moving Picture Experts Group, intended to produce high-quality, full-screen interlaced video.

MPEG2-DVD: Preset MPEG-2 settings that conform to DVD (also called digital versatile disk) specifications.

MEPG2-SVCD: Preset MPEG-2 settings that conform to SVCD (also called Super Video CD) specifications. SVCD supports higher-quality video and more advanced features than the VCD format.

Macromedia Flash Video (FLV): Macromedia's multimedia format designed for delivering content over the Web. (Note that Macromedia is currently part of Adobe Systems.)

QuickTime: Apple computer's multimedia architecture, which includes a wide variety of codecs designed for various applications.

RealMedia: Real Network's standard for low-data-rate applications, particularly downloading and streaming audio and video over the Web.

Windows Media: Microsoft's standard for low-data rate applications, particularly downloading streaming audio and video over the Web.

Figure 15.83 Choose File > Export > Adobe Media Encoder.

Figure 15.84 The Adobe Media Encoder's Export Settings dialog box appears.

To export using Adobe Media Encoder presets:

1. *Do one of the following:*

   ▲ To export the program from the timeline, select the sequence's tab in the Timeline panel or the program view of the Monitor panel.

   ▲ To export a clip, open a video clip in the source view.

2. To define the footage you want to export, *do one of the following:*

   ▲ In a sequence, set the work area bar over the range in the timeline that you want to export.

   ▲ In a clip, set the In and Out points to define the frames that you want to export.

3. Choose File > Export > Adobe Media Encoder (**Figure 15.83**).

   An Export Settings dialog box appears (**Figure 15.84**).

   continues on next page

Exporting an AAF File

Advanced Authoring Format (AAF) is a widely accepted file exchange format used to transfer both data (video and audio files) and metadata (such as edit-decision list information, including the use of dissolves and wipes). AAF helps you retain as much of your project as possible when transferring it from one system to another. However, be aware that the AAF features and data supported by one program may not always be supported by another program. If you plan to export your project using AAF, you should research (and, ideally, test) the process to maximize the data you can transfer and to prepare to re-create the data you can't transfer.

You can export to AFF by choosing Project > Export Project as AAF.

4. Choose an option from the Format pull-down menu (**Figure 15.85**).

5. In the Range pull-down menu, specify the portion of the clip or sequence you want to export (**Figure 15.86**)

▲ If you're exporting from the timeline, select either Entire Sequence or Work Area.

▲ If you're exporting from the source view of the Monitor panel, select either Entire Clip or In to Out.

6. In the Preset pull-down menu, choose the preset that matches your export goal (**Figure 15.87**).

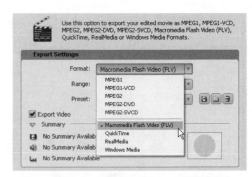

Figure 15.85 In the Adobe Media Encoder's Export Settings dialog box, choose an option from the Format pull-down menu.

Figure 15.86 In the Range pull-down menu, specify the portion of the clip or sequence you want to export.

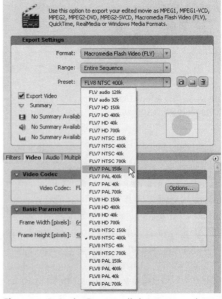

Figure 15.87 In the Preset pull-down menu, choose the preset that matches your export goal.

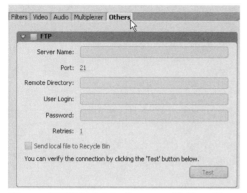

Figure 15.88 Click a tab to view or modify the settings in that category. The tabs/categories available depend on the format.

Figure 15.89 When you click Save, a Rendering dialog box appears, indicating the time required to render the file.

7. To view the settings, select the tab that corresponds to the setting category you want to view or adjust (**Figure 15.88**).

   The categories that are available depend on the format you specified in step 4.

   Consult the Adobe Premiere Online Help system for additional guidance on these options, or consult resources available from Real Networks and Microsoft.

8. When you're satisfied with your selections, click OK.

   A Save File dialog box appears.

9. Specify a filename and destination for the exported file, and click Save.

   A Rendering dialog box appears, indicating the time required to render the file (**Figure 15.89**).

✔ Tips

- In Premiere Pro, the Adobe Media Encoder's Export dialog box can crop, scale, deinterlace, or apply a video noise reduction filter to the video before encoding it to a specified format—processing known as *pre-encoding* tasks. It can also execute *post-encoding* actions, such as uploading the exported file using FTP and producing a log file of the render.

- The MPEG2-DVD presets have Quality set to 5. This is unnecessary for most video and causes extremely long encoding times. Unless the video image includes an exceptional amount of motion, set Quality to 3. If you see artifacts created from excessive movement, increase the Quality setting.

Exporting an Edit-Decision List (EDL)

As you learned in the introduction to this chapter, the primary goal of offline editing is to generate an edit-decision list (EDL). An EDL describes your edited program as a list of editing events. Exporting an EDL enables you to transfer your offline editing decisions to an online editing controller. You can export an edit-decision list using the CMX3600 format, the most widely accepted and most robust of the EDL formats.

You can find out more about specific EDL options (such as B-rolls and wipe codes) in Premiere Pro's Help System and User Guide or by consulting an online editor (the person, not the machine). Always keep in close contact with your online editing facility to ensure that you're prepared for online editing.

You can export an EDL by choosing Project > Export Project as EDL.

Figure 15.90 Exporting a Clip Notes PDF allows reviewers to enter comments at particular points in a work-in-progress. Their exported comments...

Clip Note comment imported as sequence marker

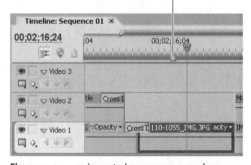

Figure 15.91 ...are imported as sequence markers...

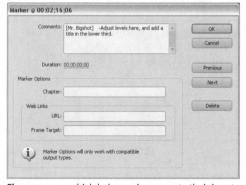

Figure 15.92 ...which help you incorporate their input.

Exporting with Clip Notes

At its best, a production is a collaborative work of art; at other times, it's a struggle among disparate visions. Either way, review and input are necessary parts of the work-flow. (Even personal projects benefit from a little constructive feedback.) Premiere Pro's powerful Clip Notes feature facilitates a collaborative process—although coming to an agreement is still up to you.

The Clip Notes feature lets you export a draft version of a sequence for review. The exported video is either embedded or linked to a PDF file (Adobe's ubiquitous Portable Document Format), which can be emailed to any number of reviewers. Using nothing more than the free Adobe Reader (Adobe Acrobat Standard and Professional work, too), a reviewer not only can see the video, but also enter comments at particular points in the sequence (**Figure 15.90**). When they're finished, the reviewers export the comments and email them back to you. Importing the comments into Premiere Pro translates them into sequence markers placed at the specified points in the time ruler (**Figure 15.91**); just open the markers to see the comments, which are attributed to the appropriate reviewer (**Figure 15.92**).

EXPORTING WITH CLIP NOTES

To export a Clip Notes PDF:

1. In the Timeline panel, select the tab of the sequence you want to export for Clip Notes.

2. Choose Sequence > Export for Clip Notes (**Figure 15.93**).

The Export for Clip Notes dialog box appears (**Figure 15.94**).

3. *Specify the following options* (**Figure 15.95**):

▲ **Format** specifies whether to encode the video using QuickTime or Windows Media format.

▲ **Range** specifies whether to export the entire sequence or part of the sequence under the work area.

▲ **Preset** specifies the relative quality of the video: low, medium, or high.

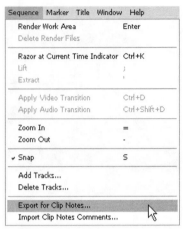

Figure 15.93 Choose Sequence > Export for Clip Notes.

Figure 15.94 The Export for Clip Notes dialog box appears.

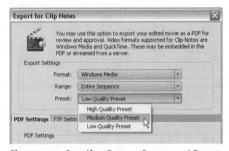

Figure 15.95 Specify a Format, Range, and Preset quality setting.

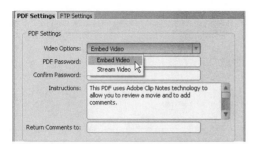

Figure 15.96 Specify whether to include the video in the PDF file (embed) or link the PDF to a separate video file stored on a server (stream).

Figure 15.97 You can password-protect the PDF file and include custom instructions for the reviewers.

Figure 15.98 If you opted to stream the video from a server, specify the location. Or, you can check Confirm URL Later.

4. Select the PDF Settings tab, and then *choose an option* from the Video Options pull-down menu (**Figure 15.96**):

▲ **Embed Video** saves the exported video into the Clip Notes PDF file.

▲ **Stream Video** links the exported video to the Clip Notes PDF file but stores the file on a server.

Embedding the video produces a relatively large file that includes the video; streaming the video produces a smaller file that requires accessing a server to view the video.

5. In the PDF Settings tab, *specify any of the following options* (**Figure 15.97**):

▲ **PDF Password**—Specifies a password that reviewers must enter to open the PDF.

▲ **Confirm Password**—If you specify a password, you must enter it again in this field.

▲ **Instructions**—Includes a custom message that appears to reviewers when they open the PDF.

▲ **Return Comments To**—Specifies an email address that the reviewers' email client program will use when they export their comments (see "To review a Clip Notes PDF," later in this chapter).

6. If you chose Stream Video in step 4, *do any of the following* (**Figure 15.98**):

▲ For URL, enter the Web address where you want the video file stored.

▲ Select Confirm URL Later to have Premiere Pro prompt you to specify or confirm a Web address later, just before creating the PDF.

continues on next page

EXPORTING WITH CLIP NOTES

577

7. To upload the PDF using File Transfer Protocol (FTP), click the FTP Settings tab, and specify the options.

To specify particular FTP settings, consult your network administrator.

8. Click OK to close the Export for Clip Notes dialog box.

The Export for Clip Notes save dialog box appears.

9. Specify a name and location for the Clip Notes document, and then click Save (**Figure 15.99**).

Premiere Pro renders and encodes the sequence to the location you specified.

To review a Clip Notes PDF:

1. Open an exported Clip Notes PDF document.

An Instructions dialog box that includes a text message from the editor appears (**Figure 15.100**).

See the previous task, "To export a Clip Notes PDF."

2. Click OK to close the Instructions dialog box and to view the Clip Notes PDF and embedded video (**Figure 15.101**).

Figure 15.99 Specify a name and location for the PDF, and click Save.

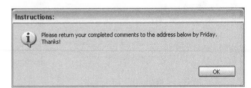

Figure 15.100 A reviewer must first respond to the Instructions dialog box...

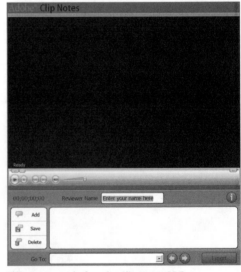

Figure 15.101 ...before the Clip Notes PDF opens.

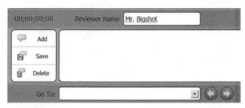

Figure 15.102 Comments are attributed to the name you enter.

Figure 15.103 Clicking the Add button or pausing the video stamps the comment field with the timecode and reviewer name.

Figure 15.104 Add your comment, and click Save.

Figure 15.105 When you're finished commenting, click Export.

3. For Reviewer Name, enter your name (**Figure 15.102**).

Your name is associated with the comments you enter.

4. Use the standard playback controls in the media player to view the embedded video.

5. *Do either of the following:*

▲ Click the Add button 💬.

▲ Pause or cue the video to which you want to attach a comment.

Your name and the current timecode of the video appear on the top line in the comment field (**Figure 15.103**). A text insertion cursor appears on the next line.

6. Type the comment you want to attach to the current frame, and click Save (**Figure 15.104**).

7. Repeat steps 5 and 6 until you've added all the comments you want.

8. Click Export (**Figure 15.105**).

An Export Form Data As dialog box appears.

continues on next page

9. Specify a name and location for the Clip Notes comments, and then click Save (**Figure 15.106**).

The saved file uses the .xfdf file extension.

10. If prompted by your email client software, modify and send the automatically generated email with the Clip Notes comments attached.

An email client prompts you if the editor specified an email address in the Return Comments To field when saving the Clip Notes PDF file. See, "To export a Clip Notes PDF,"," earlier in this chapter.

To cue to and edit comments:

1. In a Clip Notes PDF, *do any of the following:*

   ▲ To cue the video to a particular comment, select the comment in the Go To pull-down menu (**Figure 15.107**).

   ▲ To cue to the comment preceding the current frame, click the Go to Previous Comment button ⊙.

   ▲ To cue to the comment after the current frame, click the Go to Next Comment button ⊙ (**Figure 15.108**).

   The current frame of the video cues to the frame containing the comment.

2. Edit your comment in the comment field, and then click the Save button.

   Remember to resave the PDF file so that it reflects the most recent changes.

Figure 15.106 Specify a name and location for the Clip Notes comments file, and click Save.

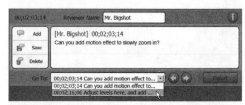

Figure 15.107 In the Clip Notes PDF, you can cue to a comment by selecting it in Go To pull-down menu...

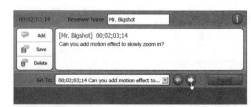

Figure 15.108 ...or by using the Previous and Next buttons.

Figure 15.109 Clicking the Delete button removes the cued comment.

Figure 15.110 Open the project from which you exported a Clip Notes document, and then choose Sequence > Import Clip Notes Comments.

To delete a comment:

1. In a Clip Notes document, cue to a frame containing a comment.

   See the previous task, "To cue to and edit comments."

2. Click the Delete button (**Figure 15.109**).

   The comment at the current frame is removed.

To import Clip Notes comments:

1. Open the project from which you exported a Clip Notes document.

2. Choose Sequence > Import Clip Notes Comments (**Figure 15.110**).

   An Import Clip Notes Comments dialog box appears.

   continues on next page

3. Select the Clip Notes Comments data file associated with your project, and then click Open (**Figure 15.111**).

Sequence markers corresponding to each comment are added to the appropriate sequence in the project (**Figure 15.112**).

4. To view a comment, double-click its corresponding sequence marker.

A Marker dialog box appears, and the reviewer's notes appear in the Comments field (**Figure 15.113**).

Figure 15.111 Locate the Clip Notes comments that correspond to a sequence in the project, and then click Open.

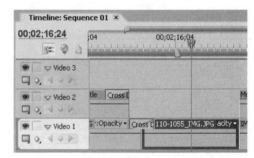

Figure 15.112 The reviewer's comments are converted into sequence markers placed at the appropriate points in the sequence.

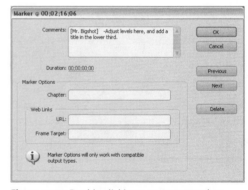

Figure 15.113 Double-clicking a sequence marker reveals the comment in a Marker dialog box.

INDEX